IN SEARCH OF GREENER GRASS

Road Dog Publications was formed in 2010 as an imprint of Lost Classics Book Company and is dedicated to publishing the best books on motorcycling, motorsports, and adventure travel. Visit us at www.roaddogpub.com.

Originally published in the UK by Matador, an Imprint of Troubador Publishing Ltd, Leicester, UK 2012.
This North American edition published by arrangement with the author 2017.

Cover typeface Dead Kansas ©Fabien Delage (www.wmkart.com)

ISBN 978-1-890623-55-5
Library of Congress Control Number: 2017933731

An Imprint of Lost Classics Book Company
The UK Edition of this book is available in eBook format at online booksellers.

In Search of Greener Grass

Riding from Reality towards Dreams and Finding Fulfilment

by

Graham Field

Publisher
Lake Wales, Florida

For Mum
who always encouraged the travel
and withheld the guilt trip

FOREWORD

I can always remember where I was and what the weather was like at significant moments in my life, so I remember that the sun had just come out, and I was seated on the terrace overlooking my vegetable garden, with a large gin and tonic by my side waiting to be tasted, when I first opened Graham Field's book.

I wasn't expecting much.

At the time *Jupiter's Travels* was first published, thirty-eight years ago, I don't remember there being a lot of competition. Of course there was *Zen and the Art of* ..., that improbable blockbuster which came out just before mine and opened the door for books related to motorcycles, but people had only just begun to use bikes to make interesting journeys rather than for joy-riding.

All that changed dramatically during the last decades. More and more people began to take off on ever more ambitious trips, and inevitably, large numbers of them felt compelled to write a book. And now of course there's a deluge of blogs as well. I'm all in favour of it. Some of them keep friends and family entertained. Some reach out to an ever-growing community of motorcycle travellers, but they all start with the same premise: "If you like bikes you will like this book or blog or whatever." In other words, they don't really stand up on their own any more than a bike does.

That's why Graham's book was such a joy. I wrote to him almost immediately.

"Even though you put me down in the first paragraph of your introduction, I think your writing is bloody marvellous. I've only read four chapters, but I wanted you to know that I am really glad to have met you."

Graham is a dancer. He moves like one and writes like one, dancing through his experiences with a light and lovely touch. He is effortlessly amusing, and I know how much work goes into that. His writing comes out of nowhere, and I am sure it will just get better. He has his own idiosyncratic view of life as he wanders around the world like a pied piper taking us along for the ride and...you don't even have to like bikes.

—Ted Simon

Ted is the author of *Jupiter's Travels* and *Riding High* (about his 1973 round-the-world ride on a Triumph Tiger), *Dreaming of Jupiter* (a 2001 ride of 59,000 miles through 47 countries on a BMW R80 GS), and *Jupiter's Travels in Camera*. Ted's books have been the inspiration for many adventure riders and travelers seeking to understand the world they pass through on their journeys. Ted is founder of the Ted Simon Foundation, that supports and promotes travelers and whose "...ultimate aim is to promote understanding, reduce tension and to favour the chances of peace between our many cultures."

Rear cover photo and above by Serdar Sunny Unal, http://serdar.world

ABOUT THE AUTHOR

Author and travel writer Graham Field was "born at a very early age, and independent travel begun shortly after he learned to crawl." During obligatory but inadequate schooling he spent the majority of his time looking out of the window and escaping into his favourite daydream—the freedom of the road. Making restless dreams become a reality has been his single-minded talent.

Graham's life of travel really started with his first motorbike, obtained way before he was old enough to have a licence. By the age of eighteen he was living in the US, working in construction, in strip clubs, and riding a 1960 Harley-Davidson. In 1990, he set off around the world with a backpack, and this was followed by challenging solo cycling trips in India and China.

For over a quarter of a century, Graham has had three constants in his life: motorcycles, travel, and diary keeping. He appeared on a national TV game show, where he announced he would use his modest winnings to ride to Mongolia. This was when all three of his obsessions came together. On a thousand-dollar KLR 650, he rode 15,000 miles east from his home in the UK—105 days on a $7,500 budget. This journey, the people met, the challenges, and the startling contrasts of both the cultures and landscapes became the subject of his hugely popular and inspirational diary-format book, *In Search of Greener Grass*.

A few years later, his KLR, with the same budget, distance, and time-frame, took him to Iraq and Azerbaijan. A "eureka moment" occurred during this journey, and that epiphany became the topic of his enthralling second book, *Ureka* [Titled *Eureka* in the North American print edition.]. His third book, *Different Natures*, takes the reader on earlier motorcycle trips from the Alaskan Arctic Circle to southern Mexico. Delving into diaries packed with tales of naivety, and at times eyebrow-raising debauchery, the reader soon discovers that Graham's mantra is "You never lie to your diary."

Graham writes regularly for *Overland Magazine*. His articles and columns are published in British national papers and motorcycle publications in both Europe and North America. His presentations are widely regarded as some of the funniest in the genre, and in radio interviews he is well known for his passion for travel and his off-the-cuff comments, which both challenge and amuse. He makes regular contributions to *Adventure Bike TV*, where he was nominated as "most inspirational adventurer." Graham has a residency on *Adventure Rider Radio*, alongside travel writers Brian and Shirley Hardy-Rix, Grant Johnson of Horizons Unlimited, and myself. He currently lives in Bulgaria, with a variety of iconic motorcycles, a cluster of KLRs, and some gold-digging cats.

—Sam Manicom

Sam is the author of a four-book series (*Into Africa*, *Under Asian Skies*, *Distant Suns*, and *Tortillas to Totems*) about his eight-year journey around the world by motorcycle.

Whatever you do will be insignificant, but it is very important that you do it.
—Mahatma Gandhi

Whether you think you can or whether you think you can't, you're right
—Henry Ford

Another town I've left behind, Another drink completely blind, Another hotel I can't find,
—Lemmy

A refreshingly cynical and humorous account of a solo overland motorcycle journey from England to Mongolia and beyond.

ACKNOWLEDGEMENTS

I've been riding and writing for over twenty-five years; this book is the result of both.

I would like to thank Lauren for believing I could do it, Sara for helping me do it, Sam Manicom for all his support once I'd done it, and Brigitte for everything else.

And as for everyone else who contributed to my good memories; the Internet information contributors and informers, the travellers, home owners, helpers, wavers, and lookers; thanks for making my view of the planet's people mostly positive. Long may it last.

Finally, thanks to you, even if you didn't read it, you at least picked it up and opened it, and that's a start.

Right, what's next...

TABLE OF CONTENTS

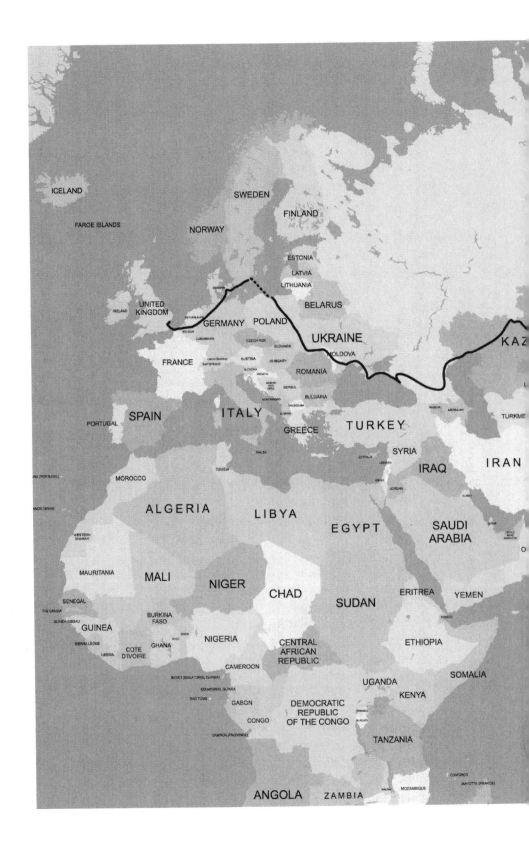

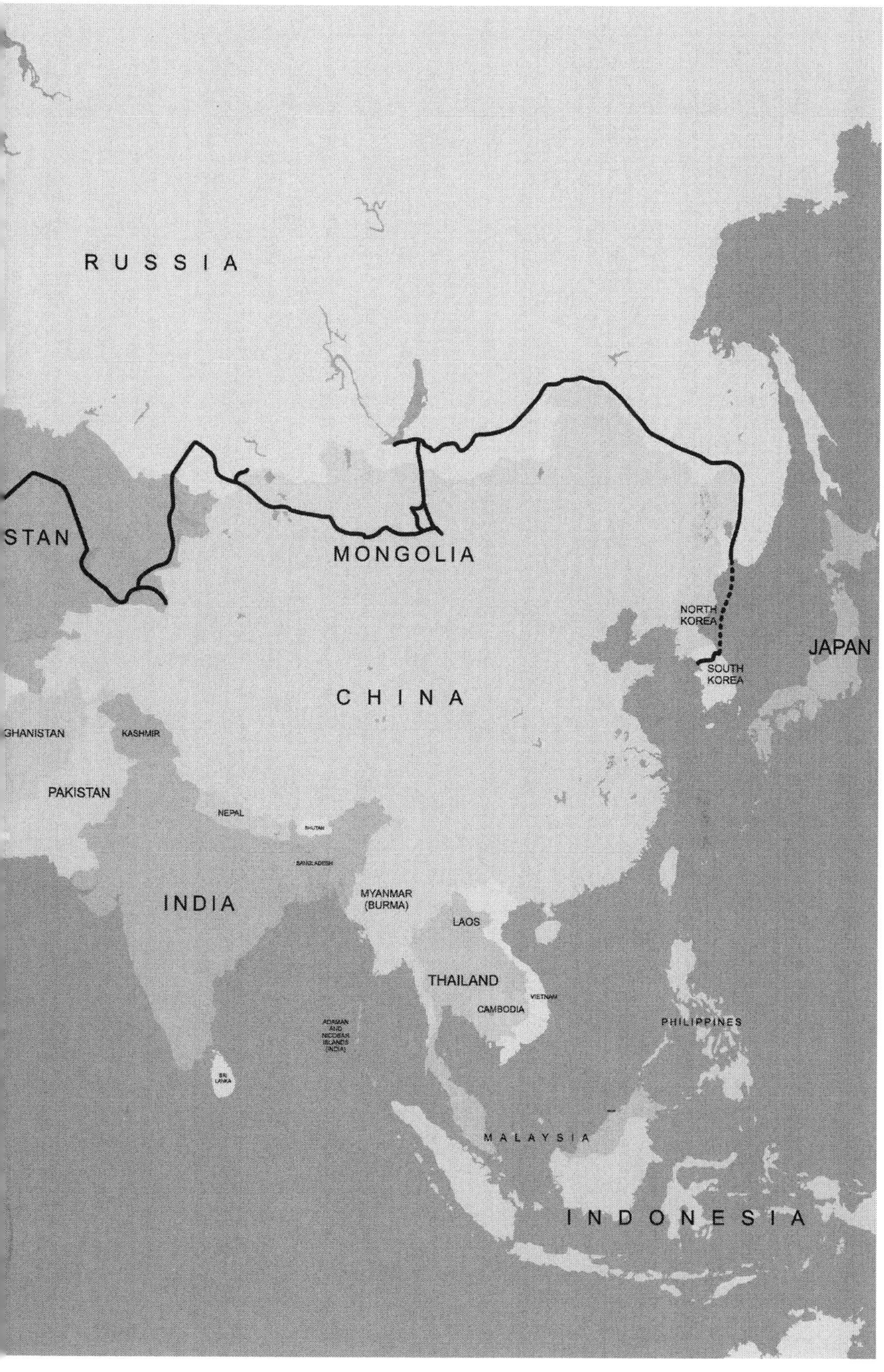
RUSSIA
STAN
MONGOLIA
NORTH KOREA
JAPAN
SOUTH KOREA
CHINA
GHANISTAN
KASHMIR
PAKISTAN
NEPAL
BHUTAN
BANGLADESH
INDIA
MYANMAR (BURMA)
LAOS
THAILAND
VIETNAM
CAMBODIA
ADAMAN AND NICOBAR ISLANDS (INDIA)
PHILIPPINES
SRI LANKA
MALAYSIA
INDONESIA

INTRODUCTION

"And after the break you're going to find out something else about this gentleman. He wants to make a long journey, on a motorbike. Have a think about where he might like to go; if you can come up with it we will give you...congratulations," said Noel Edmonds before the commercials started for the viewing public. The make-up lady waited with her brush, poised to apply yet another layer of crud to my face. The sound man came and fiddled with my microphone, and the motivational production crew told me to be more appreciative and give more consideration to the money that the banker was offering me. "It's a lot of money to some people who watch—don't disregard it."

"It's a tactic," I lied. "If I don't look like I'm excited by it, he will up his offer." I wondered if the banker could hear me.

And we're back.

"With a significant sum of money, the big journey you want to do is to...?"

"Mongolia."

"Mongolia, why Mongolia?" prompted Noel.

I clearly knew nothing about it, but then that's why I travel: to find out. Research has never been my strong point.

I babbled something about it being a wild country—challenging and an adventure from the start.

"And how much would a trip like that cost?"

Oh, I don't bloody know. "I would need a specific bike, I couldn't do it on a street bike..."

Well I'm committed now, I thought. I just told the nation of *Deal or No Deal* fans and all my friends who were watching. I cringe when I think of my response as to why I would want to ride my bike to such a place. In my defence they want sound bites, not long-winded explanations. I'll save that for the book.

So I was briefly a TV star, recognised everywhere from Marks & Spencer to Asda; even the local press had called for a story. Then in ten days I went from celebrity status to white trash. I rented out my house to save for my trip and moved into a trailer.

Man, did I pick a cold winter to live in what I would explain to anyone and everyone was not a caravan but a thirty-three-foot-long, American fifth-wheel trailer—the sort the Caravan Club frown upon in their reverse snobbery ways. But I wasn't living in it to make friends in the caravan community; I was there to live a comfortable and compact life for a year. And I did, until the winter of 2009/10 decided it was going to break records and freeze my toothpaste in its tube. I was preparing myself for the hardships of the trip, saving money and sitting in the poorly-insulated, freezing trailer. I read my guide-books and formulated a plan whilst wearing a woolly hat and fingerless gloves.

It was never meant to be a return trip. I couldn't even imagine getting there, let alone coming back. Ulan Bator was where I was heading, and that was the goal—just that. It's massive. End of story. My budget was £5,000: 100 days at £50 a day. I wasn't sure how realistic it was. It wasn't a holiday, but it wasn't an endurance test either. Some days you want a hotel and a good meal, and some days there's nothing to eat and everywhere to camp: I thought it would even itself out.

On reflection, there was a major flaw in my plan: Mongolia was an unthinkable distance, unimaginable terrain, and quite possibly an unachievable destination. But, should I actually get there, then what? Next time I do a one-way trip I will try and make sure my destination is a port, not a land-locked city in the middle of a land-locked country in the middle of the biggest landmass on the planet. Ho hum, you live and learn.

Part of the motivation to go was that my social life had gradually disappeared and no longer existed at all. Everyone seemed to get partners at the same time. They were all staying home, playing happy families. There was usually a divorcee around who wanted to catch up on the fun they'd been missing out on, and I was Mr. Goodtime, Mr. Commitment Free and Unattached, always up for anything. But there had been a lot of time alone recently, and if I was going to be in my own company, it may as well be on the road. I steered my life in this direction; it was time to go and take advantage of it.

I knew it was getting bad when the doorbell rang one morning and it made me jump. The postman had brought another eBay purchase to my door. Yep, when the ring of the doorbell is unfamiliar it's time to go out the door and close it behind you.

Inspired by *Long Way Round* was I? No, I don't think so. Mongolia was first brought to my attention in China when I met a Dutch couple who had ridden the Trans-Siberian Express. Listening to their tales of wild horsemen and staying in the traditional canvas-covered, felt-lined gers, that was the seed.

It germinated on an 11,000 mile ride to the Arctic Circle in Alaska.

So I never wanted to even mention *Long Way Round*, and I refused to cast judgement on what they did until I had done it too. But Ewan and Charley are (regardless of opinions, and there are plenty) as associated with Asia overland as much as Borat is with Kazakhstan. So I couldn't and wouldn't ignore what they did: as my trip progressed I learnt just what talented actors they are.

It was probably 2005 when I saw their series. I watched it again in the May of 2010 for research. Ooh, I thought, we have the same panniers, and that's where the similarities ended. And then the butterflies began. How the hell am I going to manage that on my own? My most challenging ride to date had been to the Arctic Circle.

Years ago I decided to get a big piece of art tattooed on my back. I'd considered this for many years. Every time my top was off I would think, "Now if my back was tattooed, would that be a problem?" After years of the answer being "no," I started to save and look for a suitable tattoo artist. I considered techniques and design, and I thought about colours and textures, size and time limits. After much consultation with the tattooist I chose, the day came when the design had been agreed and the entire outline had to be tattooed in one sitting from my shoulders to my coccyx. As the needle first penetrated the skin around my kidneys and later over my shoulder I realised that the one thing I failed to consider in all my research was the bloody pain factor.

I was wondering if I would find this happening again when I hit the road. The roads would become horrendous, and I know that picking up my fully-laden bike single-handed would be next to impossible. Removing luggage every time would be infuriatingly tedious, but I'd deal with that when I had to. For now, making it to Ukraine would be an experience; riding into Russia would be remarkable; negotiating the roads in Kazakhstan would be a daunting challenge; and if I did make it to Mongolia, it would be a massive achievement. I was not sure what I'd do when I got there. I'd see if anything was broken, bike, body, or budget, and if everything was intact then maybe I wouldn't turn around. But that was a big maybe.

Right, there's this monkey: it's a stuffed toy. Yet it's more than a stuffed toy. Monkey is a very significant character. He played a co-starring role in my TV game show. For the last three years or so I made picture books of Monkey having adventures, which I would then video myself reading and send to my daughter in

America. The idea was that she would become familiar with the English scenes from the book so that when she came for her first visit it wouldn't all seem so strange to her. It also served the purpose of teaching her to recognise my voice, accent, and know what I look like. So eventually, Monkey evolved from a toy into a character. The stories always ended with him getting into trouble, and so the catchphrase "Oh Monkey, he's so bad" was born.

I managed to find another monkey on eBay who was going to be a stunt double, but when he arrived, although identical in every way, he was half the size. He became Monklet. That led to new poignant story lines of how much fun Monkey would have with Monklet and how much he missed Monklet when they weren't together.

In my idle hours I had made a crash helmet for Monklet out of a tennis ball. It was matt black and open-face with a silver chain for a chin strap. My friends said I had too much time on my hands. Perhaps. Just think of all those trips to Matalan and episodes of *Strictly Come Dancing* I missed out on. Whilst packing the bike I had moved Monklet around, but there was no room to take him. It was unnecessary and impractical. He had a permanent cheeky smile on his face. I may havebeen forty-four, but it kind of warmed my heart to see it; particularly as he had become a common bond between my daughter and me when we spoke on the phone.

"So how's Monklet doing?" Madalynn would ask.

"Oh he's so bad; you'll never guess what he's just done..."

So at the eleventh hour, Monklet was strapped to the spare tyre with a bungee cord, and while it may have been the pressure from the elastic, I think his smile got a little bigger.

I was leaving for Mongolia; I wasn't catching a train, I'm wasn't going to the airport. If I didn't live on an island, I wouldn't be going to any port at all. If my panniers were empty and I did a right instead of a left out of my driveway, I could have been doing the usual trip to Asda. But I wasn't. I was going under my own power to the centre of Central Asia. Oh, and with the help of a ferry company too.

The Preparation

So I was riding to Mongolia alone on a bike, which I bought off eBay for £800. I was the only bidder, because it was listed in the wrong category.

"You got a lot of bike there for £800," said the grumpy owner when I went to pick it up. I didn't tell him of his *faux pas* or that I actually had bid over £1,000. He set the reserve price; I reserved the right to not feel guilty.

My bike was not love at first ride but, just like the best albums, the ones that don't grab you straight away end up being the ones you play for the rest of your life. The KLR 650 didn't pull effortless wheelies, but those weren't really a necessity for a long overland trip. It didn't produce adrenalin like my Ducati did; it didn't give me the feeling of achievement of my chopper; or have a triple-figure cruising speed of my triple-cylinder Triumph. That, I suppose, is why I bought it. I needed something that wasn't like the others, to do something the others couldn't do. It did have a lovely exhaust note, though, thanks to the aftermarket pipe—just the right side of obnoxious. Well, it was from where I was sitting anyway.

Through a winter of eBaying, the bike and all the accompanying paraphernalia stood me at only £2,000; and that included four new tyres. The idea being, that I could, in the worst case scenario, afford to walk away from it.

"Buy time, not equipment" was one of the single best lines of advice I read during those months. There was also the whole "less is more" philosophy, meaning that the less weight on the bike the better it will handle. Saying that, the more you take, the more comfortable the journey will be. There's no simple way. It's all too easy to read about all the gadgets and decide you must have them. There have been travellers long before there was Gore-Tex and Thinsulate, or even roads or engines; since man has said "I wonder what's over there?" and gone to look. I didn't need that stuff. It would only end up owning me.

I looked at the price of a satellite phone, in case I got in trouble beyond the bars of mobile reception, but it was more than the cost of a flight home. Yet another piece of equipment I didn't take.

Though the Internet makes research so easy, there are so many opinions out there that nobody can agree on anything. Just because someone expresses an articulate and eloquent argument on a topic doesn't mean that it has any validity or accuracy; you could meet this guy in a pub and in two minutes decide he's an utter prat. A posting has no personality, and ultimately, you have to make your own decisions based on your own criteria.

For example, I did the most research on what tyres I would use. Just because someone slates a particular tyre doesn't mean it's not good; they may say that it's bad in the wet or in mud, but that could just be the workman blaming his tools. If he can't ride in wet or boggy conditions, of course he's going to blame his tyres and not his inabilities. Eventually, I narrowed down all the tyre brands, taking into account mileage, endurance, handling capabilities, and of course, the price. I then discovered that the ones I wanted were unavailable in this country.

This was just one of many hurdles.

My preparation thus became an act of defiance in the face of the incompetent and the useless who put road blocks on my path. This included: the poor recommendation of a village key cutter who "deserves the business;" he wasn't even local, well not for me; an inbred idiot with no sense of urgency. Then there was the insurance company that asked if I was sure I wanted to travel to Russia—they could insure me through Turkey—and the international manufacturers of cool bits who won't post overseas. I was looking forward to leaving them all behind and replacing them with difficult border guards, jobsworth customs officials, and corrupt police.

The winter dragged on, and my preparation continued. Pannier debates no longer mattered to me: I was to be travelling alone and needed security. It would take more than a knife to get to the contents of the used but polished Touratech panniers I eventually decided on: unless it was held to my throat, of course. That's pretty much where my designer accessories began and ended.

My other accessories were more creative: the bottom of a chip fryer made a headlight protector and a bloody great lump of aluminium was turned into a bloody great fork brace. I stuck one plastic windshield onto another to give me the "extended touring windshield" which was the perfect height, if my posture was good. With my back alignment belt it should be. I mounted a chrome toilet brush holder behind the front wheel to carry my tools in, keeping the heavy stuff low and spreading the weight. It looked really good, but my ingenuity ended before I could find a use for the now homeless toilet brush. Nothing happened by accident in my garage, apart from the cuts and bruises from sharp edges and unexpected left-hand threads.

It wasn't so much *Mad Max* as crazily minimalist. I already had compact camping equipment from when I cycled in India and China. Not *through* China or *around* India, let's be clear. It wasn't for charity or anything. I just wanted to do it. I hung off the back of trucks up hills; I got on wicker boats across rivers and sat in the back of a pick-up truck when I was just knackered; I took it on trains when the scenery looked bland. It's not the easy option: when you're not riding it your bicycle turns from a physical pain in the arse to a metaphorical one. No one wants to transport it. It's not like you can stuff it under your seat like a back pack. On a train trip from Goa to Delhi I had no choice but to sleep with it on my top bunk. Bloody thing.

I did suffer my fare share of hardships in my 10,000 kms of cycling: icy mountain roads in China, sadistic traffic in India, and dehydration in Thailand. From foot to pedal to throttle, I was slowly making life easier. Or was I?

That was yet to be seen.

Over New Year I was in Colorado to visit my daughter and to pick up a large capacity fuel tank. It was big and green and a little bit smelly. I picked up a lot of other parts there too, because KLRs are a religion in America and all sorts of cool stuff is available. I decontaminated the tank to the point that I could, and did, put a lighter in it; there was nothing flammable left, just the smell. I then put scented fabric softeners in it; the kind you put in the tumble dryer with your clothes. An acquaintance of mine recommended it; he used it when he sent pot through the post. Tried and tested.

My friend was waiting in the airport car park for my confirmation text to say the box containing the tank had been accepted. It was "The owl is in the barn, all is well." Or so I thought. Whilst waiting at the departure gate I heard, "Will passenger Field please come to the podium and make himself known." Bollocks.

"You called me?"

"That gentleman over there would like a word with you." That gentleman had a gun and didn't look so gentle.

"Mr. Field?"

"Yes."

"Your check-in luggage, there is a fuel tank."

"Yes, that's right."

"Well you can't do that. It's flammable; it's a prohibited item," he spat.

"It's not flammable, it's been decontaminated and you could put a lighter inside it."

"That's not the way we test them, sir; it has been removed from the flight. I will be reporting back to Homeland Security, and you may very well be prevented from catching this flight. Furthermore, this could impede any future entries to the US."

Well, are you keeping me here or at home? You can't threaten me with both.

"Oh great," I texted my friend, "the owl has been removed from the barn."

So paranoid American security was doing what it does best: scaring people and terrorising them. I waited. The boarding started: "Will first class passengers, passengers with children, anyone needing assistance, and bikers who are a threat to the security of this brave nation please board at your leisure."

I waited until my row was called. Now feeling like I really was hiding explosives, I tentatively walked to the gate and onto the plane. Where I would normally be told which aisle to go down, I was greeted by the head stewardess. "Mr. Field, we do apologise, your package has been removed. This is the policy of the Homeland Security agency and not of the airline. You may be approached by customs officials on our arrival in the UK."

Well at least I'll be dealing with people with common sense there, I thought. I sat in my seat and deleted all my texts; I'd sent and received nearly 1,000 messages. I was sure there might be something incriminating there somewhere, should a thorough search for evidence of my terrorist activities be conducted.

Upon my arrival the plane was not stormed by SAS soldiers, and I disembarked of my own free will. Through passport control no sirens went off, no lights flashed, and no cages dropped from the ceiling over me. I went to baggage claim, and there it was: my massive box, no longer carefully tied with string like it was when I checked it in. Now it was covered in bright tape that said "United States Homeland Security intercepted, defused, and made safe" or some such bollocks. I lifted it off the carousel expecting riot helmets to pop up from behind every possible barricade and guns to be pointed at me with a loud yell of, "Freeze, hippy, step away from the box that once contained an oversized tank!" But there was no reaction and there was no tank, just a big box with a mounting bracket in it and a little card saying "Homeland Security actually didn't give a damn, it was the policy of the airline and that is why your personal effects were removed." Well, one of them was lying.

Should I take the bracket out and leave the box in the baggage claim area or carry the whole thing out? It's a tough choice; I knew I was being watched. I took the box through the nothing-to-declare alley, and no one batted an eye. I was free, just really bloody annoyed that I'd let suited authority intimidate me.

So my friend went back to the airport and picked up the explosive tank from behind the check-in desk, where it had been sitting for three days. He put it in a box and sent it to me in England via the US mail parcel service. No word ever came from the anti-terrorist squad.

Satellite navigation—sat nav? I'd been a truck driver for seventeen years; I have a sense of direction. GPS means having no concept of your whereabouts in relation to what's around you: not knowing how close you are to the coast or cities unless your little screen informs you. I was doing this trip to see the sights and be free, not to watch a four-by-four-inch screen. I don't like being told what to do by a digital voice any more than I do by the luggage police. Garmin, I won't do what you tell me. I've got my maps. But maybe I'd take a compass too.

Four months before I left, I took my mum up to a funeral in Leicester. She had a sat nav in her car. Common sense tells me that the crematorium would be out of town, but the sat nav sent us right into the city centre. I argued profusely that this was an area of precious real estate; we are not going to find rolling green lawns and headstones inside the one-way system. The time-saving device had sent us to where births and deaths were registered. That was the only nail needed in the coffin that was the sat nav dilemma.

Sponsorship was also a very brief consideration. However, I read some very pessimistic views basically saying that if you don't have a high profile journey, a column in a bike magazine, newspaper stories about your trip, and a website with thousands of followers, no company is going to invest in your journey. So I didn't bother trying. On the road I found other sponsored riders who had been given every travel and navigational accessory available, just by asking. Damn those pessimistic articles.

However, I soon discovered that there was a downside to full sponsorship. You are owned and committed to your sponsors, who have expectations and want a result from the money they invested. For me the point of the trip was to escape corporate dictatorship, not embrace it.

I wanted to hide a few ignition keys around the bike. Why suffer the inconvenience of changing the ignition or being stuck in an undesirable place because you mislaid your key? I had one spare, and despite previous frustrations, I persevered and got another one cut. This time I went to *my* local, and long established, key cutter. I told him of my journey whilst he looked through his book of blanks to match my key.

"Come back at the end of the week," he said. Over the course of the week, I went through a folder of paperwork I had been given when I got the bike and discovered another spare key in it. Bugger, I thought, I really don't want to spend £6 on something I don't need. But I decided to honour my request, anyway, seeing as he ordered it in specially. So I went back to the shop at the end of the week, and he asked more questions about my plans as he cut me a quadruplicate. He then gave me the key. See, that's karma. That's a really good sign. Honour and honesty, it's the key to a trip, and that's the closest I got to sponsorship.

There were two mantras that I took with me. The first was my mum's constant reminder that you catch more flies with honey than you do with vinegar; good advice especially when vinegar flows so readily from my lips in confrontational situations. The second one I may not have left with, but I soon found out: everything happens for a reason.

The house tenancy came to an end. I moved back in, got my garage back, and really started to get to know the inside of my bike. It was time to sell on eBay, one massive sale, a fifth-wheel trailer. And when that was gone, I was ready to go too.

The lounge was full of piles of stuff. I packed and re-packed and wobbled out of the driveway on many test rides. It was so bloody heavy, I couldn't lose any more stuff. I had minimal clothes and spare bike parts, cooking stove and food, camping equipment, a bit of photography stuff, and essential haircare products. Then there were the two spare tyres strapped on the top box. I remounted the panniers further forward and relocated various things. It was going OK until I put on the maps and paperwork and then, once again, I was overweight. The only consolation was I didn't have a passenger, twice the weight half the space. I suppose I was better off.

I took the bike down to the south coast for a test ride and to meet someone who I'd been in contact with via an overland website. He was doing a similar trip on a similar bike. The journey made me realise that it was time to leave the Internet and hit the road. Paralysis by analysis: that's what was happening to me. Knowledge is only power to a degree; there comes a point when you need to get going or else there will be no adventure left—when every border crossing has been researched, every road analysed, every route deliberated, every country categorised for temperature, ideal time to travel, and best exchange rates. I could sit on Google Earth and trace every part of my route.

There was a calm satisfaction at the last stages of preparation: the quiet enjoyment of going down to the garage with a cup of tea or a beer and working on the bike. We were both nearly ready for the journey. Sometimes I just sat and looked at it. To the casual observer nothing was being done, but there was lots going on: no point in wearing a helmet if there's nothing inside worth protecting. I struck a similar pose on a stall by the bench when I was building my chopper, but I smoked back then and looked a lot cooler. So did the bike, but this project wasn't about being cool; it was about strength, endurance, and practicality, qualities not associated with cigarettes and Autosol.

Two Days Before I Leave

Right, what was on the list? Not much. Lists, my life has been nothing but lists, and for everything I cross off I add another three. If it was not crossed off now, it was either not important, too late, or there just wasn't room to put it on the bike. So I got on the Internet: more rejections to requests for free overnight stays at people's houses from Germany to Kazakhstan. I opened my profile and speak my mind about my experience of the couch surfing website; it had wasted hours of my time, not to mention crushed my self-esteem with its constant rejections. I just said I'd go back to the old-fashioned way of meeting real people on the road in the real world, instead of wasting my time in that cyber community.

In theory it had sounded such a good idea, to stay in the houses of like-minded people who were in-between their travels and sleep on their couches as I progressed across Eurasia—not only saving money but getting firsthand experience of a country from its inhabitants, having some company at the end of a day's riding. I would be swapping stories and views, eating local food, either home cooked or from a restaurant I would never find on my own, gaining knowledge, inside information, new friends, new destinations, the sites the guidebooks didn't know about. That was my rose-tinted idea of what being a paid-up member of the site would offer me.

Everybody "loves adventure and meeting exciting people" but, I was finding that when the reality knocks on their inbox they run a mile, or at least "won't be able to host on that day"—none of them. Feeble excuses, negative comments, if they even replied at all. Cynical, weary, rude, inhospitable. Was it the bike? The look? I even contacted some local hosts to try and meet them for a coffee and ask what I was doing wrong with my requests, and they too were standoffish and unwelcoming.

"Screw it, ya can keep ya couch, ya scared and paranoid *Daily Mail* reading hypocrites," was my inner defensive reaction and generalisation to the whole bloody scene.

I was feeling so liberated by my withdrawal from this disappointing Internet community, that I lost all track of time during my rant. It had suddenly gone 9 A.M. and I hadn't even logged onto the Ticketmaster site to book my tickets for the Roger Waters show next year. By the time I got to the availability of tickets I had no choice but "best available": what a scam, I'd be at the top back seats with the other genuine fans. But at least I'd have tickets for three of the five dates.

Along with the confirmation email of my ticket purchase is one from the visa place; my passport will be with me tomorrow before midday with my Russian, Kazakhstani, and Mongolian visas in it. So I book a ferry for Sunday. That still gives me three days to get to Sweden. Sweden is a very tactical part of the leaving plan: I'm going to miss the whole of the English summer. All the bike shows and festivals will be happening whilst I'm on the road, so I'm going to meet some friends for the Sweden Rock Festival. This has several benefits: not only will I get my festival fix, but now leaving home is not the daunting prospect of riding to Central Asia; I'm just off to a festival, that's all. It's brilliant on so many levels.

Well that's it, I'm definitely going now. I don't enjoy being in front of the computer all the time, but it's just the way life has become. That will all change very soon.

My speedometer cable has not arrived again. There was always going to be a last minute thing that causes stress, and this is it. I call them again, and they, too, promise delivery on Saturday morning.

On some sudden flash of common sense, I decide it wouldn't be a bad idea to get a Russian phrase book and impulsively buy a guidebook too; neither were on the list. Like my panniers aren't heavy enough without this brick of a book to carry too.

Months of preparation mean that I'm almost organised, almost on top of things, in a manic kind of way. So I can sit in the garden and flick through my Russian book. Wow, this changes everything. I only ever saw Russia as a country of transit, like Belgium, but it's got so much to offer, and why wouldn't it? It's the biggest country in the world. I can't believe I hadn't even considered it. Okay, I admit it, there are some gaping holes in my research and organisational skills.

I fear for my life, really, I can't get it out of my head. Not in a Russian mafia or rebel kidnap kind of way, but I just can't get the fear out of my head. I feel like I'm leaving something behind that will never be the same again. I have had butterflies in my tummy for a week now. They started on my first, fully-laden test ride, when the bike wallowed and wobbled: it's too heavy, I'm not confident with my control of it. All excitement is smothered by a layer of dread and I'm not sure if it's ridiculous or not. It's the fear of an accident that's due to the bike's handling characteristics, that's what I need to work on. I take off the panniers and re-drill the mounting brackets to bring the weight as far to the front of the bike as possible. But now when I dangle my legs to steady myself they get trapped under the bottom of the panniers; that will break an ankle for sure. Yet, I'm less likely to need to put my feet down if the weight is further forward. Oh God. I just have to get on and deal with it. I need a distraction, so I watch a *Shrek* DVD and go to bed.

The Day Before I Leave

5th June 2010

I get up at 7 A.M. and instinctively go straight to the garage. The bathroom scales are there next to the bike; I weigh myself at 150lbs. That's less than my luggage.

I'm really in a zone now. Well, I'm not in *the* zone, just in *a* zone. I wander around aimlessly and wait for the postman; he brings both my passport and my speedometer cable. The passport has the three relevant visas in it but the speedometer cable is the wrong one. Two weeks of waiting, two emails, four phone calls, and they send the wrong one. However, the inner cable is compatible, and that's the important bit.

I pack the panniers for the last time and take out the bike for one last test ride. For the first time in weeks I can see what speed I'm doing. The bike has also now doubled in value; I have hidden euros all over it. I photocopy a map of Eurasia and stick it on the side of my pannier; I figure I can use it as a show and tell. It fits perfectly, despite the curvature of the Earth. If I lived in Surrey or was going further than Ulan Bator it wouldn't fit: I see it as an omen that I was never meant to live in Surrey.

My mum drops in to say goodbye. Thankfully, next door's kittens come out to play and the distraction keeps the tears away. I send some texts, say some goodbyes; everyone else seems to be on their holidays too. It starts to rain, and I start to wish I wasn't going on my own. This preparation, this feeling it would be different. But I know I've always had my best experiences when I have travelled alone.

Three years ago, three of us left Colorado for Alaska. On the evening before our departure, we were loading our bikes with our check lists out on our seats. There was a strange atmosphere: I was expecting laughing and excitement, piss-taking and bonding, but there was only silence. We were all so focused on our packing, weight distribution, and load security; deep in our own thoughts and individually preparing our own bikes. Tonight is much the same; no company, but still the silence.

The fear remains. I can distract it, but I can't get rid of it. It's the fear of fatality. I never felt like this before I went off to cycle round India or China. Nervous, yes, but not this feeling of foreboding. It doesn't exactly feel like a suicide mission, but I feel like something is going to change, not just my own wondering wild eyes, but something big.

I take a bottle of wine into the bath and spout Merlot-inspired wisdom into my voice recorder.

Wanderlust: an itch that needs scratching. No itch ever got better by being scratched, just inflamed.

If I carry on like this I'll talk myself into a panic attack. If I have the need to speak to a higher being, I have none to call. I have no faith, no faith but karma. Speaking to karma is pointless, only my actions can change my karma; I am god of my own destiny. So I will travel solo without a god to talk to. I'll just talk to myself. I hope it's not all drunken bollocks like this.

I go to bed. I sweat and turn and have lucid dreams and listen to distant thunder and the rain on the roof: I wonder if I'm looking forward to the morning or just dreading it.

DAY 1

KLEVE, GERMANY, 368 MILES

So I leave my damp sweaty bed and go out into the damp sweaty morning. The storm has passed and left a humid summer mist behind it.

I try to be calculated and methodical, but I'm just manic and absentminded. I have a shower and put my underwear on back to front. Of course, I realised immediately, but it's not a good omen for the focus and concentration I need to negotiate all that's to come. I know I'm going to face bigger challenges than this.

When you move house, everything has been boxed, loaded, and you're ready to leave. You gather up the last minute things; kettle, phone chargers, and so on, and find that, because they were scattered around empty rooms, what may have looked insignificant will completely fill the car. I had a sponge bag to take, a big bottle of water, and I'm going to take some old trainers too for the festival. I'm not doing it in bike boots or sandals. This means that I now need a little backpack to carry the festival stuff in. I also get a padlock and chain. I've spent weeks trying to save an ounce here and there, and now I've put a bloody great chain on my bike. I then fill up my massive tank with 25 litres of fuel which added another 40lbs. Shit.

Well at least it's not a passenger, I keep saying to myself.

I give the last of the contents of the fridge to my neighbours. My hands shake as I hand them the leftover orange juice and milk.

"You're shaking."

"I know."

"You'd better go." I did.

I go back to the house, clean up, turn off, unplug, lock up, close the front door, and put the key back through the letter box. I get on my bike, and my neighbour points an iPhone at me and takes my photo. That would be the leaving party then.

"I wish I was coming with you," she says.

"There's room on my horse for two," I reply.

Where the hell did that come from? Well I know *where* it came from, but why?

She goes back inside. No waves, no ceremony, I just wallow out of the driveway and into the haze of an English summer morning. The front door is locked, and I don't have a key, the estate agent has. If I never live in that house again that's fine by me; I'll just keep on riding.

Last night's fear is less prevalent now, but I do feel a little conspicuous as I ride down the A12 like some post-nuclear survival vehicle. As I cross over the Dartford Bridge I'm looking at the freight ferries and thinking about the dodgy haulage companies I've worked for. I'm certainly not feeling the angst I was expecting. This is okay.

At Dover docks I am told what lane to go to. This, I think to myself, is going to be the last time I'm going to understand what I'm being told. I park behind the other bikes: the two-week European tourers, none of whom are carrying spare tyres. I draw a little crowd, and I hear the words I dare not to speak: "*Long Way Round.*" But it's all positive and enthusiastic; I'm even told that I'm brave or something like that.

The bikes board the ferry first. Fish and chips or Sunday roast? What is going to be my last English meal? When I've eaten the last chip, I send my last texts with the last of my reception and the last of my free minutes. I put the last of my English coins into a fruit machine that I don't understand; I may as well have thrown them off the side of the ferry for all the time it took for the machine to swallow them and entertainment I got from it.

I think about Monklet and how much attention he has already attracted. He's a good conversation piece; I think about his smile. If I can keep a smile on my face it will make my journey so much easier. I really must remember that.

As a truck driver, Calais was a regular part of my working week, but now I don't recognise it at all. Straight off the ferry, no customs, no stops, and I head east. I suppose I'll be doing this a lot now.

There are little differences, like the electrical pylons are a different shape to home. Then France is swiftly over, and I'm into Belgium; it all slows up as I approach the Antwerp ring road. I consider going north, but I'm trapped in my lane; but not trapped enough that I can't be barged out of it by some liberty-taking driver. Christ, that was close. I sit there for a second incensed at his audacity and then squeeze past him, sticking out my hand to push in his wing mirror. If Monklet could change his expression he would frown at such behaviour. I never intended to do any damage, it was just a warning shot, but as soon as I do it I realise I had better keep going. I'm still a little unsure of my width; I carefully filter through the traffic, deliberately trying to miss the other wing mirrors. There's nothing like an adrenalin rush to bring out the best in your skills.

The traffic soon frees up, and most cars start to overtake me again. I can't even recall the colour of my new enemy: I scan my mirrors for a car with a look of revenge on its radiator grill. A lot of passing cars have passengers pointing and smiling: that will be the effect of Monklet. I'm so glad I brought him.

Into Holland and I'm probably safe now. I go onto reserve after only 282 miles: so much for my long range tank. That's disappointing, as is the weather, which turns to rain and continues into Germany. I get to my friend's parents' house. I've only been there once before, but I find my way easily enough, and my first day's riding is complete. I wheel my bike into the garage; the toothpaste I used to get my tyres onto the rims has reappeared. Thanks to the rain and centrifugal force, I now have white wall tyres. The rain has also got into my map. Eurasia looks more like a tie-dye T-shirt now. I'm sure I'll still be able to find my way.

Day 2

Neustadt, Germany, 268 Miles

The pre-breakfast activities include looking at maps with my friend's mum. I'm told to avoid Poland, as apparently it's flooded; it's been on TV and everything. My friend's sister then arrives for breakfast, which is good for several reasons: not just because her English is flawless, but also because she's hot and laughs at my jokes. Were she not married with two kids she could be a contender for the woman who I don't think actually exists.

She warns me of Kazakhstan, as she's had dealings with those people, and her mother then says that Russia is dangerous too; both also agree that I must beware of Ukraine. Everyone has a fear and disaster story. Even on the dirt roads in northern Alaska the reports were always more dramatic than the reality. I hope that this is just the same.

I still don't have a good reason as to why I want to go to Mongolia. I really must come up with an answer; I just know I'm going to be asked again.

While my visit is all very pleasant, familiar, comfortable, and yummy, I'm supposed to be staying with a friend of a friend in Denmark tonight, so I swiftly get going. I put my boots on the wrong feet, but at least this morning the underwear presented no problem. I must be improving. I then pack up, take a few photos of the family by my bike, and say goodbye.

"Stop in on your way back."

Way back? Way back? Do you know how far I'm going? I'm not even sure I'll get there, let alone back. Despite this, I keep the printed street map of their town safe, just in case. That's how life is going to continue for the foreseeable future, I suppose: lots of brief encounters. I wave goodbye.

"Oh, what side of the road do I ride on again?"

The last image I have of them is with concern on their faces.

"No, it was a joke; it's the right, right?"

Well that was a good first stop: I now have three emergency rolls stuffed inside my spare tyres. 31 miles later I'm 29 kms from their town. Yes, I suppose there was probably a more direct way to the autobahn. Still, I continue and head north where the roads are dull and so is the sky. I'm doing a maximum speed for England, but here the Mercedes and BMWs go from a dot in your mirror to a turbulent wind that rattles your visor in the time it takes to cancel your indicator. I find myself doing double takes before my overtakes. There is intermittent rain, but there's nothing too extreme in any aspect of the day. I find I've really underestimated today's distance. I text my Danish connection that I won't make it tonight, and there's instant relief; I feel much better now that pressure has gone. I then opt for a slight change of route, more fuel, and another bun, then on I go.

I notice frying pan-sized lumps of tarmac in the road; I try to avoid the bumps, but I'm willing the roads to be this smooth in Central Asia. I fear for the metal fatigue in my panniers and the supporting rack, but either it will make it or it won't, and worrying about it isn't going to help.

I'm cold, I'm wet, I'm getting tired, and I know I will be camping for the next five days after tonight. There isn't much Germany left now. I go into a small town and find a hotel. Wow, I'm so clever, finding a hotel in a foreign land without a guidebook. Is there no challenge I can't rise to? It's not cheap, but I get my own individual garage to put my bike in. I then put *BBC World* on in my room; will you look at that, Poland is flooded. Fancy that. I've got a big bed and two duvets, it's still light outside, but it's grey and it's cold. It was a dull day, but that's okay; sometimes uneventful is just what you need.

Day 3

Solvesborg, Sweden, 182 Miles

At last, a long warm comfortable night's sleep. I start the day in a positive way by getting all of my clothes on in the right order and the right way round.

In the singular hotel breakfast buffet dining ritual, language is unnecessary. I sit at a corner table, munch my meat and cheese rolls too quickly, and wish I had deeper pockets. The hotel experience was perfect.

I then get the bike out of the garage, and I'm off. I find that the road and land soon ends with a ferry; it's such an easy transition. I'm the only motorcycle here. I pay my fee and get a coupon for free cigarettes; soon the bike is strapped down, and I'm embarking on my second ferry crossing of my overland trip. Giving away free fags is a crafty ploy, so I text my Swedish friend to see what brand she smokes. Nicotine is no longer a temptation to me, but now I'm in the duty-free shop I look at all the alcohol. I buy a big bottle of Jägermeister; well I *am* going to a festival. So are several of the other passengers. They are buying cases of beer and even have trolleys to carry them on. They are serious duty-freers; they are not spending money, they are saving money. I don't have that option; low volume carrying capacity means high volume alcohol. It's quantum drinking; it's all about time and space.

A kid with his photo ID pinned to his jacket approaches me with his laptop, and I answer his questions and do his survey. Mongolia is not a destination he has on his list.

"Yeah, okay, it's a holiday then. Tick holiday."

And then there's Denmark. It's warmer and brighter now. The kilometres are flying past; maybe they are shorter in Denmark. I've never been here before. I think I should see something, so I ride into Copenhagen. It's easy and there isn't much traffic as I head for the city centre. There are a lot of beautiful girls riding bicycles; I'm not giving the road my full attention. Luckily, the lanes are wide and the traffic is calm. I'm trying to remember the Hans Christian Andersen story but can't. Was it something to do with a mermaid? There is a statue of one in the square; that'll do. So I stop my bike in a cycle lane, jump off, and take a photo of the mermaid, with the bike in the foreground, of course. My, how those pretty faces scowl when you park on their territory. Oh come on, you can get past that, it's not that wide. I've got two wheels too you know. Well, it would mess up all my plans to get involved with a beautiful woman so soon in the trip. Not that there were any offers. If I hadn't stopped in their cycle path, they wouldn't have noticed me at all.

There are people who travel to try and heal a broken heart; dumped or divorced they walk the Earth taking with them the misery they were trying to leave behind. They tell their stories of dejection and unfairness to anyone who will listen, in the hope that someone will magically cure their sadness and divert their constant stream of lonely longing thoughts. Then there are the people who have left their loved one behind and miss them like a limb. Be it a lover or a complete family unit, the highlight of their trip will be the reuniting at the end of it. They wish to share every exciting moment with the ones they left behind, and all the dull time in-between would be so much better for them were they in the company of the ones most dear to them.

I've done both those kinds of travelling, and they are both shit. My last proper relationship ended over a year ago. I'm not missing anyone. I'm not looking for a replacement, or forgiveness. I'm not longing for a past; I'm looking forward and enjoying the moment. I'm ready for a complete change in lifestyle, location, employment, and social life. I'm travelling with freedom and nothing much to lose. If only I can just sell my house whilst I'm away...

I did have one pang of sadness; not in a heavy-hearted way, more in a pathetic way. It was when I realised that the only thing I was missing was Steve Lamacq and Marc Riley on *BBC 6 Music*. I'm not sure how liberated that makes me. I probably shouldn't have mentioned it at all.

Well that'll do for scenery and culture, time for another country. This time I get 310 miles out of a tank-full; that's better, everything is better. I cross the toll bridge into Sweden. How much? Eighteen quid to cross a bridge? Well I guess if I had a choice your prices would reflect that.

I decide to take the southern coastal route, as I'm in no rush and my friends won't even arrive at the festival until tomorrow evening. I can hear the bird song through my helmet and over the noise of the engine. I'm having a bit of extra bonus spring: everything is in blossom; the rapeseed fields are still yellow; and the conker trees have those little white flower pyramids on them, my own personal favourite symbol of the spring. The sky is blue, the roads are empty and all around are those discrete little blue and yellow gestures of national pride. The smells of the lilac drift through my open visor, and having my fingerless gloves on is always a good sign too.

I really do love Sweden. If it wasn't for their winters I could live here. There is so much space; it's twice the size of Britain and one tenth of the population. It's the perfect ride, and at 6 P.M. I pull into the Sweden Rock Festival alternative camp ground. It's not the caravan hell I was expecting: there are trees and rocks and space and no stupid rules with even more stupid people enforcing them.

I pitch my tent, drink some Jäger, let down my hair, and go for a walk. There is a really good vibe; I speak to some people, everyone speaks English. I have travelled forward 1,000 miles and back in time twenty-two years. The guys all have glam-teased and sprayed hair and scarves tied round their legs. Bloody hell; don't tell me this look is back again.

I help a girl carry her camping stuff to her site, and she gives me five beers. I go back to my tent and prepare myself for some extreme mingling. I put my Jägermeister, camera, and beers in my backpack; I walk up to groups of people, offer them Jäger, and make all sorts of new friends. I talk, I listen, and I learn bugger all.

I've never been to a festival alone before, but this is easy and it's fun. I may not be in my country, but I'm definitely in my element. I see a girl with dreadlocks that reach the floor, and I hang with her entourage. I speak my Swedish phrases for them, and the evening is a blur of laughter and alcohol. One of the girls is wearing a sash; apparently it's her hen night, and the sash says so or indicates it or something. I'm pretty drunk by now, and she's very pretty. Somehow we end up in a bar together; she tells me how she's met Axl Rose, and I tell her how I met Jimmy Page. I buy more beers; they are £10 each but, luckily, I haven't grasped the exchange rate yet.

Jäger has leaked out of my backpack and down my pants. I have her put her hand down there then see if she can smell it: sometimes my powers of persuasion are beyond necessity, not because she didn't want to, but did I really need her to? At that moment in time the answer was obviously yes. Thank God I've mastered putting my underwear on the right way. It's all getting a bit fuzzy now; her sister arrives, and we go watch a band, and then I lose the girl. One minute she is at my side stroking my hair (or was she wiping her hands), the next she has disappeared.

I use the liquor portal. The gap in the time and space continuum that leads the drunk safely back to his bed. Or in this case, my tent. And that is all I wrote...

Day 4

Sweden Rock Festival, 1 Mile

I wake up and it's light. It's always light: it's Sweden, and it's nearly midsummer. I feel awful. The Jäger bottle is by my head, and it's the last thing I want to see. There is less than an inch left in the bottom; I don't need to see that, either. How much money have I spent? Are my possessions still here? Everything except my ponytail tie: that's what I get for letting my hair down.

I lie in my tent. I need to visit the toilet block. I have things to do today. It would be better to do them than just lie here; I should divert my mind from how I feel. I have pre-arranged to have my bike locked up in the camp ground's own workshop; after so much preparation, to have it stolen at this early stage would be a little frustrating to say the least. I want to enjoy the festival, not fret about my unattended bike. So out of my panniers I get what I think I will need to survive the next four days: sometimes a stuffed toy is a conversation starter, but in this instance Monklet is not going to generate the kind of attention I'm looking for. He can stay with the bike. I follow a guy on a quad bike to the workshop. It's quite a way away; I hope it's safe here. Bye-bye, see you on Sunday. I'm talking to the bike, right? I'm then taken all the way back to my tent on the back of the quad; it's like VIP camping.

It's cold and rainy. I decide a shower might be a good idea. I buy my tokens and stand in line. The toilet/shower block is clearly brand new; the copper pipes still shine. They are mixed showers, and most people strip outside the cubical before entering, even the girls. Is it to save time? These Swedes are so considerate. I'm too hung-over, too messy, and too modest to get naked in the queuing area. I take off my top as a token gesture, as I like to show off my back piece anyway. It's tat for tit.

I put in my token, and the hot water pumps and washes away the wretchedness the alcohol in my blood had left in its wake. With a head full of bubbly and expensive hair product the water stops. Great. I look up at the immaculate pipe work and realise that the token box is wired to the hot pipe, so cold water is free. So I rinse my hair and body in icy but freely available water, whilst trying to convince myself this will make me feel better. Before I go back to my tent, I buy a cheese roll wrapped in cling film, which costs £5. I'm generally pretty organised when it comes to festivals, but on a bike loaded with necessities for the long distances to come I'm strapped for room. I would use my loaf if I had one but it just isn't an option. My chores are done; I suppose I feel better. I start to realise the other things I should have taken off my bike. Wind-up phone charger, poncho, and credit card might have been handy.

The day passes with dozing in my tent, text updates of the progress of my friend's imminent arrival, and frequent trips to the toilet block. I have festival belly: it's an inevitability but also annoying that it's on the first day. In late afternoon I get a text saying that they're at the gate.

"I'd better get up then," I reply.

"You're in your sleeping bag still?"

"No, up off the toilet."

I walk out of the cubical and focus on the first car I see, trying to figure out what side the driver would be on if I'm facing the car. It's them, my friends are here. We are so good at meeting up: Brazil, Egypt, India, and now Sweden. The organisers seem as relieved as I am.

"Show them to your camping area."

"Okay, follow me."

I run through the site: running, that's the cure I was looking for, either that or the beer that was put in my hand as they exited the car. Maybe it was just the company, but I'm ready to party again. I try to help with tent erection, but my efforts are pathetic, and they aren't best chuffed at the amount of empty there is in the Jäger bottle either. They left the tequila at home because of my contribution.

"Yeah, sorry about that, you see what happened was..."

They are so well prepared: carefully made yummy, healthy vegetarian food, created with love. I need this. They roll a joint; I don't need that.

"Let's go for a wander," I suggest.

I forget we are at different levels. I'm just feeling better; they are just getting started.

There are so many people here now. The personal feel has gone, and we trudge along in the procession. I'm not going to see the friends I made last night. I do see dreadlock girl, but I'm all dressed up in a hat and scarf, and I don't feel cool enough to say hi. That's why I don't get stoned anymore, it takes away my confidence. Am I going to spend the whole bloody festival looking for a pretty girl with Jägermeister down her fingernails and probably an engagement ring? Was she wearing a ring? I really didn't notice.

There is a massive queue for turning tickets into wristbands. I ask a security guy if he knows what time the ticket booth opens tomorrow. He says "nine," and I stand there waiting for a better answer. He means 9 A.M., not that he doesn't know. When this communication breakdown is cleared up, I thank him and wander back to my friends. See, this is why I don't get stoned anymore.

It's been a wasted day, but with my friends my requested pillow has also arrived. I put in my ear plugs and have an early night, as the music starts tomorrow. It already has in the camp site, as a massive sound system has been set up by some particularly hard-core campers. They are still going strong at 4 A.M. when I follow my well-trodden path to the toilet block. Time will tell just how hard-core they really are. Peaking too soon, the ruin of many a festival.

DAY 5

SWEDEN ROCK FESTIVAL, 0 MILES

There's no bike outside my tent: this is too soon in the trip to be without it. It was my identity, my reason to be here, and now I'm just another festival camper.

My meagre supplies and equipment may keep me warm and dry, but not fed and not independent. I have an egg sandwich for breakfast, and I'm all the more hungry knowing how limited my funds are and how expensive everything is. Festival expensive combined with Sweden expensive: it's a bad combination for my budget. Every day here is two days off my trip. My friends want to go and see the first band; I admire their enthusiasm and try to tap into it. When we get to the festival arena, the gates haven't even opened yet, so we sit with our backs to a closed stall and people-watch. Some chav kid comes stomping out swearing and spitting. The first chav I've seen in a week and he's English. I'm so ashamed of my country sometimes.

The gates open, and a band starts up. While my friends rush in, I stay outside and nurse my beer. It turns out to be a sound check, and they are rightfully embarrassed when I do casually stroll in: they win nerd of the day award, and they know it. Inside it's quite a compact venue; I can see three stages at once. This will be good. No walking Glastonbury miles will allow more energy for head banging.

I sit on a grass bank; it's so easy to take the piss out of bands like this. I'm not really into this, and I'm not sure why. Is it the cold? The expense? I looked at my Russian guidebook this morning and found the language is impossible. I feel the nerves coming back again.

People-watching is always fun, particularly at festivals, and despite the grey chill, there is still a lot of flesh exposed. Am I watching in general or looking for someone in particular? Am I going to spend the entire weekend this distracted? I meet some friends of my friends who are referred to as "reverse-a-tors" behind their backs: a couple with peroxide hair and fake-tanned skin. I put on my mask and hope no one sees through.

Every rock festival this year has a Ronnie James Dio stage, in memory of the great man. We head over for a ceremony. It could have been so much better; it's sad and wet, and my tent is calling. I doze the afternoon away, sheltering from the weather and disgust myself at my complete inability to grasp a single word of Russian from my book. I resort to looking at pictures of mountain ranges, and the nerves go away. I then go for a wander and chat to a drunk girl. As soon as I'm on my own I meet people, it's a good sign, considering the trip ahead.

As we head down for the evening session, I get some goulash soup; it seems the most cost-efficient way to stretch out my money and fill my stomach. I stand alone and watch Slayer; they seem tired or is it me? I can't seem to catch anyone's eye. When we meet up after their set, my friends tell me about the goulash all over my face. I wipe it off and stay in their company for the rest of the evening, half enjoying half the bands and really enjoying a few. A lot of them I've seen before over my thirty-year devotion to the masters of metal and all things heavy.

Day 6

Sweden Rock Festival, 0 Miles

Well, I seem to have regained control over my festival tummy, if not my mind. I want to get on the road, but at the same time I'm nervous to; my mind is always ahead of the moment I'm in, and it's pissing me off. I'm feeling pretty dirty now, and I still have two days to go. I hope my cabin on the ferry to Poland is a single one. The food we have and the money I have are clearly not going to last, nor is the beer.

Whilst watching daytime bands, it starts to rain again, so we stand in the bar watching the people outside brave the weather. A rock chick in hot pants walks past, but she is wearing leg warmers too: sex and sensibility, two essential qualities in a woman I think. I'm seeing a lot of familiar faces now but not the one I'm looking for.

It's raining hard. We trudge back; I could really use some of the stuff I left on my bike, but I don't go. I'm indecisive, grotty, and tired. I lie in my tent until someone shines a light. It's the sun. We grab some beers, go back in, and suddenly everything is better. We sit on a grassy bank, watching bands from a distance, and slowly the layers of clothing are peeled off. The fashion of the weekend seems to be red tartan kilts. It's not a good look. It takes a certain something to pull off such an outfit, and most of the guys wearing them don't have it.

This is my favourite aspect of festivals, sitting on the grass in the sun, drinking, talking bollocks, people-watching, and taking the piss; generally just laughing at everything. I then establish a four-step plan: I will finish my beer, go to the portaloo, wash my hands, and then get some Mexican food. It doesn't sound too challenging in the great scheme of things, but I'm in festival mode now, and without a firm plan I could be wandering aimlessly until it gets dark, and it doesn't get dark, so where would that leave me? However, there is an unexpected surprise as I put stage four into action. The Mexican food is Europeanly disappointing, unlike the compliment I then received. The guy stirring the refried and reheated beans turns and says to me:

"Been working on your biceps man?"

"No, not really. I'm pretty lazy, just lucky."

"Well ya looking good."

I was laughing all the way back to the grassy bank.

I have two phones: my home number and one for local sim cards. Both are dead. I haven't seen a computer in nearly a week; this would be the transition happening then. From somewhere I hear Gary Moore hold the prolonged cord of *Parisian Walkways*, and in a sea of soft focus my only awareness is that the festival has washed over me.

DAY 7

SWEDEN ROCK FESTIVAL, 0 MILES

When you can't understand the drunken babblings of the late night partiers outside your tent, they are somehow a lot less annoying. I awake to sunshine and have no idea what the time is, but I know I'm minging and the site is silent. They are so considerate, these Swedes, that they don't even snore. I negotiate the trip-wire guide ropes and take a cold, free shower. I then get a cup of tea and sit on a rock in the sun: I feel the best I've felt in ages.

It's short lived, however, as clouds start to appear and shorts are duly swapped for thermals: I retreat to my tent and let the Russian language make my eyes glaze over.

Once again, we are inside for the first band, this time by my request. When I was a truck driver, the bassist of this band used to load my truck. It's raining again, and we stand right at the front of the stage; it would be rude not to. They haven't drawn a massive crowd. It's not easy to lose yourself in the music when on the other side of the crowd control barriers a security guard stands staring right at you, three feet from your face. It's not even lunch time, and there is no one behind me. What do you honestly think the danger is here? Relax guys. I'm watching my old mate on stage, but I can feel the eyes of security burning into me. I try staring him down, but he is well practised at such tactics, and I pretend the stage has taken my attention away from him.

There was a time when I always used to go down the front. I would rush past the bar and merchandise stalls as soon as the theatre doors opened, just to get the perfect spot. I would stay there through the support band, whose name I not only knew, but whose record I owned too. I would fight to keep my position as the crush and struggle behind me would have the stage bruising my chest. I wouldn't give up my position until the headliner's last encore. I wouldn't even think about needing a drink or a wee the entire evening. I don't recall there ever being security in front of me then. I wasn't going to cause any trouble, and my enthusiasm was not alcohol-fuelled, so I suppose it was unnecessary. Perhaps they are only there now for my own safety: I may be pushing my limits standing up for so long after days of sleep deprivation and malnutrition.

In the afternoon we are sitting in the sun doing what we do best, and I see my bassist friend. He comes and hangs out with us; he rides a motorbike now too, and he tells me to get in touch when I get back. People keep asking him for a photograph; I didn't realise he was so famous, so we take photos too. Chilling with the rock stars, we're so cool.

The day gets colder and colder, the stamina is going, and the beer and food are long gone. We partied hard and peaked too soon. We lose each other, so I wander back to the tent, just in case they had the same idea. I lie down fully clothed, just for forty winks: then there is the sun again. I slept right through Guns 'N' Roses. Gutted.

Day 8

Karlskrona, Sweden, 87 Miles

I lie there trying to figure out how I managed to miss the headliners, including what excuse I'm going to come up with as to why. I feel awful; not just from the alcohol and bad food, but because the fear is back. I need to ride. I don't want to. I need to keep on going. Everyone is packing up, and that feels sad too. I don't want to move on. Well, I do. My head is not right, and it will be good to dry out a bit; blow some of that festival fuzz out of my muggy mind.

It soon transpires that my friends have missed Guns 'N' Roses too. So whilst I was worrying about what I was going to say to them, it turns out that they also peaked too soon. With the best intentions, our bodies and capabilities just aren't as rock 'n' roll as we would like.

I then find Mr. Campground, and he takes me to get my bike, telling me how they only got the shower block completed the day before the festival and how they used the land for farming until Sweden Rock decided to hold their annual event next door. Now they provide this alternative camping experience once a year, and that's all they do.

"It's better than farming," he shouts to me from the front of the quad bike.

No shit.

I take my bike back to my tent and put my phone on charge. As it accepts its charge, it vibrates around the seat happily bleeping: loads of messages. I'm not replying, though, it's too expensive now I'm out of my free minutes range. It's sad to pack up. I feel just like I did last weekend when I left my house, full of butterflies and foreboding. The difference is that this time I'm slightly more focused as I pack my bike in my methodical manner. My friends sense my state of mind and wander off to find some soup, while I concentrate on my packing ritual. They return just as I've decided there is room to strap on the trainers, just in case.

I find some beer amongst the debris of the camp site and replenish their diminished supplies before following them out. The local newspaper says Guns 'N' Roses got booed last night because they came on stage so late. They kept everyone waiting in the cold until 3 A.M., that egotistical ginger fuck. There was a time when he was punctual and appreciative of his audience. 3 A.M.? I would have missed them anyway. I'm glad I saw them in their heyday and not on this clutching-at-our-past tour.

We find a cash machine, and I give them back what they lent me; then it's goodbye. I feel empty, not excited. The sun tries to shine, and I try to appreciate it. It's always weird going back into civilisation after a prolonged festival environment, not helped by the grey cloud combined with the post festival blues. I'm reluctantly back in my own company. I'm on a downer that half makes me want to follow my friends up to Stockholm.

Sweden Rock Festival was undoubtedly the coldest, possibly the most expensive, definitely the friendliest, maybe the healthiest, and even after all that camping, still the most beautiful of festivals I have ever attended. I never did see the pretty fiancé again; probably just as well.

I take the road to Karlskrona; it's too close, too soon, too early. The port is an example of the dismal indifference you can create in concrete. It's Sunday, dead and uninhabited, except for a Polish biker. I go back into the town past the retail parks of consumer hell; the sprawl of electronic and DIY stores heaving with obedient shoppers buying their big TVs and latest fashions and gadgetry in an attempt to enhance their lives and their houses. Even though I'm not working tomorrow, I could still feel the sense of just waiting for Monday to arrive.

Some Sundays scream Sunday, and this one does.

I find a subterranean Internet café where the walls and ceilings are black, as is the keyboard, and a solitary light casts shadows over the worn keys. It's painfully hard to get my fix. I find the concert I slept through on YouTube, and the sense of loss disappears.

I then go and sit in an awful sports bar, trying not to watch a World Cup match on the omnipresent televisions. I nibble a burger as slowly as I can to pass the time. But too soon my plate is empty and reason to stay has left. I go back past the mute sadness of the shopping centre, back to the silent Sunday of the port. Seagulls screech, and nothing moves. I get my boarding ticket and my cabin key. It's a single. I can't wait for my berth.

Nothing to do now except wait; I could have got the day ferry but that would have meant an early start, sitting on a ferry all day, and finding somewhere to stay as soon as it docked. I'm sure this is better. I wait for the barrier to open, wait for the ferry to arrive, wait for the trucks to disembark. I chat to the Polish biker: he has done a three week circle, and it rained every day. He shows me his helmet cam. I didn't realise how cheap they were, but I don't think I need one. The other cars are full of rowdy, vodka-drinking Poles; I can't face any alcohol at all.

I ratchet my bike down and head for my cabin, where I do some emergency laundry in the shower and then clean myself up with the unlimited hot water. I just want to sleep, but there are noisy people outside my door. My first impression of Poland is not good, and I haven't even got there yet. But I do want to get some distance done now, just pass through and try to keep dry. My cabin is cold, my blankets inadequate, and my sleeping bag is on my bike. I put my jacket over my head and try to calm my busy mind into sleep.

DAY 9

40 Miles Southeast of Warsaw, Poland, 272 Miles

At 6.30 A.M. the ship's tannoy blasts out *Beautiful World*, but it's not: the skies aren't blue, they are colourless, and my washing is still wet. I go to the breakfast buffet; it's an awful environment, with shuffling hordes of impatience and irritation. On the plus side, I'm wearing my combats, so I can fill my pockets with supplies. I'm glad to get back to my cabin, even though it's colder than the rest of the ship.

I soon become aware that Poland does not have the euro, but at the exchange counter they want to change my euros to Swedish kroner before they change them to Polish zloty, taking a commission on a bad exchange rate with each transaction. No thanks.

I go down to the bike, relieved to see that it's still standing upright. I'm sure it feels the same when it sees me. I unstrap it, and then I'm ready to go. The Polish guy revs the four cylinders of his thirty-year-old Suzuki GSX and turns on his helmet cam for the exit up the greasy ramp. Then he's gone. I enter Poland with my senses fully alert. Hello Poland, my eighth country; I haven't even shown my passport yet.

Before I leave the port, I stop to change money. I leave my bike unattended and get my local currency. Then it's across the road for fuel. When I go in to pay, behind the counter is a wall of vodka, but before 9 A.M. on a Monday morning, it's not a temptation.

Some differences are subtle and some slap you in the face. The first thing that hits me is the smells. Strong diesel fumes pumped out from the back of slow trucks are combined with pungent toxic emissions from the factories. I realise how incredibly sterile our Western world is. Unfamiliar food smells then waft under my visor; now I know I'm really abroad.

The cars are old and always full: a poor economy stops wastage.

Poverty creates unity. We moan about our petrol prices at home, but it doesn't stop us doing solo trips most of the time. How often do you see four or five adults in a car in Britain?

I head for Gdansk, which I associate with one thing: David Gilmour. He recorded a live show here, and I have the box set at home. If I had had one single positive response from all my couch surfing requests, I may have been staying here, but I didn't, so I'm not. Just as I'm thinking how foreign everything is, I see a Tesco, visual evidence of their world domination, second only to Lady Gaga. I know which one I'd rather come across.

A motorway has been built since my map was printed, and it's all a bit confusing, so I decide to stick to the back roads. I wind round villages of old women with head scarves and long skirts walking down cobblestone roads. I've definitely gone back in time, so many people are walking; that would be why they are not a nation of fatties like we are.

I stop to take a photo of a stork in a nest of sticks on top of a telegraph pole. It's a strange site but not as strange it would seem as I am to the villagers as I point my camera at said stork. Perhaps I would blend in better if I didn't have my pants and socks drying all over my bike. I feel much better now I have all these distractions, but I still wonder why I am doing this.

I get back on the main road to Warsaw. The driving, oh my God, it's so aggressive and impatient. I have to spend as much time looking in my mirrors as I do in front of me. I leave the obligatory space between me and the car in front, but then the car behind passes me to get into the space, with no intention of overtaking the car I was behind before he cut in. They overtake straight into oncoming traffic, who then veer over to the hard shoulder: it seems to be a recognised method. So when a car comes up behind me, I have to go over onto the hard shoulder to let him pass, and if I don't notice he has come up behind me, he passes by ridiculously close. It's so dangerous until I learn the etiquette. When in Rome...

The road is lined with whores waiting to pick up motorists. So many of them, all of varying degrees of attractiveness. If you had the time and the money you could rack up a lot of notches in your steering wheel on your journey to Warsaw. They sit on stalls in clearings at the side of the road. I seem to remember hearing about this somewhere. It rings a distant bell: it should be an alarm bell. I do slow down for a better look, much as I would for a fruit and veg stall or a full skip. The difference being, skips don't smile and flirt when you think about climbing inside. Where would we go if I was to stop, would we have to erect my tent before anything else? I'm intrigued. So many questions, not least the price and the amount of custom they get. I wonder how healthy they are; they do all seem to have firm stalls if that's anything to go by.

There are other things being sold at the roadside, like pots of popcorn. Well, what looks like popcorn. I don't slow down to check, because I'm not hungry for popcorn and I'd had a big breakfast on the boat anyway. Later, I stop in a garage to try and grasp the exchange rate; I check on my washing, stretch my legs, and eat my ferry roll. It turns greyer and starts to rain. Do I want to see Warsaw? No, I want to head east, remember? This is not a European sightseeing trip. I'm in transit. I'm not really intending to do any sightseeing until I get further east. It's not what I came to see. That's why I didn't stop at Dover Castle before I shipped to Calais.

So much for the deliberation. Warsaw doesn't have an M25; the road takes me right into the city. The Vistula River divides the city in two, and as I ride down its west bank, I can see how swollen it is, though it seems to have gone down from the news reports I saw. Warsaw was not the Venice I was led to believe.

The traffic is slow and smelly; bus passengers look out of the dreary windows at me with dreary looks. Some boys in a van hoot and wave and ask me where I'm going.

"You need to be in that lane," they say.

They let me cut in front of them, and I cross over a bridge and I'm heading east again. The rain has stopped, but it's cold and grey and I'm tired. Between looking for trucks in front, cars coming up behind, whores on stalls, and popcorn, it was a pretty exhausting day.

A hotel is signposted; it's not late, but I'm ready to stop. It's a bit posh, but I'm definitely worth it. There is a solitary communal computer running Windows 95; I'm not in any way a geek or computer snob, but it does make me smile in a nostalgic kind of way.

I eat in the restaurant alone, but before I'm finished, a Belgian guy with perfect English enters the dining room, and we start chatting. He buys me beer on his expense account, and we discuss how dangerous the driving is here. We talk kids and family; does anyone have a straight-forward family life anymore? He tells me he was within a week of what was to be his first marriage and was summoned to his fiancé's house. The whole family was sitting there, and she told him she didn't want to get married, right out of the blue, whilst her relatives gave stern nods of affirmation.

"Were they there just to enjoy your humiliation?"

What a soul destroying experience. I wonder what her side of the story is. We drink and talk, and four hours pass. So much for drying out.

Biking alone is a little bit dull, and my budget is badly blown. Today was nothing special, and I still overspent. Rain doesn't enhance anything; it may make grass greener, but it goes unnoticed until the sun shines. It's unfair to judge a country when you're only passing through its grey wetness; but it's also impossible not to have an impression, and from inside my helmet, I didn't like anything I saw outside. So it's probably just as well Poland is not my destination; I'm just on my way.

DAY 10

L'VIV, UKRAINE, 226 MILES

I am woken by a text from my KLR buddy; we met through the overland website during my days of research and preparation. I asked questions, he gave advice, which then resulted in a test ride to the south coast for a visit. He left England a month before me and headed towards northern Russia. Reading between the lines, he wasn't having as much fun as he could be having. His text suggested a meet in L'viv, Ukraine. Well, that's a good way to start the day. Not that I'm ready to start it yet. I stay in bed with *BBC World*, and when I do open the curtains, sunlight streams in, whoopee.

In the dining hall I fill up on scrambled eggs and Polish sausage and blatantly take a roll back to my room. About the only way I can justify a hotel is the fact I won't be spending any more money on food. I go and check on my bike and move it into the sun to dry off. I then briefly indulge in the nostalgia that is Windows 95 again, just to say I'm still alive. Afterwards, I check out and go to load my bike; an older guy is loitering around and then takes a photo of me on his phone. He shows it to me, followed by all the others he has taken of my bike.

"Yeah, I know, I do it all the time."

Sunshine changes everything, but my head is still full of indecision. Every choice I have I agonise over. It's impossible to illuminate the uncertainty in my life.

I read once that Albert Einstein had seven suits all the same, because he didn't want to waste his brain power on thinking what to wear. I deliberate over whether I should wear jeans under my bike trousers, where I should stop to eat my stolen roll, and whether I should spend one more night in Poland or go into Ukraine.

When I'm back on the road I feel more confident and better acquainted with the style of driving. I'm fast approaching the truck in front, and rather than slow down, I just overtake into the path of an oncoming car; sure enough, he pulls onto the hard shoulder. So the system does work, but I don't try it again. I pass by graveyards and notice that every grave is meticulously maintained: they all seem to have fresh flowers on them. I wonder if they've just had a "day of the dead" like they have in Mexico, or whether there are so many deaths on the road that the flowers never get a chance to wilt.

Despite the unfamiliarity of it all, I can at least read the signs; I bet if I do end up coming back this way, it will feel almost homely.

The Polish sausage I ate earlier doesn't do my breath any favours. The fumes continue in my helmet much like the petrol ones do in my tank. 372 miles before I go onto reserve; that's the best yet. 70mpg, due to my slower speeds. I can't blame the bike for my blown budget: it's my choice of accommodation that's doing that.

I can't find a good place to eat my roll; there aren't many lay-bys, which also equates to not so many whores. I'm wearing my fingerless gloves now; it's always a bonus to have a fingerless glove day. It's so much easier to take photos, and if it's sunny, there's more to photograph, so it's a single-edged sword I suppose, which is a good thing, depending what end of it you are on.

There is a queue of traffic up ahead; I have run out of Poland. Well that's that decision made then. People are standing around outside their cars, and they indicate that I should go to the front. It's a long queue, and my exhaust pops out a warning as I tentatively ride past the wandering motorists; they are just as big of a liability when they are out of their cages. I reach the border just as the sun decides to be its hottest and shiniest since I left home. I stand in my bike gear (thankfully without my jeans underneath) and sweat. With the smell of sausage still on my breath, I start to negotiate my way out of Poland.

A bike and geared-up rider can be an intimidating sight. I've been around both all my life, and although I don't feel it, I can still understand the threat of the loud engine and covered face. It happens less these days. However, it can still provoke reactions that otherwise friendly people would not express. There is the little unexpected bonus I'm getting from bringing Monklet along: a smile breaks a scary face. He sits on the back tyre (the spare one, he's a monkey not a mud flap), and people look at his beaming smile and flapping arms and smile back. That in turn makes me smile, and before you know it, there's been a transient jovial exchange. That has to be a good thing. Smiles don't need explanation or translation.

I wait in line to get my forms and fill in the blanks. When finished, I sit astride my bike in the shade of a canopy and hand my completed documents through a window. I get the appropriate stamps, and my passport is handed back to me before being waved on. I was just pulling away from a customs booth when there's a screech of tyres and crunch of metal. I look behind; someone had got out of their car with the engine running and still in gear. It rammed into the car in front, which pushed the next car twenty feet forward: right where I had been balancing my bike five seconds before. Phew.

The entry into Ukraine goes okay; I hand my motorcycle papers to the customs official, who reads out my address to me and even tries to pronounce my postcode.

Bless him. He then says, "Okay, bye bye!" and I move forward to another queue. We have to wait by the barrier; why? Lunch time? Army search? No, because they have just painted a new white line, and we all sit watching paint dry before we can drive over it.

And what a line it is: the other side of it is a very different world. I've entered into the land of the Cyrillic alphabet, so I can't read any signs at all; there are horse and carts trundling along next to massive Scania trucks. There are workers in the fields with scythes. The roads have deteriorated even more, although the driving standards have improved dramatically. It's so exciting to have transported myself into such a different country. It's exhilarating but also very scary. The scaremongering words of warning come back into my head, and I decide that this is prime mafia-mugging territory. I have prepared for this moment: I have a mugging wallet with me. It has a photo of my daughter in it, some US dollars as well as local currency, and several expired credit cards. It looks like a good little steal to the opportunist thief, but the real bounty is stashed away in the bowels of the bike.

I find a piece of waste ground to pull over on and do my wallet switching, but a car pulls in behind me. With paranoia being paramount, I pull out again and soon I'm in L'viv. I find myself right in the city centre, and the traffic is awful. I didn't realise that I'd gained another hour, and it was now rush hour. Have I gained an hour? My clock has just gained an hour, because I moved it forward an hour, but I have lost an hour; this continues to confuse me and everyone I speak to at every time zone. The pavements are full of beautiful women, and the roads are full of ugly vehicles. Then with an overheating bike and no idea at all what any written word says, the roads turn to uneven cobblestones, and just to really challenge me, they throw in some tram lines. Oh yes, the motorcycle wheels fit in there perfectly; well, the front does. Shit. So I head out of town in some direction or other.

I would like to go back in later; there was beautiful architecture and fountains and parks and so many pedestrians. But, instead, I find a hotel out of town; I ask the price; it's expensive. I go back to my bike, I do some calculations; wait a minute, no it's not. Prices have dropped, so I take a room. I can justify it if I have to, but I don't. A band is setting up downstairs right beneath my window; every time I look out another amplifier is being dragged out of another Lada. I'm thinking, "Oh shit," but when they start up it's really good. Bass guitar, squeeze organ, and a drum. They play kind of folky Ukrainian traditional (I would imagine) music.

I eat my dinner down by the band, and I think my foot may even have tapped a bit. More players turn up as the evening progresses; they must have finished work late, I suppose. I'm really liking this. Sitting in the warmth of a foreign city and getting a little bit of local entertainment. I've just ridden to Ukraine, and I'm quite chuffed with myself. Back in my room I surf through the channels and find porn. Hard-core porn. Today has been a good day.

Day 11

Ternopil, Ukraine, 97 Miles

The sun is out, the sky is blue, and there's the click of high heels outside my room, where the beautifully dressed women of L'viv are strutting off to work. My KLR buddy, Andy, has also texted to say he is 90 kms away.

When I get down to the empty restaurant, I can't read the menu and have to do an impersonation of a chicken just to get some food. I get cheese and meats: they just wanted to humiliate me. Moscow MTV blasts out of a wall-mounted TV; the sound is intrusive, and the visuals are exhausting. I've had more relaxed breakfast experiences. I take my time and wait for Andy to arrive.

The daily indecision strikes again. Should I book another night? I take a walk and find the ring road. I did have it right in my head, I was west of the city; I'm slowly learning to trust my instincts. I walk past a street market filling my senses with the strange, the foreign, and the vaguely familiar. Babushkas sit behind the fruits of their labours and stare at me. Shoulders back, head high; yes I know you are all looking at me, but I will project an air of confidence and an image of belonging, and if I can just fool myself, that will be a good start. Back at the room I decide to pack, but I'm distracted by the porn on the TV. It reminds me of my Russian visa; multiple entry.

I ride out at midday. Andy can't find me, and I have to ride to the ring road and back again. We text, we talk, I ride up, I come back, I wait, I feel conspicuous, and then I see the square headlight and silver panniers of the KLR I envied in Southampton. Handshake and hug, we talk for two hours non-stop; well, Andy does, he clearly hasn't spoken in six weeks. He tells me of corrupt cops, fines, and border fiascos. I let him vent; it's funny, relaxed, and easy-going.

"I haven't met any English speakers in ages," he says.

"I know, you won't shut the fuck up," I say with a grin. Yeah, we're going to get along just fine. "So, in an ideal world, where would you be heading now?"

"Odessa."

"Now there's a coincidence."

"Let's ride together for a few days and see how it goes," he says.

So we ride. The roads are not good, but his opinion of them is lower than mine. It all depends on your basis of comparison. No one can agree on road conditions. I first discovered this in Alaska. Every report was more dramatic, more sensational, more horrendous than the reality. Mud was always deeper, distances longer, and weather worse. Once, on a stretch of dirt road from the Canadian border into Alaska, I got ahead of my riding companions. When I found a nice little vista point to wait for them, a lawyer on a hire bike came from the other way. He stopped to tell me the horrors that lay ahead of me and how he overcame the challenges. When my mates caught up and he realised I wasn't a sole rider, he changed the subject and then said his goodbyes. The most difficult thing I came across on that road was the crossing back into the USA, and even that was a breeze compared to airport immigration. The officer looked at my passport photo.

"You still got all that hair under that helmet?" he asked.

"Yeah, a bit thinner and a bit greyer, but it's still there."

"Surprised you managed to get it on at all," he says, with a sly smile and the authority that makes up for the lack of wit.

Yeah, nice one officer, like it, like it. Terrific race those Alaskans...terrific.

It's strange riding with someone, it takes some getting used to; it also makes me look forward to my solitude again. But I always want what I haven't got until I get it. I take the lead and take photos as I pass. Always a good ice-breaker I think; everyone likes a photo of them riding.

I keep hearing about the corrupt cops who will pull you over and relieve you of your money. They are everywhere, and despite the oncoming vehicles flashing their lights in warning, getting pulled over is inevitable.

The way we deal with passing the constant speed traps is to always find something to look at as we pass the cops. A glance down to check the engine is still there, a study of the map on the tank bag or a turn of the head to take in the scenery. Anything but eye contact, because if your eyes lock and the baton is raised, you are now either going to be robbed or become a fugitive. The best thing is to keep behind a truck, so the cops don't see you until the last minute. Of course, the obvious answer would be to actually do the speed limit, but that's a dangerous option. No one does the speed limit, so if you do, you're constantly overtaken and cut up. Sometimes this is only done to hoot and wave. Our foreign plates and spare tyres scream excitement and adventure to the enthusiastic and revenue to the law.

When we stop, we talk quickly and excitedly. The road is uneventful, but the thrill is in the strangeness of it all: the horse and carts and old Russian ex-military trucks pumping out black smoke as if they are steam-powered. We do a steady

55mph, if the road permits, and at every police check turn our heads and carry on. It's far more distracting riding as two; I'm not paying nearly as much attention. I have turned my mugging wallet into a corruption wallet, which basically means taking out most of the money and putting in a driving licence.

We head into Ternopil, realise our mistake, and duly turn around and head for the ring road. A quick discussion at the lights and Andy says go on to the next town. I say yes but mean no; I'm wet and it's gone 5 P.M. As we leave the rainy, smelly, nondescript city, a police car comes past us waving us over. I knew a pull was inevitable but not so imminent. The fat one stays in the dry while his "bitch" gets out, showing us a video he has of us doing an unrealistically high speed. It's a nice little video of us riding side by side, but he is not here to be congratulated on his photographic skills. It is a digital readout that says 85kmh in a 60 zone. He takes our documents, and the only word we understand is *protocol*. It's all bollocks, a big game. They show us a three-page report they have had to type up, logging our disrespect for the law. And when exactly did you find the time to write that then? We must pay a fine of 700 of their gold pieces; a beer is five gold pieces, so this unreasonable request is absolutely out of the question. We protest. They take one of us at a time into the car to interrogate and intimidate. It's raining hard now, and while Andy is in the back seat, I go and sit in the front. They look at me.

"What? It's raining out there. I'm getting wet."

After much frowning and flaunting of their authority, suddenly it occurs to them that for a small gift the whole incident could be overlooked. The fee drops to 200, the game has reached its conclusion, but I want to play a little more. In my mugging wallet is 180, and I show them that's all I have; with disgust and reluctance I put the last of my currency on the dashboard. I then offer an expired visa card to make up the short fall. But they are all smiles now; our passports are returned, having abused their authority to line their pockets. It's all handshakes and waves. Now who has broken protocol? We never stood a chance, but with gritted teeth to keep the dummy in, we got away as lightly as we could hope to. Corrupt cops are right down there with estate agents and health and safety officers. Fuck 'em all.

That will teach me to calculate my chickens whilst I ride. I had realised that today was about to be the first day I had lived within my budget, but it's blown again now. It's getting dark; I see a sign that starts with "Mot..." That will do. It's less than a hotel and more than a truck stop; that would be a motel then. We are shown where we can park our bikes under cover; a tiny room with two single beds for £7 each. That's more like it. In the bar/café the owner mothers us, cooks for us, and frowns as we order our third beers.

I'm a notoriously light sleeper, and thankfully, Andy doesn't snore. It's silent and warm, and the only sounds are of the occasional truck passing outside and me saving money.

Day 12

Tulchin, Ukraine, 232 Miles

I'm awoken by sun through the window instead of snoring: I like my new travel companion.

The paving outside the front of the café is made from blocks laid in a herringbone design; it's an optical illusion, somewhere between an Escher drawing and one of those 3D posters that were so popular in the early '90s. I stare at it whilst Andy loads his bike; it looks almost corrugated but is flat. I take a photo of it that will make great wallpaper on my desktop.

Out on the road we turn a lot of heads, but for all the attention we attract we don't get many waves. I persist and wiggle my hand relentlessly, and finally a wave is returned. I love that, always have.

I remember cycling through the tea plantations of Sri Lanka, and all the leaf pickers, who were carbon copies of the women on the PG Tips box, would straighten their backs to wave enthusiastically at me as I passed. People would wave, whether they were young boys playing cricket with a plank for a bat and sticks for wickets or old boys holding their gnarled walking sticks between their legs as they stay sitting on a bench in the shade of a bamboo thatch. Those Sri Lankans are a great nation of wavers. Waving has to be my favourite non-communicative recognition. Better than a friend request on Facebook without a message attached. This is real. Instant and genuine, and being the short-attention-span commitment-phobe that I am, its intimacy and immediacy is perfect for me.

Andy seems to be carrying a lot more stuff than me; it makes me feel good about my minimalist packing. I do envy his tiny laptop, though. In my time of research, I found a particularly good thread on the five best and worst things people took on their trip. sat navs and Leathermans kept coming up, as did a notebook. I have an ancient Swiss army knife and a sense of direction; I didn't acknowledge those modern day necessities. I don't think I really considered it fully. The word *notebook* to me conjures up an image of a policeman pulling a spiral-bound wad of lined paper from his breast pocket and licking his pencil before flicking through the pages and writing in it—not a small computer. Not that I brought either. But as Andy said, the notebook was a comfort thing. I had Monklet for that, but it wasn't really the same. One particularly memorable quote was "The best thing I took on my trip was my wife, when she was right. The worst was my wife when she was wrong." I can't read women any better than I can read a Sat Nav or Cyrillic, so that was another option I didn't have. But I do like that notebook idea.

I've really got the feel of the bike now; I'm weaving around the potholes with total control. It's taken 1,900 miles to get this confidence. That and less pressure in my tyres seems to help too. Now if I could just grasp the language and the road signs I would really be making some progress.

It's a stop-start kind of day. We see a German on a thirty-year-old SR500: he looks like my dentist, but that is only really of interest to me and my dentist. But honestly, the likeness is uncanny. I enjoy looking at his bike. I've owned several XT500s over the years, exactly the same engine but with an enviable, twelve-volt electrical system that generates lights you can see by and indicators that flash at less than 5,000rpm. Twelve-volt electrics, it's no wonder they caught on. His bike is vibrating apart, and he shows us all the things that aren't there anymore. He is carrying his tools in an ammunition box on the top rear of his bike; I frown inwardly at his bad choice of weight distribution. He has come through Moldova; it sounds pretty cool. Within a few miles I have decided my journey won't be complete without a trip into Moldova.

A group of touring bikes come past us all honking horns and waving, and I'm beginning to feel not so special anymore.

The thing about travelling with new company is that I'm on my best behaviour. With my two riding buddies, who I have known for an accumulated fifty-five years, I have been known to throw teddy out of the pram and have my little tantrums, but they aren't perfect, either. Methodical Rob's "I need to completely repack my panniers" is an almost daily comment, as he sticks on another nicotine patch, because every bike trip is the perfect time to give up smoking; at least for the first few days. And then there's Jonathan, whizzing off ahead in the wrong direction because he never has a map. It's no wonder I get infuriated with my two best buddies sometimes. But with my new acquaintance I have patience to spare. Days like today I could just keep on going. The butterflies and the nerves are a thing of the past now. The down side of a new companion is a change in my ritual; I would never have let myself get this low on local currency if I were riding alone.

We ride into a city to find a McDonald's for free Wi-Fi to see if we need a visa for Moldova. The place is heaving with beautiful women. I go buy some McShite while Andy surfs; there is more substance on the Internet than there is on the tray I bring to the table.

We don't need a visa, so we decide to head south to check out what Moldova has to offer. We get completely lost trying to exit the city. We head down dirt roads by abandoned factories, bumping over exposed railway tracks and into an estate of high-rise housing blocks. If this was at home I would feel very uneasy, but people are friendly and helpful, and we find our way back to the right road, no stress, no worries, and no temper.

After two months away, Andy has become very practiced in his camping skills; it will be good to break my hotel habit. We stop to get some supplies when we come to yet another tiny village. As we walk into the little shop, the young girl visibly jumps; well yeah, I suppose we don't look like your average shopper. Lots of pointing and laughing and a bit of miming, and we are sorted for E numbers and whizz off, but first a little beer in the sun.

The shed next to the shop is full of sewing machines with miserable people operating them. I'm looking through the door and thinking how lucky I am to be out here by my bike with a cold beer in my hand and not slaving away in a sweatshop. Even when the minibus comes to pick up the workers at the end of their shift, there seems to be no sign of relief on their faces, no chatter or interaction. They are just sewing machines in the material world.

The sun is beginning to drop, and we ride past fields of virile crops towards Moldova, past the plodding progress of the horse and carts: there is no urgency in this timeless place. Andy seems to instinctively know when to pull off the road, and we ride down a track to a secluded spot perfect to pitch a couple of tents for the night.

When it comes to riding capabilities, Andy and I are on similar levels, but once the camping stove is unpacked I'm out of my element. Where I have a pannier dedicated to haircare products, he has one for food, and all sorts of spices and condiments appear. Now I understand why his load is so much bigger than mine. I decide I can either watch and learn or drink and daydream; I opt for the latter and spray some red ken in my hair.

We eat well and find out a little about each other's lives, both of which seem to be having a high point. The sound of frogs keeps me awake, but in a good way.

DAY 13

TIRASPOL, MOLDOVA, 178 MILES

The frogs croaked outside my tent all night, but I feel so alive when I wake up. Although the tent's sagging with dew in the morning, the sun dries it off as I eat my sausage sandwich. My panniers look like they have vomited, but the contents go back in an ordered fashion with room to spare. There is no need to "completely repack them."

It's such a perfect morning: the shadows of trees cross the road to shade us before the sun rises to its peak in the solstice sky. There is no traffic, no cops, and no worries, just a vague destination to head for. The problem is that said destination is actually in the other direction. So once my head comes round to the practicalities of navigation over the appreciation of the day, we turn around and ride on the sunny side of the street towards Moldova.

We pass through quaint villages of old, scarved women bent double doing their manual chores. Turkeys, goats, and cows wander along the verges. As we exit one particular village we pass a beautiful girl in a backless dress. The only thing that holds my jaw up is my helmet strap; surely it's too early for that dress. How do these beautiful girls turn into these wrinkled and bent old Babushkas? And did the old men who married them notice the transition? At a petrol stop two old boys roll up in a Ural with a sidecar. We scrutinise each other's bikes with smiles and finger pointing. They have a reverse gear, but I only intend to head in one direction. That's how they deal with their hot, young wives becoming crumpled, gravity-challenged old women: motorbikes, the international distraction to all issues female.

The border village has a massive street market bustling with people; there is so much to look at and to look out for; so many wrong turns to take. We squeeze through tight gaps of badly-parked trucks and overflowing stalls.

We find the river we saw on the map that divides Ukraine and Moldova; it sort of leads in the direction of Odessa, so it seems like a good idea to follow that. There is no bridge, so we wait for a ferry in the shade of a customs border post. Our documents are passed from one official to another whilst the sniffer dog lies motionless in the dust; looks like he hasn't sniffed anything good recently. We wait with the excited passengers, who have all come from market with their rolls of Ukrainian wallpaper to decorate their Maldovan houses. It seems to be a popular export.

In the marshes between the reeds is a carpet of frogs. Every so often they start up a frog chorus and all participate; the stagnant water ripples as they reveal their hiding place, and then for no reason that I can see, it all goes silent again. It passes the time while we watch the ferry come and go on its ten-minute crossings until it's our turn to board.

It takes three hours on the other side to get processed, not because of the queue; there are only the two of us. They want to see a green card, but insurance companies no longer issue green cards. It's not done in a nasty way; it's friendly and upbeat, firm but fair. Between the immigration girl, the customs man, and a useless Russian phrase book, we slowly understand we have to go and buy insurance from that little shed over there. It was not straightforward, but still full of patience, we mime and laugh our way through the whole process. As has become the custom, every parting is done with big, friendly, sincere smiles and waves.

We are free to discover Moldova. All I know about the country is that Iron Maiden sing about it in the song *Alexander the Great*. I want to play it on my iPod; I like to play relevant songs: I played *Going to Montana* by Frank Zappa when I was going to Montana and *On the Train to Bangkok* by Rush when...well, you get the idea. So I was keen to hear Bruce Dickinson scream something about "defeating an army in Moldova" and get my history lesson from heavy metal.

We go the wrong way and ride into a village; we stop to look at the map. In a statement that is rapidly becoming a catchphrase we realise that "I don't think we are where we think we are." We are instantly surrounded by the villagers, excited children all pointing and shouting, even cars stop to help us read our map. We are invited to follow a Lada out of the situation we have created and onto the right road. We ride into a town, and I change some money; it's always a relief to have local currency. Whilst Andy goes to buy ice cream, I guard the bikes; another great thing about not being a solo rider. Probably the biggest problem is the unattended bike; it's unavoidable and very uncomfortable. It occurs to me that I might have a more detailed map of this area than my vague single page of all things Eastern European. I dig in my panniers and discover that I do and that it also covers the last three days of riding. Oh well. They use the Roman alphabet here, so I can read the signs again in this country. I can also read the faces; the people here are noticeably different in their clothing and manner. They show their emotions here much more. The Ukraine stares have been replaced by smiles, and waving seems to be a national pastime. I'm all for that. Every pedestrian waves, and even the truckers hoot a hello.

The land begins to undulate: if you can't have mountains an undulation will do nicely. We climb hills, and the views and scenery get better and better. We haven't really followed the river, but it is somewhere around. In a tiny town we take every available wrong route and end up down bumpy, rocky, dirt tracks. I'm not such a confident rider now; my feet are hot in my boots, and my helmet is uncomfortable. We can see the road we want, but it's the other side of a ravine, and we just can't get to it. Eventually we take the right road; it was the first one we had tried.

We had intended to stay in the next town but inadvertently take the bypass-cum-truck route. It's a mud track of carp-pond-sized puddles, and we manage to miss anything that may have looked like culture, architecture, or accommodation. We are just riding heads down and avoiding the holes, and then we come across the elusive river—the river of divided and undecided borders. There is a short and casual police check before we cross the bridge. On the other side are more border controls. Where the hell are we? I thought we were in Moldova, but now what are we crossing into? Are we back in Ukraine? I haven't even touched my Moldovan money. It takes hours. One particularly anal bureaucrat fills out his forms meticulously slowly, reaching for dusty ledgers on straining shelves, leafing through well-thumbed pages to find the relevant code number, which is then copied down in the empty box. The ledger is then carefully closed and replaced, and after a phone call, the next line of the form is started. There is no point in reacting; I won't give him the pleasure, so I lean back into the seat of this authoritarian's office, and when my phone rings, I take the piss out of this idiot to my daughter in Denver, who wants to know where I am. She's not the only one. After the form is thoroughly filled in, after every *i* has been dotted and every *t* crossed and yet more money has been demanded, we then have to give the exact routes we will be taking and places we will be staying. This is a bit tricky when you don't even know what country you're in. After we have both been processed, Mr. Anal gets off his fat arse and comes out to the bikes. He gets very excited when he sees my new tyres strapped on the back. No I didn't declare them, and no you are not going to fill out any more forms. He smiles; he is messing with me, but I know if I show the slightest hostility this bluff will become a reality.

There is a motel directly across from the border crossing, but it's not a motel, or if it is, it's not a motel for the likes of us. So we follow the river, and the light disappears as does any sign of civilisation, and somehow there is nowhere to camp, either.

After an hour we come to a town; there is no hotel. Well there is something like an old Russian dormitory, but it's not an option. We decide to camp, but the supermarket has just closed. Some concerned locals lead us to a hotel; it's the dormitory again. Oh, okay then. We are screamed at in Russian by the receptionist; we pay in dollars and are led past a banquet hall. It's Friday night, and there is a function on; there are countless stunningly beautiful women dressed to kill. They could all be supermodels, every one of them, and in my stinking sweating bike clothes they are as unavailable as a hot meal and a cold beer appear to be. Our bikes are locked in a dungeon downstairs. Andy goes out in one last desperate attempt to find something to eat or drink. I finally get to play my iPod, Bruce sings Macedonia, not Moldova, so I even bloody got that wrong.

Our cell is so far down the corridor that we can't even hear the music from the banqueting hall, and it's also extremely unlikely that any of the girls will wander this far away from the party. Andy returns empty-handed. Ho hum, off to bed then.

DAY 14

ODESSA, UKRAINE, 110 MILES

Next morning we wander into the depth of the hotel, through dark, windowless, musty rooms, through a labyrinth of broken hotel furniture, until we are reunited with our bikes. We push them up a ramp and into the sunlight, then ride round the corner to the supermarket. It's a beautiful fresh morning, and Saturday shoppers stare at the freak in biker boots wearing thick black trousers walking up and down the aisles carrying his basket. I don't care today. I sing along out loud to *Too Much Love Will Kill You* by Queen as it's pumped out over the supermarket PA system. I wait in line at the checkout, but they don't accept the money I changed yesterday or the Ukraine money I have either. Am I in some parallel universe? Where the hell are we? I have to go to a bank within the supermarket to change money again, whilst the unfortunate people who chose my lane are now fully committed with their shopping on the conveyer belt, waiting for me to change my money. I'm totally unaware of the country I'm in, the exchange rate I'm getting, or the currency I am receiving. I'm in the vulnerable position of holding out the notes and letting the cashier take the ones she wants.

I go back to Andy waiting by the bikes. "I don't think we are where we think we are." I don't mind the stares until we eat our yogurts and slice our loaf and they are still looking on. Come on, you've seen people eat before; now go about your business.

We head out in what is almost definitely the right direction. Every single road to our right has police and barriers blocking it, so we keep going straight. At a roundabout we are stopped and sent in what probably continues to be the right direction. There is nothing else I would rather be doing right now than riding in the sunshine. We pull off the road at a petrol station just for a drink and a stretch. The pump attendant comes over for a chat, "Mongolia? Crazy": the usual stuff.

Then another border; now we are definitely heading into the Ukraine, but it's not so simple, as now the officials are really corrupt. The entry stamps in our passports are different. The discrepancy is of great concern to the men in uniforms, and we have to deal with a double act of nice corrupt cop and high-ranking nasty corrupt cop.

"You must go back to the last border and get the right stamp in your passport," says nasty cop.

"But boss," pleads the nice cop, "let them go, please boss, let them go."

"Speak to boss, give him present," we are advised when boss had left the office in disgust at our inappropriate paperwork, "$50, I tell boss you are sorry."

More frequently these days I find myself looking much harder into the eyes of people just to age them, because as I get older I have come to realise that more and more people, especially ones in positions of power, are much younger than me. I have always had respect for my elders, which automatically makes me contemptuous of anyone who isn't. Nasty cop may just have a few years on me, but his bitch is just a boy, and he needs a slap.

I lay $20 on the table, and it is covered immediately by a big ledger. Nasty cop comes back in.

"Boss, please, they are only tourists, on holiday, please, boss, let them go." The nice cop continues to bleat and humiliate himself on our behalf.

The ledger is moved, but strangely the $20 has disappeared. So has nasty cop's reluctance to let us continue our journey with such discrepancies in our paperwork. This blatant disregard for the law, this major infringement of their regulations, which previously gave nasty cop no option but to enforce the law with all the power invested in him, now can seemingly be overlooked. He will ignore our misdemeanour and let us leave his corrupt little country which will never amount to anything. No wonder it's not even marked on the maps. They don't need a present; they need a fucking Oscar. What a bloody waste of time that trip across the border was. What country were we in anyway?

Transnistria it turns out was where we were; it's a part of Moldova, but it declared its independence in 1990, which was followed by a two-year civil war. Transnistria has not been recognised by any country but maintains its functional autonomy and has military and other support from Russia. I didn't know this at the time, and now I do I don't really care. But I do hope all those beautiful girls are happy in their independent state, and that their futures are as bright as their smiles.

I'll know more when Iron Maiden release their next album. Unless there is an invasion by America, in which case I'll get my rhyming report from Roger Waters.

We are about to enter Odessa; this is the first place I've actually wanted to see—the first calculated destination of the trip so, therefore, the first achievement. It looked a long way from home on the map. Andy pulls off the road into the dust.

"I saw the bar, perhaps we should have a drink. It would make dealing with the city easier."

I like this guy. So we stand outside in the heat to keep an eye on our bikes, and the beer tastes so good. We are attracting unwanted attention; I'm beginning to think this is not such a good area. One particular drunk, gold-toothed local won't stop shaking my hand and wants to ride my bike or at least on the back. I have to assert myself, and I discover he does understand at least one word of English. When I shout "Oi" he jumps away, and we leave before he changes his mind.

We ride into the city looking for the sea and a hotel. At some traffic lights a guy leans out of his window.

"Are you here for the bike show?"

"What bike show?"

"Follow me."

First we go to a pedestrian area where bikes are allowed to park. It turns out it is the weekend of Ukraine's biggest bike show, and we have just missed the ride out. A lot of the bikes are still parked here, and we are taken to an open street café and shown a table already occupied by some very big Maldovan patch club members. They all shake our hands before returning to their ice cream sundaes. People keep coming up to chat. An American comes to the table and starts to tell us about all the places he has been and all the people he knows. I take an instant dislike to him; he is one of those people who may have been everywhere but has seen nothing. He may know of all these people but he doesn't know any one of them, and I can see right through him. There are some Russian patch club girls looking at my bike, and seeing as this is such a friendly city, I go and introduce myself. I am loving Odessa; it's bringing out the best in me. The bikers mix with the shoppers and pedestrians, and there is no judgement, just acceptance. And the women: oh, my, God. An Italian approaches me, his pedal has come off his bicycle; do I have any tools? So I fix his pedal. He then confides "It's my girlfriend's bike," and over walks another stunning, angelically-beautiful example of the female form. Our operation creates a little interest, but somehow it doesn't feel like we are being stared at, just watched, appreciated, and accepted. I'm sure I'm glowing.

Our self-appointed host, Igor, is ready to lead us to the show. The American has wandered off to take photos of pretty pedestrians without their consent and causes a bit of a stir. We ride out of town, and the pounding music from the stage announces we have found the bike show. We pay our money, get a T-shirt and sticker, and someone shows us where we should camp. Although it's in the sun, it is explained that we will be in the shade in the morning when we most need it. We get off our bikes, look at each other, and give a high five. We have just ridden into town on bike show weekend. We have somewhere to stay, lots to see, and people to meet. I think we have just landed on our feet. From Sweden Rock one weekend to Goblin bike show the next. There I was thinking I was going to miss a summer of bike shows and festivals.

Beyond the show is Butlins-style holiday camp accommodation, where the majority of the bikers stay, and beyond that is the beach. It's perfect. We sit at a long bench-like table and party with people who have come long distances for this show. Drinking beer, talking bollocks, and people-watching: déjà vu. Afternoon turns to evening, we sit in the sun and the bands play on into the night. There are fireworks and now the obligatory beautiful women, tonight with painted bodies or dressed like sexy cops and all with perfect figures. I think we may have peaked just right.

Day 15

Goblin Bike Show, Odessa, Ukraine, 0 Miles

The sun is shining, but not on our righteous camping spot. Consequently, I'm not forced out of my tent by heat; only by my own offensive smells. It's time for some personal hygiene. This may be the time but it isn't really the place; parched dusty land with no running water in sight. I pack up my tent slowly while Andy sits in the shade with his laptop, logging the adventure so far.

I go to the bar at midday, well it is only 50p a beer. As I approach Andy's table I say, "And then at 12, Flid turns up with some beer," and that is all he wrote.

We are then joined by some of last night's stragglers, and the beer and conversation flows. On my third trip to the bar a passing police patrol catches my eye and frowns at my excess. We decide to stay another night, and I re-erect my tent. With limited water I have a shave and brush my hair and teeth. Feeling slightly better, I am approached by two topless girls with painted bodies who say, "You have an interesting tattoo, man"; my focus is torn between their pretty faces and their painted perky parts. It's hard to know what to say.

We decide to go to the beach. Apart from some marmite I squeezed onto some bread, the only things to pass my lips were beer and a toothbrush. The beach is packed with miles and miles of perfect skin. Drunken girls lie comatose on their beach towels. I need a shower, a cold one; I opt to dive in the Black Sea instead. We drink more beer and then finally eat something.

Back at the bike show the American fake joins us. This guy is an utter pervert. Yes, the women here are beautiful; I think we have established that. Undeterred, he shows us reams of photos on his camera of all the ones he has photographed, then tells us of all the dates he has had and has lined up. I wander off; Andy seems to have more tolerance than I do.

I go chat to the Lithuanian bikers; they are packing up to ride to "Crem," which turns out to be the Crimea. Everyone has recommended we ride there: it's supposedly the highlight of Ukraine biking. Andy is up for it, so it seems we will be together a little longer. We are then approached by a girl with a cigarette, no lighter, and an air of availability; it's time to get out my phrase book. But by the time I find it, I have lost Andy, and more frustratingly, the girl too. No worries, it's been a day of beer and little else. I go and lay in my tent, and the next thing I know it's light and the tent is full of mozzies, which, when I squash them, I find are full of blood. Bugger.

DAY 16

ODESSA, UKRAINE, 11 MILES

I wake feeling fresh as a daisy, albeit a daisy that has grown next to a leaking portaloo. People are packing up, and I see the stage and bars being dismantled. I think we managed to squeeze just about everything out of this show that we could. The toilets are now horrendous, though. I can't hold my breath that long, and inhalation makes me gag.

I pack up my tent again, and two different guys I haven't even spoken to come by to wish me safety and good health on the road. The camaraderie of the Eastern European biker is like nothing I've ever experienced. In England it's there to a degree, but there is too much segregation, depending on what you ride, when you ride it, and what you wear when you do. It's so much easier to segregate than it is to unite; I do it myself.

I've seen it at its lowest when I broke down in Yosemite Park in California. There was an intermittent electrical problem on my Kawasaki Concours when I was riding back from Alaska. After stopping at a vista point the bike would not start again. I had the seat and tank off, tracing wires and checking for continuity. In the two hours I was there, at least fifty gleaming, posing, Harley riders must have wallowed past, and not one of them stopped. The patriotic fashion of riding overpriced and underperforming American iron, being weekend warriors with matching embossed leather jackets and crotchless pants (surely one of the most impractical pieces of motorcycle clothing ever, but no less popular for it) has created a breed of motorcycle rider with all the compassion of a minivan driver. These people know far more about hedge funds and PowerPoint presentations than they do about the brotherhood of the road and the camaraderie of like-minded people. But my mind is not like theirs. I do have a Harley, but I don't like to mention it: I've been riding them since the early '80s, long before they became fashion accessories. There was a time when you knew any other rider was going to be a genuine bike enthusiast, who knew their machine inside out. They had to, as the bikes broke down constantly; it was a passion, a deeply embedded love. In England it wasn't even based on some obsessive patriotic obedience, it was something deep; the bikes didn't stop well, didn't go well, and didn't handle well, and in our damp climate all they did well was corrode. It wasn't about status or one-upmanship; it was about a deep desire, kindred spirits. I heard someone say once you can't love something that doesn't have a heart, but that deep throb, that vibration of a badly balanced engine; it was a pounding heart that stirred the soul. We worked on our bikes as much as we rode them and enjoyed both equally.

That has all disappeared. With reliability, emissions, and noise control they lost their character, and with corporate expansion and mass marketing they became a fashion symbol. Harley-Davidson became a toy, played with and not understood any more than the lifestyle or the riders that the posing masses so desperately want to be. When I'm asked what I ride, the last bike I mention is my chopper; say the "H" word and there is an immediate stigma attached to it these days. I don't want to have to prove what I'm not, before anyone has even discovered what I am.

So anyway, those bikers from the east are truly people of honour, and when I build my perfect country, taking every positive aspect of every country I have experienced, I will use the biker mentality of the east as an example of caring, sharing, non-judgemental, open, and honest friendship.

One such biker took me over to the Butlins to enquire about the availability of a room, but unfortunately, after he left the communication broke down, as I was assigned a double bed and then a dorm. I gave up on that little venture. It was a horrible environment, anyway, now the other bikes had left, just a Soviet high-density holiday camp; not exactly inspired, relaxing, open spaces. It was just a prison with slack security.

We rode 300 metres to the next accommodation, which was far more relaxed; still an annex of thin walls and thinner mattresses, but it had the right vibe. My tent is little more than a coffin with a high roof, so it's a real luxury to spread myself out a bit. I went off to the toilet block and washed my clothes under the standpipe. I'm sure it would not seem so idyllic if I was trying to hold down a job, but in this holiday lifestyle the romanticism of such basics is enough to make the most mundane chores enjoyable.

When I travelled in India with a girlfriend, I was the self-appointed dobe wallah, (washer person). I would sing my little dobe wallah song and, usually naked, I would stomp up and down in a bucket of laundry powder and clothes until I had squashed all the dirt out of them. One day, whilst pouring the blackened water down the squat toilet, I half noticed a dark lump follow the water out of the bucket. I checked the pile of wrung out clothing on the floor and nothing seemed to be missing, except there may have been a thin black top amongst the laundry that was no longer there. So with an open hand and a closed mouth I knelt by the stinking hole and reached down the toilet as far as I could. In a trainspotting kind of way I patted my hand and felt around, but there was nothing down there, nothing you would want to wear. So I scrubbed my hands like I had OCD and hung out the hippy rags to dry. It was later that afternoon when I heard the words I was dreading,

"Have you seen my black top?"

"I've got something I need to tell you."

She froze. The last time I said that, I had told her I have a daughter. There was visible relief when she discovered that she had not so much gained a daughter as lost a sun top.

"Come on, I'm going to take you shopping."

We decide we should go to see a little more of Odessa, so with wet jeans and T-shirts we ride into the city. It was not quite as glamorous and decadent as I was expecting. I was on a mission to change my Moldovan money, but the only bureau de change that offered that service was closed. At an open one I tried to change a 50 euro note but was told it was "broken" and they will not accept it. We wandered around. Andy seems to have an ice cream addiction; it's a good way to spend the small change that inevitably accumulates in your pockets when you're not familiar with the currency. We find an Internet café, but here in Ukraine it's still acceptable to smoke in such places, and my eyes start to sting. Also, I've only just washed my hair, so I go and sit in the real world and look at the kind of women I thought only existed on the Internet.

The ride back is the perfect summer evening riding temperature: a short ride in long shadows and no wrong turns.

Back in the room we have carelessly left the door open, and the American perv pokes his head in saying, "It's only me." He proceeds to tell us about his latest conquest of preying on the vulnerable and helpless in his fifty-year-old paedophile style. He makes my skin crawl. Another type I only thought existed on the Internet.

We are obliged to go to the restaurant with him; I don't want to be associated with him at all. I half expect a hit squad of revenge-filled fathers coming after him with guns or scythes.

He tells us of a young girl from the north that he had relations with a year ago and how she is leaving her boyfriend and catching a bus to come and see him. I don't know if he is full of shit, or is destined to have it kicked out of him. I gulp my beer and walk away. I manage not to voice my derogatory opinion of him. Later that evening, he's there in the toilet block, and whilst I'm trying to piss he continues to talk at me, now he has a captive audience. Some people just don't get it. Does he not know how much I despise him or does he just not care?

DAY 17

ODESSA, UKRAINE, 20 FEET

It was a clammy night with mozzies buzzing in my ear, but luckily I had only been bitten and not gorged on. When I got up and walked down the corridor to the shower block, I felt giddy and light-headed, so I went back in the room where I lay down again and drank some water. Unfortunately, it was too little too late. We were supposed to head off today. Fortunately, Andy is easy going and understanding, so he heads out with his laptop.

I lie on the bed with the window open and listen to the breeze in the trees, the sweeping of the path, and a distant foreign radio. I realise of all the places I've been in the last few years this is the first time I have "travelled." It's reminiscent of Southeast Asia sometimes, the sounds and smells, the squat toilets, and my inevitable runny tummy; but this feels less like a bike trip and more like travelling with a bike. I doze, but I can't ride today; I can't walk down the corridor without putting out my hands to steady me. Andy has already anticipated this and suggests a day off. He goes and gets some supplies while I read the health section of my guidebook. I have textbook, or at least guidebook, dehydration. Bleeding obvious now I think about it: it's been all sun and beer for the last three days. I think the sweaty night just depleted the last of my reserves.

Outside the noises turn to hammering, screaming kids, and rattling scooters. I'm too out of it to be annoyed, and I watch the flies buzz in circles around the light. What a fruitless existence. I'm fine lying down, the problems only occur when I try to move my head. I spend the day drinking salty water and eating marmite sandwiches. Feeling ill in cheap rooms in foreign countries: I have as many experiences of that as I do stamps in my passport. This is to say, for me it's an inevitable part of travelling. Strong mind and weak stomach: it's a symptom I regularly suffer, whether self-inflicted or innocently acquired.

I had barely completed my first week in India when I learned an important lesson the hard way: never eat in an empty restaurant. People cook their native food best. Indians don't make pizza very well, and if the restaurant is not commonly frequented the ingredients stop being fresh and refrigeration is rarely practiced. My travel companion and I consequently spent a dismal day in our room, needing to be permanently in the vicinity of the toilet at all times. As the boredom set in, we threw biscuits in the blades of the ceiling fan from our beds. If you could get the biscuit to hit a revolving blade square on, it would catapult it full force across the room, where it would turn to crumbs with its impact against the wall. It was quite entertaining for a while. I learned that no matter how strange local food looked or smelt it was going to be prepared with generations of experience.

Whilst cycling in Thailand on my return from China, I promised myself, up every hill and along scorching roads, that I would treat myself to a week on a beach at the end of my trip. I chose an island to break from my cycling and made the mistake of staying in a twee tourist village, where I felt completely isolated and longed to be back on my bicycle. I remember listening to some English backpacker one breakfast complaining about his bacon and egg sandwich not being as good as the ones he got at home. Well guess what Tarquin, you're in Thailand, eat what they eat, they know how to cook that. I bet you would get a pretty disgusting beef noodle soup in your local greasy spoon café too.

Later the perv drops by and offers his help; I'm glad I wasn't rude to him last night, as I would have felt awkward now, though maybe he is so thick-skinned that he wouldn't have noticed. He says the woman he is meeting tonight is a medical assistant, and she could have a look at me. Wore a nurse's uniform in her profile more like. I declined his offer.

After three litres of water and a pile of peanuts I'm feeling better, and we go and sit in the restaurant. Good healthy food, I'm feeling better with every mouthful. The perv is on another table with a long-legged bottle blonde. She looks cheap, not the typical sophisticated well-dressed Ukrainian lady. He comes and smokes over us as we eat whilst bragging about his latest beauty. I'm pretty sure he is paying for her company; nothing wrong with that, but we haven't paid for or requested his, so why can't he go back to his peroxide partner. We strategically get up together and leave. We have a fly and mozzie cull in the room as thunder rumbles outside. When I go out to move my bike undercover, I see a French-registered camper van parked outside. I speak to the girl who steps out of it. It looks very comfortable, self-contained, and homely, yet also quite isolating. I'm definitely travelling the way I would most choose to right now, and tomorrow I will be hitting the road again.

Day 18

Simferopol, Ukraine, 329 Miles

It's raining heavily outside, so I turn on our little TV in the corner. The screen is snowy, and there is a flickering image of a weather girl in a mini skirt. She points at a map of the country, which is covered in lightning bolts, everywhere except over us; we have a sunny cloud. She may be hedging her bets, but I admire her optimism as well as her legs. Her report is good enough for me; I go out to start loading the bike. Peter the perv is also packing up. I could just hide, but I decide to go and say goodbye. Of course, it's not that simple. He is off on a mission: the girl he was importing down from the north has been in touch. She's lost her phone and bus ticket, and he is going to ride 600 kms to rescue her, a knight in sopping armour. If she exists, she is clearly lying to him, and if she doesn't, he is lying to me. I suggest he should try choosing his route based on scenery, instead of just following his dick. He says he knows, says he should get some therapy, the first honest words to come out of his mouth.

It's a good idea in life to remember that people like him exist. It's not nice to think about, but it's good to be aware. I shouldn't care what became of him, but I can't help but wonder sometimes. I was able to do an exaggerated impression of his slimy voice, which cracks a smile with me and Andy, so he was of some use.

The cleaners are desperate to get their hands on our key, they never smile and have managed to bring the smell of the toilet into the corridor with their filthy mops. I wonder if they get a lot of job satisfaction.

This way of travelling with no urgency, for me, is a first for a motorcycle trip. I really look forward to getting back on the bike after a few no—or low—mileage days. On the way out of the city I manage to change my "broken" euro. The traffic is heavy, and the humidity is high, but we got out of town no sweat. At a fuel stop a young lad jumps out of the back of a transit van, bursting with youthful enthusiasm. His elation at seeing our bikes transcends the language barrier, he is so uninhibited, so cheerful that it's infectious. He wants us to do wheelies so that he can photograph us on his phone. Sorry, the bikes are too heavy, I point at the panniers. He's a little disappointed that I won't remove them just to perform a vulgar display of power. I feel almost guilty, but I don't want to put unnecessary strain on my chain purely for his entertainment. Sorry, too old, too mature, too responsible, too sober, but your excitement and passion is commendable. I feel like a killjoy. Now which way to Crimea?

We ride into a heavy storm too quickly to zip up and protect ourselves; before it penetrates we are out the other side onto dry road. Little Miss Mini Skirt must have run out of lightning bolts. I forgive her.

Bypasses elude us, and we manage to ride right into a town on a road which dead ends by a train station. A well-dressed man sitting in a 4x4 offers to help. He shows me where I should be going on his Sat Nav. His wrists are adorned with thick gold bracelets; his high-pitched voice is out of character but his generosity is not, not for Ukraine. He decides that we should just follow him, and he weaves through the traffic like he's experienced in high speed pursuit. We do our best to keep up through the back roads full of potholes. I'm wondering if this is a short cut or if he is taking us to where we will be shot and mugged. But it's the former; he leads us to the bridge that takes us across the Dnieper Delta. We continue on slow roads of smelling, smoking trucks, impatient drivers, and road works with no traffic lights; everyone just barges through the single lane. When the road is straight and flat, I suggest swapping bikes; Andy's is so different and so the same. We voice our observations when we swap back: his clutch is light, he thinks mine is heavy; it has to be my cable. I have a spare running parallel; I'll keep using this one until it snaps. His engine is tighter, mine is looser. His air-filled seat pad is not as comfy as I expected. He says my clutch slips, not that I'd noticed. I'm still glad to get back on my own bike, which is just as well really.

We ride into Krym, another autonomous republic, but without the borders and corruption of Transnistria. More importantly the speed traps have stopped too. We head west in heavy rain, but a low sun ahead of us bounces off the wet roads and into our eyes, disguising the water-filled pot holes. There is probably a rainbow behind us, but my eyes are squinting at the road ahead, and I can't refocus into my mirrors. We leave the clouds behind and ride off road onto tall wet grass as rabbits run from my front wheel. It's a soft and hidden place to camp. I've fallen into the comfort of company. It's enjoyable, but I'm missing the challenge, and although there is the isolation of the helmet, I seem to be missing the vulnerability of solo travel, its hardships and rewards. But I'm just having so much fun. The sky is big and contains most of the weathers we have seen today. But there are also stars above our heads, and if the moon could make rainbows it would be doing it right now.

Day 19

Sudak, Ukraine, 177 Miles

I don't sleep well fly camping; I'm too alert, too aware of every sound. Dreams are lucid with my heightened state of awareness. With the dawn comes the rain. The tent was perfect for cycling, it's small and light and compact when dismantled, but inside I feel like some fairy tale character that has swallowed a "big pill." It's okay for sleeping in or even lying awake trying to sleep in, but any other pastimes are futile. I'm coiled up like I'm going to pounce, just to write some figures down. I seem to be back on budget, but a new tent is not on the cards. The only pressing thing today is the sides of the tent on my pile of bike clothes, but I don't really want to spend any more time in it. I would like to get out. I apply the conservatory theory and decide that it is probably not as bad outside as it sounds inside. Unlike the *Daily Mail*, which sits inside so many conservatories and is as bad inside as it is outside.

Four of us met in Brazil, we split into two, and then one went home. My home was rented out, so I continued onto Chile alone, where I met a Czech, a tall thin man of little means and a liking for red wine. He missed his family, had strong opinions, a sharp wit, and a standoffish nature, but for some reason, I chipped away at his cold exterior, broke the ice, and found a very warm person. We hit it off and travelled together to a national reserve but arrived late at night on the edge of nowhere. The bus turned around and left us on a windswept beach. We took shelter in the sand dunes, and although he had no tent or camping equipment, he had no other options, so he stayed. In the night I heard the rain start; I couldn't enjoy my self-contained shelter, I only felt the guilt.

"Fliiiid?"

"Yes, Charles."

"Eetz rain ning, can I poot my pack in yor tent pleez?"

"Yes, okay, are you alright out there?"

"Yez, iz no problem for me."

I didn't get back to sleep, the rain got harder.

"Fliiid? I'm geeting wit, can I geet in yoor tent?"

What can you say? Really. There is nothing anywhere that resembles any kind of shelter. Not a tree and nothing manmade in sight.

"Okay, Charles, get in."

We sat side by side cross-legged with our knees locked inside our arms and our hands clamped round our wrists to keep ourselves in this compact position. We both ducked forward so our heads did not touch the top of the tent. It was cramped and uncomfortable, but we did have a 2.5 litre box of red wine, and to celebrate the dawn we opened it and started to drink. Charles had a watch with a barometer on it, and we looked at it every fifteen minutes to see if it had lost or gained a bar, indicating an improvement in the weather. I was torn between resentment and guilt. "Hjärterum Stjärterum," the Swedes say. "Yak tor rom fact tor rom," I say. It means where there is room in my heart there is room for your bum. Well that's how it was explained to me anyway. It's a great phrase, and although the way I say it not even the Swedes can understand, to me it's more about a philosophy than correct pronunciation. There was room in my heart and my tent for Charles; not much, but just enough. By comparison, this tent I'm in this morning is palatial.

So I move my bike under the trees for shelter and pull my tent pegs out of the ground. Andy makes coffee, but I opt for the obligatory camping food suitable for any meal, sausage and bread. I add a slice of cheese to give it a breakfast feel. Andy has some good sayings; today's is "rain before seven, fine by eleven."

The rain gets heavier, and I put on my bike clothing, even my helmet. The regulations of the packing ritual are relaxed, and the tent is just bungeed on the back of the bike. I ask Andy if he has ever known a girl who would not be whinging right now. He starts to tell me a story; at first I'm keen to leave, then I think, well what's the urgency to get on the bikes in the rain? So we stand around swapping stories and slowly loading the bikes. I'm learning to slow my pace. It's a good lesson. It seems illogical, but it makes perfect sense, and when we do fire up the bikes and head for the road, the skies have cleared and I start to dry out.

I have gone from passing fields of green crops to yellow crops to harvested crops. I'm not sure if it's the time that's passing or if I'm passing through time.

Time for some culture. We head down into Balaclava, famous for its volatile past; *The Charge of the Light Brigade* is probably its most famous event. Six hundred of the British cavalry were ordered into "the valley of death" by Major Fuck Up and Miss Communication and were shot at from three sides by Russian forces. Also, the balaclava hat with eye holes was first worn here. The lines "Theirs not to reason why, Theirs but to do or die," come from the poem Tennyson wrote about it. *The Charge of the Light Brigade* that is, not the wearing of the balaclava. Although, thinking about it, it works for both.

So much for culture. Our experience was not so dramatic as to inspire such immortal words of mortal combat. In fact, the only killing we saw were the ones the restaurants were making on the price of a fish dinner. It's a touristy little place, I see backpackers wandering aimlessly, and I appreciate our independence. I no longer have any desire to do the local train and bus thing, despite the hassles of locking up the bikes every time we walk away from them. I much prefer it to dragging a pack around a country, being a victim of dependency at every guest house and bus station. The valley of death actually looks quite nice these days; more like a flowery meadow.

Right, been there done that, what's next? After nearly 3,000 miles, I'm on a road which has bends, a good surface, and no cops. I can scrub in the edges of my tyres. We follow the cliff tops and look down at the sea on our right and up at the mountains on our left. We do manage to miss the recommended winding pass. No worries, we avoid the towns and follow the cliff top road into a black sky ahead.

We hit slow, cross-town traffic just as the deluge starts. It's unavoidable. We crawl up a hill; the road has no drainage, and the water cascades down. Putting down a foot has the water streaming over my toes and flowing in an arch down the top of my boot. But the traffic is too slow and the road too steep to balance. There comes a point, riding in the rain, when you can't get any wetter: this happens in record-breaking time. Crouching behind the screen makes no difference. I only notice the rain is running down my neck because it is colder than the dampness it replaces. A change in gear redistributes the water in my crotch. Pulling in the clutch wrings the rain from my fist. My visor mists up and has drops on both sides.

The roads are the best so far, mile after mile of coast-hugging twists and turns and probably a view too—all ruined by shitty weather. I pass the crawling Ladas just to avoid the spray. The problem with wild camping is the sleep deprivation it causes me. On top of everything else I'm tired. I've lost Andy. I want to pull over and wait, but there is no shelter. The road drops down to beach level, where there are sodden tents pitched, then back up onto cliffs. At the end of a long straight, I stop and wait. Shelter would make no difference now anyway. I'm beginning to think there is a problem; the only lights coming towards me are in pairs. Just as I'm about to turn round through the mist and spray, I see that familiar oblong headlight.

"Everything okay? Come on, not so far to go now."

We are heading for Sudak: we have been told of a biker bar there with free accommodation. We were given the impression it was unmissable. It is not. There are no signs of it or for it. Out the other side of town under a petrol station canopy I've stopped having fun. I need a room, and I need it now. I have at least learnt the sign that means room, and I lead us back into the town. I'm no longer interested in democratic decision making. I want to get off my bike and out of these clothes. I'm displaying the assertiveness of an imminent tantrum. Andy sensibly decides to follow. I see a tout holding a sign with those shapes on it that are letters that spell a word that means room/hotel/shelter. He shows us a photo album of a place with marble floors and roman pillars, imperial leather bathrooms, and orgy-sized beds.

"No, what else have you got?"

You can't blame him for trying; we did look desperate. We follow his Lada to a private house with a Nissan hut of rooms, perfect. It is perfect too, it's family run; they know a little English and give a big welcome. Some kids show us around the communal kitchen and dining area. The other guests are friendly, and once wet clothes have been replaced with damp ones and black-leather-dyed hands are clasped round a cold beer can, the hardships of the day are resigned to history. Not as tragic as *The Charge of the Light Brigade*, not as creative as a balaclava, or as inspired as great poetry, but mine is not to reason why, mine is but to live to ride.

DAY 20

SUDAK, UKRAINE, 9 MILES

It's an excellent drying day: our pile of festering clothing is hung on the line, along with tents, sheepskin seat covers, and all things material. Even when he is rung out and hung out to dry, Monklet smiles. There is an outside basin with a mirror on the wall above it; in the bright sunshine the reflection shows every little defect as I shave. I was having a good morning until that happened.

Whilst visiting my daughter in Colorado, I hired a car and drove 850 miles to St. Louis to go and see Roger Waters. I decided it would be cheaper to get a hotel downtown and walk to the venue than it would be to get a cheap one on the outskirts and get two taxies. It was a luxurious room, and the mirror door on the wardrobe was directly behind the vanity unit. With the door ajar I could see my back tattoo perfectly in the reflection, and that's a rare opportunity. Instead of enjoying this sight, however, my eyes were drawn to the flesh on my scalp barely covered by the thinning hair. I got to see what my friends just knew but never mentioned. And that day was ruined too.

I needed to replenish my funds, so I pulled my bike apart to go dig for some euros. While I was about it in the sunny courtyard I did a little maintenance. It was satisfying to have the space to spread myself out and the safety to leave stuff unattended, resulting in the satisfaction of having it all dried and repacked. My tyre pressures were significantly low: no wonder it handled so well in the wet, maybe. I checked my oil for the first time; it was low, really low. Worryingly low. Andy said with the oil I was using it was to be expected after 3,000 miles, and when I do my oil change it will not only stop my clutch slip, but a more suitable oil will not burn off like the stuff I am using has. He's very good at putting my mind at rest. It's been a relaxing morning chatting to the other guests and hearing their stories. I haven't eaten all morning, so we walk to the main street. It has everything we need: banks, supermarkets, wine shops, money changers, and of course, beautiful women, always beautiful women. I'm just getting complacent now; all the women are beautiful, and that's just the way it is.

We really must find this biker bar. Andy's bike is stripped of its entire luggage, but mine is fully loaded again, even the tyres on the back, which continue to give my journey credibility and yell "long distance" louder than my oil-consuming engine does.

We ride off and find a big castle and windy roads, probably the same ones as yesterday, but in the sunshine they are completely different. It only adds to the frustration of what we missed and how much better it could have been if we hadn't been riding through a monsoon.

It's fun, but there is no biker bar here. We ask a moped rider, and he leads us under a barrier, through a pedestrian area, and past a parade of kiosks selling the usual seaside tat; we then go on to an open-air bar on the sea front. The waitress beckons us to ride inside; okay then, and as I dismount a girl runs towards me and hugs me. It's the Russian patch club girl from Odessa. What an entrance. Ride your bike straight into a bar and get a hug. Today is a good day. So we sit in the bar and chat and laugh. The waves crashing on the beach are massive, so are the cliffs and the castle balanced on top. What an amazing place this is.

In the evening we all go walkabout; there is something missing. It's a golden mile of fairground rides, pumping music, huge open-air bars with big screen TVs, live bands, karaoke, and all those seaside entertainments. There are plenty of people strolling up and down, but none are stopping, the bars are empty, but for a romantic couple dancing alone or a bus load of spinsters singing to a jukebox. I can't help but think there's something better going on somewhere, but if there is we can't find it, and the walking starts to get tiring, and worst of all, sobering. The Russians were sleeping in the bar, so we said goodnight.

Back at our Nissan hut some other bikers have arrived and are barbequing, insisting we eat and drink with them, but it's 1 A.M., and I've socialised enough today. Our decline seems to offend them, but we decline all the same. Motorbikes are a lifestyle; it's not just transport, it's easy to let them become a way of life. Over here it's everything. Your accommodation, your companions, maybe it comes from Soviet times. All I do know is that the bond is strong, the friendship unquestionable, and the generosity unlimited. The only expectation seems to be that all offers are accepted, because a refusal often offends.

Day 21

Sudak, Ukraine, 0 Miles

It's time to go. I'm not exactly sure what time zone I'm in, but it's definitely time to go. Andy has to complete his circuit via Turkey and Greece, and I have Russia on my mind, but it's Saturday, and there are expectations for the biker bar. Tomorrow would be a good day to leave. No point in rushing.

I sit at Andy's laptop and write a mass email. I've still got some Merlot left, and the words flow readily: this is luxury, no Internet café time pressure. A lady comes by selling pastries; oh, yes, I think I'll have one of those. I sit shaded in the warm breeze; the world is at my fingertips, as is a glass of wine on one side and something yummy on the other. Yes, I'm in no hurry to leave this behind.

We head for the biker bar, seeing some familiar faces on the way; we are already recognised in this town. People thinking we are brothers, turning heads and making friends, having lots of laughs; our bikes attract so much attention and conversation. We don't ride through; we stop and take it in.

We are outnumbered by bar staff. There is relaxed and then there is just plain dead. We have a beer and look out at the promenade, which is a catwalk of beautiful, bikini-clad women. Motorbikes and bike memorabilia, castles and cliffs, sea and sand, there aren't many bars with a view to beat this one. Yet, there is the underlying knowledge that this is the last day, and in a way, I would like to get it over with. It feels like we are just prolonging the inevitable.

Lone journeys are full of hellos and goodbyes. Some people you meet are good for an evening meal and a drink, and others become travel companions for many miles. People are generally at their best when they travel, not concerned with work and the other distractions and obligations of a home life. I don't think these friendships that are born on the road are shallow at all; they may be transitory, but they are no less sincere for that—two like-minded strangers whose paths cross, meeting each other's needs and heading on their way. I may swap email addresses, but it is friendship for a moment in time. You can write to each other and recall the memories, but the encounter cannot be relived. It's spontaneous, it's luck; it may be some divine intervention beyond our comprehension as paths cross and lives become entwined, albeit briefly. You tell your best stories and in return receive inspired wisdom and quotes to enhance your life. It's genuine, it's passionate, it's real, and then it's over. It's everything couch surfing is not. And just like albums, motorbikes, and favourite places; occasionally one comes along that you know you will keep going back to. It's rare, but it happens: that's what happened with my Swedish friends.

The bar is not happening today. We get some supplies for a last supper, and whilst Andy cooks, I go get beer. Our neighbour brings us some pancakes, and I play with his girls; the seven-year-old is cheeky, but her little sister is still shy and hides from me, wanting to be seen and running off in hysterical giggles when she is. It's a little holiday community. Three of the last four Saturday nights have been like this, fretting for the next day, the borders, and new countries.

I'm scared and excited all over again, but it doesn't reveal itself in hysterical giggles.

DAY 22

ANAPA, RUSSIA, 172 MILES

Is it anxiety or a hangover? Am I feeling full of dread or dreadful? When dawn comes I just want to get up and get going, because it's agony just waiting and worrying about all that's to come. My tummy has butterflies again; I've never known a trip that has so consistently brought on these feelings. Okay, let's do it. I get up, walk to the kitchen, and put the kettle on.

When the bikes are ready, we put on our hot clothes and wave goodbye. As we go round the corner I hoot at the man in the wooden shack who has sold us our beer for the last three days. With our bikes and helmets on he guesses who we are and returns our waves, and once again, it's into the unfamiliar. We witness some of the cliffs and scenery that was denied to us when we arrived, but my mind is not focused, and my thoughts are all over the place. Soon enough we are at the fork in the road where we will part. We do one of those biker handshake-back-pat-hug things I've seen so many patch club members do over the years. It's been an amazing eleven days. Rip off the band aid, helmet on, start bike, hoot, wave, leave. Urrgghh, it's physical pain, companionship torn from me without anaesthetic.

Alone on an unknown road heading for the ferry to take me to Russia, I can feel the angst in my back, in my tummy, and in my head.

I ride east, it's what I do. The land changes to grassy plains; horses and cows wander freely, as do geese. I'm heading for my fifth ferry on this overland trip. I follow a car with Russian plates instead of my instincts and have to do a U-turn. One more police check, one more "present" wanted. But they won't accept local currency, or my US dollars; they don't want a present, they want a souvenir. When they both get an English 10p coin I am free to go. Well that was cheap, but still principally extortionate. I'm besieged by midges as I pay my fee; they crawl into my ears and nose. I hit myself trying to evict them. I put on my helmet and accelerate away from the flying insects and uniformed parasites.

Around the corner is the port. I try to find the ticket booth; it is closed until 2 P.M. Now it is 12.30 P.M.; there is no 1.30 P.M. sailing today. Let the waiting begin. I'm approached by a beggar. "Go speak to the pigs. I only give presents to people in uniforms with guns," is what my shake of the head was saying. I eat some bread and sausage and wait in line. When the ticket office opens it's quite an easy operation and quite cheap too. This makes me wonder whether they understand it's me *and* my motorcycle, but I have showed them my vehicle documents, and they seem to understand.

I once had a very rare Harley-Davidson that I bought and restored in England. It looked wonderful but was actually a piece of crap. That's why it was so rare. By the time they had manufactured just 3,000 of them, the motorcycle-buying public realised that, although aesthetically pleasing, this bike was, in fact, even worse than the other rubbish they turned out in the late '70s. It still had collector's value, however, although not in England. So I exported it back to its country of birth. Being an American-made product returning home, it was exempt from emissions control and other regulations. I did have to call the factory to get a letter stating that in its year of manufacture it met the standards required of it. I remember getting a call from the factory one morning:

"Good morning this is Harley-Davidson; may I speak to Graham Field, please?" Wow, Harley-Davidson is calling me, I've got your name tattooed on my body. It was like getting a call from my favourite rock star. They sent me the documentation I needed, and when I presented it at the local EPA (Environmental Protection Agency), the lady asked "Why have you got this?"

"Because it's an American-made motorcycle that I am importing."

"Oh is Harley-Davidson made in America then?"

Just because something is bleeding obvious to you, don't assume it is to the rest of the world, or even America for that matter.

So I shouldn't assume that because I produced my bike documents, I have a ferry ticket for both me and my bike.

It starts to rain. I put on my poncho and sit on my bike. How do they make ports so bloody depressing? This sad transition was not made any more pleasant by spending yet another grey Sunday at yet another ferry port waiting for a ferry that was cancelled. I put on my iPod, and rain trickles down my face.

Eventually, we move forward. Customs is slow, but they process me without too much trauma. I am told to go and park by the gaping ferry doors. The faces of the dockers and crew are hard; the beauty of the beach has been replaced with the brutality of docks and industry. Ain't no palm trees here, but then I never saw eye candy at Felixstowe, either. It's been an exhausting day emotionally, and I can't stop yawning. I ride onto the ferry; there are no securing straps, so I stand in the hold and hold my bike on the stand. The other passengers get to go on deck for the forty-five minute crossing. I am in the bowls of a damp, smelly, noisy, rusty, Soviet ferry. I can't judge the biggest country in the world based on this. Yes I can. First impressions are inevitable, and I don't like it.

No one ever said it would be easy, and I never expected it to be, but fresh in my own company again, every aspect of this seems so hard. First find the port. There is more than one, do I need a ticket? Is it a free service? I can see Russia from here; is it a shuttle or a ferry? Then wait, then buy ticket for me and bike, everything has to be pointed, mimed, and explained; customs and immigration procedures, then onto ferry, having to be my own personal ratchet strap holding my bike up for the crossing whilst others watch the view.

I do have phone reception down here though, so I send three texts. How much will that cost? £1? Money well spent. It's a comfort thing; I have a phone, may as well use it; I allowed for it in the budget, no point in being in total isolation.

The ferry turns, my bike rocks. If I wasn't here, it would have fallen. I made a good choice there, at least. The doors open, the ramp drops, the foot passengers run for immigration, and I ride off the boat. I'm given a form; "Can I have one in English, please?"

I was dreading the entry into Russia, but as is often the case, the things you fear most cause the least problems. People will always put the frighteners on you, telling of their terrible experience with roads, officials, and traffic. Just because it was a problem for them does not mean it will be for me, just as an uneventful road for them becomes a torturous event when I come to it. The thing to always remember is the only experience that counts is your own.

My entry into Russia was painless; I got a form in English and was helped every step of the way. They were professional and attentive. I did have to fill the form out twice; apparently panniers are not luggage, but they were searched all the same. Well I took off the lid, and they glanced inside; the toilet brush/tool holder was of interest to the customs officers, if not the sniffer dogs. I was taken to buy my insurance for Russian roads, and with a smile I was told I was free to go into Russia.

There were two problems, both of which were my own doing: I had no fuel and no currency. I could have filled up in Ukraine before I left; I had Ukraine money and time to spare. I had no other use for that currency, how stupid; I'm so annoyed at myself. I made the only problems I encounter today. I had gained an hour or lost it, and all money changers were closed.

5 kms out of the port is a checkpoint with armed soldiers. "Hello, how are you?" Oh the comfort of the correct documentation. Insurance, bike documents, visa, international driving permit. He's happy, I'm happy, I'm free to go.

I find a petrol station that takes US dollars and get some fuel. So now all I need to find is a place to sleep.

There are big American trucks and fields of sunflowers casting shadows over the road in the low sun. Okay, we have trucks and sunflowers at home, and even shadows too, but it still feels so strange. I wonder if Russia will ever seem like familiar ground. Perhaps after Mongolia.

I head for the town of Anapa and ride around as the light fades. I see tourists but no hotels. Come on, Flid, you've got to do something, stop, ask, and deal with this situation. I get out my phrase book. I see a sign that starts like it means room for rent, but the word was much longer. It's getting late, and I'm getting desperate. I open the gate and do the bed mime: hands together as if to pray but held to my ear. Not that I actually sleep in that position, but a starfish stance would only confuse the old lady. She shouts out a name, and two eleven-year-old girls come running up; both speak English. They show me the room; it's perfect, with a kitchen and the shower "where you will wash yourself." Yeah, okay sweetheart, I know, it's been a tough day.

Later they take me to the bank, so I can use the cash machine and to the late shop so I can get some food to cook. I buy them ice creams, but when we get back granny has made me soup, chicken and potato. The girls try to teach me some Russian; it's fun, but I'm so tired, let's continue tomorrow. Feet landed on again. Thank goodness for little girls.

DAY 23

ANAPA, RUSSIA, 0 MILES

The privacy of my room is so appealing; I opt for water instead of going out to the kitchen to boil the kettle. I look at my maps and guidebook and formulate a plan. For starters, I'm not going anywhere today.

The girls, Anena and Dasher, are waiting for me. They take my food out of the fridge and lay it on the table for me. I make a kind of breakfast sandwich, and they wait impatiently for my Russian lesson to begin. Anena lives in Volgograd, but every summer she comes here to stay with her gran; Dasher and her family come every year too and stay at the guest house next door, so they are best of friends. Anena has a serious nature, and it's hard to make her smile or laugh. She's talkative enough but not willing to be silly, unlike Dasher, who is scatty and has a face full of expression; she reminds me of a *Watership Down* rabbit with her wide eyes and bouncing character. The girls have even found me a phrase book, which converts Russian into English—not so useful for my learning, but handy when a Russian wants to make me understand something.

They are soon frustrated at my slow progress, but I'm quite pleased with myself. I can count to ten, I can exchange pleasantries, and with the words written down phonetically and Anena's solemn voice saying the phrases into my voice recorder, I'm learning fast. For me anyway. My favourite phrase is pronounced "wotblink" which means "oh bugger," "damn it," or "bollocks."

The girls want to go to the beach, and I am invited along. I seem to have been adopted by this family. Even the cat makes friends with my sheepskin seat cover and sleeps on it in the sunshine.

On the way out I point at the sign which almost says room to rent and ask why it's different to the word in my phrase book: "Because this word means rooms to rent." Oh those pesky plurals.

Of course, it's tourist hell down at the beach. The plastic sun beds are laid out in perfectly straight lines, stretching for miles. No one seems to care, no one sees the misery or feels the lack of freedom. The cramped and crowded conditions are of no concern to the hordes of happy holidaymakers.

It's so difficult being an older single man and playing with the girls. The world is so quick to point its paedophile finger. I'm so aware of it, it makes me self-conscious. The only thing the girls think is slightly strange behaviour is my standoffishness. I dare not make contact with them when we go into the sea. I opt for the splashing game; it's safer than putting them on my shoulders. I thought I blew it this morning taking a photo of them by my bike, but I compensated for that by showing Granny photos of my daughter, thereby disarming any concerns she may have. Maybe it's all in my head; then I feel bad for thinking it. After the second swim, we go and play in the sand, making castles and sculptures. At least there, there are other parents with their kids. I fear Granny feels I've led them out of her sight. I can't relax, I'm on my guard; when we dig each side of a sandcastle, I deliberately dig deep so our hands won't meet in the middle of the tunnel. If Anena feels something touch her fingers in the sand and screams, heads will turn, and I can't dig a hole deep enough and quick enough for the ground to swallow me. A long-haired tattooed freak who doesn't speak the language playing with two Russian girls; I suppose it looks a little strange. But I don't have the same accent as my seven-year-old daughter, either.

In England I'd bounce on the trampoline with my god daughter and her sister; we'd try to do somersaults and laugh and giggle. A friend of mine's daughters are teenagers now; I learned my trampoline tricks with them, ten years before. Sometimes I feel like I'm Peter Pan. Why should I have to prove I'm not Gary Glitter?

I'm not sure what my role is here. Have they invited me because I'm more fun than Granny, or do they think I would be alone without their hospitality? I'm getting fed up of double-thinking everything; it's exhausting, and at 3 P.M. I make my excuses and leave. I think it's best for Granny's and my stress levels; you can only stand awkward discomfort for so long.

I wander round the town; it's clean but bland. I find an Internet café and discover Germany have knocked England out of the World Cup. Wotblink. I don't mind that we're out of it; I mind that it's because of Germany. I get the inevitable gloating emails from my German friends. I remind them of the medal count in the Beijing Olympics, but that's just history as far as they are concerned.

Well, I suppose I'm hungry, I suppose bread won't cut it, I suppose I'd better find a restaurant. I opt for pizza, ordering is easy. I sit alone in an outside restaurant: sometimes it's unavoidable. I don't mind it really, and I'm very experienced in eating alone in public. After the morning I've just had, I've run out of self-consciousness.

I'm looking forward to getting on the bike again. I have a nagging worry about getting my visa registered; I'm not exactly sure what it involves or of the repercussions if I don't, but it's the next thing on the bureaucratic agenda.

I buy a big box of chocolates on the way home; they have been very good to me. It was the right thing to do; the sound of ecstatic indulgence transcends the language barrier as they devour the contents of the box. Well that's been a friendly little introduction into Russia. What a diverse trip I'm having.

In my room I watch *My Name is Earl* dubbed in Russian, although Karma doesn't need translation.

Day 24

Sochi, Russia, 226 Miles

I have a real talent for meeting good people, then leaving them. Everyone comes out to wave me off, even faces I haven't noticed before. Maybe they were waiting for me to leave before they showed themselves. I say "goodbye" and "thank you" in Russian, and the girls hold open the gates for me; the impenetrable iron gates that all the properties seem to have, that supports the sign saying, "multiple rooms to rent," also seen on a lot of other gates around here.

I wonder what they thought of me. Maybe they didn't think about it too much. Well, good, bad, or indifferent, I'm gone now. I ride out past the high-rise housing blocks. It's not a pretty sight. My attention-seeking exhaust tone turns the heads of the labourers, painting railings and digging holes in the road. I feel embarrassed to appear so free and wealthy, but I worked for this trip, and it's because I have first-hand experience of painting railings and digging holes that I can empathise.

At the bike show last week I was asked what I do for a living; when I answered, they looked at my hands. "You have a woman's hands m'lord"; yeah I must admit all the cuts have healed, the black nails grown out; they are looking a bit girly.

The lesson I learnt this morning was that it is actually quite a good idea to get to the bottom of your panniers every now and again. Not necessarily completely repack them, however, there is no point in carrying stuff if you don't know you're carrying it. I found a ratchet strap I didn't know I had and relocated my clothes to where the pillion would sit. It meant I had room for my food in the pannier, and what I didn't realise until I got on the road was that it provides additional lower back support. It's one of those win-win type things.

I approach the town of Novbriska; I don't think I need to go into it. It rains, roads flood, and cars splash puddles at me. Traffic is slow and it's all turned miserably grey. A van hoots at me; the lads have a "where the hell are you going?" kind of expression on their faces.

"Sochi, which way is Sochi?"; take the exit to your left at the roundabout over yonder old boy, best of luck, toodle pip. That's what they meant, clearly, as it makes my compass say east again. There is solid traffic on a bridge. I could go down the middle, but I'm not sure I should. Then, with only a few weeks warning, my clutch cable suddenly snaps. I bump up onto the pavement; it is the most painless fix imaginable. There is already a spare running parallel, and swapping them over takes only minutes; I adjust it up and I'm ready to go again, like a Formula One pit stop. And, man, is my clutch light now; Andy was right about that. I skip through the stationary traffic and divert off round the docks and up the hill, where I can stop to look down at the city and its bay. Yep it's ugly. On I go.

Following the Black Sea coast means every town is a seaside town; I don't even like seaside towns. Give me mountains any day. Maybe it's an Essex thing or a Colorado thing, but I'll always choose snowboarding over sunbathing or surfing, mainly because my surfing experiences have usually resulted in lungs full of water and shorts full of sand. I'm fed up with seaside tourist towns: it's not the real country, and it's not why I'm here. In fact, why am I here? To register my visa, and that's about it. From the sign posts I see I will make Sochi tonight, and that will be the last of my seaside towns as I head into the landmass of Eurasia.

The white lines painted on the road are as slippery as ice when they are wet. Whether they are chevrons, crossings, or divide lines, they are all lethal; it doesn't take many scares before I start making sure I am vertical when I cross them.

Sochi is going to host the Winter Olympics in 2014. This road is awful; there are constant road works where they are upgrading for their big event, with a procession of crawling trucks mainly carrying steel for the stadium and Olympic Village. Combined with the Ladas, who obediently follow crawling trucks uphill rather than cross the solid white line, it's all very slow going.

I don't know what the penalty is for crossing the line, but it is surely at least crucifixion of the driver and his immediate family. No one attempts to cross them, yet give them a blind corner with a dotted line, and they fearlessly overtake into the unknown. I pass a few trucks, but nothing changes. I breathe the same black exhaust fumes, only from a different vehicle. The only things that pass me are the black Mercedes with no number plates and tinted windows; they overtake anything, anywhere. They are obviously above the law and possibly death-proof too.

I'm becoming more aware of my instincts and am learning to listen to them. When a line of cars takes a left fork at a signless junction, I don't automatically follow if I feel I should bear right; it saves me a few U-turns. I come to a particularly dangerous junction, where the traffic lights are out of sync; they have all the traffic stop at the same time, and then all the lights turn green together. If you can't even assume the lights are correct, you have to ride very defensively.

I ride into Sochi; the wealth is instantly evident. Hummers, limos, Lexus, and Porches. Marinas of expensive toys moored, with expensive women lying on them.

I've never been to Cannes or Monte Carlo, but I get the impression they are like this. For the first time this trip I use my guidebook to get a hotel. It's expensive, but it does include a ticket to Waterfun World, whoopee. It has secure bike parking, and when I finally get to it, the room is lovely too. That shower after a long sweaty ride is blissful. In the full length mirror I realise I may be living fast, but I've left it too late to die young and leave a good-looking corpse. If I'd have known this were going to happen, I might have got a pension plan.

My father always used to say, "You don't go on holiday to save money;" this isn't exactly a holiday, but I'm in a rich town. I will only be here one night, might as well live it up a bit, that's what credit cards are for. I have a nice room, so I'll go off and do nice things. I'm not drinking cheap beer out of a brown paper bag tonight.

I go for a stroll down the prom, and I see a cyclist with his bike fully loaded. Without a second thought I ask where he's from. He has cycled from Germany in a six-month circle that will take him up to Moscow before he starts to head back. He has stopped at this restaurant because it has Wi-Fi, so he can download tomorrow's co-ordinates onto his laptop and into his GPS, all of which are charged from a special dynamo. Wow, I didn't have this stuff when I was cycling, in fact, I still don't. We decide to have a meal together. He was brought up in DDR so was taught Russian for five years and, therefore, is a little better than I am. It's the classic example of meeting someone on the road who is the perfect company for an evening. We eat healthy fresh fish and drink wine.

We end up in a bar watching a World Cup match. Some locals buy us drinks, congratulating us on our achievements. All I did was twist a throttle, but I know how it feels to push pedals round. I don't miss it any more than I do painting railings.

DAY 25

CHADYZENSK, RUSSIA, 144 MILES

It's been a while, but I remembered to take my little day pack with me to fill up at the all-inclusive breakfast. Unfortunately, it isn't like that; I get a bowl of porridge and a cube of scrambled eggs that looks like quiche. Oh well. My visa registration won't be ready until midday, so I walk to a shop I saw yesterday on the way in called "Notebook City." I look at the displays: £300; I really can't stretch to that. As a consolation I buy a Sochi Olympic T-shirt.

I wander past Waterfun World; it's actually better than I thought. I have a free voucher to go in, but on my own it would just be Water World. I load my bike and take one more shower; got to wring every last ounce of luxury out of my room. I sit in the lobby and wait for my visa registration to arrive. Eventually, I get a piece of paper, and I'm still none the wiser as to what it says, what it does, or why it is. But I've got it, and I can leave the seaside behind and head for the hills.

The Caucasus Mountains are Europe's highest range. There is a tiny road on my map that takes me right across the range to the town of Maykop. It doesn't really matter how slow or bad the roads are, I can't wait to get in the mountains; I have supplies to camp for a few days if the going is slow. I find a mountain road: it's windy and scenic and there is no traffic, then it enters a village and ends. Wotblink. I go back to the main road and try another road, no luck. I'm already sweating, and whilst looking at my map, a lady who speaks English comes to help. The only way is to take the coastal road back 100 kms.

So I have to double back along the stinking, slow-truck-filled, exhaust-polluted, Lada-crawling, coast road. Everything is annoying me. The potholes, the erratic driving, my squealing back brake, my hot sweaty clothing, and the constant stares I get. I keep missing second gear, and the sole is flapping off my boot. Bloody BMW boots. I should have trusted my instincts; anything BMW breaks.

Then I put my foot down in cow shit. I can't get comfortable on the bike because of my clammy clothes, and on top of all that, I have got a sore throat from all the fumes.

All this is making my riding style far more aggressive than usual. I'm not playing the passive waiting game today. When I come up behind something, I overtake it, I even lean a bit on the corners; yeah baby, I'm so bad. Five hours to do 100 kms, five hot uncomfortable, grumping, swearing hours. I think it's safe to say I've had enough of the Black Sea coast now. When I do find my right turn it is at broken clutch cable bridge. All that way just for visa registration; it's not been very fulfilling. There is not nearly so much traffic on this road. I stop and take off my crushing helmet, look at my flapping sole, eat out of my panniers, and feed some sausage to some stray dogs that show up. They are very timid but grateful all the same.

Why am I so down on BMW? Well, it's like this. At school you automatically hate what your friends like, just so you can take the piss. My mate liked BMWs and Rainbow, I like Harleys and Motorhead. So I took the piss out of the constant changing singers in his band and bikes that were wider than they were high. He likewise made fun of Lemmy's three-minute songs and "hardly driveable" motorcycles. It's just what you did.

Fast forward twenty plus years, and my riding buddy has a GS. Whether we are in Germany, California, or Alaska we always end up in a BMW dealership because of some mechanical problem. I didn't need any more ammunition, but when it comes to BMWs, it's the gift that keeps on giving. It's just a personal thing. I don't hate them, I just don't like them. When I was trying to decide on a bike for the trip, I tried to keep an open mind, but there was no way I was going to take a BMW. Then like I didn't have enough reasons, I was recommended a GS website, for its sales of other bikes and all things overland. I find you have to be a paid member just to look at the "for sale" ads. What other site charges you to look at what they are selling? If my computer had a least favourite sites icon, that site would be right there with couch surfing.

I feel a little better after my snack stop. I feel myself relax and start to enjoy the ride again, although my arse has had enough for one day. The discomfort has nothing to do with distance, it's all to do with distraction. I don't feel or notice my riding clothes when I'm enjoying the scenery, but when things get slow and stressful all the other things start to irritate me too.

To eliminate any further stress, I fill up with petrol before I need to and top up on water too. I'm back to tiny villages again and winding roads and, at last, some mountain views. Then the road turns to dirt. Today things just won't keep going right, just when I start to enjoy it, my satisfaction is taken away. I persevere and get back to tarmac; I even get a fleeting glimpse of a snow-capped mountain out of the corner of my eye. But then it's gone. It wasn't enough to take my breath away but it was encouraging.

I practise what Andy taught me; I go down a tiny track and find an orchard to camp in for the night. I seem to be quite well hidden, I can see the road, but the road can't see me. I hang my stinking clothes off branches and put up my tent. It's all very grassy and green; I was hoping for a better view, but it's late and I won't be doing much viewing. I cook potatoes with mushrooms and pilchards. I don't particularly like this bit. Andy loves it, but I've done it before on my cycling trips. I cook alone and eat alone and wait for a time when I can justify going to bed. It's dull and it's boring; I'm not much of a solo camper.

I look at my maps; it's so daunting, so far to go and no idea what to do after Ulan Bator. Back? Forward? Fly home? Home? I was looking for a new life, remember? I just haven't found anywhere I want to live it yet.

I look at my boot to see how and why the sole is flapping. The good boot has a moulded sole: it can't flap; it's impossible. But now I see the problem; I just don't believe it. The sole is flapping because it has been sliced very carefully, and a 12mm strip of rubber has been glued onto the base of the boot, then the sole has been stuck back on. I've been walking and riding around with a built-up boot for nine months and I haven't even noticed, nor has anyone else. No wonder I keep going round in circles. How could I not notice? When I bought them off my friend's mum in Colorado I wore them on a 2,000 mile trip to California and back. Through an English winter, and all the way here, and I never bloody noticed I had a built-up boot. My foot has a wedgie.

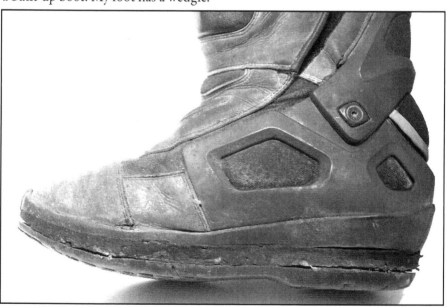

Day 26

Kislovodsk, Russia, 286 Miles

I woke with a start at midnight because someone was shining a light in my tent. It was just the moon; I wish it wouldn't do that. The next light was the sun. It was an uncharacteristically good sleep. I get out of my tent, and it is heavy with dew. I see a man very nearby spraying the trees. I know he's already noticed me; my blue tent in his green apple orchard is not easily missed.

He comes over to me; he has a massive sickle. He is not happy, but thankfully he is not grim either.

"Camping okay?" I ask, possibly twelve hours too late. He nods his acceptance, if not his approval.

If that was a welcome I don't have long before I will be outstaying it. I wrap up my dewy tent, have a yogurt, and decide it would just be bad etiquette to leave a steaming turd in his orchard. So I start the bike, wave my thanks, and carefully negotiate the wet slippery grass.

The two-wheeled track is now slick from the morning moisture; I'm not feeling confident, and sure enough, the bike goes down, my first drop. I turn off the engine and contemplate briefly. No damage, but a smell of petrol, and with adrenalin-enhanced strength I lift it back up. I wish I hadn't put that extra 25kgs of fuel in it.

When I was preparing the bike in the garage, the weight was becoming a bigger issue the closer I got to my departure date; I did wonder if I should lay it down and see if I could pick it up again. I'd spent so long getting everything just right I didn't want to risk bending or denting anything, or for that matter putting out my back before I even started the trip. That would be a feeble reason to not go. So I never did the test. I decided I would deal with that when it occurred, and I knew it would. It didn't bounce, but it didn't break either; the ground was soft, and I had the knack and the strength to bring it back upright. That was a reassuring way to start the day.

All through yesterday's frustrations I was trying to think about the smile and how important it is. Look at Monklet. Remember how it's done, I told myself. This morning when I dropped the bike I trapped his tail; that made me smile. I'm feeling a little low; I'm hoping the mountains are going to lift my spirits.

There are a lot of police checks today, the standard shack on each side of the road. Barriers, police, and armed soldiers stand around, their rank and hierarchy dictating whether they are in the sun, the shade, or sitting inside the shack. My rarity breaks the ranks, and they all stand around me, not in an intimidating way; it's just a break from the mundane. They seldom speak English, but I can guess the questions now; how many cylinders, the engine size, the distance I've come, and always how big my fuel tank is. I draw numbers on the dirt in the tank to answer their questions; it's always friendly, the paperwork is just a formality, and it's quick and efficient. No corruption, just doing their job. It's no inconvenience to me at all. Lately it's been the only human contact I get.

I pull off in a flowery meadow down to a river to have a sandwich and to do what I didn't have time to do this morning. I wonder what all these mozzies and flies do when I'm not here. As I squat behind the bike, a truck pulls off the road and comes straight towards me. I really don't want to be rushed. I hurry the job and finish the paperwork, which unfortunately gets caught on a bush and waves like a flag; look at me, over here! The truck takes a side fork and reverses up to a pile of rubbish, and then he hydraulically tips the bed of his truck up; seems he's come here to dump as well. When I ride back past him, he has a big smile and wave for me. Annoyingly, I left my side stand support behind in my haste to leave, but I didn't discover that until later.

The road improves, the traffic decreases, the scenery is more dramatic with grassy hills and mesas, my spirits lift, and the temperature cools. The problem with the mountain range is that the Russians don't seem to have built roads into them, only around them. The white peaks stay on the hazy horizon but never seem to get any closer. I ride through foothill villages; the styles have changed. The women still have beauty, but it is discreetly obscured by head scarves and long skirts; even the young girls dress like babushkas. They are less than a day's drive from the flesh-exposed seaside, but I've gone back in time again, and bikinis and notebooks have been replaced by shawls and water pumps. I prefer it. I don't feel like I can stop and integrate, but I can pass and appreciate. Now the road really starts to wind up the mountains. I stop to look down the valley at the tiny villages I have come through; the dwellings look like little white mushrooms that have popped up on a hill and rolled to the bottom of the valley. It's a very peaceful place, with a simple way of life; they gather their wood and stack their hay, fetch their water and tend to their livestock. Modernisation does not appear to be missed or needed. This mountain wilderness would be so much more relaxing had I not entered into it on an empty tank. I come to a ski area, which usually indicates the top of a mountain.

I ride over the pass and coast downhill to save fuel. I get to hear nature's noises: waterfalls and rushing rivers, squawking birds and rustling trees. It's like cycling but without the effort. I do remember some benefits of the bicycle.

I ride into Kislovodsk; I'm beginning to question this guidebook. I've been using the *Lonely Planet* for over twenty years; I'm familiar with the format. It is the same reason I don't switch to an Apple Mac. I'll stick with this because I don't want to start from scratch with a new system, even if it is better. The advantage of the *LP* is you can use it two ways: if you want to stay away from the procession of gap year backpackers just go to a town or part of the town they don't recommend. It's easily done. I live in a touristy town but I never see any, and for thirteen years I lived less than a mile from our Norman castle and Roman theatre.

But I wouldn't mind some company, so I head for the "recommended" hotel. Are they having a laugh? Not for the first time, I'm beginning to think the researchers were either taking bribes or just sat in a bar and made it up.

And surely, if you are a receptionist at a hotel and someone comes to the desk, I don't think it would be too presumptuous to assume that that person may possibly want a room for the night. However, I am handed a mobile phone, and the receptionist's friend translates my request to the receptionist. Surprisingly, I want a room for the night. I unpack my panniers, and some mushrooms fall out. I kick them into a bush. I am led to my room by a moustached, smartly-dressed, and incredibly anal hotel manager. I have to do some laundry: my bike trousers have become offensive. I scrub them and my jacket and hang them on my balcony.

I wander into town, glancing back at the hotel, mainly so I will recognise it when I return. Amongst the rows of identical balconies it's easy to see which one is mine; it looks like a dobe wallah has moved in. The pedestrian tourist area is awful, it lacks charm, style, grace, tranquillity, taste, planning, and forethought. In fact, it has no redeeming qualities at all. If the guidebook's researchers even came to this town, it was only to take a hefty backhander from the café they recommended. I sit outside and look out at the road. A vehicle slowly goes past in the centre, spraying white lines in its wake. There are two big cylinders on the back of the truck, one containing paint, the other perhaps Teflon. When I get back to the hotel, the manager had neatly lined up the mushrooms on the wall by my bike. I thank him and tell him I'll be having them for breakfast.

Day 27

I'm glad I don't have a morning ritual that I'm dependent on. There are no cigarettes, no tea or coffee, or food available, and I don't really fancy bruised raw mushrooms. My packing process has become a piece of visual art; it's as fun to perform as it is to watch. It's methodical, thorough, efficient, and best of all, not sweat-inducing. It's very satisfying. So is finding my way out of the city first time. I have to appreciate these little victories; it's daily practice for nearly four weeks now. I've become a smooth operator.

Soon I'm on the road to Mt. Elbrus, Europe's highest peak. I haven't been in Russia a week yet, but already I've become accustomed to the unusual—the cows blocking the road, donkeys standing in bus shelters, babushkas and old men on their horse and carts, ugly high rises. Even the foreign alphabet is beginning to make a little more sense.

I ride into the canyon and follow the river. It's beautiful, but for the rusting pylons and farm machinery. It all seems very serene. Even my bike seems quieter, or maybe the rising altitude has changed the pressure in my ears. The temperature drops as I get nearer to the snow. That is the only evidence I'm going uphill. A twist of the throttle is the only energy I use. I'm inclined to forget about cycling. However, the experience makes me appreciate the power of my engine all the more, and I feel a thrill of desire.

Round every corner it's becoming more picturesque; snow-covered rocky peaks, pine trees, and a foaming river at my side. I'm hoping I'm going to see some travellers at the end of the road, maybe even a bike. It adds to the excitement. There are signs in English: hotel, camping equipment, rentals, it's all looking good.

Then the road ends at the base of Mt. Elbrus. How disappointing; it's somewhere between a quarry, a scrap yard, and a building site. A man with tanned hide for skin and '70s sunglasses comes up to me. I thought he was just another well-wisher telling me I'm crazy to ride this far, but it's a car parking attendant, and in this international resort he demands fifty rubles in one language, Russian. "What? This bit of litter-filled gravel is a car park?" My first impression of this place is him, the second is a bunch of tacky stalls. I can see no reason to get off my bike, let alone stay. "You know what? I don't think I want to park, in fact I've seen enough. I'm leaving." They certainly know how to take natural beauty and turn it into an eye-sore. It's definitely about the journey, not the destination; it's so discouraging. I go down the road and stop to eat yogurt. I throw the carton on the ground when I'm finished; it's a statement. It's hard to put into words, but it was something to do with their lack of respect for the scenery, their country, their environment. Everywhere is rubbish, half-built monstrosities, and decaying machinery.

My mood has changed 180 degrees with my direction. On the way up this canyon I was in awe and full of excitement, now I'm full of disgust, disappointment, and yogurt.

I didn't have huge expectations for the mountain range, but it still let me down. The guidebook has overrated everything I've seen so far. Have I outgrown the *Lonely Planet*, or have I out-experienced its writers? Maybe they write for a different generation now, for the easily satisfied and less critical. Perhaps I should have seen Russia purely as a place of transit and not as a place to sightsee. I'm heading east again. I think I will not change that.

The mountains return to their hazy distance, where there is still hope and promise, but in my mirrors I know it bears no reflection of the reality. I'm given relief from my negative train of thought at a police check. The only barrier I can't get through is the language barrier. Having checked my documents with neither of us understanding a single word each other spoke, one gold-toothed official says "Barack Obama" to me. We both laugh, and I'm free to go.

The same comments at the petrol station.

"Anglia? Crazy."

I'm beginning to concur.

I'm getting bored; it's dangerous. I consider what I would be doing if I were at home right now, 4.30, *Deal or No Deal*? Fuck that. I've just got to ride on through it or stop and let in what it is I am passing by.

Having overtaken a fair amount of the inevitable slow trucks and crawling Ladas, I stop at yet another junction and check my map again. I had also overtaken two off-duty cops; they stop to give me a telling off. I carry on, and they catch me again at the next junction. They instruct me to follow them out of town; I don't want to leave. I'm looking for a market to get food or maybe a room to stay the night. I've already done 300 miles today; I'm tired. But at a safe and anal 30mph, I am led out of town to the road I sort of told them I was looking for. "Well thanks for that guys; see ya." So much for fresh food at a local market; I get fish fingers and beer at a tiny supermarket. Then I go find a hidden place to camp, which has not been used before and therefore is not covered in plastic bottles and any other rubbish deemed unworthy of packing up and disposing of thoughtfully.

The thunder rumbles, and I pitch my tent under a tree, more to be out of sight than out of the rain. I manage to fry my fish fingers, drink my beer, and get everything washed up before the heavy summer rain starts to fall. I get into my tent; I've had more exciting Friday nights. This would be one of those low phases.

DAY 28

ASTRAKHAN, RUSSIA, 447 MILES

I'm woken by two stray dogs outside my tent. I instinctively sit up and growl at them, and they run off. Hmmm, would seem I'm in need of human company; I'm turning into Dr. Dolittle. It's a nice, easy day. 400 kms to Astrakhan; then I will take a day off before crossing into Kazakhstan.

I definitely picked the right place to stop for the night; the landscape quickly changes to flat, arable farmland. Even if I had found somewhere to pitch a tent I wouldn't have been hidden, and it clearly rained a lot heavier here than it did where I stayed. But that was yesterday's luck. The crops have all been harvested, fields ploughed. I wonder what the farmers do now; it's only the beginning of July.

The sporadic signposting has got me again; somehow I have managed to leave the main road. This is pointed out to me at today's first checkpoint, but they show me an alternative route on my map. No worries, I can go up the side of the Volga Delta; it's as broad as it is long. Those lazy farmers certainly haven't bothered to irrigate this land in their spare time. It's hot, barren, deserted plains. I have a slight feeling of recollection in my head, but trying to recall adequate information is futile. If I could find some shade I would stop and check my book. There is no shade, no trees, nothing, but I'm getting a niggling feeling, so I stop anyway. The *Lonely Planet* can't be accused of overrating this area. Well this ought to keep the backpackers away; in a boxed section I read snippets like: "An area of political unrest, like walking in a minefield, pleasant until you take the wrong step, weekly reports of shooting, bombings and kidnappings, particularly foreigners who fetch a higher price." Oh great, and all I have to protect me is a throttle, an offensive smell, and phone reception. I decide to use one of my weapons immediately. I text a friend and tell him where I am, where I'm going, and that I will be safe in two hours, when I will definitely text again. Everywhere is deserted; petrol stations are abandoned and have been for some time, hoses ripped from pumps. What houses there are, are either boarded up or in ruins. It's a little scary. The few vehicles I see have number plates from places like North Ossetia, Azerbaijan, Georgia, names I know from news reports and not the holiday programmes. The cyclist I met in Sochi said he was going to be coming this way, or so he thought.

Those smiling officials at the checkpoint had different uniforms on. Were they leading me astray on purpose? There are yellow signs on the side of the road. What do they say? A warning? Danger signs? Probably best I can't read them. I haven't seen yellow signs before. I could have turned round. I'm not sure why I didn't. Perhaps I didn't want to lose face back at the checkpoint. No other reason comes to mind. If you're going to go through hell, it's probably best to keep going. I dare not trust any more "officials," but if I keep riding when I'm being waved at to stop will I be shot in the back? If I do stop, will I be mugged or worse?

In the heat haze ahead two trucks are stopped on either side of the road. I watch a single figure walk across the road. An ambush? I pass at full speed; no wire had been strung across the road at neck height. I'm suspicious of everything now. On top of all this heat and fear the sky is full of locusts or crickets, and they splat big yellow puss over my screen, which I cower behind; they hit like hailstones on my legs.

I find a petrol station; it stands alone, but it is operational and open. There are several men standing round their parked cars excitedly studying a map. Are they discussing no-go areas? I keep on my helmet. If I'm thinking this is disguising my nationality, I've not considered my bike with its British plate and Union Jack sticker. In my alarmed state I miscalculate the amount of petrol I need and don't get a full tank (you pay first for the amount of fuel you require). I have enough now to get out at full throttle, which isn't much more than 70mph. I long for my Triumph for the first time this trip, which could get me out of here at 140mph; I'm overtaken by a tinted-window Mercedes with no plates or form of identification.

I reach the T-junction, and I'm half-way. A few huts are all that depict the village. I hurtle north. I'm so thirsty but dare not stop to drink. There is nothing around, just hot parched land. Why would people fight over land like this? Or perhaps the fighting left the once fertile land this way. With a second's warning the dots ahead become another storm of locusts and they hit like golf balls on my perfectly positioned windshield. The impact is loud, and I feel the spray of their yellow innards touching my dry cracking lips, exposed through an open visor.

Even if I dared to stop, I could not capture this on a photograph. To anyone who wasn't here it's just barren desert. But in this moment, in this environment, knowing what I've read, paranoid of every vehicle and having seen evidence of once-inhabited places, there is doubtlessly trouble here. I'm not sure how serious, or how recent, but it looks like a war zone to me. When I come to the river and the checkpoint, I'm sure my relief is evident. Yes, I was scared, but in fairness most of that yellow is from the splattered locusts. I was informed and scared, not just cowardly.

I'm back in stable Russia. I'm greeted with a gold-toothed smile. Is he saying congratulations you are safe? No, the official has some bad news. The road is no more, I have to take a different route. I will now be taking the third side of a rectangle, a total of an extra 300 kms. It's so hot; I stop in the shade of an abandoned petrol station's canopy. Something catches my eye. Is that a big bird nesting in the top of the building, or is someone looking out at me? I take bread and sausage out of my hot panniers. I eat, rehydrate, and feed a stray dog, then text my friend; I'm still alive and safe.

I picture his Saturday morning routine; fresh orange juice on the patio, Planet Rock on the radio, the bright green of his postage stamp lawn surrounded by the privacy of woven fence panels. Well I'm not bored any more. Careful what you wish for. I wonder if he has any comprehension of what I just rode through. Do I for that matter? Was my fear justified? Was his complacency?

Okay, deep breath let's get this over with. I ride a few more miles, and then the road just ends; what the fuck? It turns to not just dirt but deep ruts and sand as far as I can see. I can't ride this, it must be wrong; I go back to the tarmac. But the only other choice is to go into a village. So I go back to the dirt track; my compass says west, I want north or at least north-west. It's not a matter of how many times I nearly drop the bike, it's constant. I'm not riding, I'm balancing. It's a continual struggle to keep it upright. I can't do this; I turn back again. I've been riding eight hours in extreme heat now.

There is no one around, and I'm not sure if that is good or bad. I usually see some kids come running out to see the source of the thumping single-cylinder exhaust note. There is a fisherman by a small stagnant pond. I show him my map; he points to the village. I ride round the dusty tracks of the abandoned mud and tile houses and find hard road. There is a broken down truck with its bonnet up; the driver is pouring water into a steaming radiator. I can't get enough confirmation at this point; he is likely to be more informed than the fisherman. He indicates this is the right road, but that it will turn to dirt. He is right, but at least it's level dirt; I reduce my tyre pressures, and it's not too bad at all. I take it easy. It takes a lot of concentration, and I'm already mentally exhausted from today's events. Eventually the surface turns to tarmac again, and unexpectedly the bike coughs. I've used up my tank of panic-pumped petrol; I only have about ten miles on reserve. I've been doing 30mph and third gear; yeah that makes sense. I find a small village; a Chinese-looking person is wandering about. I point at my tank. I need petrol, and he points at a container, "No mate, I don't want to ship it home," but, sure enough, inside the twenty-foot container is a petrol pump, and across from it is a hut with a mirror window. A grumpy Mongolian woman with gold teeth sits inside. I can picture her now, but if the window was mirrored and she didn't smile how do I know what her or her teeth looked like? I do recall she didn't seem nearly as pleased that I was there as I was to be there. It's a Mongolian village; it's amazing, even the roofs are up-turned like Chinese roofs. I could take some photos of my bike in front of them and go to the beach for three months— just tell everyone I made it to Mongolia.

There is a completely different vibe here; I like it. I stop at a little shop for water, it feels fine to leave the bike unattended as I go into the shop. People still stare, but it's not threatening or intrusive, it's gentle and inquisitive—the Buddhist nature. I really love the adventure of this wild open space; I have a full tank and supplies again. The discomfort of today's distance is of minor concern with so many distractions. The unknown, new experiences; this is why I came, it just took 4,000 miles to get to it.

I get some brief cloud cover before the over-exposed plains ahead, and then I'm back on the right road, the one I accidentally split from this morning. I still have over 200 kms to go; that was one hell of a diversion. I see a signpost in English; it says Moscow is 1,700 kms away, but more importantly Atyrau is mentioned, my first evidence of Kazakhstan. Now *that's* really exciting.

So finally, after over 700 kms I get to Astrakhan. Twelve hours; it should have been five hours and 400 kms. But what an adventure. I can't find a hotel. I'm so hot, so tired. I ride round and round the town; this is when accidents happen. After an hour of stop-start traffic lights and false hope, I find one; it's expensive, but justifiably so.

The woman opens the big metal gates for me to bring my bike in, but she can't lock them again. I help her line them up, and she slides the metal bolt into my thumb, full force. It bursts and bleeds instantly. That entire road, all these dangers, and it's the hotel that breaks my skin. She rushes me to a sink, puts iodine on the gaping wound, and puts on a bandage. It's so big it looks like a cartoon throbbing thumb. It almost hurts as much as I made out it did. I take a shower, wash away a day of fear, mystery, and excitement whilst she cooks me a dinner made of pork and guilt and brings it to my room.

Those are the days that stay with you, the tales they want to hear when you get home. But I could never make them really understand. It's personal; it's why I'm here.

DAY 29

ASTRAKHAN, RUSSIA, 0 MILES

As I come back to consciousness, I make a mental list of all the things I need to do today, the things that stop me sleeping any longer. At the top of the list is water; I'm sure my levels are very low. So I duly head out with my too hot and too tight jeans on, because I'm not sure this Sunday city will accept cut-off jeans. I do like to try and make some effort to blend in. I'm not carrying an extensive wardrobe, but I don't want to look like I've wandered off the beach.

You can only get away with that in Rio, where voluptuous girls in dental-floss bikinis walk the pavement and pop into department stores and boutiques. It's a thin line between acceptance and offensive; I guess that's why it's called a Brazilian.

Anyway, around the corner from my hotel is an aptly named convenience store; I get a big bottle of water and right next to it is an equally convenient Internet café. Inside it is quiet and cool, so I indulge in a long session, free of time and cost pressure, whilst consuming my two litres of chilled water. The guys even printed me out a map to show me where I can change my oil tomorrow.

So, hydrated and communicated, I wander off down the bank of the canal. I find the big shops I passed several times last night. One is a DIY shop, so list in hand, I go inside the multi-storey complex. Oh my God, I'm in B&Q on a Sunday. I find the plug converter I need and get out quick. I walk past an English pub that isn't open; how very authentic. I wander on. The town is situated on the side of the River Volga that flows into the Caspian Sea. In the centre is the walled kremlin on top of a hill. There is more than one kremlin in Russia. A kremlin is a fortress, which once was a place of safety for the town's people. It's a good landmark, but despite that, although I'm not lost, I become temporarily unaware of my position within the city. The white walls of the fortress look the same from every side. Just when my feet are beginning to complain in my worn out and holey trainers, I stumble across a market. It is vast and has everything; everything, that is, except what is on my list.

I have a Parker pen. I've had it over ten years; I found it in the glove box of a pig-ugly Yamaha Venture I rode through ten US states in two weeks. At the time it was all that was available on my budget. Buy it or don't go. It was Yamaha's version of a Gold Wing, and it was bloody awful. I don't think I have a single photo of it, that's how ugly it was. It served its purpose and was quickly resold. But I kept the pen. And over the years I have put in many refill cartridges.

Once it ran out on a train journey through Odisha, India. Whilst walking a busy street in a nondescript town, I saw, standing in a row of shops with signs written in Hindi, one English sign; it said "pen hospital," and they had my Parker refill. But that's the chaotic magic that only happens in India. Russia does not have that kind of magic, nor does it have impact adhesive for my flapping sole.

I love markets in foreign countries: the smells and sounds, the multiple cultures selling their strange-looking foods, the dead animals hanging from butcher's hooks, and weird-looking fish on beds of ice. I'm getting close to the caviar capital; all things luxurious and essential are available. There are so many stalls selling the same things but still seeming to survive. It's a great little excursion, and when I'm spat out the other side of the market, I see I'm by the canal that goes past my hotel; and on the walk back I see an oil shop. Perfect.

In the evening I make a trip to the English pub; it's utter shite. There is Wimbledon on the TV, and the camera pans to Cliff Richard. If I'd had any homesickness that would have cured it. The place is dead, and no one seems to speak English. So I return home, having stopped for some convenient bottles of beer. I sit on my balcony, looking out at the canal with my iPod on, and watch the sun go down.

I have the inevitable pre-border sleep, erratic and restless, because I'm crossing into Kazakhstan tomorrow.

DAY 30

ATYRAU, KAZAKHSTAN, 252 MILES

Whilst I'm loading my bike, I am approached by a man who says "good morning" in excellent English and introduces himself as Jacob. He says he is an economist and in the same breath tells me he doesn't want to talk about it, but he does want to talk. I have to change money, and he insists on escorting me to the bank. I question his motives, but he seems to just want a break from the usual Monday morning routine.

As we walk past the fountains and benches outside the kremlin walls, we use the beautiful women as a common interest. He says I don't look my age; he is only thirty, married, and not getting any sex. I said right now I'd kill for sex, and we both burst out laughing and can't seem to stop. We are giggling like little boys with a porno mag. We have just met and are stone-cold sober. He in his suit and me in T-shirt, tattoos showing and hair down; we are chalk and cheese, but we have found common ground in just five minutes, and the passing beauties frown uncomfortably.

My bike is parked outside the dining area, and I have some spectators as I load the last of my gear. I don't mind at all, I think I can feel their envy. I might even be feeling some lust. I'm feeling good this morning, fresh and confident. I tighten my straps tighter than necessary for my dining adorners. Monklet's eyes pop. I can be such a wanker sometimes.

Every weekend I'm aware of what festival I am missing at home and feel a little pang, especially if I'm camping alone that night; but a Monday morning packing up my bike in the sunshine, whilst my festival-frequented friends are dragging their burnt and abused bodies back to work, makes me glad to be where I am, doing what I am doing.

The gates of doom are carefully opened, and I wave goodbye and head for the oil shop. Yes, they have motorcycle oil; yes, I can change it here. Well that is easy, not cheap, but I have good quality oil and some spare to top up with. I'm even given a rag to wipe my hands on. "I think a tip is in order young man; much appreciated. Good day to you."

It takes me two bloody hours to get out of the city of Astrakhan. It's not a big city, it just has a complete lack of signposts, and then when I find one it takes me to a major junction, which has no signs at all. I look for the road most travelled, but it's not necessarily the one I want. I turn round in the end to go back to the centre and try again, only to see signs for my destination in the direction I've just come from. Urrgghh.

I want to open up the throttle and just pass everything, riding like an idiot to vent my frustration at the wasted time, but I scream at myself that I'm feeling fit, I have not yet had any negative police encounters, the bike is running fine, and if I stay another day it is no problem. Get this in perspective and calm down. If you have an accident now you only have your tantrum to blame. And it works, to a degree... I fill up with petrol; I pay on my card for the first time. I have to sign three times, and how much is that going to cost me? I change more money, the oil change had drained my funds, and one way or another, I will be back in Russia. So, having finally got on the elusive right road I reflect that everything got done, but it was done irritably, sweatily, and with difficulty.

I stop in the shade and have a sandwich and drink. I'm filthy again with sweat, oil, dirt, and dust. It's like this most of the time. I'm just getting used to it. The fresh clean entry into the morning lasts until the first red light, and then it's all over until the next available shower. It's already 1 P.M., but I'm glad to be looking forward and not going round in circles anymore.

For the next few miles towards Kazakhstan I find it's actually very hard to find anything to worry about. But, of course that is short lived. I come to a long, narrow, temporary toll bridge. "See," I say to myself. "Lucky you changed money, eh?" It is a wobbly affair, but I'm used to them. At the other end is a choice of direction and no clue as to which one to take. Is this a road trip or a relationship analogy? It takes five directions, and I ask three people before I get it right, and then I get the hell out of there. It's about relationships, isn't it?

To the border; exiting Russia is easy. They don't even want to see my visa registration; all the unnecessary miles I rode and the expense I encountered. Typical.

So, I'm out, but I'm not in, just a long bit of road. I'm in no man's land. What would happen if I came off here? I see a small red velvet cushion at the side of the road, perfect for my bony aching arse. But why would someone throw out a cushion here? What's inside it? I decide it is best left, and then along comes Kazakhstan. Not too tricky. Only one clever little bureaucratic fee to pay, and I haggle and get it for five quid. I don't think insurance is compulsory. The man in his underwear, who gets out of his bed in his little hut to fill out my form and take my money, doesn't seem to think it's important to go to the insurance boy in the next shed to purchase a certificate. And that's good enough for me.

The heat is really oppressive now. The officials seem to get great pleasure in watching you bake in the queue, when they could so easily let you into the shade of the inspection area. One uniformed man is most interested in Monklet; I show him some photos of my daughter playing with him. Everyone can relate to family. If I hadn't had Monklet with me, I wouldn't have showed the photos; if I hadn't shown the photos, I wouldn't have made the connection and perhaps I would have been left baking in the sun a little longer—another bonus I didn't consider when I strapped him on.

With documents stamped I pass through the barrier and am besieged by money changers and other vendors. I get an okay rate and buy a bottle of frozen water off an enterprising kid on a bicycle, all the time trying to keep an eye on my panniers and possessions as the crowd surrounds me. It's times like this that a loud exhaust note is a bonus. It disperses the throng better than bad breath.

So, wet and sweaty all over, but for a numb horizontal strip on my chest where my frozen water is stuffed inside my jacket, I head into Kazakhstan, whooping in my helmet at my achievement. What a change. Russia, Ukraine, and the ones before were Western, despite their individuality, but I am instantly in a hostile desert. There is a line of mud huts with painted window frames, corrugated iron roofs, and blue wooden doors. Power lines go to the huts; I bet it's not to charge their iPhones. There are camels roaming across the road. CAMELS ROAMING ACROSS THE ROAD!

I have ridden my bike to where camels wander freely. Lizards scurry off the hot tarmac as I approach. There is nothing on either side of me, no trees, nothing but parched, dry, inhospitable desert. I make a mental note to carry more water. The road is okay, but there are big potholes without any notice, so it's probably just as well there is not much to look at. I need to keep my attention on the road ahead. I hit one, one in 5,000. Not too bad, but tell that to my wheel and spokes; they just don't like it. I blended in in Russia, well to a degree. People spoke Russian to me, assumed I was of their country; now the faces have changed, the hair is black and the skin dark, the dress is all encompassing and the beauty is discrete.

There isn't much to see but so much to take in. Then three bikes come the other way. We are such rare creatures out here; it's not a matter of a wave or a hoot, we stop and shake hands. They are three Germans, and before my side stand has bedded into the dust, the subject has got round to the World Cup. They give me the usual reports of bad roads, expensive hotels, and worse heat to come. Two of them are on street bikes, a Yamaha Fazer and an old, double-overhead cam Suzuki, both on street tyres. No wonder they thought the roads were impassable. One golden bit of information was that at the end of the day they just pull off the road 500 metres and camp; I'm not sure I would have had the nerve to do that. I also learn the meaning of two words I have probably heard already, "cuda" where are you from? And "acuda" where are you going? Everybody asks those questions; I already know the answers.

"You don't have many stickers on your panniers, man," one of them says.

"I have to cross borders singlehandedly, check my visas, buy insurance, pay bribes, find water, food, petrol, change oil, change money, all the time trying not to leave the bike unattended or out of sight. I have to put my camera on a tripod if I want a photo of myself. I struggle with language and luggage, lifting my bike when I drop it. Doing my laundry, inflating and deflating my tyres, depending on road surfaces. I have to navigate by maps, look for accommodation, and then negotiate rates for single-occupancy rooms. And when I'm not doing any of that I'm riding my bike. Stickers? No I don't have many fuckin' stickers."

They joke that I face certain death ahead, and they will look out for a report about me on *BBC World*.

"Use the cafés," they say. "Russian for "soup" is "soup," and it's always hot, healthy and full of well-cooked tender meat."

It's good to chat. After fifteen minutes of intense interaction, I realise how different it is to ride alone; not better or worse, just different. Mentally they are in a different place than me. It's not just beating Argentina, it's that in my helmet is reflection and analysis. In theirs is a break from the company. I've done both kinds of riding, and although I envy their companionship, I wouldn't change it, not right now. I'm taking everything in, right in, deep inside "there's a journey going on inside my head man." But really, I think how some people get up in the morning and habitually turn on the radio or TV, instant stimulation, and when, if ever, do they have time for reflection? It's an important time to have, but like anything, it's best in moderation.

I suppose I could turn around and camp with them tonight, but I'm not going west, and anyway, now I have exhilaration to keep me company. It wasn't much, but it was good to have contact with like people after a long and not so good phase in my trip. I know that has all changed now. It changed when I put my Russian guidebook back in my panniers.

So the camels become common, as do herdsmen in the fields. The cars hoot and wave, and smiles are back on the faces.

I stop as a train track crosses the road and as the ancient heavy engine drags its cargo across my path. I focus on the stationary car in front of me. There is a Pink Floyd sticker on the bumper. How cool is that? I sing *Learning to Fly* in my head for the rest of the ride.

I've reached a country I've read about in advance, my guidebook is already well-thumbed. I'm still ecstatic at having made it this far. My bike clock has gained another hour, and the desert skies turn brilliant reds in my mirrors as I enter Atyrau. The diversity of this oil-rich country becomes instantly apparent. Enormous international high-rise hotels, wide clean streets, vast squares surrounded by multi-storey banks, and people of every description playing in fountains and under flags and banners. There are gold-roofed churches and round-topped mosques, and best of all, the occasional signpost. I find a landmark, and I cross the Ural River from Europe into Asia. I ride straight to my desired hotel; they even speak English. The gates are opened for me to park my bike. This Central Asia guidebook works well; that Russian one was useless.

I go to the market for water; it would appear I overpaid at the border, but that's not really a surprise. I go across the road for beer, barbequed lamb, and chips, and it's absolutely perfect. First impression of Kazakhstan is good, very good.

All the fear has left me now. No more morbid thoughts. The next unvisited country for me will be Mongolia, but there are still a lot of miles and challenges between here and there.

DAY 31

ATYRAU, KAZAKHSTAN, 0 MILES

A day off. I don't need it, but I like to acclimatise and find my feet in a new country and do my research before I go forth. At least that way I know what I'm missing.

There is cloud cover today; it would be the perfect day for riding, but it's a good day for walking round the city too. I do some bike maintenance, more a check over really; the tyres are showing signs of wear, but generally it's holding up very well. That's the peace-of-mind mechanics over with.

I walk into the city, but it must be siesta time as the place is dead; not the vibrant buzz I saw last night as I rode in. I take some photos of churches and mud shacks in the shadows of glass-and-steel tower blocks. This is possibly the first scenic photos this trip without the bike in the foreground. I find a computer shop, but notebooks are still £300. Well this is dull.

In the list of famous rivers that run through my head, the Amazon, Nile, Ganges, Tigris, and Euphrates, the Ural was unknown to me; it's not spectacular, but it's a major border and a division of continents, so that makes it exciting to cross, despite its characterless appearance.

Back on the Asia side I walk down the concrete path that is the river bank. Up ahead of me are two very big, very drunk guys with their shirts off, built like Soviet housing blocks. It's one of those do I slow down or do I divert? kind of dilemmas. I don't particularly want to do either. I haven't got a lot to lose; my valuables are back at the hotel. So I maintain my pace. As I approach, some drunken instinct kicks in, and they turn and see me. I've assumed their frame of mind, I don't think they are going to be a problem. I'm an instant source of entertainment to them. They shake my hand vigorously, ruining any chance I may have had of becoming a virtuoso. We don't know a word of each other's languages, but they do have gold-toothed smiles of genuine friendliness, albeit born from a bottle. They want a photo and accost some passing weakling to take their phone and take a picture. I get a bear hug strangle hold; God they're strong. But if there is a hostile bone in their bodies it's buried beneath affable muscle. They're grateful and boisterous, and I go to leave then think, "Hang on, I want a photo too." I turn back, and they already know. The weakling is summoned back, and now I've got a photo of me being crushed by two Kazakhstani hulks. I think that's a genuine smile on my face. There isn't an ounce of chav in them; I would never put myself in that situation in England. I continue at my previous pace, and when I dare to look back, they are miles behind. Phew, and that would be my first real interaction with a Kazakh.

The Internet café is full of gamers; Internet cafés are fast becoming a thing of the past. Everywhere is Wi-Fi; not much good without a PC of some sort.

In the evening, being a creature of habit with a liking for chips, and also because I've already done a lot of walking today, I go back across the road from my hotel for my usual. I'm instantly invited to join the owner and his friends at their table. A fast-talking youth then introduces himself to me. He insists he is not involved with the mafia and can help me with whatever I need. Well, I never suggested you were, and I seem to have successfully procured my chips without owing anyone any favours.

Well I do need a laptop; no problem, he has a connection. No, I don't need a connection, my hotel has Wi-Fi, I just need a laptop. Oh wait, I see what you mean. He says he is very drunk and has been drinking for three days. Really, is that all? I've been drinking since 1979. I'm feeling facetious this evening. His wife has been completely left out of the conversation now. He invites me to his birthday party tomorrow night: "There will be many girls." My kebab is not as good as last night; he starts to get into a domestic with his wife. It was kind of him to offer, but I think I will simply say goodnight. He insists he will meet me in the morning to take me to the laptop shop.

There is football on my TV, and whilst surfing for something in English, I find the MotoGP. Perfect...and then it's 3 A.M. What happened?

DAY 32

ATYRAU, KAZAKHSTAN, 0 ACTUAL MILES

I call the lad who isn't in the mafia and hasn't been drinking very long; he's as keen as he was last night. He comes to meet me, and we walk in the blistering heat to the laptop shop.

There is one notebook: it's pink, and the sticker says it's 61,000 of their gold pieces, however, we are informed that it's actually 50,000, which is about £230. It has Vista, Office, and a built-in webcam and microphone. It's perfect. The girl is not exactly what you'd call helpful. Maybe she thinks we like this kind of non-service, us English; no, we just accept it. They won't take credit cards, so I get a fist full of Tenge whilst they start it up. It turns out it runs XP and the Office is a thirty-day trial; it's actually a reconditioned notebook. It comes with no discs (having no disc drive) or paperwork of any kind, and if I don't keep the box, which is the size of a pannier, any warranty is invalid. It will still be fine. I'm handed over from miserable sales girl to miserable money taker. I would never have been able to manage this without the help of mafia boy; he says he will be round to see me later to install an anti-virus and Office for me, as soon as he's tended to some business. I don't want to know. Thank you so much.

Back at the hotel I get online. And that is when I lose myself. I see what Andy meant about a comfort thing. Instantly, location is irrelevant: I have air conditioning, *BBC World*, and an Internet connection. I could be anywhere; I'm not alone, I'm not travelling, and I'm not in Kazakhstan. I'm just back in an all too familiar cyber world. I chat on MSN and Skype, contact my mother, mates, and my daughter; I download my photos, I check emails, and information websites; put photos on Facebook and contact other overlanders.

Seven hours have passed. I have seen nothing of the city; I've been nowhere. Mafia boy has been calling all day; he's been really busy. I don't want to know.

He turns up in the evening, I have bought him some beer, but he won't take anything. He is an honourable guy from where I'm sitting, with a beery haze in a cyber-world. I'm not sure if today was wasted or needed. There was one thing in the world weather I was looking at: the temperatures in Kazakhstan, and I'm beginning to realise just how hot it is in mid-July. I can't decide if going south will be hotter, because it's south, or cooler, because it's the mountains; just what I need, another quandary.

Same place for dinner. The football is on, and the place starts to fill up. I have a little interaction with some rowdy youths, but they are all friendly. It seems friendly is the way they all are, no matter how they look, how they behave, or how much they drink. They are simply friendly, and that's all; that is all that there is to it. I spend the first half of the game trying to work out who is Spain and who is Germany. I head to my room at half time only to fall asleep and miss the only goal. But it's the one that matters; Germany is out of the World Cup. That will be the end of those smug emails.

I spent the day in a virtual world where I left my loneliness behind. I don't want my trip to turn into this; I want to keep my head, my bike, and my experiences in the real world.

I have butterflies again to get back on my bike, and that's what reality is all about.

Day 33

South of Bayghanin, Kazakhstan, 239 Miles

The day starts with a flash of brilliance: I can use that foam packing the laptop came in under my sheepskin seat as extra padding for a bony arse. My ingenuity gives me a feeling of great contentment.

When I go down to load my bike, there is an American-registered 4x4 parked in the compound. I assume it's a diplomat's car, but the two Americans who own it are on a round the world trip, well across it anyway. They shipped it from the US to the UK and are heading back home in an eastern direction. It's really good to talk; I haven't spoken much to proper English speakers for a while. Well, obviously they don't speak proper English, but it's quite good. They say my choice of road to Aktobe is bad; they are doing two sides of a very big triangle to avoid it. I don't care; my mind and route are set, and there is no alternative as far as I'm concerned.

The inside of their vehicle is immaculate: soft, clean, and comfortable. They said regulations in Iran meant they had to have a guide or chaperone with them at all times. They missed him now but not the massive watermelons he kept buying and bringing into the car, a potential sticky bomb. I'm delaying them, so we swap numbers and say goodbye.

I'm loaded, ready, and really excited. I fill up with petrol and go round two thirds of the ring road to get out of town. Just when I thought I was wrong, I find the right road. I love my digital compass; it's a little bit of confirmation when I don't trust my instincts. It turns itself off after five minutes, so I'm not drawn to the screen all the time. I just press the button now and again, and it basically says yes or no. I trust it, but I don't rely on it. I bought it, like everything else, on eBay, but it came from Canada. It's capable of doing so much more, but I don't understand any of its other functions, and I prefer it that way.

The road to Makat starts out smooth, although there is a gradual decline in the quality of the road surface. I slow the pace accordingly and pay more attention to the conditions. My bike is quite agile, so I can veer round potholes, but it requires constant effort, and it's mentally and physically tiring. Some potholes I just stare at, like a rabbit in the headlights. My lack of reaction wakes me right up as I pound down into them and bounce up the other side. I'm impressed at the way the panniers and rack stand up to this abuse. To think, I used to check them after every bump at home; now I just assume they are still there. They can look after themselves; I have other things to concentrate on. There isn't much of anything about, but I do see a brand new petrol station. It's not even open yet, and I stop in the shade of the canopy and take photos of passing camels.

I ride into the town of Makat, where I decide to fill up; I've already used one third of my tank. There appears to be just one petrol station, and they only have seventy octane. I'm not putting that in my tank, even if the engine will run on it; it will do more harm than good. The main road runs alongside the railway track, but it is completely dug up, there seems to be no alternative to the troughs and trenches of sand. Some is compressed; I try to follow the car tracks. I'm not even sure I want this direction, I don't have control at all. I should deflate my tyres, but my optimism says hard road will reappear; in reality I lose my grip, and I drop the bike. Once again from some unknown place, strength is summoned, and I lift it up again. I hate sand. I try to use a path at the side of the rail track; it's as bad, maybe worse.

Not only did I not get petrol, but in my deliberation I took the cap off my tank and didn't screw it back on properly, so now petrol has soaked my tank bag. Brilliant. I stop and ask directions and am bombarded with advice I cannot understand. Helpful but abrupt directions are thrown at me, and I miss every one of them. The roads end, tracks fade away. The most promising road leads to a power station and then ends. I go back to the village and ask again; that power station seems to be the most popular option. So I try again, aware that I'm making no progress and using precious fuel all the time.

This time I ride around the back, where there is a truck parked. The driver points out over the grassland. It's not a road, it's not even a track, it's nothing, but he is a truck driver, a brother of the road, and I've run out of options. So I follow the direction of his finger. A man is walking around out there, and he points at a row of telegraph poles. The ground is a corrugation of humps, I continue further and then, totally unconvinced, I return to the man. He insists with rigorous hand motions, so I try again. There is nothing out here, nothing but heat and a hazy horizon. Ruts and grassland becomes my route, heading for a row of telegraph poles that depict a path, which turns into a track, and meets some gravel, and eventually turns into a road. There must have been an easier way. There is a bucket on a post, and painted on it is the name of my destination. I suppose that's all the confirmation I'm going to get. Over that next hill I will reduce my tyre pressures; over that next hill is paved road. I laugh out loud. It's taken one-and-a-half hours to do six miles.

I feel the ache of stress leave the bottom of my spine. My mood is as volatile as the road conditions: dusty road—dirty fun; smooth as silk road—mind accelerates to other places, potholes and sand, and the concentration exhausts me.

There are place names on my map. I assume they are villages, but my expectations are higher than the head count. I ride into a few of them looking for petrol, water, top ups, opportunities; not in desperation, not yet. But they are nothing more than a gathering of wooden shacks and a scattering of a few old cars in varying states of disrepair. If there is a place that sells supplies, anonymity is its priority. A few more wasted miles. It's a relief to be back on the main road. Smooth roads are as sporadic as the signposts. I'm up and down the gears, not sure what range I have now.

Sometimes the road is so bad that the vehicles have made a better smoother track at the side of the road. I ride on that, wondering if the road has improved. Back on the road of stones and gravel with holes and bumps, the dust track does seem better, so I go back. It's almost fun; it would be if I wasn't playing Russian roulette with a tank that was running dry—always something to worry about, always. The road improves, then disappears, and then it's back again.

When I get tired of 20mph washboard dirt, I try taking the speed up to 45mph to even out the bumps. It's a theory I know works, but I've only applied it in hire cars, not my own vehicles. It works, but I feel the vibrations still; I have little control and wonder how the fasteners and racks are coping with this abuse, so I slow down again.

I know I'm running out of fuel now. I divert to a tiny village. The heat is so intense now that I have taken off my bike trousers and replaced them with combats. Keeping my Levis for best, they could do with some new genes here too. I follow yet another Lada to a dusty area, where there is an old Russian tanker. It's not so much parked as abandoned; a black hose comes out of the top. I'm told this is my fuel. A lady approaches with her hand outstretched. How old is this petrol? What octane? What price? And how do I start the flow? Suck? No, I don't think so. I'll take my chances. There is always something in short supply: confidence, company, patience, language, sense of direction. This afternoon it's petrol.

So I get back on track and stop at a small dwelling, which the hand-painted sign is optimistically calling a café. There are a few old trucks outside. Inside are barefoot truckers and a couple of van-driving youths who speak a little English. They tell me the only petrol is back the way I came 200 kms, or onwards 300 kms. I don't have enough fuel to do either. I stand outside in the shade of a truck and drink a two-litre bottle of water. I'm crushed; what am I going to do? If I turn back I've quit; congratulations, Kazakhstan, you win. I've dropped my bike twice this morning, I can't find my way, and when I do I have no fuel to get there. I'm disheartened by my dependence; I'm defeated by the road. If I keep on going I simply run out of fuel and then what? Stranded in the desert? What to do? What can I possibly do?

I have a firm talk to myself; I have no one to banter my options with, no one to bounce off. Fuck it, I'll keep going. When I run out I will take off my tank and hitch. So I keep going. I deal with it.

It feels so fatalistic; I'm just going to run my tank dry. I'm riding into a desert, stepping off a cliff, going over the top of the trench Blackadder-style. Well maybe it's not that dramatic, but it is to me. Back on the road I'm so focused on what I want to see, that I'm not sure if it's hope or reality when I see the canopy up ahead. Could it be the liquid I so desperately need in this desert? Could it be a petrol station? I get closer; it looks like one. Is it open? Does it even have petrol? Yes, yes, and yes. All of those; it's clean, pristine, straight out of my highest hopes. From the pump flows life blood into my bike, my trip, my hopes, and my survival. In the squeeze of a trigger I have been given an extension on my life. I'll give the van drivers the benefit of the doubt. Last time they came down this road the petrol station may not have been here.

The only other building is a hut/café, and I order soup, because I know now it's the same word in Russian.

I'm so hot; a little boy has followed me in, staring at me from a safe distance at the corner of the room. I take off my boots and make a "phwoar that stinks" gesture. He giggles, so I continue talking to him, accentuating my tone of voice. I get a reaction and then get my soup.

All is well again. Full tummy, full tank, empty land.

I'm back on the dirt roads with renewed vigour, confidently speeding down the tracks. I'm a jet fighter, but my vapour trail is a cloud of dust behind me. I can't photograph this stuff; it's one of those moments again. It would mean nothing without the hardships, the compensation for endurance and tough decisions.

Fulfilment evolves from persistence, and it comes at a price. I paid my dues; I reap my reward. A petrol stop has never been so dramatic.

The dirt road branches off and reconnects; there's no traffic. A trail in the distance up ahead becomes a truck, and when he approaches me he switches sides, so I pass him on my right. Through his consideration I avoid his dust cloud.

My shadow is long, and my day is complete. Where shall I camp? I pass the endless steppe of parched grassland and infinite horizons. I can pitch my tent anywhere I want to. I think I shall cammmmmmmmmmmmmp here. I pull off the road and ride a little way, there is a dry river bed, and I can park in the dip out of sight. I put the bike on the side stand, and this will be my home for the night. I pull off my boots and my other sweaty clothing. I can't seem to stop undressing, and I run around naked in the warm breeze as the red sun falls. The stars appear, the gentle wind keeps the mozzies away, and I bravely sleep with my tent open.

This is why I am here; this is what I came for. Some people who know have said "Why here? There is nothing there." Exactly, nothing but me, me and my thoughts, so clear I could see inside my head, if I didn't keep my helmet on.

DAY 34

AKTOBE, KAZAKHSTAN, 194 MILES

That was quite possibly my best night's camping ever, in a totally-isolated-nothing-but-the-sky-and-all-its-tricks kind of way. The setting sun was so big and so close that, had the developers of 3D TV witnessed it, they'd realise they haven't even gotten close to recreating reality; but how many have witnessed this reality? Then, just after midnight, up came a crescent moon that was so large that I lost all sense of space perception. I thought it was a bush fire until it rose and took shape. And the stars: that infinitive night time sky that is such a rare sight for us Essex inhabitants. There are no new sequences of words to describe the star-infested heavens, be it romantic, factual, or awe inspiring; everyone has been moved to stretch the limits of their vocabulary and their thesaurus. Does anything else but falling in love drive even the most illiterate heathen to put crayon to cardboard in an attempt to convey the rare but inevitable feeling inside that occurs when one night one finds oneself free of light pollution and looking at a sky full of immeasurable hope and possibilities? Google it, I've got a ride to write about.

I pack my bike with my iPod on. Firmamental experiences require appropriate music, so listening to David Gilmour's *Big Ol' Sun*, I go about my ritual, the difference being that this morning I'm out on soft steppe; the side stand sinks, and the bike falls over. That is that little self-indulgence cut short; ear phones out, iPod off. Reality check.

"Concentrate; you are out of sight and all alone. Get this bike upright and back on the road." Well it was good while it lasted.

A herder has brought his herd into view; I think they are goats or they could be cows, and he is further away than I thought.

In an extravagant manner I use the last of my wet wipes for my morning bathing. Being industrious, I'd bought a back-up pack, which I break into for my face and neck. Unfortunately, I don't know they are scented, and now the inside of my helmet smells like nappies; clean nappies, but nappies nonetheless, or some other artificial stink-removing scent.

There are eagles at the side of the road; some just stay perched on a mile marker as I pass, some take a step back in a minimal sign of respect. There is no urgency in my day. I enjoy the varying surfaces. I just take what comes as it comes. I pass a dead camel on the side of the road; those things are massive. That really would make a dent in your radiator grill.

I remember in Australia the kangaroos would gravitate to the road at night, because the tarmac held the heat of the day when the outback night time chill descended. Even the truckers with their heavy-duty "roo bars" would try to avoid the impact. Not in the name of roo preservation, but because they were big heavy lumps of meat that would mess up the most armoured of trucks. But what really got me was the wombat practice. Like guinea-pigs on steroids, they are a slab of muscle and fat with bad eyesight. The trucks would almost go right over the top of them: almost, but not quite. They would usually get jammed under the sump and be dragged down the road until they wore down a bit and the bloody mess would tumble out from behind the trailer. Travelling through the outback I would see these long red skid marks; I came to expect I was about to come across a dead wombat, with bloody stumps for legs. It's wasn't until I saw a live one in a reserve that I realised they were actually quite cute: stupid, but cute.

I consider the air-conditioned luxury the Americans are travelling in, and how the motorcycle is luxury to the cyclist, and I wonder what a 4x4 driver dreams of. Maybe the freedom of a motorcycle, maybe a chauffer-driven Hummer. Or have they found that illusive contentment?

I pull into a town; on the dusty main road I find a busy little market where I can replenish my supplies. Everything on display is behind the counter, which goes around all four walls. I wait for a service lady to be free, I point, and she picks stuff off the shelves for me: bananas, yogurt, bread, etc. I think this is how "supermarkets" were in the old days, before self-service and trolleys. It's still got a personal feel in a tiny village like this; God forbid you needed condoms or Canesten. Everyone would know you were getting it, or got it. No surreptitious scanning at the self-checkout.

An old boy pulls up on a Ural with a sidecar as I load my bike, and he shakes my hand. So many handshakes, so many smiles; my laughter lines are full of dust. I appreciate the simplicity of these little towns. The pretty girls squashed into tiny buses with mobile phones pressed to their ears; the endless goats, geese, camels, horses, cows, and turkeys that wander across my path; the cattle herded by men on horseback, but somehow the term *cowboy* does not apply. These are tribesmen almost, scratching a living, not living a romantic dream. They are there for the moment, as am I. So I try to live in the moment and appreciate it, because it can never be reproduced, and I'm not sure how much longer it will last or if I'll ever be back this way.

The humidity has gone, and the temperature may even have dropped, so the sweat has ceased for a while. It's time to dig out the lip balm; my smile is cracking in this dry air.

I approach Aktobe almost with sadness. After my time in the desert, it feels strange to be in a city; the adjustment into wilderness is far easier than the one into civilisation. Traffic lights and police. Cars and commerce. I don't like it, but once again, the diversity of this country is remarkable. From a deserted desert to a cosmopolitan city, it's an almost instant transition. I go right into the centre of Aktobe, not for sightseeing but to find Wi-Fi. I just want to see if there are any potential travel companions in the area and if I have had a response to my request: "In western Kazakhstan heading east, can speed up, slow down, or in the case of Astrakhan, I'm quite good at going round in circles too."

Sure enough, there is the Wi-Fi sign; I have to consider security again. I park in view of the picture windows, then go and order an awful burger with fries. I overhear English being spoken, and without a second thought I go to its source. I'm not looking my best, windblown, sun-scorched, iodine-stained, and with wild desert eyes. My girly hands are now dirt-ingrained, cut, scarred, and hardened; tanned where the fingerless gloves don't cover, callused where they do. And on top of that is the faint aroma of scented wet wipes, but I don't care about that. I know I look like I have come from one steppe beyond the city, but I'm on a mission to get my information and get out again. I would never have had the confidence to do this in the old days, but I walk up to the table and meet an American peace worker and her friend, a Kazakh student. I ask what time zone I'm in, that's always an ice-breaker. They have a friend who "just loves to help;" they call him, but his English is not so good, so they will stay and translate.

"Okay, thank you."

I go back to my laptop. I hadn't considered the pinkness; it was of no concern in the hotel room, but in a Wi-Fi restaurant I'm a little self-conscious. The walking contradiction of a budget traveller, filthy dirty, slightly scented, with pink communication equipment. *I* wouldn't talk to me. No one wants to ride with me, either, it would appear, although I do get a message from some Brits in a Landrover, telling me how bad the road to the Aral Sea is: 180 kms of sand and no fuel at all. Shit, the feel-good factor is a delicate thing out here.

Gennadi is an older man, very smartly dressed and with a quiet but assertive demeanour. He scans my map and shows me which roads I should take. Going to Aral is out of the question as far as he is concerned. Of course, I can go, but I would be a crazy suicidal fool to go alone. He makes it quite clear, through the interpretation of the girls, that he will only give his advice and offer his services if they're taken. He shows me another route that takes me through Astana, the extravagant capital, which I also want to see. I was wondering how I could combine it into my previous itinerary.

I am to follow him to a hotel, so we all go outside; the girls get in his Lexus, and I follow. We go out of town, off road, am I being taken to be mugged? I follow suspiciously, and I end up at some strange holiday getaway. I am more ordered into a room than checked in, and there I am left with the promise of company later.

I'm so isolated here: I feel trapped, captive. My day has suddenly turned sterile and boring, and it's only 4 P.M. on a Friday afternoon. Maybe we will all go out partying this evening; that American was pretty hot and clearly unattached. Could she tell I scrub up quite well? Does she care? Maybe I'll not see any of them again.

I check his suggested route; I suppose it could be okay. His words, combined with the message I got today and my recent experience with sand and lack of fuel, have taken the bravado out of my wanderlust. But nobody, *nobody* can ever agree on a clear and unarguable definition of what exactly a bad road is.

I go and drink an expensive beer outside the attached restaurant; they put on awful and loud music, just for me? I get a text message from my local Kawasaki dealership. The spare spokes that I ordered in the spring have come in. Good work guys; what a service. A wasp flies into my beer. I go back to my cell.

True to his word, my Lexus driver returns, and his English seems to have improved dramatically. He buys me dinner, gives me advice and phone numbers of "fixers" on my intended route. Is this to keep tabs on me? I even speak to one of his connections on his phone, who will sort a hotel and a tour for me when I arrive at his city.

Gennadi takes emergency numbers from me, in case he has to inform my next-of-kin; this is becoming very strange. Then his daughter and her boyfriend arrive, they study in England and have excellent English. I can't pay for anything; the rest of my travels round Kazakhstan have been arranged and taken care of.

I'm given so much advice, and it's getting a little patronising: don't drink the water, talk back to the police, or eat bad food, but it's all done with the best intention. I'm so suspicious, but I am coming to understand that I have found genuine people, with hospitality that extends beyond my cynicism. I don't really get it, but they fear for my experience as a lone traveller in their country. They want to take care of me, that is all. I have to promise I will call any time with any problem, so that they can fix it for me.

When they have just about taken every last bit of adventure out of my trip, I am told I will be met in the morning by the daughter, Anastasia, and boyfriend, Yevgeniy, and they will have a Kazakhstan sim card for me, with credit on it. At 11.30 they say good night. I go to my room wondering what the hell has happened since I pulled into Aktobe.

DAY 35

SOUTH OF DENISOVKA, KAZAKHSTAN, 364 MILES

Thanks to the security guard my bike is still there, but he's probably responsible for relieving the monotony of his night shift by playing with all my switches. It's not a big deal; I just feel a little violated. Would he have done the same in an unlocked car?

I ride to the petrol station, which is the rendezvous point. I fill up and wait. There are lots of onlookers and lots of handshakes. It's just a modern morning on the outskirts of the city—no evidence of the land I travelled through to get here. I'm just waiting in the shade. If I was trying to keep a low profile, I would be failing, but I don't mind the attention. I'm waiting for someone to say, "Didn't I see you on *Deal or No Deal*?" I feel like I have celebrity status just by having my bike with me. When there is no more interest in me and I'm left alone, I wonder what sort of car they will be in; a nice little VW, I expect. As I wait in the shade two bikes go past with the trademark aluminium panniers that scream overland traveller. They are the equivalent of the dreadlocks and pierced eyebrow of the gap year backpacker. I'm torn, do I wait for my "fixers" or chase my potential new riding buddies?

I go buy an ice cream, and they turn up in a sporty Mercedes. I don't know the model, but it ain't no Golf. They are late, because they got stopped for speeding and had to pay off the policeman. With the honour and reliability I have come to expect, they have a sim card for me, so I put it in my phone and take their numbers. What have I stumbled across here? I'm instructed to contact Yevgeniy's parents when I get to Almaty, as they will put me up. Sometimes thank you is so inadequate.

I apply the tortoise and hare strategy. The two bikes that passed will stop, inevitably, and if I don't stop to drink, I won't need to stop and piss, and if I keep a steady speed and don't stop to take photos, I will catch them up.

In Alaska I got a puncture and had to plug my tyre; it was a bad fix, and I had 150 miles to ride to Anchorage, where I could get a new one. I had to ride at a steady 50mph to stop the plug from flying out and to minimise damage if it did. I rode with two other bikes, who would overtake and then stop for a drink or a wee or whatever. I just plodded on, and they would take ages to catch up. It's the same as the trucker doing a constant 56mph without stops; I would frequently catch up or be re-passed by the speeding motorists who couldn't maintain momentum. My strategy works perfectly, as there, at a bus shelter are the two bikes, so I pull up and say hello.

They are a German couple just come down from Russia on identical Yamaha XT660s, with identical riding clothes and identical helmets with built-in intercoms. They have helmet cams and sat navs and satellite phones and a big SLR with an even bigger lens. They carry spare petrol and more water than a prenatal class—thirty litres of water and five of petrol. How different my trip to Aktobe would have been with those supplies, how dull. They are one week into a six-week trip to Mongolia, where they will ship their bikes and fly back home.

I sit with them in the stinking, shit-and-fly-infested shade of a bus shelter, where they are resting. They are so well-equipped and informed; they know and have so much that I don't. We are joined by two drunken guys, who stop their old Russian truck to come and say hello. They shake hands and pose for photos. Shirtless and gold-toothed, they breathe their alcohol breath through their smiles. I help them to push start their truck; it's got to be ten tonnes easily, and with a jolt and a black cloud of exhaust it bursts into life and they are off.

Nearly two hours have passed, and the Germans are on a tight schedule, so we ride together. I'm waved to ride between them; I feel a little inadequate in my fingerless gloves, combats, and a map. I have a scratch on my camera lens, a hole in my left boot from gear changes, and tape holding my right boot together; and today I noticed my tyres are full of cracks. I didn't feel challenged, but now I'm riding with such technology and researched organisation, I really do feel like I took a left one day on the way to Asda and ended up here.

Well this sucks. I was happy when I was riding alone. Now I'm in pursuit and being followed, and I know I'm being talked about too. When I showed them my built-up boot, I got a frown, when I was expecting laughter.

"How did yoo not know dat one of yor bootz waz higher dan the other?"

I only said it for a giggle, now I just feel a bit stupid. The ride is smooth, the scenery dull, it's not as hot, and there is farmland around us now.

When we stop for petrol I suggest a café, as I'm hungry. Riding with others, I can't have my bread and sausage stops, I can't even let go of the throttle to do up the flapping Velcro on my glove. I've lost my freedom to dither. This recommended road may be in good condition but it's boring.

I take off my boots outside and enter the café; they are impressed, I can tell. We sit on the floor round a foot-high table with a plastic tablecloth on it. The food and service is good and simple. Bread, water, and tasty soup; it's perfect. They have not been in one of these cafés before; I don't tell them this only is my second. They encourage me to stay and camp and ride with them. I know they have discussed this in their helmet intercoms. Why wouldn't they? I should feel pleased that I'm likeable, but I feel I was tested and judged. Which, of course, I was. That's how you decide on companionship, nothing wrong with that. Couch-surfers do it all the time; they just draw the wrong conclusions.

They are all right. The only thing I don't want is "sympathy companionship." Tell me if I spoil your plans, but actually I think maybe I enhance them. I've travelled as a couple, not on bikes, but it's the same principle I'm sure; you just don't attract company as a couple, and interaction is half the trip. We do have some fun; we are a spectacle. Wherever we are, be it on the road or parked by it, there is always a mobile phone pointing in our direction, filming and photographing us.

Back on the road my position within the formation is centre again; I try to stay behind and am waved forward one position. If I take the lead, I am soon passed again. It doesn't matter; it's just an inherent need to be contrary. It may be childish and rebellious, but it's those little acts of defiance that give me the illusion of freedom, and it works for me.

There are suicidal birds that fly out of the fields as we are passing, right into our paths. I duck behind my screen to avoid impact, and one hits my hand. A lemming without a cliff will think and fly laterally. Near death is everywhere. Marmots cross my path as eagles look on from their nests in the trees.

I feel protected but happily independent, glad to have the company, but not for too long. They ride hard and fast; it's more evident when the road deteriorates again, and I find it hard to keep the pace. They are on a different time budget to me; I feel pulled from the front and pushed from behind.

The sun turns red, I catch up Stephen in front and suggest stopping, because it doesn't seem to be on their agenda. This is my favourite bit. We just pull off the road and pitch our tents. I take photos whilst they do oil checks and charge batteries. The girl is an excellent rider, far better off-road skills than I have, but it's hard to compliment a female biker. If I say I'm impressed, she'll think I assumed she would ride like a girl. I didn't and she doesn't, but I keep shtum. I make rice with tuna and garlic; it's the best camping meal I've made. I'm really pleased with it; I keep insisting they should try some, but they don't seem that eager.

"Really, you should see the shit I usually cook." They bring out bratwurst and other supplies from home.

"How long does that stuff keep?"

"Ve left six daze ago, ve ave five veeks to get to Mongolia, our food vill not run out."

It's already 11 p.m. as I pack up my stove. I manage to burn my leg on my mozzie coil; great, avoid a bite and get a burn. They say they want to be up at 6.30 a.m.

"What?"

DAY 36

NEAR SAWMALKOL, KAZAKHSTAN, 325 MILES

I hear the sound of production. It's 7.30 A.M.; I'm late, but I don't care. I can get up, packed, and fed quick enough. I don't really have much to say. I'm travelling independently with company, there is no communal spirit, and I don't think they have time for that. I chew on bread when I'm packed up; they are still charging their phone and camera batteries.

We discuss the plan for the day; they have decided that, although they were going to go directly east, they can afford the time to go down to Astana with me. I'm not sure if that's a good thing or not. I like the company, but they have high-mileage ambitions. It's still early; we'll see. On the road we go through agriculture before we go into town; best we stopped when we did then. We pass a lone and loaded cyclist: I always stop for cyclists.

"Need water?"

He is Spanish on his way to Australia; not much to say, he is deep inside his head, I can tell. I congratulate him on making the World Cup final, but he is unaware. He is fit and tanned, but I think there is damage inside.

Later we pass a bier haus: outside is a huge statue of a beer drinking character in lederhosen. It's too much to pass up, and we turn around. The yard out the back is a kind of truck stop; a driver is asleep on top of his cab, and others simply lie on the ground. I suppose it's just too hot in their cabs. I see a Tesco trailer. I see a lot of European trailers out here, obviously sold to Kazakhstan haulage companies. This isn't Poland; there is no Tesco here, yet.

They order German food, and it's good; the place is German run, and I have my first beer in four days. I could easily drink this Sunday away, but Stephen doesn't like the taste of beer. We have ice cream for dessert; it's good, this being on holiday. We attract the inevitable crowd and take it in turns to talk and answer questions.

Like the cyclist in Sochi, Stephen was schooled in the DDR and speaks Russian. He can read it too. Very handy. I'm also learning some useful words by being around him, but the sounds of the shapes they call letters is too much to retain.

Time is whizzing by, and with all their gadgetry, they are constantly stopping to charge batteries. No wonder my tortoise-hare thing worked. They are so well researched and disciplined, I feel like a sloppy-seat-of-my-pants traveller next to them.

Then I find my tank support brackets have broken. I need to do maintenance on my bike. My back aches; I can't ride these long days. I don't have to.

When I travel through endless cities of high-density population, be it Bombay, Bangkok, or Birmingham, I wonder how there is enough food to feed everybody. It's seems such an unmanageable task, but out here where the fields of crops reach every horizon I think, ah, that's how, and I no longer fear for the city-dweller's hunger, or at least I can think about something else now.

I've actually managed to take the lead; we head into a city, and there is a comprehensive sign in English giving every direction and the distance. Typical, just when I get to travel with the Sat Nav fraternity I get directions I can understand. I take us round the ring road, as if I knew anyway where we were going to go. I'm obliged to call one of my fixers in this city, just to say I'm okay. I call and get no answer, phew. I text instead, and just to be sure, I text Gennadi too; he is relieved I have company.

We have stopped by some fruit sellers—all women and all drunk. One in particular has wild eyes, a cowboy hat, and a loose top with loose breasts underneath. She takes my hand and leads me off to her stall to see her watermelons. How could I possibly refuse a drunk girl who wants to show me her melons? Without the language I can still make inappropriate comments and raise a cheeky smile. I have my hands full, and photos are taken of my fruity purchase, and we laugh and flirt.

I think the Germans are wondering who the hell they have picked up, and so am I. Despite this, they seem to be having fun too. We secure a watermelon in the centre of their spare tyres. There is a river opposite where lots of people are swimming and lazing around. A guy in Speedos comes up for a chat, and we both laugh when we compare each other's dress. I'm in bike clothes: gloves, helmet, jacket, and boots, and he's barefoot in budgie smugglers. One of us is dressed inappropriately.

Convoys of wedding cars pass, covered in flowers and hooting their horns, waving and shouting as they drive past. It's all so upbeat, so fun, so friendly. What a great place; what a good day. Would I encounter this on my own? Maybe, but a bit wearier. At a petrol stop even a cop is friendly; sometimes you can just radiate, and it comes right back at you.

Now we have mileage to do; it's going to be long and hard. My back already hurts. I calculate mileage in my head, and the mood changes. I can't do this. They want to do 300 kms to a national park; I need to take it easy. The road deteriorates, and I slow down. We stop for supplies, and I have to do my chicken impression again to get eggs. I seem to be unable to be the straight man with other straights, it just brings out the fool in me. I don't think they mind, they may even enjoy it. Outside the store are ten-year-old boys on mopeds, revving their engines and doing wheel spins. I pretend to race with them, down on my bars, all cheeky grins and noise. They take the lead, and then with a twist of my throttle and change of gear, I wave goodbye.

The road is rough, and my companions stop; they have realised we won't make our target, good, but that means camping and so more provisions have to be bought. They have a plan for a meal they want to cook. Into another village, and Stephen takes over; he's got intentions and can communicate them. He asks everyone, and we ride round and around, and the place has only got about three streets. But he perseveres, and we find the store. I get impact adhesive for my boot but still no eggs.

It's time for the best bit: pull off into a grassy meadow, into the shade and shelter of some trees, and the riding day is done. They have a small larder in their panniers. With my tablecloth poncho and cutting board, I have something to offer. They make an amazing spaghetti bolognaise, followed by watermelon for pudding. I offer to do the washing up, while they take satellite readings of our coordinates. They document them, and then they are transmitted to people at home, who can log their position and progress. I text my mum, "Just had a fab spag bog." I really need to clean out my panniers; I have had a Marmite leak. I hate that.

Day 37

Astana, Kazakhstan, 311 Miles

I've got a tent full of mozzies, but they haven't bitten me for some reason. I had heard that they don't like blood with alcohol in it, but I proved that theory wrong when I passed out by a water tank, which was home to a million mozzies, at a full moon party. I woke up with a body that looked like a 3D map of the Himalayas. Not this morning. Now my body is a temple of purity and abstinence, as opposed to its more customary amusement park status. those fickle mozzies don't seem to be hungry for my uncontaminated blood.

I wander into the woods for a Forrest Gump, whilst the Germans perform their morning constitution of charging and transmissions. A tractor trundles past us with a trailer full of farm workers; we wave but get no response. It's a Monday morning. They are on their way to work, and we are on our way to Mongolia; I think I can sense some resentment.

Whilst we camped last night, the World Cup final was played in South Africa. With my notebook and their communications equipment I bet we could have watched it somehow, if we knew or cared. More watermelon, and I wait for them to plug in, turn on, and tune in, then we're off. This is my other favourite part of the day: fresh and rested, cool and comfortable, with the sound of an enthusiastic engine in the clear morning air.

Soon we come to a pristine, smooth, brand-spanking new piece of deserted dual carriageway. It's so new that I can still see the stencils where the white lines are sprayed. The bus shelters still have plastic on them; if only I hadn't gone into the woods this morning I could have christened one of them. The Germans don't think that's funny at all; they don't do bus shelter humour.

We turn off to Lake Burabay and follow a dirt road that takes us to a barrier, where we pay our entry fee to get into the national park.

It's okay: rocks and pine trees. The smells and scenes remind me of the Rockies, and I get homesick for Colorado. The problem is there are too many tourists squashed into too small of a place. The open spaces in this country are amazing; the cities have a beauty too. However, this over-hyped and over-developed piece of natural beauty has become a contradiction by over population. We stop by the lake, and a constant stream of traffic passes us. Well I'm here now, so I go to the shore, strip off, and jump in; it's cold but refreshing. Right, been there, seen it, done it, got my T-shirt wet, let's get out of here. We are all of the same opinion when it comes to tourist hell. We are out the other side of the park in no time; it really is small, no wonder it's so crowded.

We see hotels everywhere; it's so ugly. Then we are stopped by police. Stephen is in front and gets a five minute interrogation. Based on his law-abiding documents, we are all judged to be of no threat to this resort of repulsion. Once we are a safe distance from the holidaying masses, we stop for a kebab, shezlic it's called, a shish kebab; vegetables and barbequed meat. It's a national delicacy here and in Russia. It's my treat; they fed me last night, that's the way it works. Well, in my head anyway, but they seem awkward with it.

Back to the perfect road. It's now a three-lane motorway, but there are still fruit stalls lined along the side. You just don't get that on the M1. We ride three abreast on this empty highway, and I take their photos, the first they have of the two of them together. I haven't seen roads this good since I left Scandinavia. It's just a motorway, but it's so remarkable after what I've been through. My mind is free to wander, no attention needed.

We pull off into a rest area full of vendors. Once again, our arrival is met with smiles and intrigue. Everyone has a smile, whether it's from behind the window of a Lada or a Lexus. There is always encouragement, always good will.

This time the commodity is honey, and girls from the stalls want photos of themselves sitting on the bikes. Usually I would not be so keen, but it's all done with such politeness, excitement, and enthusiasm I can't possibly refuse. I have perfected the high kick to get my leg over my luggage. I show them how it's done; it almost becomes a competition, full of giggles and blushes. The Germans have their honey; I almost got one too. I wink and wave goodbye to a particularly pretty face with a longing look in her stay-here eyes.

With the new road comes big American trucks as we head to the high-rise wealth of Astana. I'm really excited to see this extravagant city. I'm becoming aware of how scruffy I look as we approach the glamorous jewel in Kazakhstan's crown. We were kings of the countryside, but we are peasants in the city. The sand roads were beyond my capabilities; this silk smooth surface is beyond my expectations.

We stop outside the city to decide on a hotel. Then I get to indulge in the luxury of satellite navigations.

"Ve have not ze time to take zee wrong direction." Best I don't lead then.

I follow the leader straight through a city of giant TV screens on buildings, spectacular fountains, and outrageous architecture to our hotel of choice. In the parking compound is the Americans' 4x4 from Atyrau. The receptionist wants more for one person in a room than for two people in a room. They can't make me understand why I pay more than the couple do. It's beyond logic, and it's really bloody irritating.

"I'll pay the same."

But no, it has to be more. I'm not staying here on principle.

It's dark now, we have passed through another time zone, and it's beginning to rain. We can't find another hotel, and I feel a bit guilty, but I'm not going back to that stupid hotel. It's too late to be picky, and when we find a very expensive and very luxurious place, I have to concede and take it. I have to spend two days' entire budget just to get a room.

These high-mileage days have taken their toll on my bike, my back, and my budget. I can't keep the pace. My budget is based on finance, not time; they worry about not making their destination in time, and I worry about not having the money to get to mine. After a shower, I'm all ready to go out and explore. I knock on their door.

"You coming out?" They were in bed.

"Oh, oh right, okay then. Er, see you tomorrow then." Well that was disappointing.

Day 38

Astana, Kazakhstan, 0 Miles

I wake at 7 A.M. and look out the window; sure enough, there is Stephen loading up his bike. They are not going to see anything unless it's from the saddle. It seems strange to me, but maybe they are more focused on Mongolia than here, much like I sped through Poland to get to Ukraine.

They come to my door, and I let them use my pink Internet connection whilst I go down to my bike, detach and bring up my Marmite pannier. They offer to take me to breakfast, so I jump on the back of a bike, and we go in search of a café. After several failed attempts, we settle for coffee. It takes them so long to lock up their bikes, no wonder I caught up with them in the first place. Whilst we sit there, Stephen warns me about my visa stamp and that I should get it registered and how, in fact, insurance is compulsory. He then warns me of heavy and dangerous traffic in the south of Kazakhstan and recommends a route in Mongolia. I have to stop him in the end; this is information overload. So with a hug and a wave I wandered back to my room, helmet in hand; it was an easy goodbye. We had some laughs, well I did anyway.

I look in my passport; my visa doesn't have the stamp that theirs had, so I go to a posh hotel with a built-in travel agency. They tell me they could register it, but I've exceeded my seven-day deadline, by one day. I'm told I have to go to the immigration police, which sounds ominous. I get a taxi; I'm panicking a little. I arrive there at 1.10 P.M. They close from 1 P.M. until 2.30 P.M., so I walk off to find insurance, as recommended by another posh hotel.

Luxury hotels are always good for advice because someone will always speak English, and they can provide the service that high-paying guests expect. All I have to be is polite and grateful, and I get all the help I need, just to get me out of their gleaming lobbies.

I have a map drawn for me, and I follow it to what I was told is an insurance company. I sit in a queue until I am seen, and am then directed downstairs to another office. I produced the last policy I had as an example of what I need. A girl types, one-fingered, on her computer; I have the feeling it's not right, but I don't have the words to question her actions.

"I'll be back later."

I walk back to the immigration police; the place is now bustling with people, all holding forms and various documents. It's a chaotic place; a big room of tables and pens and blank forms in Russian. Through a door are the officials in a row of cubicles. They are all safely behind glass, so they can be as rude and unhelpful as they like without fear of retaliation. An armed guard stands at the door, and eventually, in a system that does not involve any logical form of queuing, I am sent to my allotted official.

She is the proverbial bitch and says that I need a translator, so I call my fixer and pass the phone to Superbitch. There is a long, heated discussion. When I get the phone back, he tells me he will get me help, whilst the fascist dictator yells at me to go outside. I'm sure she knows what she is, no need for me to voice it to her. I try to fill out one of the forms on the table; I'm helped by the thronging and infuriated masses, and although I'm sure it's wrong, I take it back to the evil woman. She continues to insist I have a translator.

"Where am I going to get one of those from? I'm on a bike."

"Go to your embassy!" She shouts.

I'm not having a very good day. I go back to the insurance place. I have to pay 1,500 gold pieces for a sheet of paper, and it's not insurance; it's a translation of the example certificate I gave them. For fuck's sake. I'm hot, sweaty, and stressed. I am staying in a place I can't afford, to pay a fine I can't determine, until I get a translator I can't procure, and I can't leave until this stamp is stamped in my passport. For all my efforts so far all I have is an English translation of an expired Russian insurance certificate. I'm watching my trip being cut short with every bill, and I can't go anywhere.

I get a taxi to the British Embassy; it's just over the bridge. I could have walked that. My passport is my rite of passage. I've never dealt with embassy employees before. I thought they were only there for when you get caught at an airport with two kilos of cocaine up your bum.

I get a lift to the appropriate floor. Even seeing the flag is comforting. A woman is behind a glass screen.

"Do you speak English?"

"I am English, what do you need?"

"A hug?"

"Having a bad day? Wait there, I'll send someone out."

I speak to a lovely man, typically English: polite, understanding, sympathetic, attentive, and utterly useless. I'm glad there was no coke found in my bum with him representing me. He will get it all sorted out tomorrow and recommends an insurance place. In fact, he has a Kazakhstani employee write on a Post-it note in Russian that I need to buy motorcycle insurance.

The insurance building looks promising at first; a security guy leaves his desk and takes me to the right office, which is empty apart from a girl and a phone. The company has moved premises.

I give up on the day; it's been awful. I was so looking forward to this city, and it's failed me in every way it can. I walk along the river towards my hotel. The south of the river is where all the stunning postcard scenery and elaborate affluence is at its most evident. I wonder if the Germans even saw it; I get a tantalising taster, but I will save it for later. My feet are killing me; these trainers are worn out and give me blisters.

When I cross the river, an older lady is standing on tip toes looking over the railings like a little girl. Actually she's probably younger than I am; I forget how old I am sometimes. She says something to me and points at a big fish trapped in the reeds; we both watch it, and I wonder how symbolic it is. She insists on walking with me; she points out we both have our hair plaited. Her only words of English are "I love you." I respond by counting to ten for her in Russian.

Day 39

Astana, Kazakhstan, 0 Miles

This room may be excessive beyond my budget, but when I'm trapped in bureaucratic hell, it's good to start and end my days in comfort.

It's a beautiful morning. I'm rested and refreshed and ready to continue with my registration procedure. I am early at the immigration building, so I sit on the step outside, and my mum's words go through my head: "You catch more flies with honey than with vinegar." I must maintain my smile.

As 9 A.M. approaches I try to coordinate my call to the embassy with my turn at the cubical of non-cooperation. Sour Face doesn't look like anybody told her "I love you" last night. I fix my smile, say good morning, and hand her my phone with my embassy translator on the other end. When it is handed back to me I am told that they will have to send someone down, and then the phone goes dead. I have run out of credit. So I continue the call on my UK phone. How much is today going to cost me?

I feel reassured now the cavalry is on its way, so I sit outside and listen to my iPod and people-watch. I specifically got all my visas in advance to avoid these sorts of bureaucratic delays. I'm as much annoyed at myself, for listening to someone who didn't know what they were talking about, as I am for the stringent enforcement of rules. In actual fact all I am guilty of is simply being twenty-four hours too late in getting a stamp in my passport. Not a huge threat to national security in the great scheme of things.

After an hour, a black Range Rover turns up with diplomatic plates, and out of the passenger side steps my saviour: a slim young girl in a summer dress, with hands full of paperwork. I think she can see my relief and appreciation. She has never done this before and seems a little nervous. Her innocence and beauty seem more prevalent than her official power and capabilities. I'm torn between the role of victim and protector. Don't mess with my angel; she is here to help me.

First I show her to the cubical of negativity and revulsion. It seems to go all right. I feel all powerful, now I have my embassy with me; like my big brother has turned up just as my lunch money was about to be taken. We are directed down a corridor, and we wait outside a room where the extremely naughty are dealt with. When we enter we are faced with a very strict and serious Vietcong-looking man with four stars on his shoulder. He is shouting at people in his office who have three stars. He then turns to face us. My lady shows him all her documents; she is very qualified and armed with some lovely looking certificates and much authority. He looks through her paperwork. As they exchange words, he actually breaks into a laugh at one point.

"That's a good sign," I think to myself, "Maybe she can get me a private cell." I stand quietly until we are both ushered out.

"What did he say? It seemed to go all right. Why did he laugh?"

"He laughed because I am over-qualified to be doing this."

No he didn't, he laughed because you're the prettiest thing in here. We must get all her documents photocopied for him. There is a place round the corner. She offers to pay, but I want phone credit here too; anyway, the British tax payer shouldn't have to pay for my photocopies.

We then go back to the office where Mr. Flirty Four Star seems satisfied and we are given blank forms. Basically, the forms say I admit to being a criminal, I am fully responsible, blaming no one, and will accept whatever punishment they see fit to impose, be it fine, incarceration, deportation, or life; how can he give me life when he clearly does not have one to give?

"Just tick the yes boxes; I apparently have no rights in this country." Back to Mr. Judge and Jury. The fine will be a minimum of 14,000 Tenge, that's £75. What can I do? Haggle?

"They will know for sure tomorrow."

"Tomorrow?"

She goes back to the cubical of sadistic suffering.

"It can be done today: the fine will be 14,150."

An extra quid? Why those liberty-taking bastards.

But they won't take my money. We have to go to the bank and get a money order. The bank is packed; no problem, there is a machine that will print a money order. I just have to feed my money in. But it's only for account holders, so we go back to the queue. We will be in line for over an hour. By then the immigration police will be at their hour-and-a-half lunch break. My little helper finds an armed guard who will let us go to a different part of the bank for a small token of our gratitude.

"Step aside, darling, I'll handle this one," I would never say. The gun-wielding guard put my 500 note in his pocket, and we are processed. She is appalled, my embassy aide.

"I have never had to do such things before."

"Really? You should travel with me; it happens all the time." No, honestly, it's an offer; but she doesn't pick up on it.

We get back to Mr. Four Stars of Mayhem before his lunch sabbatical. My passport will be ready at 4 P.M.

The chauffeur waits in the air-conditioned Range Rover and takes us back to the embassy, whilst my over-qualified assistant puts my credit into my phone for me. Would it be inappropriate to offer to take her for dinner? Her fingers are ring free. No, I don't want to live in this city.

My embassy came through for me just for this minor infringement of not registering my visa within seven days. It was, they said, the first time this had happened. I'm sure as more tourists come, if this stupid rule remains in force, a lot of people will be paying a lot of fines, and the embassy will be besieged by tourists. I'm discovering that Soviet mentality is still very much a part of officialdom, but the Kazakh public are very different from their northern neighbours.

Inside the guarded compound of my embassy I offer my inadequate thanks and say goodbye.

I head back to the place that used to be an insurance company, and I get a map drawn for me to their new premises. The security man suggests I take a photo on my phone of the logo of the company I am looking for; good idea. I feel things are getting better.

Twenty minutes later I am leaving an air-conditioned insurance office with a valid certificate, for the cost of £2. I walk back home and pay for another night; I'm not even counting anymore. I go early to immigration, as I have nothing better to do. My passport is returned with the precious registration stamp in it. I then call the embassy and thank them, and then call the 4x4 Americans who were the ones who told me visa registration was not necessary, to let them know what they were about to go through. After nearly forty-eight hours, I am free to see the city.

I decide first to go to Khan Shatyr, a 150m-high, leaning shuttlecock of a structure that was designed by Norman Foster. It contains shops, cinemas, pavement cafés, a golf course, beach, and all other essentials in life. It's very impressive from the outside. Inside it's like Lakeside with a different roof. It's bloody awful; it's a shopping mall, full of posh shops and pushchairs. I hate this environment. What was I thinking? In the supermarket, I buy paté and bungie cords and that's me done.

There is a spectacular view from the steps looking east towards the shiny and symmetrical city, but my trainers threaten to shred my feet if I attempt another step. I jump on the back of a crowded bus back to my hotel and jump off again before I have to pay.

A little victory: I finally get something for nothing in this fine city.

Day 40

North of Balkhash, Kazakhstan, 342 Miles

This hotel is so good. Not only do I get shampoo and conditioner, but it's such good quality that I actually use it.

Back to the bike: I have been able to see it from the window of my room, but other than that it's been abandoned for the last two days. I decide I will ride around this beautiful city, seeing it from the saddle and taking a few photos; being built from scratch means it merges together in a consistent and harmonious way. I ride past the Bayterek monument, which looks a bit like the World Cup trophy but is actually a symbol of the Kazakh legend. The ball at the top is, in fact, an egg that contains happiness and desire, a bit like the inside of my helmet; it is very photogenic, unlike the contents of my helmet. I ride on under an arch in a fourteen-storey, white, terraced building block with gold-mirrored windows towards the Pyramid of Peace, where I am flagged down by a policeman. I have to obey the man with the baton: when it points at me, I must pull over. He was most excited, but not in a good way. I had ridden too close to the presidential palace and broken protocol.

"Oh come on, I'm just a tourist. Please?"

"Pleeeze, pleeeze!" he mimics, and shouts his incomprehensible babblings, before demanding my passport.

A plain-clothed man gets out of the police car and spouts to me in Russian, like I would understand the same spiel if it came from a man that was not in a uniform. Then they both went back to the car and started to fill in forms. I'm fuming. Screw this city. It's been nothing but bureaucracy, fines, and authorities. I was so looking forward to being here, and it's been shit. Now I can't even leave. I just wanted to look at the architecture. I was ready to explode at this cop: "Maybe it should say on the visa that you don't want tourists, because that's the impression I'm getting and so will everyone I tell." But I keep my big offensive mouth shut; it's getting easier with practice. I decide the pen is mightier than a string of abuse; I get one out, along with the business card of the man from the British Embassy, with the intention of taking the cop's number and making sure he knows what I'm going to do with it.

The two men deliberate over the forms in the car, and I sit on the bike. I wonder if I ride off now without my passport how smart of an escape plan that would be.

I get a text. It's from the American 4x4 drivers; they are at a northern border town, and they, too, have had to get their embassy involved to sort out their failure to register their visas. Kazakhstan is such a diverse country, it has many faces, but the face of authority is very stringent, unnecessarily so I think in the case of well-meaning but uninformed tourists.

Then the plain-clothed guy gets out of the police car with the forms and into another car, and leaves. The cop comes back with my passport and explains the way I should go to the Pyramid of Peace.

It turns out the form-filling was for the plain-clothed guy, who was not a cop at all but had also broken protocol and was getting a ticket, so I'm free to go. I'm so relieved. I shake his hand, and he almost drops his precious baton of power. Slowly and respectfully, I ride back in the direction I had come from. Relieved that my big offensive mouth remained shut; it would have only antagonised the situation, and I won. Phew.

I think it's time to leave Astana.

It's so good to get out of town and ride through the steppe, as opposed to riding a step-through. As I ride south the driving standards deteriorate, cars pass so close I could kick them. I'm not sure if they are inquisitive or just don't care. After they pass me, they pass the next car with more space. It's really annoying me.

As I head south the temperature increases, and I feel the delirium of my brain boiling inside my lid. I have experienced this before, riding through Arizona in July. I know the signs, like when I have painted too much gloss paint, and I know the thoughts I am having are from a mind in an altered state. When a car jumps out from behind an oncoming truck and I have to take evasive action, it's with spaceman movements that I avoid a head-on collision.

I stop at a café and eat a dead animal, tender from being on the boil all day, not unlike my mind. If someone else in the restaurant is eating I point at their dish, if not I just have soup. Luckily I'm easily fed; my diet is as diverse as the last customer's order.

I see two bikes coming the other way. I wave and flash my lights, but neither of us seems like we want to stop. It's the wrong time, the wrong vibe; I'm glad to be out on the road again, and I'm enjoying my own company and being back in the wide open space.

Due to three horrendously expensive days in Astana, I'm trying not to think about money. Today's mental calculations are how much further my tyres will get me and when I will change them. It will be a treat not to have to carry them anymore, but they are an insurance policy that I'm reluctant to discard. The daily strapping and retightening is a pain. I read about the problems of tyre creep before I left. The article said you are most prone to suffer from it on sandy terrain with low pressures. The tyre can creep round the wheel taking the tube with it, ripping the valve off, resulting in an instant flat tyre. However, tyre creep was never mentioned in relation to trying to keep the bloody things in position on your top box.

Up ahead are hills. It's early to stop, but I ride off road, up and down the rocky hillocks. I'm hidden from view at the expense of having no view. It will do for tonight. I go to a peak for phone reception. It's amazing. Wherever I have been on this trip I've had reception. In Kazakhstan I have had a full five bars, even when there have been no signs of civilisation anywhere. In this country of vast, open, unpopulated space, I'm never isolated. Yet on my English Three network I never get reception, whether it's at home, in the high street, or on the train to London. Whilst the other commuters talk on their phones, all I get is a text to say I have a voice mail. If my phone does ring, my conversations don't end with goodbye but "Hello? Ya still there?"

I thought it was my user-unfriendly phone, which I dislike as much as my network, but it's not the phone, it's my useless phone company; this contract has been the longest eighteen months of my life. They could learn a thing or two from the reception I have got in Kazakhstan.

Yevgeniy, boyfriend of daughter of fixer, has texted me; his parents are expecting me, and although they don't speak any English, they are looking forward to meeting me. I still don't get it, not really; hospitality like this is beyond my comprehension.

I sit at the top of a hill with my camera and tripod waiting for a sunset that doesn't happen. I don't need to cook because I've eaten, so I'm a bit challenged for entertainment. It's hot still; I lie on top of my sleeping bag in my tent. Then it starts to rain, and I have to close the door, and my breeze has gone. Suppose I'll try and sleep then.

Day 41

100 kms North of Almaty, Kazakhstan, 389 Miles

The heat of the sun gets me out of my tent at 6.30 A.M. when I'm still half asleep. What half I wonder? The half that does calculations and co-ordination it seems; I trip over guide ropes, drop my keys, and open the wrong pannier to find food. Somehow, a basic survival instinct eventually takes over, and I manage to put bread in my mouth and slowly become more responsible for my actions. I even manage to get the top box shut first time without anything sticking out from the side—a challenge at the most lucid of times.

I take the track to the road and head towards Almaty. I'm looking forward to this city by the mountains. Anywhere with snowy mountains is my idea of perfection, but the two things that bother me are going south when I should be heading east and staying with people who speak no English. However, this trip is all about seeing and experiencing the country, so that is what I am going to do. I know that staying with any native family wherever you are is such an insight into their everyday life. A day in someone's home is far more enlightening than a week in a hotel with a conducted tour every day.

The sign posting is so good now, so good that I miss Balkhash completely by using the bypass. I half wanted to visit it, but the half of me that did is asleep now because it was up so early this morning. It's ironic that the Germans I rode with were so desperately short of time but wasted so much of it pratting about with time-saving equipment. Now here I am on my own with no time limits and going faster than I need to. I'm just too quick and efficient in my daily operations, packing, refuelling, and eating.

It's the same at home; I microwave a meal, and with no distractions while I eat it, I find I have troughed it in less time than it took for the microwave to go "ping," without even noticing the taste. The only meal that takes longer to eat than it does to prepare is breakfast cereal.

The road follows the side of the lake; it's a big lake, the fourth biggest in Kazakhstan, so it's a significant size. I'm not in any hurry to get to another city, so I divert off to swim in Lake Balkhash and, once again, find that the "special" areas are the most disappointing. At the shore is a tide line of plastic bottles and broken glass. Despite this, the water remains a clear turquoise colour, and I can see the truck tyres lying on the lake bed. I strip off to wash, and I get bitten by ants as I make my way through the rubbish. The dirt road here was the highlight of the dismal detour. I quickly retreat in the opposite direction.

Well, now I have an answer for my query as to what the temperature will do as I head south to mountains: hotter, it gets much hotter.

Back on the road I see some bikes coming towards me. It always causes a little thrill of hope and possibility when I see other riders. I'm ready to brake and turn around, but although they wave, there is no brake light when I turn my head to follow them. As the day and the miles go by so do northbound bikes; their luggage is for a long weekend, not a long summer. I'm beginning to think I'm missing something. I hate thinking I'm missing something, especially when it is bike-related.

All along the side of the road are people selling fish, smoked or dried and salted; I keep saying I will stop at the next stall, but I don't. Then I leave the lake, and there are no more stalls. I'm not in a hurry. Why do I do this?

In a small forgettable town I stop at a market of fruit and veg where a brave ten-year-old boy comes up to chat. He speaks good English straight out of a text book but pronounced perfectly. I wonder if he has ever had the chance to practise with a native speaker. At first, with my ever-present paranoia, I wonder why he is coaxing me away from my bike. I want to keep it in my sight; I then realise that he wants to be in the vicinity of his mother's stall as we have our conversation, to show off his expert linguistics. I happily oblige. And I'll have those last two bananas while I'm here, please.

The landscape is changing, all the trees have gone. I hadn't noticed their absence until I saw one standing alone. I'm not sure how long it would have taken me to realise otherwise, not having a hammock with me.

It is so hot now, I have already changed to cooler clothes, but I have to ride with my legs splayed because the heat from the engine is so intense it's burning them. I stop in a stinking, shit-filled bus shelter, just so I can put the bike in the shade to cool. Flies buzz around me, cars slow to stare, and it's altogether a miserable and uncomfortable experience. I hope my bike appreciates it.

Further down the road I cross a river. It would be a great place to camp. I eat at a café; I'm getting good at this now, familiar with the method of ordering and not so surprised with what I receive. I even get an ice cream for pudding. It's medicinal; I'm overheating. I ride down to the river, but there is nowhere to camp, as it is fenced, segregated, and restricted. If these people had net curtains they would be twitching now.

I go a little further and then leave the main road off to where the river must run. It has been dammed, and there is a vast reservoir where there once was a canyon. It's beautiful but intimidating, as beauty often is. But a faint heart never won a fair camping spot. There are steep cliffs and hidden ravines. The shore line is inviting, but the route is illusive. I walk down, it's very steep; I'm definitely going to camp here, but not right here. I ride on carefully as the land undulates; sometimes it is a bump, sometimes it's a gorge.

I ride down a slope that is too steep; I say "ride," I mean kind of locked up my front wheel and slide down intentionally. The sun is going down, and a storm is blowing in. No worries, I can see it will pass. I get out my poncho and sit on my bike, totally exposed on the side wall of a canyon. To one side is the downward path of loose rocks, to the other a cliff face and deep water below. Along comes the storm, thunder rattles round the canyon, and the wind blows like a demon. I straddle the bike, still fully clothed in helmet and boots, and don't ride the storm out. I'm wet. It doesn't matter, though; it's still warm, and I will soon dry out. Then the wind changes direction 180 degrees, and my poncho shelter turns into a sail, and it blows me and my bike over. Bollocks. So in pissing rain on the edge of a cliff with a bellowing poncho pulling at my legs, I get under my bike once again, and I lift it up. Just at that point my phone rings; urrgghh, I'm out of hands. It does make me laugh though. What the hell am I doing?

The call was from a Swiss guy who has seen my plea for a travel companion. He is two days from Almaty coming up from the south. This could work out well.

The storm turns into a rainbow; clothes dry and my bike is upright again. It's hard enough in this place to find a flat spot to put up the tent; as for getting tent pegs into the ground, it's impossible. So I gather rocks to stop the tent from gusting off, and after the poncho experience, I decide not to tie the tent to the bike. I don't want to stand there like a child who let go of his helium balloon watching my bike paraglide away under my tent.

So I climb a little to photograph the sunset and become aware of just how steep this incline I descended in the name of a "perfect camping area" is. How steep? In the gradients "versus" surfaces equation, with loose-jagged rocks on the side of a steep canyon this rates as "bloody steep." And that's enough to lose sleep over.

Even an emergency midnight snack of Marmite on stale bread under a black poncho of night, pierced by a million points of star light, doesn't take away the daunting prospect of tomorrow's first 500 metres, most of them vertical.

DAY 42

ALMATY, KAZAKHSTAN, 72 MILES

First light is so beautiful that I have to get up and take photos. Then a storm blows in, so I go back to bed. When I make my second appearance into the day, I walk the path again that I will have to ride. I've done it three times now, and every time it gets steeper. I move some particularly sharp pointy rocks, which have puncture written all over them. Additionally, this heat hasn't done much for my food supplies. I scavenge through the panniers for something to eat and throw out a squashed banana, an over-ripe melon, and some sweaty cheese. I'm generally almost superstitious about throwing out food, but I'm only an hour from the city.

I don't so much pack up as mentally prepare myself to ride back up again and out of the canyon. Despite the heat, I put on all my protective clothing; armoured jacket and the thick bike trousers with padded knees, all to soften any impact. I think about leaving a message to be found if I can't get it up, something along the lines of, "Awfully sorry, this has never happened before."

I drop my rear tyre pressure, warm up the bike, and give myself a firm talking to: my motivation is to not hurt myself. I could take off my panniers and make three trips up so the bike is lighter, then ride it up to meet them, but in my laziness I convince myself that I need the weight over the back wheel. I need speed and confidence, and a little control wouldn't go amiss either. I have my phones strategically placed so, whichever way I fall, whatever leg is trapped under the bike, I can still reach a phone. People have done greater things on lesser bikes. I'm about to push my limits, find where my capabilities end. Like Evel Knievel, I survey my ramp.

Okay, I have to get into second gear by this point; I can't let off the throttle until that point. I have to bump up this rock and not take that route because it will lead me over the edge. What a prat I was for coming down here in the first place.

Okay, let's go, hard on the throttle. I accelerate up the track, into second gear, faster than seems sensible. I hit the loose rocks, stay on the throttle, bump up the ridge, and the wheels don't collapse. "Don't throttle back you wuss, stay on it."

I pounce onto the second part of the track and lose balance. I stop.

"Why did you stop, you idiot, go on, go on." I go on, the rear wheel spins, rocks fly, traction is sporadic; I leap forward, a little bit of control. Yes, I am riding this bike, I am negotiating its direction, and I'm up. I've bloody done it. I've got it up. No apologies. I went up better than I went down. I'm so pleased with myself and with the bike.

Right, take off some clothes and pump up the tyre. I feel elated, but there is no time to wallow in self-congratulation.

I'm still quite a way from the road. I have a tiny dirt rut to follow; I ride past a shepherd with his flock of goats. Then I see, bounding through the long grass, his ferocious dog foaming at the mouth chasing after me. I have to ride fast down the dusty track to escape his hungry teeth. Do I really need this? Can I not revel in my accomplishment for a minute? No, not if I don't want my calves pierced by rabid fangs I can't. So I ride to the road and do a few miles before I allow myself a brief period of euphoric reflection and mental celebration. Now back to the challenge of the day.

I look up to see snow-capped mountains on the horizon; I wondered when they would turn up. Trees have started to make another appearance, then fields and marshland. As I get closer to the city I pass by a purple lake. I stop to take a photo. As I lift my helmet I realise it smells as unnatural as it looks. That is some seriously toxic water. If anything can live in that I don't want to meet it, or eat it for that matter.

The road's surface worsens, the signs stop being in English, and the traffic builds.

As I ride into Almaty there are no road rules left at all. Lanes mean nothing, the cars swerve, they cut me up, they come straight at me, pass me and then stop. When in Rome...I ride like an idiot too, and I get along just fine. I get in the right lane to beat the line of stationary traffic turning left, then turn left in front of them, whilst holding up the traffic behind. Okay, see, I can do this too; other drivers seem to expect it; expect it or feel the impact. I'm on my brakes, on my throttle, and on my guard. I'm on two wheels, and I'm on a mission, same one: I don't want to feel pain.

I've been camping for two nights and sweating for two days: I don't think I'm ready to meet the parents yet.

In the centre of the city I see a woman holding a sign that means room for rent. I stop my bike by her, get off, and let her lead me to the room. We cross the road, and then we walk through the concrete gardens of high-rise housing blocks. I have left my bike unattended and unlocked with tank bag, camera, and passport all there for the taking. I've already decided I don't want the room before I have even seen it. With every step I just want to get back to my bike. It's a dingy, musty, apartment on the second floor of a tower block. If I was staying a month I could bring out its potential, but for a single night it's unthinkable. I half walk, half run back to the bike; it's still there all intact. That was not a smart move at all.

So I decided to spend my first night in Almaty in a Soviet-style prison of a hotel. I stand at the desk sweating, whilst the receptionist chats away to the security guy; am I invisible? I'm sure you can smell me, even if you can't see me. I turn to walk out and get a reaction. The receptionist only learnt English so she could be strict and abusive. The misery of communist Russia is recreated perfectly.

"Do you want cheap room or not?"

"Can I see cheap room?"

"No."

"Can I see expensive room?"

"Yes."

It's shite.

"I'll take the cheap one."

"You pay."

"How much?"

"I told you," she snaps.

"No you didn't."

"I told you the price."

"No you didn't. You said cheap or expensive; you didn't say a price."

"Bla bla bla."

"I'm sorry I didn't catch that."

"Give me money."

Bitch, your beginning to piss me off, I didn't say. I give her money.

"Room 435."

It's the shittiest, furthest from the stairs, smelliest room with the most mozzies, thinnest mattress, and the worst view, next to the construction zone, with constant banging and drilling, she doesn't say.

My guidebook says to unplug the phone to avoid prostitutes calling,

"How much is cheap one?" But I don't pay for sex, at least not directly. With the investment of time, emotionally, physically, mentally, and financially in an indirect way, but not in the money-on-the-dresser kind of way. But just out of interest, how much? I unplug the phone. Anyway, the hooker would be all sweaty by the time she reached my room.

The parking attendant suggests I take everything off the bike, which is a pain at the best of times, but in a hotel where I am on the fourth floor, with no lift and at the end of three long corridors, I don't want to make that trip the six times it would take. I manage it in three trips. I take what's important and Monklet is relieved of his guarding duties at the insistence of the car park security man. So as not to make him feel inadequate, I take him off with the intention of washing him. He still has yellow puss on him from the crickets he headbutted in Dagestan. Now drenched in sweat and utterly filthy I manage to burn my hand on the exhaust when I'm locking up the bike. Wotblink.

I go for a walkabout. Almaty is the former capital city, and it's got an established elegance about it. It has a mature beauty over Astana's young lust. It also has character: wide boulevards and street cafés, it's almost got a Parisian feel about it. I stop at a coffee shop with outside seating and Wi-Fi. I don't know anything about designer coffees, other than they are overpriced and over complicated. I order an iced coffee because I think I can't be embarrassed by choices I don't understand. I save all my embarrassment for opening up my pink notebook. I really am still ridiculously self-conscious about it. The street has boutiques of labels that mean luxury, pedestrians are dressed smartly and climate controlled. I don't fit in on any level: language, dress, beverage, or laptop. I try to hide in a cyber-world.

In the evening I have a disgusting fast food pizza and go back to my room ashamed at myself for not being more adventurous in my eating habits. I kill all the mozzies and turn out the light. A mozzie buzzes in my ear, and the light goes back on. This goes on for two hours until midnight, when I get dressed and go down to my bike to retrieve my mozzie spray and coils. The city is alive and kicking now, but I'm too tired to participate. When I open the door back into my room the stale heat is stifling. I open the window and light four coils and lay on the bed with no sheets covering me. Come on mozzies. If you can get past the smoking coils and the spray, you can have a bit of me.

DAY 43

SUBURB OF ALMATY, KAZAKHSTAN, 12 MILES

Well, I haven't been bitten, the mozzie coils didn't set the room on fire, and my bike is still there; that's about as much luck as I need for the day.

With the bike all loaded I ride the two blocks to the railway station, park in the shade, and call Yevgeniy. I was hoping I might be met here, as it's nice and central, but no, that's not the plan. I'm given directions I don't understand to meet people I don't know and stay in a place I'm not sure I want to go to, but I'm invited and therefore feel obliged.

I'm met on route by yet another big flashy car. Yevgeniy has said his aunt will be there too, and she speaks English. When someone says "aunt" I picture a grey-haired spinster in a camel-hair coat. One of us is wrong: either my image of what an aunty looks like or his definition of what an aunty is. Surely he means cousin. Just one more young and beautiful woman in a trip full of beautiful women; she really is well-dressed and has clearly made quite an effort this morning. What effort can I make? My panniers are not full of choice, but at least they're not full of decaying fruit and spilt Marmite anymore, either. That's the extent of the effort I made.

The driver of the flashy car is Yevgeniy's father, a friendly, welcoming, healthy-looking man; he is probably about my age but a hard working family man as opposed to my lifestyle.

So I follow their car out of the city, trying to remember the route we are taking. I have a good idea I'm heading for somewhere nice. With every turn I'm thinking, yeah, this is looking okay. We go down side roads that have fewer properties and which occupy bigger lots. We eventually stop, and two big iron gates open automatically and reveal a white marble house three stories high. Everything is marble, tile, or hardwood, and the smiles are as welcoming as they are genuine.

I have met the family: Mother; twelve-year-old sister, Dacha; Dad; and hot girl of questionable relationship to Yevgeniy. Her name is Ann, and although her English is very good, she says "Da" instead of yes. I at least understand that much of their language, and she says it in such a sexy voice.

First I am led to the shower, which is more like a personal nightclub. I'm shown how the radio speakers work, as well as the mood lighting and the built-in fan. They neglect to show me how to actually turn the water on. I then hear my name being called. I open the door in a towel; that's an ice-breaker. Yes, I'm a tattooed, hairy freak, and I'm in your shower. They show me how to turn the water on with sheepish smiles. As the sweat and filth wash away, I rock out to Lady Gaga, who is all over this country like paparazzi over a disgraced politician. World domination, I'm all for it.

Lunch is served on the marble veranda with beautiful tiles and Roman pillars for railings. It consists of large quantities of meat, fruit, chocolate cake, and even some beer.

It's time for show and tell. I get out my photos that pretty much sum up my life: the house I live in, the pubs I drink in, the daughter I have, playing with Monklet, kitchens I've installed, bike preparation. It was a brilliant idea to bring these fifteen photos: everyone can relate to work, house, and family. It gives me material; I can make them laugh. The atmosphere is relaxed, and is this girl flirting with me?

Later we get into Mum's 4x4 and we go to the mountains.

This city is situated in the shadow of a mountain range. They are right there, ,big and imposing and snow-capped. No foothills to speak of, just a vertical wall of rock that looks impenetrable.

She drives so badly, no indicators, swerving, never looking in the mirrors, stopping for me to take photos in the middle of the road. God, I hope I never meet her when I'm on my bike. People hoot at us, cut us up, but she is oblivious. She talks on the phone, and she can't even steer the thing. When we get to the mountain hairpins the wheel is yanked at the last minute, and we are slung to the side of the car. She puts it in first for the incline and keeps it there, revving it to 6,000rpm; the engine is screaming to be put into second, but she won't listen. It's appalling. I try to cover my disgust at her driving with gratitude, but it's not easy. I did not come all this way to be killed in a 4x4.

We get close to the snow, and I get to see the stadium where the Asian Olympics will be hosted soon. Luckily, it rains, and so we turn back, but even downhill it's kept in first gear, until we miss a vista point; then we reverse uphill, and the clutch burns like bile in my throat.

We then go to the city to buy supplies and stickers; yes, finally I get a sticker for my pannier. I've forgotten my wallet and have to borrow money off Ann. How embarrassing; they do all this for me, and then I have to borrow money. Either that or say I don't want the stickers after all this effort to find them.

The rain in the mountains has been a storm in the city, and there is no electricity when we get back to the house, so we go out to eat. I'm taken up the mountains again, this time to a complex surrounded by pine trees; we walk past stretched limos and caged animals. Yurts are scattered around a restaurant and kitchen area. We are assigned a personal waiter, who shows us to our very own yurt. We are made comfortable, and all kinds of traditional Kazakh cuisine is brought out on endless plates of strange-looking but beautifully-prepared delicious food, like liver, fish, and cheeses. Finally I have something positive to say about horses: they are very tasty. And still the food keeps coming. We half sit, half lay on the carpeted floor around a large low table; it's such a relaxing vibe. With one translator and so little in common it's amazing how the conversation flows. Unfortunately, Ann can't drink because it's Sunday night and she has to work tomorrow.

They have all been to England before. Ann didn't like the taps, and she can't believe we have individual hot and cold taps.

"I thought it was a joke. How do you wash your hands? Do you have to keep moving them from one tap to the other?"

"Well, yes, I suppose that's how I do it when presented with such problems; I don't consider it a huge inconvenience in life."

Of all the problems my country faces: overcrowding, traffic, constant surveillance, ASBO drinking, terrorist attacks, and debt, it's the taps that turn her off it. I can't stop laughing.

She then mentions her boyfriend for the first time, and I hope she doesn't notice my disappointment. I'm told to stay until Wednesday when the son comes back from northern Kazakhstan. It's awkward as hell. I offer to pay for food and am left in no doubt that I am the guest.

"Kazakhstan tradition;" I wish I hadn't ordered the beer now. I feel so privileged, so humble. We are all tired from the food, them of hosting, and me from being attentive and on my best behaviour.

I say goodnight to Ann, who is returning back to some lucky bastard, and I am shown to my room. It's a little different to last night: a huge bed, hardwood floors, two double wardrobes, and full size bay windows, with net curtains that billow in the cool evening breeze. I've found myself in a beautiful house. How did I get here? This is surely one of the benefits of solo travel.

DAY 44

Suburb of Almaty, Kazakhstan, Miles—Pushed into Sun and Back

When I get up only Dacha is in the house, as she is on her summer holidays from school. She produces steamed dumplings and meat pie for breakfast. You have to be adaptable when you travel without the language. She has nothing to do, no friends, no company, just a big TV. Well, this is a bit awkward.

I decide I am going to work on the bike; she can watch if she wants. I take off the luggage and then decide I am going to clean it, not because I want it to look all shiny and stealable, but because I have nothing else to do, and it's a good way of checking every bolt and fastener.

I walk to the shops for some cleaning products and come back with two ice creams and oven cleaner. Dacha doesn't take sweets from strangers, but the oven cleaner brings the wheels up nicely. I discover one loose engine mounting bolt that I can't do up, due to little spanners and dodgy thread. Other than that, we are both fit and ready to go.

Not wanting to be outdone, Dacha decides to wash her cat; she starts by nearly drowning it, and having survived that, she tries to suffocate it in a towel. Should a twelve-year-old be left unattended? Should I leave her unattended? Who's responsible if the cat is killed? I'm just considering going to buy beer, escapism seeming like the best option I can come up with, when Father comes home.

We are taken to another fine restaurant and meet Mother. I speak to Yevgeniy on the phone; I tell him yesterday we did Kazakh tradition, today it's English tradition, and I'm paying. When I hand the phone back to his father and the message is relayed I see a frown appear on his face. It is their privilege to pay and

147

treat me. Once again, I've offended my hosts. If I had no conscience I could happily keep taking but I do, and I can't. Other than oven cleaner I've spent nothing today.

I am driven back to the house, and then everyone disappears. I stroke the cat for a while. They've all gone to bed. I suppose I will go to my room then. This is weird.

DAY 45

SUBURB OF ALMATY, KAZAKHSTAN, 26 MILES

This morning, Mother is still around when I come downstairs; has she cooked twenty sausages, just for me? There is also fruit, cheese, tomatoes, bread, biscuits, and sweet cakes, and then she fries three eggs. Just for me? I sit on the veranda and drink coffee: it's almost relaxing.

I have to go to the station today to meet the Swiss guy. I want her to write the address of this house down, just in case I get completely lost on my way back and need to show this address to someone. Instead, she draws me a full map and then insists that I follow her to the main road.

I'm riding in combats and trainers on a very shiny bike. I'm not looking like the bona fide overlander; no top box or tyres, and my panniers are half empty. Man does my bike fly along today. I wish I could always travel so light, but I need my camping equipment and all the other stuff I have left at the house. I've never been able to travel super light.

I met a Lebanese guy in Indonesia once who worked as a miner in central Australia. His entire luggage weighed 2kgs; he was moaning about how it was now actually 2.2kgs because toothpaste was only available in large tubes. He was an absolute pain in the arse. He was always borrowing something. Coincidently I bumped into him, watching a sunset by a river in Laos eight years later. I didn't ask how much toothpaste he had left. People who brag about travelling light are usually about to ask a favour of you.

One New Year's Eve evening I sat in the Wetherspoons in Gatwick Airport, with a boarding pass for Goa in my passport and no checked luggage. All I needed were sandals and a sarong for two weeks on the beach, and I was wearing the sandals. Slowly the idea dawned on me that because I had no luggage checked I could turn around and walk out of the airport. I started to feel like the few people who decided they would not board the Titanic. Then I found myself back on a train full of revellers going to Trafalgar Square, whilst the Gatwick tannoy undoubtedly called my name to board a plane to India. A few days later, I was back at the airport with checked-in luggage and this time committed to my destination to see my daughter. So travelling light is a non-committal, yet co-dependent way to travel. There were no reports of any Indian flights hitting icebergs, but there was an unreported incident of some ice being broken the other side of the world between a father and his little girl.

I find my way to the train station where we will meet without any problems.

I've already checked Greg's website, mainly to see what he looks like, so I know who I'm meeting. Duly, up bounds a tall and muscular guy of about thirty who is probably good-looking if you like that kind of thing. More importantly, he is on the same wavelength as me; he rides a BMW, but apart from that, he seems okay. We find a café to have our meeting in.

I feel quite proud of myself because I ordered in the restaurant and communicated with a local about the map, showing where I've come from and where I'm going. I have just a few words, but I'm getting somewhere.

Greg speaks good English, has good humour, and I think he will be good company. We will ride together to Mongolia, and we are both relieved and excited. We are of the same opinions, budget, and destination. He says he will start looking for a big skull sticker because he, too, doesn't want to be associated with a pink notebook. What I didn't ask him about was his time schedule. I can't leave until Thursday, as I'm obliged to meet Yevgeniy, which I want to do anyway.

At his border crossing into Kazakhstan he met up with two fully-sponsored Austrians, with whom he is staying at the moment. They are also heading east but in a different manner. Alarm bells should have gone off when he said they were scared to camp at the side of a lake in the vicinity of a fisherman smoking pot. As Greg said, "Is there anyone more peaceful and less threatening than a stoned fisherman?"

It would seem my ordering skills are not so good: I thought I ordered eggs just for Greg, but I got a plate as well. That's five eggs so far today, and it's not even noon.

On my way back to the house I find a mechanic who can tighten my engine mounting nut; it requires some effort, even with a long ratchet bar, but it's not going to come undone again, ever. I only have a 1,000 note and he only has a 200; we swap notes, the problem is fixed; he thinks I'm mad, but I think it's a bargain.

In the evening we go to the family's other residence, a flat in a housing complex; very different but very homely and with home cooking too. They haven't properly moved into the house, yet they have a lot of history here, I can just tell. The way they move around the cramped interior. They are as much a part of it as the faded photos and peeling wallpaper. The kind of things you just don't see when you've lived in a place that long. I've seen so many of these ugly housing blocks from the outside. I have wondered what kind of homes they are. Established. They are not rented, not transitory, not vacant, not subsidised, not sub-let, not charity or welfare presents; they are unpretentious and established homes.

Father loves Chelsea; we watch them lose the Champion's League. We are both drinking, and when he takes me back to the house, his driving is more erratic and aggressive than ever. Pink Floyd plays on the CD player. Ah, we have something in common; he has seen them live too. I think that's what he is trying to tell me.

DAY 46

SUBURB OF ALMATY, KAZAKHSTAN, 61 MILES

This morning Dacha has laid the table beautifully out on the veranda and then produces pasta and sausage.

"Lovely, thank you, yummy."

I've decided that today I'm going to have another go at seeing those elusive mountains, without cloud or rain or life-threatening driving. They feel like a back drop I just can't reach. I catch the odd tantalising glimpse of this Tian Shan range but they are as hard to see as the Caucasus were. I want to immerse myself in them and get the thrill of the scale and beauty of them. I love mountains: they are right there, and I can't see them properly.

I find my way up past the yurt restaurant, and then just as the air is cooling and the view looks promising, the road has locked iron gates across it. I'm not even going to approach the keeper of the gates, in case I get fined again. Besides, all my documents are back at the house.

I know Kyrgyzstan starts up here somewhere, but I'm pretty sure it's not yet. I have to turn back. I manage to find the other road to Chimbulak and the ski resort area that I came to in the 4x4. It is actually steeper than it looks; perhaps I was a little harsh on Mother's driving. There is a toll barrier, but I'm not asked to pay. So far, so good. It's getting a bit cloudy, but I'm optimistic. I ride past a white river; getting better. I'm increasing in altitude all the time. I pass a couple of girls hiking, and we wave. I'm enjoying the new road, and then round a corner it turns to dirt; deep loose gravel, too steep to even put the side stand down to take a photo. I ride round a few bends, but it is unnecessarily difficult, so I turn back.

Well that's that then. My little ride out didn't amount to much. Glad I'm not trying to actually get to Kyrgyzstan. On the way back I stop for a photo and the two hikers pop out of the undergrowth. They are locals but speak English; they photograph Monklet, and I sulk so they photograph me too. Have I got a blog? Do I have an email address? We swap email addresses; another piece of paper misplaced somewhere with another address on it from a forgotten origin. What I need is a proper book to put addresses in, a kind of address book. Another brilliant idea that I probably won't do anything about.

Back into the city, and it starts to rain, which turns into a storm, which floods the road in less than five minutes. I get back to the house, but the power is out again, which means the electronic gates won't open. Consequently, I have to take off the panniers to get the bike through the side gate. Well I'm soaked now anyway, so it makes no difference. The whole time Dacha holds an umbrella for me, which is a lovely gesture although completely useless. I wish we could communicate. I go to dry and change, and when I come back down she has put two lounge chairs together on the veranda and put blankets on them. She's so sweet. We sit and watch video clips she has downloaded onto her phone; I don't really have many appropriate ones I can show her on mine.

At last Yevgeniy arrives: I can talk, I can communicate, and I can convey my thoughts. What a relief. Considering how little time I spent with him before, we actually get along very well and have a good laugh. We go out to buy a plant for his parents. I end up getting a tree that barely fits in the car. Dacha is not impressed as she sits in the back in between the branches and covered in leaves. The parents seem to like it, though, and even if they don't, it's finally something I've given them that they have to accept, because I can't get it on my bike.

It's as much an adventure to get off the bike as it is to ride; I'm so pleased to have the time to experience this. It's hard and embarrassing at times and a constant learning experience, but I can't be impatient to get to Mongolia. I have to remember it's the journey, not the destination, that makes the trip what it is. Having the time to get off the bike and let in the country adds another dimension. I feel I can talk about Kazakhstan with a little more depth to my insights than just the scenery and the authorities.

I've never seen Borat. I started to watch it but I don't find cringing funny; if I did I would wake up laughing every morning after a night of heavy drinking and outrageous comments and behaviour. Comedies often stereotype cultures and countries; *Fawlty Towers* did, but somehow that's okay to me. Maybe it's because when it was first on TV, Spain was an almost compulsory holiday destination, and people knew there was more to the country and its people than just Manuel. Khazakstan does not benefit from such knowledge. I have never encountered a country of such friendly, generous, hospitable people who are intelligent, informed, interested, and intriguing. The country has a harmonious blend of east and west, modern and traditional, which I feel is not suitably recognised in public perception. I feel a deep and often irrepressible anger when I mention Kazakhstan, and the immediate response is "Borat." It brings on an uncontrollable rant, as I stick up for this misunderstood nation often too vocally, assertively, and passionately. I found it's a bit of a conversation stopper. Just don't say the "B" word to me.

DAY 47

CHARYN CANYON, KAZAKHSTAN, 159 MILES

I have mismanaged all my free time. Consequently, this morning I have so much to do before I go and meet my three new riding companions.

I could have spent an afternoon calmly exploring what the bazaar had to offer, but now I am rushing round it with Yevgeniy looking for oil, luggage straps, and water containers. There is no enjoyment in this hurried search for essentials. I'm out of time and out of patience. I'm not going to find this stuff with these self-imposed deadlines. And I still have to get food supplies.

We then whizz off in the 4x4 to the store, where I grab a basket and irritably fill it with my usual staples of sausage, bread, and bananas. I'm failing to keep calm at the confusion at the yogurt counter, and then Yevgeniy says to me, "I wish I was coming with you," and that was all it took.

"Thank you. Thank you; for a minute there I was so tied up in my list and lateness I forgot I was living a dream. I'm preparing to ride off into the unknown with some new companions. The sun is shining, I'm back on budget, I have a foreseeable future of work-free, self-indulgent wanderlust, heading to canyons, lakes, and mountains. The highlights of the trip are just about to begin. Mongolia is imminent, and I'm stressing over yogurt? I lost sight there for a minute, but now I see again how lucky I am. Thanks for that, I'm okay now."

I call it Piña Colada Syndrome. One morning in a tiny, open-air restaurant next to the Indian Ocean, I was sitting in the shade watching the waves, having just finished my fresh fruit and muesli breakfast. I wore just a sarong, as the warm sea breeze maintained the perfect temperature. I was chatting to some new friends around the table at a higher level of relaxation that is only obtained during prolonged stretches of absolute inactivity. We unanimously decided it would be a waste of a perfect morning if we didn't celebrate it with a cocktail. I felt sure that something fruity could be seen as a justifiable extension of my breakfast, and so arrived my Piña Colada. As we sat and laughed, conversation flowed along with the alcohol in our bloodstream. I had the misfortune of losing my pineapple chunk off the end of my cocktail stick into the depth on my glass. Immediately wanting to draw attention to the horrific luck I was suffering from I said, "Oh no, my pineapple has fallen into my drink." Then I paused as I heard what I had just said; "If that's the worst thing that happens today, it's a pretty good day, isn't it?" Piña Colada Syndrome. There will always be something to moan about if you choose to.

I send a text to Greg: please wait, I'm on my way. I didn't want to lose my riding buddies before I had even met them, not that they could be considered buddies if they wouldn't wait for me.

So my bike is packed, photos are taken, and hugs and kisses are exchanged. They have just one more chance of generosity, and this time it is three bars of chocolate and a waterproof cover for me and my bike. I ride away from yet another example of the limitless Kazakhstan hospitality. It had been a little bit of luxury, but more importantly, I felt just like a part of the family, rather than a guest in the house. I realised it more after I left. This goodbye was made much easier by the fact that I knew twelve miles down the road were three hellos.

I ride fast, weaving through the traffic, until a cop sounds his siren: shit. I slow down, and he passes. It was a warning shot: "Don't take the piss in this city." It's bloody ridiculous in this place of lawless drivers, these renegades of the road rules, but there had to be some decorum, I suppose. That's why I didn't get a ticket, just an audible warning.

I then go to the railway station car park, and there they all are: Greg and the two Austrians I instantly dub the Touratech twins. They are fully sponsored, have brand new BMWs, which are fully loaded with every accessory in the Touratech catalogue. On top of that, they have sponsorship from Nikon, which includes a £6,000 camera and free Orange phones and calls, as well as laptops, satellite phones, navigation, and tracking devices. All their clothing and camping equipment had been given in the name of sponsorship. Web cams, helmet cams, monitors, spotlights, compressors, dry bags, tank bags, tyres; they even have their names and blood types sign printed on their bikes and helmets.

The reason I instantly knew they had all this equipment was because, when I pulled up in the car park, the contents of their panniers were spread out all over the ground. They were hitting a dent out of a sponsor-sticker-festooned pannier with a sponsored rubber mallet. Apparently, the bikes had ridden into each other at the lights, and they were repairing the damage. So, I thought, they may have all the Touratech equipment, but they don't have the touring technique.

Despite this, they are friendly, and we four set off out of town, which is another luxury, because I'm following them and they are following their Sat Nav. They could also be followed on Google Earth and via their website. This is techno riding, and on my eBay second-hand bike, with my used and abused everything else, I really am once again the scruff of the crowd. But with so much visual overload it's hard to tell: four bikes carrying eight spare tyres, four laptops and six phones, web cams, helmet cams, etc. I bet the first space flight had less sophisticated equipment.

I'm finding it very hard to focus my thoughts. As a solo rider, I have deep and focused trips into my mind, whether I like it or not. I analyse, reflect, and understand. This is sensory overload, and I'm drowning in a sea of shallow and insipid thoughts, focused on logos, sponsors, and equipment I didn't even know existed. I'm constantly on camera, from behind and in front. How the hell did I ride into this? I just re-realised I was living the dream, and now I'm having it filmed too, as well as photographed in twenty megapixels through a lens worth more than my bike and all its contents. So I don't need to focus and take it all in for later recollection, it's all here on memory sticks: my real time reality is being recorded from three angles simultaneously.

It takes me a while to believe this, for it to sink in, and Greg is obviously having the same things going through his helmet too. I see him punch the air. We were both one, now we are four.

After an hour I'm getting more used to it. We have left the city behind, and there are mountains either side of us; we are attracting a lot of attention. Everybody waves, and I wave back, but the Touratech twins don't seem to. Maybe they are fiddling with their equipment. Every car that passes is photographing us with mobile phones; I'm a celebrity again. Is it going to be this way all the way to Mongolia? I'm almost fifty days into my trip. Half way. How much further will I go? Vladivostok? Vancouver? South America? Greg is going all the way. If I can just sell my house, I don't have to stop.

We stop at a café. The ordering seems to get a bit confusing, and we end up with only tea. Suddenly being four, some kind of organisation is required, but I'm the new kid on the bike; I'm not stepping up and making the suggestions. A little leadership would save a lot of time, but nobody wants to tread on anyone's toes, not yet. We have three different nationalities, two different languages, one destination, and four very different individuals with their own agendas. There are the sensible Austrians, committed to their sponsors to produce a presentation upon their return. One is a photographer and the other owns an independent film company. There is young and reckless Greg pulling wheelies and doing wheel spins and me, the budget scruff, the token Brit. I've just come along for the ride.

When I produce sausage and bread out of my panniers, it's a big hit. Feeding four instead of one soon diminishes my supplies. It's like having guests round for lunch. "I'll just have to pop to the shops."

When the scenery gets dramatic we pull over for a photo shoot. We take it in turns to ride up and back, being filmed and photographed professionally. It takes a while, but we only stop at scenic places, so there is plenty to look at, and I like to take photos anyway.

A lesson hard learned whilst travelling to the Arctic Circle; my travel buddy had bought himself a brand new digital SLR for the trip. Being a new toy, he was photographing absolutely everything, and so I was taking fewer and fewer photos, thinking I would just get copies of his. Unfortunately, his camera came with a cheap and nasty memory stick, which corrupted, and between us we have just one photo of the Arctic Circle trip that I took on my phone. "Insurance" they say here when the locals take a second photo: a very wise practice.

We were riding to Charyn Canyon, a mini Grand Canyon and probably Kazakhstan's most famous natural beauty spot. Well, there is a picture of it on the cover of my map, so it must be good. At a rest stop, three Kazakh bikers pull up, coming back from a camping and fishing trip, rods fastened like jousting poles on their bikes. They say they will lead us to a great camping spot on the river inside the canyon, and then we are seven; seven bikes riding the twists and turns of the rocky terrain, how amazing. Fifteen miles of dirt road, all of us with our dusty trail blowing across the bottom of the horizon. They even negotiate a discounted entry fee for us, and then pay it themselves. Oh those Kazakhs. Is there a more hospitable and generous nation on the planet?

We are led to the rocky path that leads us down into the canyon. It looks familiar. The Austrians will not go down there.

"Nat don dees vills," one of them says. I think he means "not on these tyres."

Okay, so they take us to another place where some vodka-drinking, watermelon-eating Kazakhs are partying. I walk down the track with one of the Kazakh bikers to view the canyon. There are balancing rocks and stalagmite pinnacles and the river flowing alongside the narrow dirt track. It's not inaccessible, it's as idyllic a campsite as anyone could hope for, and we both agree. He is so friendly and so open; I can see it in his face. I tell him about all the bikes I saw last week heading up to Balkhash. He says it was a big bike show, which has a wild reputation. Sounds brilliant. I knew I was missing something. He wants us to stay at his place later, but we are going the other way. I explain my dilemma with my new companions. For the first time, I am seeing the downside of travelling in a group. Decisions are not made easily, and compromise can have a high price. This I thought would not be an issue in Eastern biking philosophy, and he is disappointed, almost offended that I wouldn't consider going back the way I came to honour his invite.

I want to camp in the canyon, but I'm a new and lone voice in the group, so we camp in the shade of some rocks on a bit of green under a beautiful sunset. It is perfectly acceptable, but knowing there is a big orange canyon 300 feet down that track is a bit frustrating. We cook pasta and all try to outdo each other with what we can produce from out of our panniers. They may have superior stove and super light cooking equipment, but I have a chopping board, spatula, and chocolate. I may be travelling without the catalogue of touring accessories, but I can function without a titanium saucepan.

I was doing okay on the "look what I have here" stakes. And when they say "man your bike is soooo cool," I think, yeah, it is, isn't it? I made it that way, ride it that way, live with it, and love it that way, and I'm impressed but not envious of what they have, and that is a good feeling to go to my sleeping bag with.

DAY 48

Not Far from Charyn Canyon, Kazakhstan, 225 Miles

I'm keen to get up and ride down the canyon; I take photos out of my tent as the sun comes up. That's when I notice everyone else is up too, up on top of the hill to get reception on their phones and downloading photos onto laptops, clearing memories, and editing footage. Before I can decide whether I'm disgusted or impressed with this dawn procedure I am handed an espresso which sways my judgement. I played my ace last night with my chopping board.

Greg and I take off our luggage to go down the canyon, and just to ease any pain and increase my confidence, I empty the last of the bottle which was last night's beer. I can see what the Touratech twins think of my dawn procedure. We are photographed as we go down. I just kind of do a controlled skid most of the way, and then we ride the bottom of the canyon. It's a short but exhilarating ride, at last a Kazakh highlight that delivers. No people, no rubbish, no signs, and no rules. I can't imagine being able to ride a motorbike through such incredible natural beauty anywhere else. Not that we are doing any damage: there is none to do. We are respectful of the environment. We are in a world of orangey red; the rock, the dirt, and the morning sun glows and radiates.

We ride between steep walls and hanging rocks, towering formations rise each side of us; it's hard to grasp the scale. I'm using my old faithful SLR, which has been in the panniers for most of the trip, but I'm newly inspired, having seen the Touratech twins' equipment: it's time to put the compact away.

The canyon ends for us when the river takes over. The walls have narrowed, and the river brushes both sides of them. The orange is enhanced with the greens of life; trees and grass shelter from the winds and are nourished by the river. This would have been such a privileged place to camp. I'm so glad we came down here and didn't have it denied us, but nagging in my mind is getting back up again. So after a little wash in the river, we head back. I lower my tyre pressures whilst Greg goes up; he makes it look straightforward enough.

There are lenses pointing at me, and I concentrate, stand on my pegs, and ride up like I'm in total control, because I am; my skills have increased quicker than my confidence and my awareness of my abilities. Seven weeks on the bike, 7,000 miles, of course I'm going to get better, it's called practice. I didn't only get out of the canyon, but I enjoyed doing it. Yeah, I want more of this. Ari gets out his compressor so I don't have the inconvenience of pumping my tyre back up with my bicycle pump.

On the dirt road out we stop for another photo shoot, ride solo, then ride in formation; it's a bit of a cheat when we ride bumpy paths just for the pictures. Then along come two French cyclists. They are three days into a year-long trip and they are fresh and keen, enthusiastic and happy. It's gratifying to be in their company. Sat navs seem to be as common place as websites. Am I the only one who has neither?

We ride on. Greg goes through a deep puddle, and the tidal wave of muddy water flies up and I ride right into it. I don't care, it's all on video, it's all fun.

I was shown by Riso, the film maker, how the video camera works; it runs continually, and he has a monitor on his tank bag that shows what the camera sees. Every ten minutes the camera wipes its memory and starts again. If he presses a save button, the last footage is kept safe and the camera continues. It's ideal because you don't know when something worth recording is going to happen; this way you capture it all and keep only the good bits.

We are heading to the Chinese border; not only do I not have to look at my map, I don't have to look in my guidebook either. All the research has been done. I'm just following the camera. We ride through tiny magical villages that are so unaffected by the progress of modern life it's a road of regression into the past. Milk churns are pulled on little trolleys down the streets; they are pumping their water from communal pumps. People just sit around, no urgency in their lives, back to basic needs; survival is enough and everything else is a luxury. An old man in a suit rides his donkey down the street, and everyone we pass smiles and waves. I want to stop and photograph and talk and laugh with them, be a little part of their lives for a moment in time. That interaction is priceless; this is so far from the tourist track. It's real life, it's what I came to see, but we ride right through. Strange we should be missing such photo opportunities. It soon becomes apparent that scenery is one thing, but interaction is not what their trip is about. In Kazakhstan it's what everyone is about; everyone wants to shake your hand, take your photo, ask where you are from, look at your bike. But oh well, I follow.

Suspicion enters my mind. Why am I being videoed? Why are the villages so perfect and dream like? How come there was a suited and bearded old man passing on a donkey just as I passed? Why was there a village meeting at the water pump for my moment of transit? I was a lone traveller. Now I'm on camera my experiences are recorded. Is this all staged? It feels like something from *The Truman Show*. How did I fall into this? I've never travelled a road like this before. I wonder if it will have a happy ending.

I was concerned that the introspection I enjoy would evaporate with the constant stimulation of company, but clearly the opposite is happening.

German is spoken most of the time, and when a decision has been made, I'm informed in English. I'm feeling more and more isolated from the group.

We reach the barbed-wire fence, which has China the other side of it; up ahead is the last village in Kazakhstan, our destination, or at least it was this morning.

"If ve vant to get to de lakes in de mountains ve shod turn around to git dare before dark," says Touratech twin number one, who is Riso.

Oh, okay, well I guess we will turn around then, but I stay at the back of the formation and stop in the village to talk to a boy on a horse. He parks (or whatever you do with horses when you're not eating them) it next to my bike for photos, and briefly I am alone with the locals to admire their gold-topped church, take in the smells, and see the weathered faces, wondrous eyes, and unassuming smiles. I will not be deprived of these experiences, but I must remember I would never have gone down the canyon alone. These are the pros and cons of mass biking.

The others wait outside the village in the safety of the open space for me to catch up.

"We will be going back past that market, the only one we have seen. Should we not stop to get supplies?" I suggest. It is agreed, and we ride straight past the market without stopping.

I have come to realise that "if an opportunity is there it's best to take that opportunity, if it's there." It's Vinnie Jones' words in *Lock Stock and Two Smoking Barrels*, and it's become a bit of a mantra for me, especially after the unnecessary stress I have caused myself in the past by not buying fuel, getting passport stamps, and changing money when I had the chance to. Riso needs fuel; his first fill up in Kazakhstan. He doesn't understand their system and thinks they are the stupid ones.

"Just say 'da pony'; it means full. When you give them your money, fill your tank and go back for your change," I explain.

An old couple come up to me for a chat; they are very polite and point at my map. They can't believe I've come from England. I think perhaps the old man visited once. They seem genuinely grateful for my time. The pleasure was all mine. We get some supplies and fill up, except Ari, who doesn't need fuel yet. I know what this will mean but keep my mouth shut. We will all stop for him later, and if we don't all top up then this leapfrogging will continue.

So we head for the mountains, and once again we stop and German is spoken. I decide it's okay because I can stay in my thoughts without distraction. Then it is announced that it looks a bit like rain, and we should not go to the lakes and go back to the canyon. What? It's rain, that's all, and it will pass, if it even comes at all. This day is becoming a day of things we nearly saw. I consider going up alone, but I want copies of the photos that they have been taking today of me riding like a demon out of the canyon.

A convoy of cars, a wedding party, passes us hooting, shouting, waving, beckoning, it's a daily occurrence; everyone gets married in July, apparently. I look forward to seeing what is left on the shelf in August, with the desperation of an expiring sell-by date. I see no point in suggesting taking the invite to the wedding party. So I follow again, but I'm not going back to the canyon. When we stop for Ari to get fuel, I suggest we camp up in the hills.

"You meen off de road?" comes the shocked reply from Riso.

"Er, yes off the road, like our bikes were built to do." I ride over a few hills as an example in case my suggestion was lost in translation. It is considered and decided to be an okay idea, and we then ride away from the hills. I'm getting a little tired of this. I stay behind. I wouldn't even have known about the lakes and the Chinese village if not for them, so it's not really a loss is it? It's more a tease.

The others do find a good site, but as I go down the track, I have my worst fall so far and am flung off the bike. I'm okay but there is damage to the bike. I get to the place where they have stopped, too close in my opinion to other inhabitants. While they drink beer, I sulkily fix my bike. It's okay, but the windscreen has broken a bit and so has the brake lever protector. I'm also pissed off that riding in a group, I'm still pulling my bike out of a hedge and lifting it up by myself.

Whilst I'm kneeling on the dirt fixing the damage, I notice that a little weed plant is growing by my hand. When I'm done I have a beer, lighten up, and go to the river to wash. There is a field of marijuana; no one had noticed it, you can smell it as well as see it. It smells too pungent to be hemp, and it's not random enough to be natural. Regardless of its origin and intended purpose, it has very photogenic qualities. I let down my hair and stand in the middle of some plants with peace sign fingers; everybody agrees it's going to be such a good photo. I can use it on Christmas cards, Facebook profile pictures, the cover on my book.

When the riding is over and the beer flows, the fear of the day seems to be left behind; the threat of the village locals, the possibility of getting wet, the irresponsibility of camping in the hills goes, and all is calm again. We discuss travelling on together, everyone seems happy to. I'm sure I will adapt and be flexible, maybe this can work; there's always going to be teething problems with any new relationship. I've been very single-minded lately.

I can't sleep and spend the night reading my guidebook and seeing what we had actually missed today. It sounded pretty good.

Day 49

Taldykorgan Kazakhstan, 255 Miles

Insomnia: one bad night's sleep does not automatically guarantee a good night the next or even the next. Sometimes I use it constructively, but here in the tent my choices are limited. My map says we are only about an hour away from the reservoir I camped at a week ago: it's a slow circle. I'm not in any rush.

I go to the river. Once my feet have adjusted to the numbing cold, basically by becoming numb, it's not too bad. I perch my sponge bag on a rock and have a total body overhaul. It's a very fast flowing river; I have to lean forward to keep my balance. It's a constant struggle, especially with the higher flow coming from both sides of my vanity unit rock. Even at knee height it's trying to pull me downstream. I could end up back at the place I wanted to camp at last night if I'm not careful. It's the kind of fast flow that makes me wonder if just out of sight is the sheer drop of a thunderous waterfall. But this isn't a movie, just a river, so I get on with bathing. Washing in a river in morning sunlight is such a primitive and refreshing way to start the day. Although vibrating triple blade razors and three kinds of conditioner and hair treatment perhaps take the authenticity out of my ancient practice.

My necklace breaks as I wash my hair; I have caught the cord between my fingers but the pendant falls into the river. I can't try to retrieve it, in case I spill my precious Red Ken in the river and waste it. The pendant is a flat white square of stone with a Nepalese symbol carved in it. It's my second one. The first one I bought in Nepal, and when it broke I missed it so much that I got on eBay and found a similar one which came from Canada. So it was quite well-travelled before I even got it. The water is clear, but the river bed is distorted by the current. The flow is so fast that the pendant would have skimmed off downstream as soon as it touched the water, but there is something pale, a squarish shape down there on the stony bottom. I bend down, put my hand to where I saw the glimpse of hope, and I pull up my pendant. It is truly a miracle. That was beyond hope, luck, or logic: that was divine intervention. I'd drop it again to prove it, but you can't dis a miracle.

Without unknown forces working in my favour, it would have been one of those experiences which make looking for a needle in a haystack a preferable challenge. A haystack has boundaries; a river is practically infinite. I've faced more ridiculous challenges; I was once in a situation when a stoned girlfriend, who wore contact lenses, jumped into a swimming pool with her eyes open and lost a lens. She somehow convinced me to look for it. With the gullibility and stupidity of a stoned mind, I put on my mask and swam around under water. There was something that could have been a lens, a small circular transparent convex disk, but when I swooped my hand towards it, the motion I made in the water sent the elusive lens shooting off in the wake. It was an exercise in futility, and eye contact with the lens was never made again.

The sun has come up over our camp ground, so I sit on the bank to dry off and retie my necklace. I listen to my iPod and inhale the aroma of fresh marijuana plants as the dew evaporates from their pungent leaves with the intensifying sun. I'm packed up and ready much too soon; I spent the night waiting for morning, and now I'm spending the morning waiting as the temperature increases beyond comfortable.

I go and soak my bandanna in the river, and it makes for a cool neck as we start back down the track. No one seems very interested in my skid marks in the dust and flattened undergrowth where I came off last night, but I'm interested to follow the tyre tracks and try to work out how the hell I managed to swerve off the track, up a bank, and into a hedge.

So much for my concern that travelling in a group my thoughts won't go so deep; it isn't the case as I'm finding myself increasingly isolated from the group as German is spoken more and more. This is the worst of both worlds; in a group you don't meet so many people. You are less approachable by individuals, but you do have constant company. But in this group, I'm excluded from the company by language. I try to see it as a plus. It could be good that I'm not being distracted by needless chatter, but in fact, I am riding with resentment, and that's not fun. It's pointless. I like all the photos and videos, but what's the point of having them if I'm not smiling. I've had plenty of emotions in my helmet on this trip, but resentment is by far the worst. It's wasteful of my location and destructive to my enjoyment.

How the dynamics of the trip have changed. The challenge has gone; the excitement, the adventure, the daily interaction with everyday people.

The Austrians seem afraid to integrate; they are abrupt and rude to the constant questions of where we are from. They don't return the waves we get, and I'm wondering how badly I need a photograph of this.

"English or German?" Riso barks at the locals who speak to us. It's horrendous. I'm embarrassed. I'm convinced that the root of the rudeness is fear. I think he has left his comfort zone and is obliged, through sponsorship, to do what he would rather avoid. This isn't the Alps. There is more to the trip than just scenery, but he is not seeing it.

I'm wondering if I would be better off riding alone than alone in a group. I expect to not understand what's going on around me in a country so different to my own, but I should be more informed of the plans within my riding companions. The problem with this negative thought spiral is it's only going in one direction, and it's going fast. Now I can find fault in every action.

Are their riding practices self-preservation or anal retention? Why do they brake so hard for a cow that has finished crossing the road into a field? Do they think it will reverse? Moo, walk backwards whilst giving the appearance of going forward? Why at this town don't we take a left at the roundabout, take the bypass, and use some common sense instead of blindly following the Sat Nav directions? Do you really need a coffee after just one hour of featureless riding, or are you saving face?

The road out of town is dug up and impassable, but they persist because their Sat Nav tells them so. There is a perfectly good road running parallel, or we could just go back to the bypass, but there is no room for deviation from the dictator of direction. I hate sat navs. The road improves as far as scenery goes; it's baking hot, but whenever the land turns to snow-capped mountains which reach the sky I'm happy. I'd be even happier if I was riding towards them, instead of on the scorched plains alongside them, but they lift my spirits, and once again, it's time for some more video footage. I think to myself that I will get a copy of what they have and then make my own way.

It's been a hot day's riding; there are miles of dug up road, it's as if the entire budget for the improvements were used up in destroying the surface, ploughing it up, and now it remains in this unusable state. No sign of any machinery or workers, just mile after mile of excavated tarmac. That's an example of things I see daily and don't understand; it doesn't bother me; it raises questions, but not resentment. I don't mind not knowing the reasons behind destroying a surface that used to suffice and now is unserviceable.

Twenty minutes from the town that is today's destination, Riso stops because he wants some chocolate. It's not done in a quick, wait here, jump off, run in, get chocolate, back on bike, eat as I ride, considerate of everyone else's hot and exhausted states kind of way. Everyone has to stop, find a place to park, remove helmet, gloves, unplug intercoms, etc. We draw a crowd; there is no shade and clearly no consideration to anyone else. Can't we just find a hotel and then satisfy our own personal cravings? I'm not in the mood, not after today. I ride up the road and stop in the shade of a tree. In any group a natural leader will emerge. Riso is not a leader, he is just the one who does what he wants, when he wants, or in the case of Charyn Canyon, he doesn't do what the others want.

It's as if he read my thoughts, because I'm appointed the leader to find a hotel in the city. Thanks for that. You lead us along the straights, and I'll do the tricky bits. So I ask a few people, but I'm not getting on very well; we find ourselves on a road out of town. So I think let's turn around, but the Sat Nav says there is a road up ahead. Yes, quite possibly, but the town is now behind us. Am I leading or not? Because I'm not going to work in conjunction with a Sat Nav. I use logic.

Whilst we are stopped having this discussion, a BMW driver winds down his window; the Touratech twins ignore him. He speaks good English.

"You have come from Almaty, yes?"

"Err yeah."

"I saw you on TV."

"We were on TV?"

He says a traffic camera picked us up leaving Almaty, and they made a news item out of it, but I don't believe him for a minute. I do, however, have absolute confidence in his offer to lead us to a hotel. I've been in Kazakhstan long enough to know these offers are as genuine as they appear; he takes us back towards the city (imagine) and to a hotel. It's very nice and very inexpensive. He checks us in, insists to the reception that we remain anonymous to avoid the authorities getting wind and making a song and dance (literally) of our arrival. I'm still not convinced, but if he thinks it's necessary...

They have a suite of rooms that will accommodate all four of us, but I opt for my own room. I need some space. Our man, our new leader, says he will be back in an hour and says we should come to his house.

"We have to do some laundry."

"No problem, do it at my house. We have a washing machine."

"We have to eat."

"I know, my wife will cook for you; it is our honour to have you as guests."

"All four of us?"

All four of us have to discuss this; it's not to the liking of us all. So I do my laundry in my room, then go and buy us all beers and go to their room. I take my laptop to get some photos and videos, but the good videos for some reason were wiped, as were the photos of me in the weed field. All the other photos downloaded, but not them. I don't believe them.

It goes back to when the Touratech twins feared the pot smoking fisherman; they deleted those photos; they didn't want them in their possession. Which is fine, but they could have offered them to me before they deleted them. So I have stuck around and followed them to places we never got to, and of the places we did go photos were taken which no longer exist. Why am I here? Our finder, our fixer comes back with watermelon for us.

The Touratech twins have declined an invitation to stay and eat in a local's house in favour of going to an Internet café to update their website; they have passed up a chance of a unique experience to write about some place we didn't go to. I've had enough. It's Saturday night in a new town, in the company of a gracious local, and you want to waste it in an Internet café. Fuck this.

Our self-appointed tour guide is being so patient, and I chat with him in this environment of gamers and bloggers. I'm hungry, I want to see the city, and we are sitting in a virtual hell. My now well-practiced skill of keeping my mouth shut is really paying off.

I beckon Greg outside.

"Look, I'm going to go it alone. This is not why I came; this is sterile, safe, adventure-free, bland, and boring techno travel—all based on what Riso wants and no regard for anyone else's wants, needs, or likings."

Surprisingly, he is of exactly the same opinion. He is embarrassed and ashamed that they speak German all the time and is happy to split from them too.

"Oh right, well okay."

But we should probably tell them nicely when the time is right. Greg doesn't want to feel like a traitor, and I don't want to feel like I've given ultimatums.

Our man takes us to a restaurant, orders for us, and we pay for him; it's the perfect situation. We would never have found such a place, and he drives us everywhere. Once again, with the introduction of alcohol and the absence of motorbikes, the company becomes congenial. We are then taken for a night-time guided tour of the city sights, shopping centres, statues, and monuments.

"Do you want to go to a night club?"

"Do we?" Well kind of.

Do I want to keep drinking? Yes. Do I want to look at women? Yes. Do I want to listen to loud music? Yes. Have I got to work tomorrow? No. Do I need sleep due to an insomnia attack last night? Yes. Well I still seem to be in favour of it. Okay, just one drink. We pay our entry fee and are unfashionably first in as the doors open at 11.30.

Our man insists it will soon liven up, and he's not wrong; he also tells us in this town there are four women to every man. Yeah, all right. I was told something like this in Brazil. That there were five women to every man, and I only shared a room with four girls, and I never did find out who had got my fifth one. But the dance floor is full of girls, and my body is full of alcohol and head is full of rhythm, and soon enough I'm ready to get on the floor and boogie. Well, at least jump around with a smile on my face. I call it dancing; it's certainly full of passionate enthusiasm, if not rhythmic timing. And once I've started I can't stop. I'm a sweaty, matted mess, but I'm having so much fun.

It's so obvious we are four out-of-towners in a small town with the same girls and same boys at the same club. We are as strange as my dancing technique is. Greg is in his element: more used to this kind of thing, he dances with the hot girls and has the moves. I never really got that bit understood properly in my head. My hair just covers my face, and I jump around in the direction of a smile. And there are lots to choose from.

All of a sudden its 3 A.M. and time to go. We stand outside, and fights break out. I seem to have an audience, so I tell them how much I love their country and spout endless bollocks to a crowd of drunk and intrigued locals who have nothing better to do. If they are waiting for words of wisdom, they are in for a long night, or morning, whatever. My feet are blistered, my calves are swollen, my back aches, and I'm in need of Ibuprofen and a big bottle of water. We are driven back to our hotel, but we have an entourage, including the really hot—dance like a porn star—girl who Greg was dancing with and whose name I not only caught but actually remembered. It all goes a bit fuzzy, and she is in my room. Impulsively and drunkenly I get anybody who is not the hot girl to leave, and it's just me and her.

Right, well, um...so...what's a nice girl like you...she had already played her ace and exhausted her English, and my counting to ten and saying the word for potato would just confuse her. She wants a cigarette, really? In here? My laundry is drying all over the room. Shit, where did that sudden pang of practicality come from? Okay, you can smoke in my room all over my clean clothes, seeing as you're hot and sweaty and all that. But she has no cigarettes and wants to go to the shop. Oh man, my feet are so sore. I'm not walking to the shop; you go. I'll wait here and tidy up a bit. And the next thing I know it's 7 A.M., and someone is banging on my door.

DAY 50

NOT LEPSINSK, KAZAKHSTAN, 205 MILES

A fat weird guy from last night is standing at my door. Yes, I vaguely remember you, he is full of apologies and desperation; he thought he left his phone here.

No, no phone, no hot girl, no clue as to what happened. He has been up all night, he calls his phone from my phone, a friend answers it, he knows where it is now, apologises, and goes. Could you not have done that earlier? Maybe his mind is as dulled as mine. I've had maybe two hours sleep, the sun is streaming through the window, and flies are buzzing in my ears. No more sleep then.

I take the Ibuprofen I wanted last night and try to swallow them with the last of my water. It's not enough, and they stick in my throat. I lay in my bed trying to swallow them down; what to do? I'll go to my bike; there is water there. The others are all there, packed up. They say they knocked on my door.

"Really?"

Well if they did, I didn't hear, maybe hot girl did too; if they didn't, then they don't want me to tag along. I'm hungover, sleep-deprived, dehydrated, very confused and insecure, and very bloody frustrated. What happened to the hot girl, they want to know; I want to know. Damn, damn, damn.

When the others realise I didn't get laid, I realise why I'm not getting any sympathy for my pathetic state. There is a café next to the hotel. We seem to be in there ages. I drink water, lots of water. I'm not sure why, but for some reason I decide it will be easier to stay with them than face the confrontation of telling them I'm not. It would seem like the perfect time to stay in a nice room with the company of my hangover. We do have a very short and easy ride today to a place of mountain lakes, glaciers, and valleys of wild flowers nestled between snowy peaks.

I'm wearing my combats. It's too hot for proper clothing. We need supplies. We ride out of town past the immense supermarket we were shown last night, one of the town's significant sites. I apply a new tactic; I turn round and go into the car park. And eventually the others follow.

"We need supplies agreed?" Well here is an opportunity.

True to our muddled ways, we each take a basket and double up on everything. I do treat myself to a plastic plate as a fifty-days-on-the-road gift to myself. This will make meal times so much easier. At the checkout we reorganise into a trolley. I had initiated a travel pot, but once it ran dry no one seemed interested in replenishing the funds. And in my commitment-phobe style, thinking I was about to break ranks, I didn't insist, so that was the end of easy transactions. So we all fiddle about with our wallets at the checkout.

As we try to pack all our purchases on our bikes we have the inevitable crowd taking photos and shaking hands. I don't mind this, but I can see Riso is ready to explode. He was left out to guard the bikes, while we spent so long in the supermarket. In my evil twisted way I'm happy about anything that makes him unhappy. Now I'm just here for the taunting and torture of the Touratech twins.

I feel so vacant, my mind is mashed, mystified, unfocused. I follow them and still manage to go through a red light. I'm trying to figure out last night. I'm so sore, so achy, so shit. And the Ibuprofen are still stuck in my throat and are burning like my unanswered questions.

Riso wants to take the alternative route. I'm too tired to argue, just sit on my bike and turn the handle that makes noise and speed happen.

He's OK when he's calling the shots, and now he wants a shot of us all in a haystack with our bikes parked in front. Ooo yeah, that's really gonna capture the spirit of adventure biking, I sarcastically think in my cynical and dehydrated head. Ari is a little more aware. He says, "A goodbye photo," as he sets up his tripod. We all pose in the haystack like a bunch of gay bikers. Is this the kind of adventure BMW and Touratech want to promote? Because it's not the kind of back road I want to go up.

We are overtaken by a hooting car; it happens constantly. I wave instinctively. He drives a bit aggressively. I look. He is wearing a uniform. Shall I stop? Now he's getting quite agitated. I stop. We are near to the Chinese border again. I know we are supposed to have a border pass permit to be here, but that is not the problem. I call a translator on my phone; it's revealed that the road ends, so we have to turn back the thirty miles we just rode. I don't want to play this game. I want to sleep.

Back to the main road, it's now 3 P.M., and we are only half an hour from that lovely room I barely slept in.

The rehydration has taken effect; I'm stopping to piss constantly and am enjoying the ride again. I see a Land Rover with English plates; it's someone I have been in communication with via the overlander website. We stop and chat excitedly. The others had seen these guys at the supermarket, but I was not aware. Another German conversation I was not party to.

Riso wants to leave, "Ve have a place to be." I'm getting really fucked off with him now. We take another wrong turn, double back, and meet the Land Rover again. Every person we ask contradicts the one before; I think there is the village and the reserve with the same name but different directions. We get a couple of reliable and concurring routes suggested, so we all head the same way together, but soon leave the Land Rover behind. We are heading to the mountains at last. It's beautiful, low sunlight, yellow fields, hills and valleys, clouds and shadows. It's stunning. But with only an estimated 30 kms to go, the road turns to track, the track to mud, the mud to rocks, and the rideable to the unrideable, puddles of indeterminable depth. Slippery rocky surfaces; I can only just do this. This road is not going to take us to the natural beauty the guidebook promises. There is no sign it will improve, but we are close to a river, we just can't get to it. Riso is shouting in German to stop and turn back, but I don't understand or care or obey. I ignore him. He's used up his daily demands, as far as I'm concerned. Greg and I continue through puddles and mud, and there in front of us is a vision of beauty. It's not the girl from last night, but the perfect knoll. It's idyllic, by a river, lush green grass, overhanging trees, and even a picnic table. Too good to be true. Too perfect.

The ground is flat and soft, the tent pegs slide in like...like, really easily.

Some people are arseholes when they drink. Riso stops being an arsehole when he has a drink.

I try to steer the conversation round to my leaving. I look at the map with him, it has the opposite effect. I seem to have made myself more committed.

I'm hoping the Land Rover will show up, but it's unlikely, and I don't see them again. I have their number but no reception. We eat and drink; the food is good and plentiful. The mood is good and upbeat. We tell stories and have a really good night.

The Touratech twins tell me how they achieved full sponsorship, how they presented their proposal, and why it was accepted, basically.

"Not many people do adventure biking in Austria; ve are promoting it." Maybe their "adventure" will impress the Viennese, because it means nothing to me. The full moon disappears behind clouds, our illumination becomes strobing lightning, and thunder starts to rattle the sky. I go to my tent and sleep like a dead man.

Day 51

Ayakoz, Kazakhstan, 256 Miles

It's hard to leave someone when you are going in the same direction on a single road, with nowhere to stop.

Maybe it was an adjustment period, maybe it was much needed sleep, maybe it was the sound of a running river or the freshness of the post-storm morning, but my cynicism and intolerance have gone back to more manageable levels.

There is the sound of a motorcycle engine, and a Ural with sidecar trundles past carrying two old boys, a dog, and fishing rods. Well that stole our thunder. How the hell did they just negotiate that track on that bike?

Ari climbs up some rocks to photograph us leaving, riding what to us is a challenging road. We go through deep new puddles recklessly to bring up spray, so he can capture it with quick shutter speeds and wide apertures through a long-distance zoom in mass megapixels. We are posing and riding in a way that exaggerates the hardships.

I've got water down my boots already, but I don't care. I woke up differently today. Riso won't ride through the puddles. He seems to have an aversion to water, be it rain, rivers, puddles, or lakes. He avoids them at all costs; perhaps that's why he chose to travel through a part of the planet furthest away from any sea, sandwiched between Russia, China, and Mongolia. Perhaps it comes from living in a land-locked country.

I'm sweaty from all the waiting around and wet from the puddles. We come to a river. There is a potential to cross it. It's not necessary to, but it would make a great photo. I volunteer to do it. I learn a lot of lessons in a very short time.

1. Water in rivers has a strong current that messes with your steering in an unpredictable way.

2. Always put your electronics in plastic bags and take phones out of pockets.

3. Don't put yourself and your bike through unnecessary hardships.

I ride into the river. I instantly lose balance, it's beyond correction, my speed is too slow, the current too strong; in fact, this is a textbook example of making every mistake possible in one go. And I go down. Right down, bike on river bed down, me totally submerged. I come up smiling, but I'm not in a good position. Greg comes straight in to help me, Ari for some reason stops taking photos but doesn't come in the river, and Riso reluctantly paddles in. We lift the bike up; it's still in gear. I have to turn off the ignition, find neutral; saturated, we start pulling it out.

"Quick my feet are getting vet," yells Riso. This is fuckin' priceless, I'm not quite sure I'm hearing this; my bike is dead as are my phones, my camera, and my voice recorder. I'm fully clothed in my bike clothing. I have been immersed in freezing river water, as has my bike, and he is complaining about his feet? I don't think I need any more confirmation about his character. I think he would leave me dying if there was room on his horse for two.

Miraculously, and without taking out the spark plug first to drain the water that surely went in to the cylinder via the exhaust pipe, the bike starts up, but all electronics are dead. Water has got into my top box and one of my panniers, and my tank bag and its contents are soaked: maps, guidebooks, phone cards. It's a bit of a disaster. I pour water out of my boots. And once again, there are no photos of the event. Ari stopped taking photos as I went down, and there are no more until we were pulling the bike out. So I don't even have a keepsake of my stupidity. The whole point of going in the first place was for a bloody Kodak moment. This would be another ideal opportunity to let them go and spend a day in the sun drying everything out.

I do believe "everything happens for a reason"; that reason is not always apparent at the time, but it all makes sense in the end. That was the end of my compact camera's life, right there. It drowned. But thankfully, my SLR did not come into contact with water. It stayed in my tank bag, and every photo after today is of a superior quality to anything my spontaneous little compact could produce.

We ride out to the main road, my boots again full of water. The warm wind is doing its best to dry me out, I'm flapping like a loose sail in a typhoon, but I am drying. So much for the glaciers, lakes, and valleys. I was a bit preoccupied and forgot it was once a destination. Now I'm just focused on drying out.

We stop at a café, and I strip, much to the amusement of the staff. I ring more water out of my boots and hang everything off my bike in the sun. The staff are lovely. They take us one at a time into the kitchen and point at our choices. One waitress in particular is very huggy, touchy, feely, and holds me tight when posing for a photo. How much are those gold teeth worth then? They really do put their money where their mouth is in this country. I eat stuffed peppers, dumplings, and rice, and my boots drip from my mirrors.

We ride out into flat, featureless steppe, but it's the lack of anything around that is the appeal, and I'm enjoying the dry heat as it evaporates the moisture and lightens my load during 100 non-stop miles. A remarkable achievement when riding in a group.

We are still doing the leap frog fuel thing. I hadn't realised the Touratech twins had stopped. Greg is so far in front I can't see him. I stop and wait at the side of road. So this is how it feels to be alone. I go back. They are at the petrol station.

"They are a bit nervee here," says Riso. "They vont give us any fuel until ve pay."

"YES, THAT'S HOW IT WORKS HERE, it's the same in Russia, so try and get used to it."

We are heading into Ayakoz: it's a garrison town. I live in one; it doesn't bother me. First impressions are not so good. Sprawling barracks, barbed-wire fences, and the black smoke I've been watching as we approached is from a burning car. We pull up together, no one wants to stay, but there isn't much choice. Barren steppe or this, I lead us into town. It's the arse end of a beautiful country. Some gold-toothed gentlemen point me in a direction. I find the train station, always promising, and there is a hotel. We pull up at the same time four Poles in a 4x4 do. They have come from Mongolia. They could use a dip in a river. The hotel is perfect, cheap, and awful. I share with Greg for the first time. I put my phone back together. It works. I don't deserve it, but I appreciate it. I try to scratch my phone credit cards to reveal the sequence of numbers and credit my phone account, but they are still damp and disintegrate before I can expose the code.

This place is awful. One thing about Kazakhstan you have to admire is its diversity. The place is devoid of any hope or care. The rusted peeling railings contain wild overgrowth, which was once a park. The streets are dust and mud. Nothing has seen any form of maintenance in a very long time. It's a place that never had glory. Restoring it to its former misery is the best anyone could hope for. It's dilapidated; I've seen better ghost towns. The hopelessness hangs in the air. The decay is everywhere. The pavements are cracked, and weeds grow through and displace the paving stones. The dust and potholed road leads nowhere worth going to. As we walk the street to find a market, the futility of existence surrounds us. It's so depressing it breeds abuse, and the evidence is everywhere.

We sit outside our hotel bar on plastic chairs by a broken table, drink a beer, and make a meal out of the mega supplies we purchased. It's a grim and hard environment. And then comes along the first and possible only Kazakh in this country who is unpleasant. He is an old man, drunk from a lifetime of escapism that got him trapped here. He has the stance of someone who is mentally and vertically unbalanced. He stumbles out of the bar and leans over us. He's a dribbling, incoherent drunk. He carries nothing but a bad vibe, and he spreads it effortlessly over our table. With his lifetime of wasted experience, he spouts his babblings in an aggressive and dominant manner. He is a product of this desperate town. We are too much of a visual stimulation to be left alone. He staggers a few steps away but is drawn back to taunt us some more. He has stopped our conversation and replaced it with resentment, and he can feel it. The mood is getting darker; he can't be spoken to in any language. He is beyond any lucid reasoning, but he can feel this and intrudes too deep into our protective space. Voices raise, and nothing good is going to come of this. You can't hit an old man; any physical contact will not be seen as defence, and then he violated my most holy of sanctums. He pulls my hair—my instant piss me off button. I'm out of the chair before I can seize control, my eyes full of anger, fists clenched. Thankfully, my reactions catch up; now I'm standing over him I can see he is nothing. I just want him gone. Some women come out of the bar. They've probably been watching it all. They shout at him, and he staggers away, and we thank the women, but the looks we get say we are the intruders and why should we not be the source of entertainment, regardless of what form it takes. This is an ugly place. It breeds contempt, and it has a brief incubation period.

We sit in the bar. It's time to download pictures. I buy my first bottle of vodka this trip because they have no beer. It's a cheap bottle, less than 50p. I expect the worst as I put it to my lips, but it's so smooth it doesn't burn, doesn't make me wince; it's good, it's pure. It's palatable. God it is so smooth. What have I been missing. This stuff is excellent. Riso leaves to get his computer, and instantly he becomes the butt of our jokes. Ari seems so relieved to vent. So one bad apple it would appear. I feel sorry for Ari. He's committed via sponsorship to see it through; he set off with a bad companion.

As photos are transferred to memory sticks and hard drives, we are told by an angry babushka from reception it's time for us to go to bed. Download still has twenty-four minutes to go. We ignore her, and then three bolshie and very authoritative police come and force us out of the "hotel bar." It could get very nasty; I know when it's time to submit.

"Come on, let's go, NOW, don't argue, come now." Oh will you look at what just happened, leadership qualities have just emerged. It's just I can sense it, maybe a past experience. Sometimes you just know you will only win in a situation if you let it look like you lost.

They demand our passports. We walk quickly to our rooms, ignoring their requests.

"Lock your doors and don't come out." Where is this coming from? From inside the room it sounds like the situation had become a non-event, but it could have got very nasty in this strange and incestuous little town.

Greg and I lie on our beds and make fun of Riso and giggle and laugh. We laugh all the harder when we realise his room is the other side of this cardboard wall. We feel a need to stay for the sake of Ari; with familiarity comes obligation.

DAY 52

SEMEY, KAZAKHSTAN, 226 MILES

As I sink a dry sock into a wet boot, I'm hoping the day will get better. As we pack, along comes this morning's audience of one—a smartly-dressed man, who says "good morning" and then asks for a present. This town is not typical of Kazakhstan. For anyone coming down from Russia into this country this will be their first impression. It is not a true representation, just an unfortunate location.

I spot a bolt coming out of my sub frame: this is serious stuff, and it reiterates the fact I need to slow down and do more maintenance. I want to. I don't want fleeting glimpses, I want experiences. More integration and less Tourateching. The other three bikes were all new this year. Their accumulated mileage is less than my fourteen-year-old bike has done. My bike is not old by any means, but it needs to be nurtured a bit—a different style of riding and a different strategy when stopped. I don't mind doing it, I enjoy it; it goes back to riding old Harleys. It's satisfying to see a symptom and cure it before it becomes a crippling disease, but I have discarded my routine checks to keep the pace with the others.

I got a text from the Germans I travelled with; they are in Mongolia now and really having a hard time. This is useful communication: this is a side of technology I can appreciate and justify. They report lots of sand, lots of falls, it's tough going for them, and they were way better riders than I am. Although that was before Charyn Canyon and my new-found skills, oh and my ride into a hedge, when I was flung off. Good days, bad days.

We have to stop for fuel as we leave the town, and again, I have to remind Riso that he has to pay first.

I fret about Mongolia and the sand as we ride. I can't do sand; I don't want to do sand. I don't enjoy it, and I don't think I want to learn how to.

The day turns dark, cold, and cloudy; it's the perfect weather to match my anxiety and thoughts. Nothing is guaranteed, and maybe I can't reach my destination.

The coolness is a novelty at first. We stop at a café for coffee and dumpling soup.

I get out my jacket lining: it was removed in Poland six weeks ago, but it is soaked from my river crossing yesterday. I pack away my fingerless gloves, only to discover my proper gloves are also saturated, and I squeeze out the water and put them on along with my heated grips. How can the weather change so quickly? If this had happened yesterday, I would never have dried out to the point I'm at now.

My heated grips are no match for my wet gloves, and my hands are getting colder. I've got on every dry layer I have now. We haven't gained altitude, we are just heading north. We stop by a lake, and an icy wind of moisture skims the white cap surface and blows a shiver over us. My feet and hands are wet and numb. It's only the disbelief in the changed conditions that's keeping me going. I'm also distracted from the chill by the apprehension I have now for Mongolia.

The rain comes, and the road surface gets worse. But in cooler temperatures it's easier to concentrate on dodging the potholes, and it's a welcome diversion from my cold, damp extremities and discouraging thoughts. Then the road turns to mud. It's filthy fun. No point in trying to stay clean or dry. I'm enjoying it. Looking down, my boots and trousers match the engine and frame: all the same dirt-encrusted colour. It's so evenly sprayed up from the front wheel. I can't get a finish that consistent with a spray can.

Then, as if my mind has the power to give itself peace, I see a single headlight up ahead, and as it gets closer, the silver of panniers become visible. It's an Australian couple in their fifties, maybe older; they have just come from Mongolia. They mark their route on my map and say it's hard, but not so hard it's dangerous. More importantly for me, it's tried and tested, it's scenic, challenging, but passable. They tell stories of broken legs on the route the Germans pencilled in for me.

Whilst they all chat, I wander off to wee, and when I look back, I see the awesome sky over us. I've been concentrating on the road all morning, and I've only just noticed this dramatic collage of weathers: white and grey clouds separated by clear blue optimism hanging low over the long grass. The day ahead is drying out, and we have come through the worst of it.

They tell us the road ahead continues to be hard riding, but their bikes are clean, and when we leave, the conditions instantly improve, and they are about to discover the reason we are all so filthy. Nobody ever can agree on the condition of the road.

From a morning of fretting and freezing I go to an afternoon of anticipation and thawing.

When the scenery can't be captured, and the sun is not evaporating your bodily fluids so they don't have to be replenished or disposed of, stops are few and progress is fast.

The last nail is hammered into the coffin of this group when we stop to talk to a German-registered 4x4. The driver speaks English to me until Riso interrupts our conversation with German. I know it's time to let him wander the rest of his journey oblivious to people's feelings and locals' offers to hospitality and invitations. I'm done with this rude and offensive guy. As with the last 4x4 we stopped for "we have a place to be," but I guess that doesn't matter now we are speaking German. "English or German, English or German" I no longer care. I don't want to hear another word from him.

We are heading for Semey; it's the nearest town to where the Russians had their nuclear-testing zone for forty years up to the early '90s. Nearly 500 bombs were exploded. It is the perfect place to split company. Riso is too afraid to stop here, let alone stay two nights, and that's exactly what I'm going to do. It may seem extreme to contract radiation poisoning, but I think it's far preferable to the alternative. Riso is speaking in German to Ari; it's something to do with a map. I have one, and I know exactly where I am going and where I will stay, and he would too if he spoke in a language I understood.

Inevitably, on entry to the city without Sat Nav instruction, they take the wrong turn over a river bridge. I go the right way. They couldn't turn round if they wanted to. It's petty, it's inconsiderate, it's unnecessary, it's all the negative qualities Riso has brought out in me. I no more like what I have become than I do what he is.

When we get to our room, Greg's phone is ringing. Riso is screaming at him. I'm a little embarrassed at my actions: it's easier to stoop to someone's shortcomings than it is to rise above. But there is an evil little satisfaction knowing it took him an hour to find the hotel.

Later, clean and dry and warmed, I go to the lobby and come across a Finnish guy, a lone biker on his way home from South Korea. He has not seen or spoken to anyone on his Trans-Siberian ride. I'm beginning to see more Europeans than I would like. We will meet for dinner.

It's time. We have been joined by the Finnish guy, who is so pleased to be in company after a solo ride from Vladivostok, however, Greg and I are forced to tell the Touratech twins that we are missing the challenge. A group of four is too big. It's met with resentment and anger by Ari, who has feelings, and with indifference by Riso, who is oblivious to anything. The Finn is photographing us all, simply pleased to be in company, despite the atmosphere. It's almost funny, almost, but the pressure is unbearable; all I want to do is go. We are stuck at the table. Poor Ari, he is stuck until the end. We were his opportunity to enjoy the trip. We've hurt his feelings, and his disappointment is obvious: it's unfortunate. He knows why we are leaving.

They saw my bike this morning. I can't keep their pace. I have routine maintenance to do; it's not all about the company. My bike has to come first.

DAY 53

SEMEY, KAZAKHSTAN, 4 MILES

We meet for the last breakfast. The Finn is already there. The menu causes some comic relief. Butter is creamy. The hard is raw. Porridge is rice. And other mouth-watering delicacies.

Despite these temptations, I get ham, eggs, and a roll. My choice is so enviable that when the Touratech twins turn up they order the same. Riso has, since I first met him, managed to confuse every waitress we have encountered by over complicating the simplistic. He excels himself this morning, and five more breakfasts arrive along with five more coffees. We manage to effortlessly consume the lot, and when the bill arrives, he says, "Vell ve didn't orda all dis food."

"But you ate it all," observes the Finn quietly. It's a refreshing unbiased observation; it's validation of my resentment. I remember there are, in fact, two types of traveller: ones I like and ones I don't like. I've been a bit focused on the latter lately.

We cough up the extra money; Riso has remained an arsehole to the end.

We go out to the bikes and say our goodbyes, and off they go, taking their arsenal of photos and videos with them. The whole point of prolonging this ordeal to the nasty bitter end was for the photos I never got. But do I really want so many reminders of the last week. It had its moments. It's better than working. But I was not obligated and perhaps should have cut away earlier. I hoped things would change but then realised four was too many, regardless of the personalities.

It's that deceptive colour of the grass again; I never can see it's clarity until it has faded into the distance. The teachings of the road are varied. The introspective personal discoveries are as valuable as the people and places along the way. I hope not to put myself through a similar situation again. See the signs and take a different route, even if the destination is the same.

The Finn has the same bike as the Touratech twins but a Scandinavian humour. I'm still wearing my Sweden Rock Festival wristband.

"How did you go to this festival if you are riding to here?"

"I did the festival on the way."

"Well this is serious stuff," he says and takes a photo. It feels so good to laugh. It's too bad he's going in the other direction and going today. But we are not left alone. Two French guys and a Russian girl show up in Ural outfits. They are on their way from Moscow to Ulan Bator. They were supposed to be four, but their friend was killed in a mountaineering accident only a few months ago. So they are riding in his honour. It's an emotional trip; the Russian is the bereaved girlfriend. They have a very comprehensive tool kit that is spread out around the bikes, "And ve af to uoo zit ever ree day," I'm informed. Straight out of the factory in Moscow and falling apart already.

I speak to the receptionist and photograph her by my bike because she asks. You can't fool me, darling, I know I'm one of many. She shows me on a map where I can find a mechanic. I'm not sure I find the right place, but a confident and competent man instantly sees the broken tank support bracket and other damage. He bodges it in the same acceptable way I would if I had his garage at my disposal. I'm asked if I want to use the shop's computer to surf the Internet whilst I'm waiting. It's so typical of this country.

Greg and I manage to talk ourselves out of cleaning our bikes due to the imminent oil and tyre change in a few days, so we may as well do everything together.

Greg has met an American on a KTM. I've lost my special status. I was unique, now I'm as common as a backpacker on the Koh San Road. I have no identity anymore, and I don't like it. We are going to meet him for dinner, but in the meantime we have the rest of the day free, so a small drinky is in order.

The American is doing his journey alone, using the coordinates of someone else's trip. Road for road, hotel for hotel, right around the world. As we eat he says to me, "What I love about you Brits is you all have Tourettes. I just start swearing when I'm in your company."

I didn't think I was that bad. I try to use it for emphasis, as opposed to punctuation.

We swap stories and information; it just feels like back-packing. He says Semey is a funnel everyone passes through to and from Russia. He has a point. I hope we are soon spread out again. In Semey they don't ask you where you are going; they tell you.

"Mongolia?"

"Yes, that's right." There is no surprise or admiration in this town, and no evidence of the ill health they suffer from either, other than a very large graveyard I saw on the way in yesterday, which appeared to be regularly frequented.

The ongoing problems with health and births here from the radiation are well-documented, but as an outsider, slightly informed but not actively seeking, all I see is another town where all the women are beautiful. They look healthy enough to me: in fact they glow.

Day 54

Barnaul, Russia, 293 Miles

The funnel flows freely, and the procession we are a part of is spaced out enough to keep the illusion alive, and we can pretend we are intrepid adventurers still.

Now we are two, and it's twice as good now the numbers have halved. The most noticeable thing is the speed in which things happen, whether it's packing, parking, or picture-taking, it's not a mammoth operation. It feels strange to leave so quick after a stop; it feels wrong. Have we forgotten something? It gets to the point where an engine is left running for a wee stop. Decisions are instant and democratic. It's so easy when you only have two to please.

We have a change in landscape to match our temperature; we are now amongst pine trees as we head out of town. There was no gradual transition, just thermal grassland on the approach over a radiant river into the nucleus of the city and fall out the other side into forest; followed by the border. It's not busy or confusing, but like every border before, it's not comfortable either. They are always too hot, too wet. Today it's too cold, not freezing, but I contemplate digging in a pannier for my woolly hat. We leave Kazakhstan, and the hour changes, so we wait for Russia to finish its lunch. Without any shouting or pointing we go through the barrier; the insurance place is conveniently located inside a café. And shezlic and insurance is simultaneously prepared for us. The girl wants a photo by my bike, another one for the album, no doubt. It's as if they have been told to make us feel special, but we know we are just part of the parade, and we even know who is behind and in front of us, and in which direction they are travelling. I didn't find my hat, love; you can't pull the wool over my eyes.

So I'm back in Russia; I'm trying to remember how it was, but it's a bit of a blur after three weeks in Kazakhstan. I can't remember the differences or the exchange rate.

The land is green, flat, and farmed and otherwise featureless.

We ride right into the city of Barnaul—the usual Russian babes, but this time there are smiles and waves. I don't remember this in western Russia. When we stop for food we get smiles, chats, and laughs; even security guards are happy and interested.

Another refreshingly new experience is getting a room and not being tired and sweaty after the ride.

Being two is much better, but I'm missing my solitude a bit; the hardships and adventure, the accomplishment and reward. Already the company is taken for granted.

DAY 55

BARNAUL, RUSSIA, 25 MILES

I've got border lag; that extra hour is a killer. Oh the hardships of the road, and people think I'm over here having fun. My body clock thinks its 7 A.M., and I'm having to get up.

I was sitting in a fast-food Mexican restaurant in a small town in Missouri where everyone knew everyone else. As I sliced my burrito with my plastic fork I overheard the welcomes of a local homecoming. "Oh you're back. When did you get in?" The lady in question had just flown back from California and "had the worst jet lag," she "suffered so badly from it" she told her friends and admirers. And they all agreed sympathetically, although they could clearly not relate. Two hours. There are two time zones from this town to California. I just crossed one coming from Colorado, and next week when the clocks change we will all have to suffer half of her jet lag. On top of that she had had to drive the 100 miles from the airport back to Hicksville. I smiled into my refried beans. Even if you had just stepped off the space shuttle, you can't compete with a conversation like that. The woman had the restaurant in awe.

So I'm not in search of sympathy, despite barely getting nine hours sleep. I'm made of strong stuff; I'm hard core, I force myself out of my double bed and into the hot shower, then down the corridor for the inclusive breakfast. It's a slice of bread with some ham on it wrapped in cling film. It is taken fresh out of the fridge and cooked especially to order for me on a thirty-second microwave setting. A wonderful piece of Russian cuisine served like a frisbee with the warmth of Siberia. And it tastes like it looks: it wasn't fresh before it suffered its transparent bondage. The greasy film peels off the bubbling ham like sunburnt skin. The bread, challenged by gravity, the sudden change in temperature, and being saturated with drained fluids of dead pig, has lost any cohesive qualities it may have once possessed. It crumbles onto the cardboard plate. My fingers burn with scalding fat, the last warning to abort the breakfast mission before it made contact with my mouth? I'm not that hardcore. Wisdom overpowers instinct, and I go and warn Greg of the dangers of the all-inclusive breakfast.

Some of the hotels have a twelve-hour-stay special offer, hence our haste to leave. Our bikes had been locked in a storage shed, and due to a shift change, it takes a while to find someone who has a key. There's a hose pipe in there, so we cheekily take the opportunity to hose off Kazakhstan's mud onto Siberia's tundra.

I didn't think this area counted as Siberia, but the locals seem to think it does, and who am I to argue. We find the motorcycle mechanics' unit inside a business park. Greg had been given vague coordinates, and his primitive navigation system meant that, with the roads that are available, we have to get to the dot on his screen: it works pretty well, other than the off-road bits where I lose a padlock I didn't snap shut. Annoying, a small inconvenience, but mainly just annoying. Wotblink.

The bike unit is a motorcycle graveyard; it feels like more bikes die here than come out rejuvenated. The mechanic speaks no English, but he seems capable and willing, if perhaps a little brutal. Most importantly, we instantly become his priority. So I strip to my shorts and then strip my bike of luggage, tyres, tank, and seat. I remove the last of my euros. It's nearly time to start finding ATMs and really draining my resources.

When I take my tools out of my toilet brush holder, they are wet from river water, and my new spark plug is corroded, but it's a hot dry day and a quiet spot. I can spread myself out and dry everything off, and I rediscover the contents of my panniers.

For the next six hours tyres and oil are changed as various people come and go. My oil consumption is increasing. I hope with this thicker grade it may not disappear so fast.

The day is productive, the shop is convenient, and it's one of those situations where you really don't know what the end bill will be, but you have little choice or room to haggle. We turn up unannounced and keep this single mechanic busy all day, meeting only our needs.

Greg has knobbly tyres, which incidentally were given to him in the name of sponsorship just by asking. And a sticker on his panniers that said "Continental" was his only obligation for the gift. They had been wrapped in cling film for the trip and were fresh and new-looking; the protection had a far more preserving effect on this rubber than it did on this morning's rubber-consistency ham. So although we both have new tyres on our bikes, he benefits from a sexy black look and new rubber smell; all I've got to show is deeper tread and nipples from the mould. He discards his tyres. I'm more cautious; my old ones still have a few thousand miles in them yet, and I'm not ready to throw them away. I've been debating this moment for weeks, and now it's here I'm playing safe and keeping my tyres just a little bit longer.

One of the visiting bikers speaks a little English. He has a quotable phrase, which I can't remember but was along the lines of, although more poetic and concise than, "Russia is three countries. The unfriendly Muscovites, the indifferent Russians, and Siberia have people of warmth." It certainly seems to be the case from what I've seen so far.

It's time for the bill; the oil is more than the labour. How can it be so cheap? So basically you worked all day and all you earn is enough to change your own oil? Is this a favour? Is this the going rate? Is this a sideline? Because surely you are not earning a living. A fire pit of plastic bottles and discarded bike parts is torched to signify the end of a working week. And as the black smoke rises, we say our thanks in Russian and are led to a supermarket for supplies.

Our host pushes a trolley full of lids and leathers, whilst we fill another with all we think we will need to survive Mongolia. It's a very well-stocked and modern market. I've found myself in sausage heaven. I don't know what I'm buying, but I've learned that anything but the cheapest tastes good to me. There is a whole aisle of them; it's so long, I can't photograph it all on my phone.

We spend more on food than we did on our bikes. We are not pleading poverty, but I still feel a little guilty handing over our rubles to the cashier as our biker helper looks on. I can't understand the equation of today's labour costs in relation to the general cost of living.

I've not replaced my wheel properly, the brake is binding, but no time for that. On new tyres we are led across town, speeding down back roads to avoid rush-hour traffic to a hotel. Our Siberian biker says we must go to the biker bar tonight, and he will see us there.

I've managed to get really sunburnt today; flesh doesn't get a lot of exposure on the road.

What a productive day; everything got done. It was painless and inexpensive. The relief is revealed in exhaustion. I would love to have the biker bar experience; I even feel obligated to go. The mind is willing, the head is in agreement, but the burnt and tired body won't cooperate.

Despite slight evidence of deteriorating, the bike is ready for the next leg. The ultimate ride to the dreamed of destination. I'm about to ride into Mongolia.

DAY 56

YOR, ALTAI, RUSSIA, 215 MILES

I wake up full of Mongolian motivation, which is a bit premature because it's Saturday and the border is closed at the weekend. I bounce down to my bike, and the binding brake is fixed in no time. A market has set up next to the hotel. Everything is available just like before I left Almaty, and just like when I left Almaty I feel time pressure. Priority number one is find a padlock: it's not too tricky. I have a proper conversation. I can ask how much. OK, I don't understand the reply but there is definitely a "two" in there somewhere.

"Biker?"

"Da."

"Ar din?"

"Da," well strictly-speaking no, I'm not alone, but ya gotta keep ya options open.

"Make me your wife," the fat, flirty woman indicates, much to the amusement of the gathering of girls, any one of whom I would stick around for. I put my arm around her; everyone laughs. It's a happy Saturday morning market experience. I stand tall and tilted in my bike boots, confident from the company and compliments.

"Ciao."

"Ciao, baby."

That's one of those little buzzes you don't get in company. Can I maintain the best of both worlds now?

We are going to need money, lots and lots of money. I don't know what to expect in Mongolia, and rubles have got to be better than waving a credit card around.

We ride out to the bustling main road and stop at an ATM. Greg seems to have a knack for spotting them. But then with my pile of euros I haven't needed to. Money changers have been my source of local currency.

191

Whilst Greg is in the bank, a policeman comes up to me. He's not unfriendly, but something is on his mind. He leads me back up the main street I have just ridden down and shows me a sign with a picture of a motorbike on it and a line through it.

"Oh right, I get it." Time to start apologising. I show him my documents, and he seems content. "Can I just use the ATM while I'm here?"

"Don't push ya luck sonny," was the unmistakable reply.

So we go down a side street. Now the route we were taking last night to get here makes more sense.

We end up in the centre of the city trying to look out for banks, trams, tram tracks, traffic, and "no motorcycle" signs. And of course, the ever present distraction of the stunning, tall, slim, well-dressed, high-heel wearing, perfect calves, long-legged, flat stomach, push-up bra, flowing hair, enhancing make-up, sharp cheek-bones, pouting lips, and strutting-like-the-pavement-is-one-long-catwalk Russian women. Trying not to look is like trying to kill yourself by holding your breath. Eventually your mouth is going to open: in this case it's jaw dropping. And on top of all that, I have a desperate need to urinate. The kind of desperate that, even of sober mind, doorways and trees all become possibilities.

This is how accidents happen.

I opt for a triangle of green grass with a solitary tree in the shadow of concrete housing blocks. It's not private, it's not hidden, but this is a desperation I cannot control. This has probably been my favourite Russian place so far. I like it here. I wonder what the winters are like.

We have got our money and now, without looking over my shoulder, just thinking ahead, we are ready to leave. We just don't know where we are now, or which way we have to go.

I figure it out with my guidebook map; we go right by our hotel and realise the road we want is the one which our policeman guards from his control box in the central reservation. I'm not going to try and find another route. We just did a massive circuit of the city to get back here. So looking anywhere but at the direction of the copper we ride past, trying to hide behind a bus, and are on the road out of town, over the Ob River, and towards the Altai Mountains.

Now for the first time I notice my wheel wobble. My front wheel really needs to be balanced. I take off the old weights, but it doesn't improve it.

This is the road to the city inhabitants' weekend playground, and it's very busy. There are multiple lanes of fast-moving traffic, but the preoccupying issues of the last few days have all disappeared. It's getting hard to find something to worry about. The companionship is good, the bike is maintained and prepared, and my panniers have dried out and are full of food. I have currency, and I'm heading towards mountains. It's warm enough to put my fingerless gloves back on and cool enough my burnt back isn't uncomfortable. The road is good enough I can speed up out of my wheel wobble. And I'm heading for Mongolia. Contentment is illusive and short-lived, which is why it has to be appreciated.

A car passes so close it makes me jump. A hand out the window offers me a water bottle. If it had not surprised me so much I may have accepted, but my automatic reaction is no thanks, and as he drives off it occurred to me it could easily have been vodka.

Something flies up off the road. I don't see where it comes from, a stone spat up from the wheel of a car or maybe it was a wheel nut. It fires into my shin, just above where my boot stops. The pain is instant. It's one of those moments that remind you of your vulnerability. If that had come up higher and through my visor would I be a speed bump now?

The traffic is erratic. They are driving like idiots, overtaking dangerously, and then cutting in front to go at a slow and sedate pace. This is because of speed video cameras; I find this out when I'm pulled over. The baton is waved right at me, there is no ducking away from it; I'm the intended victim.

We are taken into an office where big fat cops sit on chairs in front of computers, and we are shown a video of ourselves overtaking the drivers who had just cut in front of us. 93 kmh in a 60 zone. Our speed is excessive; we are looking at a big fine. Or at least we would if we spoke the language. I understand the fat controller is not happy at the baton waver for bringing him two foreigners who don't understand a word. As with all the Russian authorities I have come across, they are doing their job, not looking for presents. So we can't be processed if we can't understand the formalities. Mr. Baton gets a bigger telling off than we do. And full of gratitude we bow our way out of the fine building and back to our bikes. That was lucky. Lucky I didn't have vodka on my breath too.

The road splits, and the traffic disperses. Once again, we are going through hillside villages, past farms, and alongside rivers and a slower pace of life; a life that as I pass through I witness like a photograph—a single moment captured. Two different lives flash together for an instant, and like lightning, it will never happen again in the same place. The kids playing in the street look up to wave, an old man walks his cow to be milked, a babushka hangs out her washing.

Then a Lada passes and hoots and waves to say we have taken the wrong turn and have to go back through the village for a second moment in time, a little more washing on the line, the cow closer to the barn, and the kids less interested than they were a few moments ago. Never say never, you never know what is around the next corner. Could even be a U-turn.

The road gets hilly, and the countryside is more sparsely populated—ideal camping territory. I take a track that leads into some trees; it's looking good until two barking dogs come chasing after me. In a two rutted track I try to turn the bike around whilst kicking out at the rabid dogs. Engine revving, balance barely sustained, half expecting to see a gun-wielding local coming to see what all the noise is about. I bump into a rut and spray up mud in my hurry to stop trespassing.

The second track is harder to ride: uneven and muddy. It gets tougher as it continues and there are no signs of flat ground, so another U-turn is in order, only to discover the beer cans had broken free of the bungee cord and punctured on the rocky ground. It's alcohol abuse, and I'm ashamed, disgusted, and annoyed.

The third track leads to a mosquito breeding ground next to a stagnant lake.

The fourth looks promising. A lush green field and haystacks to hide behind, but at the entry is sloppy deep mud, and I get stuck up to my axle, and boots instantly fill with brown thick water when I put my feet down to balance.

I see a hotel sign; it's a one-street village with a few rooms above the bar. It's perfect. The barmaid, landlady, cook, and receptionist looks nervous, but she needn't be.

Once we have got out of our nasty biker clothes and come back down clean and smiling, she makes us food and pours us beer. There will be a do tonight she seems to be saying. In this one-horse town? Do what exactly?

We sit on the wooden steps to our first floor accommodation and watch satellite dishes and power lines obscure a beautiful sunset. Some giggling teenage girls are hanging out a safe distance away, texting and chatting. They eventually come over to us.

"Photo?"

"Yes, of course." We go down the steps to meet them, and I'm handed a phone. Oh right, you want me to take a photo of you all. No that wasn't me farting, it was my ego deflating. I suppose I deserved it.

Sleep is intermittent from the pounding bass of the all-night disco downstairs. If only it hadn't been such an exhausting day.

Day 57

Near Chemal, Altai, Russia, 254 Miles

The more I read about compulsory visa registration for this area, the more confused I become. But the lake sounds worth the ride; "a relaxing place to catch your breath" the book says. I'm sure I could cope with some of that.

As we are packing up, some bolshie Russian bloke comes barging into the room, loud and animated. I thought one of the bikes had fallen over and go to check. No, he just wants us to leave. Well what the fuck do you think we are doing? He stands over me whilst I put on my boots. Where are the cleaners hovering mop in hand? Where is the impatient line of new guests wanting their beds? There aren't any, are there? You're just a bastard.

I load my bike but have left my jacket in the room, so I go up the stairs. But he has locked the door into the corridor. No, he indicates come down here. So I sit on the top of the stairs and stare at him until he comes up. Whilst talking over him to Greg, he comes up, unlocks the door, and I get my jacket. "Understand now? And we would be gone by now if you hadn't come and disrupted our packing procedure." I know I could have done this with smiles and pleasantries, but I'm not wasting my smile on this git.

Then whilst we pack he tries to make conversation with us. I think he may be a victim of inbreeding. The Siberian hillbilly; Billy Bob Bollockski, gets in his Lada and goes back to his mother and sister, and we finish loading up.

I pull away and fall off immediately; my flustered departure and broken routine had meant I left my disc lock on. No damage, but my anger levels went up another notch. Now where's that tranquil lake?

We stop at a café, and stone-cold soup is brought to our table. I'm not sure if it's customary or if the microwave has broken. The waitress comes back with a handful of souvenirs she tries to sell us.

And why would I want to remember this place? But for some reason I do.

The brown stagnant river the road followed last night turns into a wide, clear, fast-flowing one with lots of camping possibilities. You never know what's around the next corner. Well we did, we just got tired of the anticipation. Despite the hills and the pines, the raging river and twisting road, for some reason it's not doing it for me. Maybe it's because we are just killing time. The sun comes out and things brighten up, but I think after two months on the road it's easy to stop seeing the scenery, and comparison isn't fair. The reports I heard of this region was the surprise of the mountain beauty, when only a transit route to Mongolia was expected. I expected mountain beauty as part of my transition into Mongolia, and the surprise is that it's not that good.

On the outskirts of Lake Teletskoe my disappointment becomes horror. It's tourist hell. Horse rides and a token camel, yaks and yurts and endless stalls of the tackiest souvenirs. It's awful; the lake is polluted with jet skis, rowing boats, and cruisers. Where's the tranquillity? When am I going to catch my breath? The roads both sides of the lake dead end. There is no getting way from this ugly over-populated blemish on the Altai. I'd rather go to a public swimming pool. At least I'd expect that to be loud and crowded. Why do people come to a place of peace and natural beauty only to turn it into a tacky resort?

We are of the same opinion, and we turn around and head back against the flow.

We ride hard and fast, scrubbing in our new tyres on the bends. Greg has the power, but I have the handling and catch him on the corners. His knobblies are wearing down quickly. My choice of tyres was not taken lightly, nor were they free, and I'm reaping the rewards on this road. With no signs or sun to navigate by, just good judgement, we get back to the Katun River that we will follow to Mongolia.

It's formidable and fast-flowing, creating rocky walls and dramatic gorges. We have a choice: east or west of the river. The latter goes to the border, so the east will be less crowded; wrong again, it's non-stop resorts—rafting, horse trekking, holiday homes, and tacky tourist entertainment. And where's the bloody snow-capped mountains?

We opt for an organised camping ground and find an OK spot. I have bought some 5% beer, and we have one as soon as our side stands bed into the ground. On an empty stomach, like it says on the can, 5% of me is instantly pissed.

"That's better, I've had a crap song in my head all day," I say to Greg.

"Me too, what was yours?"

"Bangles, *Eternal Flame*," I sheepishly admit.

"Mine was, *Somewhere Over The Rainbow*."

"You win," I tell him.

We have lots of good food to eat tonight. Camped right next to the river, and under a blood red sunset, we have the highpoint of a disappointing day.

DAY 58

NEAR TASHANTA, RUSSIA, 233 MILES

As we ride out of the camp site, I realise we actually got the perfect spot, that is assuming you want to be anti-social and isolated. Holiday camp community is not the kind of integration I want to experience; I lived in one for a year saving for this trip. With strange looks, styles, habits, and choice of mobile accommodation, it was easy to keep myself separated from the social scene. I think the same rules apply here too.

We cross the bridge and the roads are empty, as is the land. Hilly and uninhabited, for the second night running we made a bad bedtime choice. The new scenery brings with it a new song; my eternal flame has been extinguished and replaced by the *Dark Side of the Moon*. My version of the *Great Gig in the Sky* only sounds good to my ears, and that's with a helmet on. When we stop for a coffee, Greg says he is over his rainbow and into *Estranged* by Guns 'N' Roses, so we are both happier for our new internal songs.

David Gilmour has played the soundtrack as I have lived my life: that's what I would tell him if I ever met my idol. Be it doing up bicycles to sell in my summer holidays from school to the slide guitar on *Medal*. Wrapping presents in my bedroom in the Christmas of '79 listening to *Comfortably Numb* for the first time in between power cuts. Performing it in Earls Court with the band, or Hammersmith Odeon on his own, in stadiums and arenas around Europe. From the Royal Albert Hall to Wembley Stadium, and at Live 8 in Hyde Park. Even standing outside the stage door of the Mermaid Theatre in the rain, because I couldn't convince a Radio 2 DJ who had been stood up that I would be an ideal date for the show. No one else had a spare ticket. His music has played through every significant and insignificant point of my life, in a truck parked in a Norfolk lay-by to hear the first ever playing of *Keep Talking*, as I rode a camel through the Thar Desert somewhere between Pakistan and India where frontiers of desert sands drift. Hiking in the chill of an empty winter Zion Canyon in Utah. Through the amphetamine-fuelled late '80s and the *Final Cut*. Blasting out of my van in a Glastonbury camp ground and through tinny speakers on a Thailand beach, tripping on mushrooms. With sadness in a motel room in Memphis when I discovered Rick Wright had died and again when my friend was laid to rest to Clare Torry's howling vocals. With artwork inked into my skin, and from double albums to MP3s, I think it's safe to say I hold an eternal flame that burns for all things Floyd.

I got this bike; I can ride it when I like. It's got a top box, a bloke that sings, even if it doesn't sound good. I'd write about it if I could, but I'm bored of it.

So we are stopped at this café. The labourers outside, whose only job seems to be keeping the plastic seats warm, get up and wander off like skiving workers in slow motion caught by the boss. Whatever their purpose, their reason to be, it's not of great concern to them. We sit outside in the dampness of a misty day, and out of the grey come two bikes. A hazy vision, two French guys in their sixties, compact panniers, no tank bags, tyres, water containers, nothing showing that isn't contained. One rides in trainers. How do they cook? What about spares? No camping equipment? They are doing a lap of the world; they order coffee but can't wait for it to arrive. But where are your tank bags?

"Our whyfs av dem, for wen day weel fly owt to ride wid zus, day may only av de's for luggage."

"But, but but...." So many questions

"Wee must go now, time iz money."

I turn to Greg, "That was a hallucination; that didn't just happen." I blame it on the coffee.

We continue on and pass the other French guys on Urals. This is a procession, and we are five years too late. It's not a funnel, it's an egg timer, and we are in the waist. On an atlas, eastern Kazakhstan touches western Mongolia like an hour glass on its side. With China to the south and Russia to the north, it would all make perfect sense, but we aren't at that border. One day there will be a concrete flyover there with the Monkaz café selling pannier-size stickers and bratwurst, Wiener Schnitzel, tarte au fromage, and egg and chips with HP sauce. But for now it's just another Altai Monday. We've had our hallucination, our uniqueness is an illusion, and we just need to swallow our pride, adjust our vision, and see this for what it is. This is not the road less travelled, it's the modern day equivalent to the hippy trail: it's the bikers' trail.

It's sad when I think of the anticipation, the nerves, the daunting challenges, which my basic winter research brought to my mind; the admiration and butterflies my plans generated. And now I'm just one of the crowd. Like riding to the Kent Custom Bike Show in '83 whilst the rest of the world stayed in and watched *Live Aid*, we strayed from the main stream. I may be different in my choices, but I'm not unique.

But the roads still sweep through rolling hills and pastures of wild flowers of frustration that cannot be captured on camera. They can only be witnessed first hand, which is why I'm here, isn't it? Disheartened, but not disinterested. It could be worse. I could be that sheep up there in the middle of the road with a truck coming the other way. Too quick for anyone of us to react, it stands petrified on the centre white line. The truck brushed by one side, as I pass by the other. It was a lamb sandwich, wool of death. If sheep can produce adrenalin, that one must be vibrating right now from its close shave of sheer terror.

At a petrol stop some bikes turn up from the other direction. "Oh just go away" is my burst balloon reaction. But they are here to change my mood; I just don't know it yet. They are three Russians, been for a long weekend in Mongolia, like ya do, and are on their way home, full of life, and elation from their trip.

"We are going home now our trip is over. Is there anything you need? Bike OK? Need food?"

"No, everything is fine, just using a little oil that's all."

"Oh, I have oil; I give you oil," and he unstraps most of his clumsy luggage and gives me a litre of good-quality oil. It's a gift, of course. I'm humbled again by the strength of Russian biker camaraderie. My form of transport alone makes for unquestionable acceptance. It's my favourite aspect of Russia. I do have to perform for his video camera, though.

"Hello, my name is Flid, and I'm from England. I've just met my new friends here. I'm off to Mongolia actually, toodle pip." I had just tapped into a barrel of mindless bollocks that I was happy to continue ranting at the camera, but they seemed to have all the material they needed. I was ready to open my top box with a hand on each side, smiling and saying, "I hope it's a blue."

I do things quickly, whether it's packing a tent or filling a tank. I'm always waiting for Greg, but on the road when I stop to take a photo he's gone. I try to see it as a plus. I can do my own thing, but somewhere not too far way I have a riding buddy. But I don't want to be pulled through Mongolia by his impatience. I bought a guidebook; there are places I want to stop. I'm in no hurry. When I cross that border my destination has been reached, even if my trip is not complete. Greg has the Americas still to go, and it's driving him at a faster pace than I would like to ride. And my bike is falling apart; the compass has broken free of its cable-tie and duct-tape mounting. A spotlight has fallen off. I never use them. I don't ride at night, but they look good. And I don't want them hanging off the bars like a bauble off a Christmas tree. My digital rev counter has stopped working, another eBay purchase. This one came from Ukraine; a country that meant nothing to me at the time. But because I stretched out my journey across the country it means so much more to me now than just chicken Kiev. Just as I want Mongolia to be more than inner one side and outer the other. These thoughts bring back the desire to ride alone; I weigh up the pros and cons.

We are low on food again, and due to a lack of communication, neither of us is carrying water. I don't like to travel this way. It takes away your independence and your options. No spontaneous camping until we replenish our supplies.

We find a village; it seems popular with hikers. I'd get a room here if it was just me, a break from the cold of our increased altitude. In the general store they sell smoked fish. Having missed my opportunity in Lake Balkhash, I buy some now.

The weather is deteriorating, and we pull off the road down a steep and rock-encrusted embankment to the side of the swelling river. The wind is fearsome and the clouds low. We may be sheltered from view, but we are exposed to the elements.

With the tents up, I try the smoked mackerel on bread. It's very tasty, but I can't get that smell out of my hands, and cold river water just turns to droplets on my grease-coated fingers. We have beer, but in this cold, whisky would be so much better.

The rain comes, and the cold has exhausted me. It's still light when I go to my tent. The temperature is only just above freezing, and the river nearby with its splashing white froth makes it seem even colder.

The wind blows so strong that my tiny tent is even smaller. The sides cave in to the force.

I sleep for eleven hours, and demons fill my dreams. Severe weather always makes me dream. I wish my house would sell. I don't want to go back there.

DAY 59

OLGLY, MONGOLIA, 144 MILES

I couldn't find the snow-capped mountains, but snow-capped mountains found me; only fifty feet above where we're camped, when the swirling cloud lifts, there is an icing sugar dusting of white along the rocky range.

It's one of those get up and jump around mornings, not with snowy excitement but to circulate blood around my chilled body. My breath, hands, and panniers still smell of smoked fish. I throw what's left in the river and scrub my pannier lid that I cut the fish up on. Somewhere I read about the blandness of Mongolian food, so I have carried with me a tiny pot of spicy seasoning. This morning I see the top has come off, and my heated waistcoat that sits as padding at the bottom of my pannier is a little hotter without even being plugged in.

Rather than riding directly up the bumpy embankment, I follow Greg at an angle. I'm really not alert enough, complacent in my company. My front wheel hits a rock, and I go down, dropping my bike with the wheels facing uphill. I can't lift it up. There is no way. With all my strength I can only get the bike level with my waist, because I'm down the hill from it. I can't get the extra height to lift and can't get under it to push it up. I consider dragging it round 180 degrees. It would maybe spin on the pannier but would really dent it up. There is petrol coming out of the tank. I try to lift it again, but the angles are all wrong. I look for other options, taking off the pannier I can reach won't make a lot of difference; the problem is the angle, not the weight. What would I do if I was on my own? I would do what I did in the canyon last month; I would be careful and calculated. I deserved that victory as much as I deserved this predicament. And where the hell is Greg? I have nothing better to do except photograph it and wait.

Greg eventually turns up. He had gone on to the road "enjoying the ride." It still takes all our strength to get the bike upright. But no damage is done. I do love my KLR. We look after each other; it's a give and take relationship. As we ride up towards the road, a shepherd has brought his flock out to graze. I ride away from them and parallel to the road until I'm well past. Greg takes the track that heads towards them.

From the elevation of the road the mountains look stunning with their new coat of snow. I stop for pictures. Greg catches up. He had been chased by the shepherd's dog. It was really vicious apparently.

"Really? Who would have thought it? I'd watch out for that next time if I was you." But it does make me realise I might be a bit foolhardy to attempt Mongolia alone.

This is the beauty that was eluding me. There are clusters of Christmas trees and a twisting wild road. The cloud is moody but uneven, giving glimpses of a snowy mountain range then wisping back down as if to bring my attention back to the rugged terrain that I'm riding through.

One of the few faults of the English language, apart for the illogical spelling of so many words, is that there is only one word for snow and there are so many different kinds of snow. My theory for this is, the language, English, comes from England, and we don't get a lot of snow. We don't have vast ranges of mountains and deadly frozen winters. One word will do for a weather condition we so rarely get. Now rain, on the other hand, we have plenty for that. Drizzle, sprinkling, showers, spitting, pouring, torrential, sleeting, freezing, hailing, cats and dogs, and thunderstorms. I don't like to ride in rain, but if I did I could describe what type it was very accurately. Today I'm just riding past snowy mountains. They may improve the scenery, but they leave my language lacking.

There is a forty-foot tanker trailer overturned at the side of the road; it's back on its wheels, but it's rolled right over. The tank has split, and bitumen has poured out but frozen in the atmosphere. It's like liquorish, suspended animation. It looks like it's in motion, liquefied and flowing, but it's not. I can stand on it and touch it with my tongue. I'm glad I wasn't coming round the corner when this driver overturned his truck, and I'm wondering when we are going to hit the dirt this load was intended to seal.

The terrain is harsh and desolate now. Vast cold tundra, inhospitable, wild, and beautiful, the remoteness made all the more evident because, at this moment in time, we are the only two grains passing through the narrows of the egg timer.

We reach the border village. I'm sure if there wasn't a border it wouldn't be here at all. Wooden shacks, mostly boarded up. A little store that has only rice and biscuits, so I buy rice and biscuits. No fuel, no café, not many signs of life at all, and no sticker shops: I see a gap in the market. It's time to cross into Mongolia.

There are two vehicles in front of us at the crossing: the Urals with sidecars again.

We are processed. This time my visa was not registered and again it's not checked.

Then a stretch of no-man's-land, a concrete strip of road to follow to a modern two-storey building which is Mongolian immigration. It's a little chaotic, but there is productivity amongst the chaos, and we are stamped and let loose. We continue and then a gate, just a gate the other side of which is Mongolia.

The change is instant. Yaks and camels wander the grasslands; eagles stand on the trail, reluctant to move, and when they do the wings span the track.

There is nothing but compressed dirt to depict a road. No signs, no markings of any kind. Perhaps this was where the tar was destined for. A whistling wind blows across this barren wilderness. Another time zone, but it's completely irrelevant; this land says survive or die, don't snivel and threaten to sue. Your actions are all you have; take control of them and responsibility for them. I'll never be a nomadic tribesman, but I hunted and gathered my rice and biscuits and it will have to see me through to the next town, of which there is no clue as to the direction or distance. My sterile West has left me in awe and unprepared for this. I can go in any direction; it's lawless and helpless.

A visa alone does not give me the right to be here: I'm an intruder, not a tourist. I have been spat out the narrows of the hourglass, and I'm standing staring all around me. And then it starts to snow. The third of August, and it's snowing.

I'm here; I am here. I've just ridden my bike to Mongolia, and I'm scared and exhilarated, nervous and victorious. I'm unaware and aware of it. Thrown in the deep end of wild, western Mongolia.

The track has forked, I've got a map, and there is a settlement to the east. I haven't grasped the scale yet. What depicts a village? Come to that, what depicts a road? I'm grasping for a reality; nothing could have prepared me.

I am approached by a man on horseback. He rides up from out of the hills. I don't know what he was doing before I got here, I don't know why he is here now, he probably doesn't know why I am here; I'm not sure I can answer that myself right now. Wrapped in a long, black, fur coat tied with a colourful scarf, and a weather-beaten face of leather skin and deep wrinkles that told a hundred stories, none of which I know or could ever understand. I don't understand the first thing of his life. We are worlds and times apart. There is no comprehension of each other's lives, but I ask if I can take his photo, and he agrees. This wild man on his horse has ridden over to check me out. I have to assume he is friendly. I'm on his territory; I'm vulnerable, not armed with language or knowledge and certainly not weapons or wisdom, and he could have all of those. To reach his age in this land I think he must have. Knowing how to select shuffle on my iPod doesn't make me smarter than him. Not out here.

All I have is a throttle to get me out of any danger. His interest in me is short. Perhaps he's seen the likes of me before. Perhaps we all look the same to him. Whatever his reason to ride off into the vast and deserted landscape was, you can bet it wasn't because his favourite soap was about to start.

Even without the photo, I will never forget that old man on his horse; his face had the mystique of Mona Lisa's smile. I couldn't read his eyes; I couldn't gauge his mood. I didn't know his intensions. I failed to be who I am because I felt so out of my depth. If I could have been me, I would have been something to him. He didn't say anything, and he didn't stay long. He was a product of his environment, a proud man who knew what he needed to, and his understanding of me was not a necessity in his world.

I would like to hide myself and my bike, be the unseen voyeur for a while just to try and understand what I'm seeing, get a grasp of the lives, the hardships. A little understanding would make a big difference. I can only respect him because I assume he deserves it. In his land in this environment, awe and respect is all I have.

These white boys on bikes with their baby faces and electronic boxes, who pass through his land, must be the cause of many laughter lines around the stove inside a yurt over a bottle of vodka. And we deserve to be. If I ever meet David Gilmour I will try to remember how I felt in this man's company and not be so intimidated. Him with his axe or me on my chopper, we couldn't cut it in this country.

I need to head south. I climb a mountain and follow a track. All I can see is mountains. I follow the dark soil of a single track.

There is a row of telegraph poles; it's as good a thing to follow as...well, there is nothing else to follow. When I reach a peak I can see nothing but white-topped mountains all around. I suppose this is what I expected, but I'm still blown away. I think it's the absolute lack of any kind of security: no ambulance, no breakdown service, no food, no shelter. If I'm stupid, I will die. High visibility jackets and warning signs won't help me here. Better get in touch with your survival instincts, boy. The eagles will peck out your eyes before ya wheel stops spinning if you come off here.

To the south is some evidence of inhabitants, and from my high altitude vantage point I think I can see a strip of black tar, and off to the west in the distance a few vehicles and workmen. Is that guy holding a theodolite? Oh shit, just in time. I'm here just in time. Next year it will be paved and bypassed, the year after will be sticker shops. But for now I will put air back in my tyres and ride the new road into Olgly, where all the grains from the narrows of the hourglass gravitate to.

If ever there was a day of two halves this would be the one.

When I arrive in a new country I like to stay in a hotel and acclimatise for a few days. But I quickly discover that Mongolia does wilderness very well, but the towns and cities are awful. A lot of people drink a lot of vodka a lot of the time.

This town is in my guidebook, so we try to find a recommended room. The first place is awful. We ride round the square. There is that hallucination again, two French-registered bikes parked side by side. The next place is expensive, but they promise Wi-Fi, towels, and hot water. It would be good to brag my achievement to the world and get the smell of fish out of my hands. We take their last room. We can ride our bikes round the back for secure parking. The gates are opened for us, revealing four Romanian-registered KTMs, for fuck's sake. As I fill out the forms at reception the Urals turn up. That's ten, ten of us in one town on one night, ten bikes. Funnel? Hourglass? It's a fuckin' corridor.

The room has no towels. but that doesn't matter. because there is no water at all, hot or cold, no Wi-Fi, and no power to charge phones and camera batteries.

Back at reception they suddenly don't understand English. They get that I want my money back, and I get it.

We throw our stuff on our bikes and head back round the square. If awful is the only choice, at least it can be cheap. Round the corner and on the pavement with a phone to his ear is Riso, a Touratech twin smiling his stupid smile and waving. You can't make this shit up. Oblivious as ever, he tells us where he is staying and how there is room in his yurt for two more.

We opt for the shite hotel. We throw our stuff in the room and go walkabout and find an Irish pub. If ya gonna mess up ya day, you may as well screw it up completely.

We eat good food and order a second main course, we drink whisky, and when the bill comes we pay the price.

When we get back to the hotel, we are told to move rooms. I don't mind not understanding wild nomadic horseman, but I resent not understanding snappy little receptionists who make me pack up all my stuff and move it next door.

Well how can I sum up today? Varied, definitely varied.

Day 60

North of Achit Nuur Lake, Mongolia, 137 Miles

I wake at first light; I'm wide awake and have things I want to do, namely washing myself and my clothes. There is a stinking toilet down the corridor. The door has no lock, and of the three toilets, two are blocked. I wedge the door shut and have a strip wash using the dribble of cold water from the only tap. The place is filthy, disgusting, but it's that or nothing, and nothing is what I've had for the last two days. I wash some clothing in the sink too. No one tries to get in the door. I could use the musty carpet air to replace this pungent stench I've locked myself in. But I do feel better for my efforts.

At 9 a.m. we wander around the town. The bank is a clean, smart building, and they have a guard who enters the cubical with me which contains the ATM. Are you really necessary? Smart-suited bankers sit behind their desks; I can't imagine how they got to work keeping so clean. The streets are mud and puddles, the market hasn't opened yet, neither has any café or food store. There is no urgency in this place. I manage to get some bread. This will have to do.

I pack my bike and hang my washing off the panniers. Greg is taking forever, as usual; I'm not sure what he does because I'm always focused on my own packing. I'm not the one in the hurry, but I'm always first to be ready. A few people approach me—different country, different audience, same intrigue. One man in particular, wearing glasses and a baseball cap, speaks excellent English. He is an engineer and works all over the country on various projects. He flies from job to job whilst his two co-workers drive the truck with the equipment in. He is an intelligent, informed man; I show him my intended route on my map.

He produces a book, a page-by-page map of this un-navigable country. It states distances, bridges, river crossings; it names every village and what townships have fuel. I'm so impressed. Where can I get one from? He gives it to me. Wow!

Big WOW—you have no idea what this means. You have, with a single gesture, completely changed my trip. Thank you so much, and if that were not enough, he gave me his card and number to call if I have any problems or need translation. In the right location at the right time to the right person. I'm not part of an endless procession, I've still got exclusive qualities to this man, and I couldn't hope for a better gift.

Another country full of goodness and generosity. From the Ukraine onwards it's been a journey enhanced by the goodness of human nature. My gratitude, once again, seems so inadequate. It may be just a map to him, but to a map reader on a motorbike it's a life line.

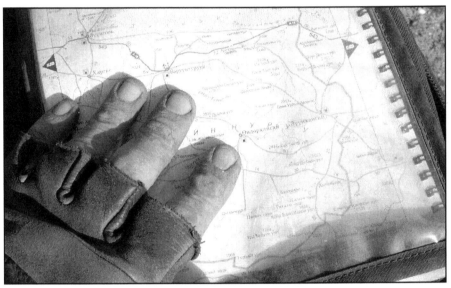

The map is written in Cyrillic. But that's a good thing. I don't have to read it, but the people I stop to ask directions do. It's perfect, and it fits in the map wallet on my tank bag.

If there is a downside to this, and trust me I will always find one, it's that this map gives me more independence and my owning it makes Greg more dependent on me. He has no map, no Sat Nav to speak of, and no guidebook; in fact, I wonder how he thought he was going to get across this country.

We ride past the market. It's still closed; I will never find the plastic water bottle I want. I also want some whisky to celebrate my 10,000th mile that is approaching. The alcohol shop is open, of course, but Gordon's Gin is £2, and by comparison, whisky is £20. That would explain last night's bill at the Irish pub.

At the petrol station we ask a few people directions. South of town, everyone seems to agree it's south. It doesn't really correspond with my map, but I'm yet to discover what appears on the map as a dark green motorway-type-road is in reality. Having to go south to get north is possible; there may be a river that's uncrossable or a road that has been washed away. I point at my north-east destination, and everyone has pointed south. The thing is I don't want to go the long way round;

I want to go the way I can see on my new map across these mountains, over these rivers. But we go the way that they all point.

It is dry, bright, and cloudless; we ride along the bottom of a wide valley. Grass scrub is the only vegetation; there are white ger camps at the sides of the foothills.

A yurt is a white, canvas, circular tent, felt-lined with a stove in the middle. It has a wooden door frame and door but no windows. In Mongolia their yurts are called "gers." And they are as much a part of the landscape as the yaks and eagles.

It's wondrous, it's timeless, and as the dusty miles pass, I slowly take it all in. Those Australians, who told me of this route, said that by approaching Mongolia from the west you are thrown into the wildest part of the country, and I think I'm glad I did it this way because my senses are reeling. Greg is always way out in front, and I can get the feeling of solitude, not loneliness, just space around me to appreciate the space around me.

We ride up a hill. There are no rules, no fences, no barriers, no division of territory: We are so conditioned but slowly become aware we can ride wherever we want to, like a kid running round a departure lounge having never experienced such limitless confines. And as if we were flying out of the airport, from our increased elevation we can see the mountainous terrain that surrounds us, the dusty track we have come down, and the southerly direction it continues to go in. We eat the first food of the day, and it's already 1 P.M. A trail of dust appears on the horizon, and we watch it get closer and pass, hidden from view from our hillside vantage point. I think it's that hallucination again.

Back on the track a lone German bike is coming the other way; he seems weary and reluctant to stop. The reason why is because he had already seen the Touratech twins and both pairs of French riders this morning. He has no humour, he has seen more travellers than locals. He confirms we are going the wrong way, so we ride back with him. He says he rides very slowly. And he does—the self-preservation of the solo rider or maybe he just wants to get rid of us. I wave and let him have his privacy back; he has eighteen miles left to enjoy it before he reaches tonight's overland congregation.

I don't mind heading back. It means we are leaving the tourist track. We try every direction out of town. We try asking locals but they are so drunk—slurring drunk, dangerous drunk, unpredictable drunk, lean-against-your-bike-until-it-falls-over drunk. They point in every direction and then ask for money. The spectacle we create starts to generate interest, and like zombies sensing living flesh, they start staggering towards us from all directions. It's time for a loud exhaust note and a sharp exit.

I stop asking drunks and use some common sense and a basic sense of direction back through the town. North the way we came in yesterday. There are police everywhere lining the sides of the roads, even putting up barriers and diversions around one building. Once again, I have no clue as to what is going on around me.

Now I'm on the right side of the river and on the right road, which was next to the petrol station I filled up at forty miles and four hours ago, but I'm stopped by the cops. The presidential convoy is coming down this road soon, and until they pass, I'm not going anywhere. So I wait, and sure enough, in a cloud of dust and a scream of sirens, a convoy of police cars and 4x4s goes past. I take photos of the first few, but there must be twenty vehicles, and I just put on my lid and wait for the word. When the last car of the motorcade passes and before the dust has settled I'm allowed to go. And this is it. The road is amazing. I can see why the president would want to travel it. I follow rivers through valleys and snowy mountain ranges on the horizon, no signs of life, or of civilisation, of anything. Just a vast and endless timeless land.

And best of all we have left the procession of bikes behind by taking this alternative route. All thanks to my man giving me his map.

Sometimes it seems like I've been here before. It's just how I imagined, only more so. The scenery is distracting, but the road is bad. Big rocks lie in wait to reshape my wheels if I don't pay attention. My bike is taking a pounding, I wonder if I will even get to Ulan Bator, let alone past it, but I don't really care because I've reached my destination. And I love every mile of it. I can't imagine the bike will be worth much if it does make it to UB. It would seem silly to spend more than it's worth just to ship it somewhere. The journey is far from over; these decisions tend to make themselves.

Although I'm riding alone most of the time, I still consider the commitment-free advantage of not having a riding buddy, and as those thoughts start to appeal I ride into some soft sand and nearly lose my balance. I suppose I'll stick with Greg then.

I stop by a river; there is no sound, no pollution, just a river with sandy banks. Then what looks so beautiful from the side of the road crosses in front of me. It's a wide river, and it's got some very deep ravines. A 4x4 van has tried, and failed, to cross it and is stuck in the current. It's the first vehicle I have seen since I left the town, and it's stuck. With my boots off, I walk back and forth, looking for a hidden boulder that will bring me off. It's my first unavoidable river crossing.

I've discovered that photos and videos do nothing to show the vastness of a river crossing, but stand on your pegs behind the bars, fill your boots with water, soak your feet, slip your clutch, lean against the current and judge your path, avoid the rocks and bump up the far bank, and the feeling of achievement is immense.

I haven't killed my phones or cameras, I just crossed a river, and I'm onward to the next obstacle.

Greg is getting increasingly annoyed that his brand-new bike is getting wrecked; I'm experiencing increased fulfilment I have made it this far with a collection of second-hand parts amounting to £2,000. We are in very different places. It's not that I don't want to keep riding, it's just that I don't have to; I'm celebrating achievement, whilst he is contemplating failure. I'm so glad my bike does not own me. This trip is done on a budget out of necessity, but I'm continually reaping the rewards of the freedom on having nothing much to lose.

We approach a tiny village: it's a square of huts and wooden buildings with roofs of corrugated iron and positioned like a wagon train to keep intruders out. But if that was the idea behind the design, there is no evidence of it in the hospitality we are welcomed with.

The German 4x4 who I spoke with en route to Semey, until the Touratech twin interrupted in German, had just trundled in ahead of us, with a Swiss-registered truck and family of four. We were the talk of the town. There was no discreet passage through. Like buses, we all arrive at once and stop in the dusty square. Greg is happy to meet some fellow countrymen, although they speak French, not German, so the common language was mine.

We create a scene. Two old men are looking at the bike, laughing, and making fun of each other. One wants to put my helmet on, and when he finally squeezes it onto his head, he play fights with his mate, probably lifelong buddies. And when I take their photos and show them, they thank me.

I go into the little shop that sells shoes and clothes; no bread, but dried noodles. Even here they have dried noodles. I have carried dried noodles I bought from Tesco for nine weeks and 9,500 miles as an emergency food. and they are available here. It's not that the noodles I carried were heavy. but they take up precious space in my panniers. Well, I'll know next time.

Now I don't feel like an intruder. I feel like a circus that has pulled into town; the old men come for the matinee performance and wander off to let the kids have their turn. One girl speaks English and is pushed to the front. "Do you even have an address? Does the postman come here ever? Could I send you photos?" I don't understand so many things. But I can laugh. and I can speak with tones which make them laugh. And the brief encounter as my personal circus pulls out of town will fill all of our minds tonight.

I didn't speak much to the Europeans. I enjoyed my local audience. But it was decided we will camp together tonight, parking our vehicles in a circle out on the wild frontier.

Since we left the town this morning this has been the most populated area I have seen. There are two riverside ger camps in sight, but these trucks travel slowly, so we stop in sight of them, and pretty soon we have visitors. A man of indeterminate age and very bad teeth, which are revealed in a constant smile, arrives on his horse; he has the traditional riding boots and thick felt coat, tied at the waste with a green scarf. His skin is dark, and in a hard life kind of way, he looks radiant, healthy. He is here with his friend and two children, who soon lose interest, but he sticks around. After some mutual and incomprehensible banter, he offers to let me ride his horse, and I'm trotted off over the steppe like a…like a biker on a horse, let's be honest. I'm no more part of his world for this experience than he has become part of mine, as he giggles from behind me when I open up the throttle and show him how many horses I have under my tank as we ride around his endless back garden. So we've shared our most personal possessions.

And now, as I unpack and erect my tent, blow up my Thermarest, and pull out my sleeping bag, he laughs at my pathetic nomadic possessions and accommodation.

We sit on the grass, the sun is low and bright, and our shadows stretch out to the east as his horse is left free to wander. He brings out his perfume bottle: it must be perfume. He asks me to sniff it, "What the top?"

"No dumb arse, take the top off." He does it for me, and some powder is attached to the stick. "Sniff this." Oh right. Now I understand. Sniff, snort, hit, bam, wow, cool. Stick around, I like this snuff stuff. No one else is participating. Don't frown at me, I'm just accepting hospitality.

We cook our pasta, and our visitor hails his horse and leaves. In the spirit of barter we trade bread for beer, and everyone's needs are met. When it gets dark we all go to the warmth of the German camper for vodka under a twelve-volt florescent light. They want to be in Singapore by Christmas and will fly out their children to meet them. A seed is planted in my head. We laugh and chat like the old travellers we are; backpacks long exchanged for more independent and comfortable forms of travel, still hungry for wonder and a thirst for new experiences, but our desires are met in ways the guidebooks don't describe. The tales we tell are not of our university years, but how we travelled before we had our engines, and Internet, phones, and iPods. When a backpack contained fifteen cassette tapes, rolls of film, new and used, because the weight and bulk of developed pictures was too great. Unsure if your camera was working until you got back home to Boots. Travelling miles out of your way, travellers cheques stashed in hidden pockets, to a poste restante to see if you had mail. Not better or worse, just different and just how I want to be at this moment in time. I wouldn't want to travel any other way. Once again, I'm doing exactly what I want to.

DAY 61

FURTHER SOUTHWEST OF NARANBULAG THAN I THOUGHT, MONGOLIA, 135 MILES

I slept soundly in the safety of the posy. It's a relaxed morning, and I walk down to the river to wash. It's everything yesterday's rancid toilet wasn't: fresh and clean, with mountain views, privacy, and sunlight. I know of no better way to start a day. I'll take this over towelling robes and power showers any day. Washing my parts in a river, blown dry by a summer breeze, and putting on clean underwear, I've never felt so fresh.

I reconsider the idea the Germans gave me last night.

When a friends fiftieth birthday party was approaching, in a divine flash of drunken inspiration, I thought a stripper would be a great idea. In the cold sober light of morning, when I considered the implications, some of the guests, his mother for example, I was less convinced of my faultless plan. This indecision continued for several weeks of drinking and sobriety, and eventually the conflict was over with a short Google search, a few clicks, and a credit card number. I was, she was committed...I ordered petite from West Thurrock. I think perhaps that has a different meaning in Thurrock to the rest of the world. Must be a Greys area. Either that or I was the lucky one who happened to order when she was running a promotion of buy one, get 25kgs free.

It all worked out pretty well. His mother was removed before the clothes were.

Last night's divine flash of drunken inspiration in the camper van was, rather than removing the mother, I decided it would be great to fly her over for her seventy-fifth. This morning the river was colder and far more sobering, but the idea remained.

I decide to check my bike for loose bits, whilst I wait for Greg to pack up, so my clean hands are soon greasy dirty again.

The track starts dry and dusty, then grassy and rocky, over streams and through boggy mud. It's breathtaking: gers and herders on horseback with their blushed cheeks and puzzled expressions, which crack into smiles as soon as I smile at them. These hardened faces are so ready to show their friendliness. I just have to be the one to initiate it, and waves are exchanged when smiles are too far away to be seen.

This area is so unspoilt only goats cross my path and the shadows of eagles overhead.

I'm having possibly the best day's riding I have ever had, the most fun you can have in first and second gear, cross countless rivers and streams, over mountains, through ruts, bogs, over rocks, and over every peak another view that leaves me knowing that only witnessing this first hand will ever really do it justice. Rolling green hills, fir trees, and fresh snowy peaks, its beauty is so inviting and not the inhospitable climate I was expecting. Well not today.

There are no other overlanders; we did see two Australian hikers who hadn't seen another westerner in ten days, lucky them.

"Ya know wats app nen in da crick eet?"

"What cricket?" I haven't seen a TV in probably three weeks. What a strange and stereotypical encounter. Probably another hallucination.

Out of the blue, eagle-territory sky a seagull appears. It's so unexpected and puts a song in my head. I end up playing the whole Bad Company album on my iPod and listen to the lyrics of the songs like never before. It was written for this ride, this morning, this terrain; it's perfect—riding down this rocky road, wondering where it might be leading, riding on to the bitter end.

I take tracks with confidence, cross rivers with hope, the map seems quite accurate, a huge lake appears, and the two-wheel track turns into a proper trail, not sealed but established. We are off the tourist track. It wasn't too difficult. It doesn't take much.

I spent a week of winter sun in Hurgharda, Egypt, one year, an awful place, a town built purely for tourism: Burger Kings, KFC, and English pubs. But go two blocks away from the main street, that's where the Egyptians live and drink their tea and play their backgammon. And even in this holiday hell you can see a bit of real life. No pyramids, but at least you're amidst the local people.

Hiking the well-trodden Annapurna trail in the Himalayas, the irritation of the procession took away any pleasure. But a late start one morning followed by an early stop, and the next ten days were spent out of step with the masses, and an isolated tranquillity followed us for the rest of the hike.

Thinking outside the guidebook. That's where I like to take my trips.

One of Mongolia's more famous sites is the twin peaks of Kharhiraa Uul and Turgen Uul—the two 4,000-metre mountains that are popular with the more adventurous hiker and also with my Swedish friends. We tried to plan a meet-and-climb, but dates and destinations were too vague. I was obliged to get some photos of me and my bike with the peaks in the background, both of which they last saw at the Sweden Rock Festival (me and the bike that is. Obviously you couldn't see the Mongolian mountains from the festival). I would have photographed them anyway. I used my tripod and self-timer because Greg had gone on ahead not even knowing what he was missing. Here I am again enjoying the journey, whilst he's blinkered to his destination. I do love my mountains. He is Swiss. It perhaps means more to me than to him. I'm frustrated he's missing it; he's frustrated I'm not.

The trails are smooth and plentiful, they criss-cross each other, and I give my front wheel the freedom to choose the path it wants to take, whilst I watch the scenery go by.

I don't recall such a perfect ride; I am literally enjoying every moment of it. The music in my head, the deep blue sky, the beauty that surrounds me, and a comfortable temperature. I punch at the air. I yell out of my visor. Every road I've ridden, all the preparations I've done have brought me to this point. Complete and utter satisfaction, enjoyment, and contentment. Nothing is missing. Every ingredient is present. It's a rare experience in my high expectation life style. Often happy, seldom content. Today right here, right now I have both.

The track goes up a steep hill; I stop again for a photo by an Ovoo, a stone cairn with a pyramid of weathered branches and blue cotton flags blowing in the wind. Spiritual and photogenic. I'm shown by some passing Mongolians, who have also stopped to get out of their car, how to toss the painted stones three times to bring good luck and show gratitude to the spirits. I think they deserve a little thank you after the experience I just had. From this summit I can see the dirt track wind down through the valley and no tell-tale dust trail to show what happened to Greg. The reason for that, I find, is a truck with a flat tyre. The whole family are transporting their ger to relocate. We take it in turns with a bicycle pump to inflate the tyre. It's hard work lying on the grass under the truck holding the pump on the valve with one hand and pumping with the other. We have all had several turns. I get my pressure gauge and put it on the tyre. The end shoots out like it's spring loaded. I show my surprise and then the gauge. I think, guys, it's got enough air in it now.

Sadly, the mountains turn to plains, the heat increases, and then we come to a real road that takes us to Ulaangom. I follow Greg, and he passes a petrol station and then a market, and when he passes a sign that says "steak house" in English, I stop. The only patrons are drunk youths, half asleep on the tables and half watching '50s-style cartoons on the TV. But that does not detract for an unexpected sizzling steak.

At this point I would really like to slow the pace. It's not a pretty town, but it has an Internet café and a supermarket. It wouldn't hurt to spend some time, but Greg is not of the same opinion. It was at this town the Australians said to head south. This sealed road could continue east, sealed, smooth, fast, and direct all the way to Ulan Bator. But that's not why I'm here. I can feel Greg's dilemma, but I'm not worried, he can do want he wants, he is counting the days until he gets there. "Maybe I can do it in three," he has said; maybe I can do it in fourteen, I think.

This isn't working. Neither is finding the right road out of town, they keep coming to an end. The map indicates it's paved, but it's not. When we stop looking for a paved road, we find the one we want.

It crosses the widest, deepest river so far. I stand and look at it. There are many places that it could be crossed, but I'm not sure I want to try. As we stand there waiting for something, a moped comes along, and without a second thought, he crosses in front of us. I clap my hands, I'm impressed. He thinks I'm a twat, but I don't care. Greg follows the moped's route and gets across. I'm still unsure. I take another route, my boots fill with water again, but I make it to the other side. I stop to empty my boots, and Greg keeps on going. He's obviously pissed off; this road is neither paved nor direct, and his bike is getting beaten up. The road and scenery may not be as good, but why rush? It would be good to cool down and wash in this river: he could really use it. It's an opportunity; it's there, it should be taken advantage of, in my opinion.

The map is really accurate. There should be a turn-off in 18 kms, and there is. The track forks. Then I need the next left in 25 kms, but it doesn't materialise. Greg is way ahead as ever. He doesn't even know where we are supposed to be going. I pass a dried, white salt lake. I'm supposed to be north of that. I've come too far. Greg is off in the distance. A pet hate of mine is people taking the lead when they don't know where the hell they are going. Do I sit and wait for him to come back, or do I try and exceed a comfortable speed on this bumpy track to catch him up? Pain in the arse. When I do catch him, I show him the map; it wouldn't have hurt to show a little interest in it before he took off in the wrong direction. I keep my mouth shut and just say we should go back past the camels and do a right. That should take us in the right direction. It sort of works. We make our own road and find some tyre tracks in the grass that lead to dirt and then split into three and almost continue in the right direction, almost, but not quite. We want to be going southeast, and we are going south. I want that setting sun to be shining on my shoulder, not on my arm. It teases a little in an easterly direction and then goes south again.

There comes a point when I have simply got it wrong. I'm not where I think I am, and at dusk I climb a hill to try to see the big lake by the small town to give me a sense of direction. I'm not sure if what I see is hope or a mirage, but it's so much further north than it should be. So we make camp; I'm feeling some petulance. This adventure is just what I came to enjoy, and I don't mind the navigating, but I could do without giving a pep talk, but as I ride around our designated overnight stop, I do see something that could be a road east to follow tomorrow. It may be a dry river bed, but it's rideable, whatever it is.

Tomorrow, like cowboys in the Wild West, we will make a route that feels like the right direction.

I'm so torn between the vulnerability of doing this alone and the freedom of going at my own pace. I put my boots on my mirrors to dry over night and pitch my tent.

For all the things that aren't out here, I still have a phone signal and text my mum, "Fancy commin to Mongolia for ya 75th?"

Day 62

Pushed out of Surginu, Mongolia, 197 Miles

I open my tent to see a herd of horses has come here to graze; I'm not sure how wild or free they are. Maybe someone rounds them up every now and again. And when they are not being owned and restricted, they are free to come here. Much like myself.

Greg is ready first; he really must be in a hurry. I realise I would rather be the one waiting than the one being waited for. There was a strong and consistent breeze last night, which means I slept well, because the wind blew away all the sounds that usually wake me up, and also my boots are completely dry. I think this calls for a clean pair of socks. Shame about my feet.

I lead the way to the track I saw last night; it is a dry river, there are a single set of tyre tracks on the sandy bed. I can't believe I'm riding on sand by choice, but there is security in knowing that it has been used once before since the river ran dry. Pathfinder was just a phrase until I got here, now it's a skill, a necessity, an achievement. The river bed just disappears as I go up a hill. I can't see what I was looking at last night. No signs of water or habitation. All I can do is have faith in my map-reading abilities, use my instincts, and head the way I think is right. The sun is in the east, I'm going in the right direction, generally. The lake is massive: whether it comes into view from the north or south of me, I think I will notice it.

I make my own road, simply head across the grassland in the direction I feel is right. Eventually I'll come across tyre tracks.

I suppose, being nomadic, a ger is moved, and after several trips have been made into town a track is created. If I follow that it will lead to another track that will get wider and dustier and lead me to town. I like that theory; it gives me hope. But I'm not sure it is a reality. It keeps me going across uninhabited land. I'm willing a town to appear out of the heat haze, but it doesn't. I've still got about 200 miles range in my tank before my eyeballs become appetisers for the eagles.

I pass a solitary ger. I have to ask. There's having convictions in your instincts, and then there is just plain bloody-mindedness. Despite the popular myth, I'm secure enough in my masculinity to ask for directions. As a truck driver it was always easier to ask than it was to find somewhere to turn a forty-foot trailer round. However, this isn't a petrol station forecourt on the Newbury bypass. This takes a little nerve. In fact, I do what at the time seems like the strangest and bravest thing I have ever done.

I park my bike away from the settlement; it just seems intrusive to ride up. I take my map, and I walk towards the ger. The family watch, the dog barks, I stoop to the ground to pick up a stone that isn't there, the dog falls for the bluff and backs off. Steps take forever, my sole flaps, my heart pounds, my eyes scan, and my face holds a prolonged and ineffective smile like a wedding photo.

Finally I'm close enough to exchange facial expressions; my nervous and non-threatening smile is now only held in place by cramped muscles. It's probably as painful to watch as it is to wear. I indicate back to the bike. Show the map. Their intrigue bridges the gap, and they look at my map. "I have to go past the camp and do a right." OK, OK, "spar-cee-bar" thank you; it's Russian, but it probably makes more sense than my cramped and distorted face. The boy calls to the dog not to bite me as I take the long walk back to my bike, sighing hard, but now with a natural, beaming victorious smile. Whilst I put the map back in the tank bag, two of the girls have mounted their horses and come over to watch, not close enough to speak or photograph but just to satisfy their curiosity. I wave, and slowly, after a little thought, the wave is returned, and all is well.

I ride past the camp and do a right, and sure enough, the flattened grass turns to track. I go right past another ger, I stop again. They have the entire contents spread out on the grass. They are either moving off or moving in, or maybe they are just looking for a contact lens. I'd really like to see inside one, as opposed to seeing the inside of one spread around outside. With a moped parked outside, somehow they seem more modern and less intimidating. The whole family gathers round, friendly and helpful, and indicates to go the way I was. This map, being Cyrillic, is priceless. I point at my destination, they read my destination, and then they point towards my destination. It's clear; it's simple and fool proof.

The track gets wider, my speed increases, and then I go down a hidden dip really hard. My tyres come off the back, and my top box mounting sheers. That was stupid of me. I have to reposition the straps that previously held the tyres to the top box; they now hold the top box to the rack. I couldn't avoid the dip, but I could have avoided the damage.

Soon the path merges with an unmistakable road, still dirt but a major route in comparison to anything else ridden today. It leads to town. On the outskirts I stop to re-strap my luggage again.

A man on a moped comes by and stops to help; he offers me a padlock, but my damage is a bit beyond that. He has a long, brown, cracked, leather coat that matches his face, he has a cheeky smile and all his wrinkles face upwards. He has his daughter with him, and soon as he has bothered to stop, in a life that has nothing too pressing to do, he sits on the ground cross-legged and starts to smoke his pipe.

He's such a character. "Can I take your photo?"

"Yeah, if ya wanta," his puzzled response indicates. He thanks me for taking his photo or maybe the thanks are for showing it to his daughter and making her giggle. "Look, your old man is in my camera; isn't he cool?" So we ride into the name on my map. No wonder I couldn't find it: there is nothing here. Nothing much, just a store to get water from and excited youths point us to the big cylindrical tanks they call a petrol station. They run alongside us as we ride to the disappointing monstrosity. I don't really want to put that in my tank.

"Oh you'd be wanting that one then" is what the pointing to a place with pumps would imply.

It does have pumps, but I wouldn't call it a petrol station. The boy attendant seems perplexed that I'm not satisfied with 80 octane. My mate pulls up on his moped, his pipe extinguished, his daughter dropped off. His indications imply that 80 octane will be just fine. And where exactly did you get your education on KLRs 650s? OK, OK, just 5 litres then. Thank you.

I'm getting used to no road signs, getting used to using instinct. It's a gift that is not used in our sterile Western world. Signs tell us hot water is hot and wet roads are slippery, narrow ones may have oncoming vehicles in the middle of the road, and low bridges are indeed low.

We really are crippling ourselves, denying our natural ability of judgment. I'm getting mine back. The hard bit is having faith in it and obeying it. But if the society

I come from has its way, like our tails and appendix, it will become something we once had, stopped using, and lost. Common sense and survival instinct are invaluable. The stupid thing is political correctness prevents useful signs being posted. "Beware chav hang out in this subway" would be useful information to people who can read and pay tax.

Instead we have created a breed of dysfunctional idiots, whose only chance of employment is to dream up rules and regulations stating the bleeding obvious, then enforcing them with ridiculous signs, and making us aware of their risks in long-winded, patronising courses and seminars, the only function of which is, apart from giving these self-appointed dictators of the clearly apparent who offer nothing to the running of society a purpose, is to prolong the life expectancy of the morons who should, by the laws of survival of the fittest, be long dead. They now continue to drain resources purely by being kept alive by signs telling them the basic functions of life. Risk assessment? The risk is soon we will have a generation of people who can't see it if it's not high-visibility, won't feel it through their gloves and hard hats, won't hear it past their ear plugs, and will only be able to proceed in life if there is a sign telling them what to do every step of the way. Health and safety is nothing but a self-generated, crippling virus created by the worthless cowards who need to justify their existence. It's done at the expense of the productive people, who pay their wages. If I had my way, I'd have all of them shot.

We pass the lake; it's a popular spot. Holidaying Mongolians, they appear to be a strange breed. Of course, go to the hot springs and lake, why not? But perhaps because they see holidaying is a bourgeois Western pastime, they wear clothes they seem to think the people they emulate would wear. Somehow Bermuda shorts, baggy T-shirts, and a high five-ing joy doesn't make them Californians on muscle beach, just Mongolians in ill-fitting clothes, but they seem happy. We continue on in the hope of coming to a less-populated part. But the road takes us away from the lake. We do get a second and third chance later, but now we have a distinctive path. Greg is out in front and not stopping. We should have taken the opportunity when it was there. I really could use a wash now.

I missed the mountains when we came out here onto the plains, but now we have mud flats, and camels loiter on the dry cracked land, and the sky is bigger than ever. It's certainly a varied landscape.

The challenge of navigation has gone; the well-driven road has turned to washboard. As the heat increases, the mind wanders. I realise I am doing 50mph and planing across this vibrating road. I'm even leaning on the corners. I get right into the zone still concentrating, but totally into the feel of the bike on the road. It's just as I realise I'm in the zone that I tend to instantly leave it and throttle back as the forks and rear shock bottom-out yet again on a misjudged pothole.

We pass two Ladas, both Czech-registered. I wave as I pass and cover them in my dust. Then when we stop for a slice of sausage on side-stand bread, they pass by hoots, waves, and smiles. I call it "side-stand" bread, because if you park on soft ground and your side-stand sinks, you can cut off a slice, put it on the dirt, and your side stand won't penetrate the surface. When there are no rocks or cans available, it's a crusty alternative.

There are trees up ahead. We agree if it's a river we will stop for a wash and laundry, relax, and camp early, but when we cross it is just another dry river bed. It's been a week since my last hot shower. I'm dusty, filthy, stinking; ground-in dirt beyond the capabilities of the wet wipes. They just take off a layer of crud before I eat my daily bread.

The next time we pass the Ladas, we stop. Six Czechs in two Ladas, four boys, two girls, on a mission to buy gers and export them home, thereby helping the local economy. It's very charitable and makes me feel like a selfish motorcyclist, which I suppose I am.

The input, stimulation, and exchange revitalise the thoughts in my helmet. It's either that or the biscuits and jam dip they put on their bonnet that I tuck into as we tell our stories. I apologise for how filthy I am. They had stopped at the lake and said it was crystal clear water: so refreshing. So that's something else I missed.

I was feeling OK, but now I'm better. Back on the bike I start waving again at anyone I see. Clouds get grey and drift to the ground in isolated rain showers making rainbows ahead of us. Then the path turns away from them, and I'm saved from the soaking I was expecting.

We arrive in a tiny town as the light fades. Petrol first, before it closes.

92 octane is a relief to find, then look for a store. The shop is not selling bread, and the café is not serving food. I get on my bike, and it doesn't start. The starter button does nothing. I begin to pull it apart but get the inevitable audience.

Nothing is working. I managed to kill all the electrics. Before I blew that fuse, at least it was bumpable. Now I have nothing. The Ladas arrive. They find an open café and order us all food. I can't fix it, not tonight with fading light and audience. I'm tired and so dirty. Electrical faults have to be considered, meditated on.

I push my bike to the open café and have dead animal noodle soup. It's perfect, but I'm pre-occupied. The locals have seen the contents of my panniers, and I can't leave. But I can't camp here in this town. I will have to stay awake, vigilant by my bike all night. In yet another act of limitless kindness, the Czechs offer to not only push my bike out of town but to share a camping spot too.

We try to tow it, but the rope snatches, and I fall off. It's not a big deal anymore. I fall off about twice a day now: both me and my bike are used to it. Like reaching top gear, it doesn't happen often, and when it does it's barely worth remarking on. As long as the two don't happen simultaneously. We tie a strap to Greg's bike, and he tries to pull me, but the strap wrenches my arm and crushes my hand. They take it in turns to push me. It's dark now, and I can't see the road. Ironically, it's the only time I've ridden at night, and my spotlights don't work. With deflated tyres for better traction on dirt road, they push me out of town onto the steppe. I follow the path the Ladas make over the undulating ground. And then as the wind blows in a storm, we industriously erect out tents in the shelter of the cars. Lightning strobes in the distance as we retreat to our Gore-Tex and aluminium sanctuaries. The wind blows so forcefully I don't think my tent will take much more. It breaths in and out so violently, snatching at the stitching and straining the poles. The gusts and the flapping fabric are deafening, and I wonder if my bike has been blown over outside. I trace the wires of my loom in my head until they weave a dream.

DAY 63

20 KM WEST OF TOSONTSENGEL, MONGOLIA, 119 MILES

When the red dawn arrives both bike and tent are still standing. Once again horses meander through the camping area, grazing for their breakfast feed. The dramatic sunrise and passing wildlife make me grab my camera before I grab my tools. I have the morning all to myself, and I want to keep it that way.

I move my bike away from the tents, spread out my poncho, and quietly and methodically start to take off what I need to get to the wiring. Strange I should favour the middle of the barren steppe over a town to work on my bike, but I've never worked well with someone looking over my shoulder.

I replace the fuse I blew last night, and I have power again. I get down to the starter button connections, I bypass them, and the bike fires up.

I may not know my bike inside out, but I know me, and I know when I work at my best—refreshed and alone. Electric faults require thought before they require tools. However, my celebration is premature.

The starter button works, and then it doesn't; it's rapidly turning into an intermittent electrical fault, the worst kind to try to track down. The Czech who is the mechanic of the crew and me spend the next three hours tracing wires, bypassing connector blocks, and getting nowhere. Despite no common language, we respect and understand each other's ability and work well together. I do discover several bolts that secure the engine in the frame have gone; those misplaced fasteners alone make it worth the struggle of removing a full 25 litre tank.

We try replacing my CDI, an expensive black electrical box, with my spare one. Do I want this to be the problem and use up my spare? The bike still doesn't start. I'm not sure if I'm relieved or not. The others are so patient; they pack up and make coffee and breakfast. I think my helper is going down the wrong route, so I

224

go and eat and leave him to it, as I would want to be left. Then when it is his turn to eat, I undo his work and the bike fires back up again, but it's not a victory, as we don't know what we've done. The entire operation has been pleasant and relaxed.

I pack up the bike and tell them I would like to buy them lunch if they have the time. They leave first, as their progress is slow. My bike is held together with ratchet straps, cable ties, and bungee cords, my boots with duct tape and glue, and I don't even want to think what's holding my underwear together. My hand ached all night and this morning from the wrenching of the tow rope. I am so filthy now: dust, dirt, sweat, and grease. My clothes, boots, jacket, and trousers, and even my sleeping bag, is filthy. My tent which was full of debris when I lifted it up to shake out the mess with my head inside it, stank too. I'm just a mess.

Those Czech girls were pretty, and I've never been so filthy; it's been the first female company for a while, and I'm minging. Out on the road my bike feels strong. Maybe it's the mounting bolts I replaced, maybe it's psychological, but it seems willing to press on, embarrassed at its little failure.

Within five minutes of hitting the road, there they are broken down and bonnets up. They insist we keep going. I've slowed Greg down enough already, and we ride the dirt into a black valley of rain. Last night's rain didn't turn the dirt to mud, it just laid the dust to rest.

Once again I'm riding alone. There is a broken down truck up ahead; I've learnt this is contact best avoided. The drivers are usually drunk whilst waiting recovery, and before now they have thrown stones or waved tyre irons. But as I approach this one, a woman walks across the track and flags me down. She appears to be no threat, and so I stop but keep my engine running. I'm unsure of her motives and my starter button's reliability.

She speaks good English. She just wants to have a chat, her daughter is in the cab. When she gets stuck on a word she shouts to her daughter, who translates in perfect newsreader English.

She tells me of the healthy lifestyle: everything is organic, no crop-enhancing chemicals in anything here—not the bread, meat, milk, or the arkhi, a fermented mare's milk that is sold on the side of the road. But it's true the crops and grass grow naturally and animals graze upon it, and it's all pure and chemical free. She tells me the scenery will get mountainous again, and the people here are good. I'm invited to eat with them; a stove is set up by the cab, but somewhere in the distance I have a riding buddy. I should probably catch him up and tell him what he missed today. It was a positive and informative little encounter, and I'm all the richer for it. Greg is up ahead, saving time that would have been better spent.

I've leant the Mongolian word for food and what the letters look like. It looks a bit like the word *ryan*, well it does to me. I see it painted on a piece of wood outside a ger. I'm hungry, it looks like rain, and I am dying to see the inside of one. Three opportunities in one, I'm taking them all.

The sky turns black as we go inside. I try to wash my hands at the little basin inside the door. My fingerless gloves have left them ingrained with dirt, blood, and stained with grease and oil, yet dry and cracked with windburn.

Inside the door I clumsily remove my boots; I think I have the attention of the entire ger. Hail and sunshine take it in turns to come through the roof. Carpets are hung from the walls. The kitchen area is nearest the door, where several women busily chop veggies and meat. Beyond the kitchen, beds continue around the circumference, with bright orange, painted wooden cupboards, desks, and dressing tables. If Genghis Khan was to walk into one today the only thing he wouldn't recognise from his childhood would be the solar panel outside, which charges the car batteries inside. Other than that, they've remained unchanged for centuries, they are ideal for the climate and lifestyle, and perfection cannot be improved upon.

A family have entered before us; they occupy the beds and every other area. The log burner is in the middle with a big pot on it (central heating). There is no menu, no choice, and no need. I'm hungry. They have food. I simply sit and wait my turn. It smells good, and when oblong stainless plates are served up with a kind of noodle and potatoes and onion with meat, it looks so yummy. I hope it tastes as good as it looks. But it's not for us. The other family ordered first. One of the diners speaks a little English.

"How much are your bikes worth?" I love to brag about my bargains. I couldn't make it sound cheaper without losing credibility, and still I'm not believed. He relays what I say to the others he sits with; they laugh and scoff, and he comes back with "They think you are not telling the truth." But I am. Just because you don't believe me doesn't mean it's not true.

He doesn't know the name of the animal we will be eating and does a little impression. Looks like a chipmunk to me. I run through every animal I have seen. He knows all the names. It's not cow or yak or horse or goat, and still he lifts his wrists to his chin, fingers pointing down, eyes wide, and sticks out his front teeth making a sucking noise with his saliva.

"Rabbit!"

"No, not a rabbit." I really don't know, but I'm enjoying this game. Maybe round the next corner we will see something at the side of the road meeting his description, only it will be wiping tears from its big sad eyes because we have just eaten its mate.

The stove is fuelled with wood and shit, and when one of the ladies empties her plastic water bottle she routinely opens the stove to put it in, then has second thoughts. Perhaps it's the presence of the foreigners. I give a little inner sigh of relief then she has third thoughts, the same as the first, and it's thrown into the flames anyway.

I'm so hungry, getting impatient, and then realise where I am. It feels so normal, relaxed, and comfortable; sitting on the floor, I lean back against the bed and appreciate the moment.

When the food is served it does not disappoint. It's perfect food for the weather. It feels like an English Saturday afternoon in November. All it lacks is a hypnotic football commentary on the TV, which has always induced sleep in me. I yawn and wait out the storm as the sides of the ger resist the flapping the wind outside tries to cause. It feels so normal in here. Babies are passed around and eventually put to the breast to keep them quiet. Family life goes on amidst the uninvited diners, who would occupy every corner, if only a round ger had corners. Bones with meat still on them are stored under a bed, and children of different ages stare with varying degrees of intrigue.

Two hours have passed since we arrived. Even Greg seems happy to be still. We ask for the bill, and the Czechs arrive. The mechanic gets under one of the cars, another breakdown. I order their lunch and pay the ger owner for six more meals. We can't wait another two hours.

Big waves goodbye. I'm being videoed and photographed as I pull away, but with one hand waving, I stall the bike. It jolts, and I lose my balance and fall off. Backwards roll, and I'm back up on my feet. Two steps forward, and I lift the bike up and get back on. You'd think I'd be getting better after all this time, but I'm just getting better at falling off. What an exit.

The rain has turned the road to mud, and it's really hard going; actually it's soft going, that's the problem. Ultimately it's slow going, especially at the bottom of a hill where all the water has gathered. I drop the bike a lot today. My stomach turns in a knot, and I need a toilet quickly. There is nothing out here at all. All I can do is ride off the track and squat by the side of my bike whilst my bottom explodes. I don't think at this point I could possibly get any more filthy. If the rain comes back, I'm just going to get naked and soap myself down in it, and then I'll have to put the same grimy clothes back on. But despite the low grey sky, the rain and hail are staying away, as does the need for another emergency bowel evacuation. The road returns to a level within my skill range.

There is a celebration on the horizon. My eyes are more focused on my mileometer than the ruts, bumps, and puddles, and at the moment it turns to 27,217 miles I stop, because I have just done my 10,000th mile. We toast vodka and take photos. I'm not looking my best, it has to be said, but somehow this mile marker is all the more authentic for the state I'm in. Greg puts a drop of vodka on his finger and offers it to the smile that Monklet has worn from the day we left. I pat my bike and toast to the next 10,000 before we set off again. It was quite emotional; I wasn't expecting it to be. Out here in the grassland of the Mongolian steppe with a herd of horses roaming just over yonder, I have travelled 10,000 miles from my garage. Not in a straight line, admittedly, but it was never about being direct, just a general movement in an easterly direction.

Back inside my helmet, I recall leaving my house and the first few miles and "Two little boys" comes back in my head. Aarggghh.

A VW camper van comes the other way, with Argentine plates. We both turn our heads as it passes, and now its Greg's turn to come off in some mud. The van stops and reverses back. The South American driver is all freaked out, "Are you OK?" We are taken aback by his concern.

"Yeah, we do it all the time." He is shocked by how blasé we are about it. We tell of the 10,000th mile and how we celebrated with vodka, and then it makes sense to all of us. Why we fall, why we feel no pain and don't even care. We ask if they have seen a river. Hygiene is top of the agenda now. They say they have seen a few.

When we travel on, all we see are dry dips in the land. If he thinks that's a river, he's going to have a shock when he comes to what we have crossed.

We are going to be camping au naturel again. Just as we are about to bump off the road towards some inviting pines, a moped carrying two locals comes the other way. The rider has a helmet on, but the pillion has long straggly hair and growths on his face. He swings a bottle of vodka in one hand and is clearly shit-faced. I'm pretty sure he had some of Genghis Khan's genes in him—not the fearless and calculated warrior bits, just the straggly hair and scary face, exactly the kind of guy who you don't want knowing where you are camped. We let them ride out of sight before we leave the road. The wet grassy ground has deep corrugations and gives the bikes a final battering of the day. I manage to stall mine as the rain that has been threatening all afternoon hammers down on me. And the starter decides to perform its intermittent failure. My tyre levers have fallen off from the vibration, and if I hadn't stalled here, I would never have noticed they were missing or known where to find them. Trying to bump the bike is futile, and as a rainbow bridges the valley the button performs again, and I bump over to flat pasture and the shelter of a pine forest, silent and out of the wind. I try to clean myself from the moisture of the grass, but total immersion is the only hope for me now.

Dinner resembles breakfast, and the sun sets like it rose, a sliver of bright red under a sky full of darkness.

Day 64

Wrong Side of White Lake, Mongolia, 136 Miles

It's a cold dawn. There is a frost on my tent, and from where I lie in my sleeping bag I can see the contours of the range of mountains below us. The valleys are filled with cloud, there are the first traces of an orange sky, above that the colours turn to deepest blue with wisps of night time clouds, and where the sky is still black there is a sliver of moon. If I move my head it looks like it's hanging from a pine tree branch, the last light on the Christmas tree, the cones have all gone out. I occupy myself trying to photograph it, but it's moving across the sky quicker than my tripod will move around my tent.

As the sky lightens it disappears, and if it were a competition Greg would be losing by another point. Being a bad sleeper can be so rewarding. The sun comes up, and my tent begins to steam. I read my guidebook, consult my map, and I formulate a plan.

Back a little way is a road that takes us past Mongolia's most sacred mountains, through valleys and ending in a ger camp with hot water and laundry facilities. It sounds like an ideal destination and a beautiful ride. I know I am going to really have to sell this well to blinkered Greg on his unstoppable mission.

We have coffee, which warms my tummy as the sun warms my bones. It's a beautiful morning; I take a breath and embark on my promotion of the scenic valley road and the prize at the end of it. "Sorry, did you think I asked for penetrative anal sex with you? Because that's the kind of reaction I would expect for such a request, especially with my lack of personal hygiene lately." He doesn't want to go any direction but east. What really annoys me is that he won't even look at the guidebook. He has no wish to even see what it is he is missing. He is just hell bent on getting to Ulan Bator. OK then, we will compromise. Up ahead is White Lake National Park. It is en route; we will stop there. I had read about

230

that too, and it sounds interesting. Lake, volcano, and mountains can't be bad. I think I'm trying to sell this compromise to myself now. There is an atmosphere now, and we pack up in silence. I really wanted to see that valley. Am I ever going to be here again?

When we first met and discussed our riding habits, budgets, and destinations the one thing that was never mentioned was our schedules. It's very important they are compatible too; I won't make that mistake again.

We find a smooth track that takes us back to the road, not the corrugations of last night. I really want to take a left and see that mountainous corridor. What's stopping me is nothing to do with commitment to Greg but the worry of not being able to pick my bike up when I drop it. I will drop it, it's a daily occurrence, and now I have my intermittent starter problem too.

So we head east. We come to a town, another western town with dusty streets and horses tied to posts outside general stores. I call my mum. She has applied for her Mongolian visa and has looked up flights. Based on the hotels I have seen, I think camping is a better option for comfort, although not really that practical for someone on a crutch.

We get food and fuel; I would like a Mongolian sim card. I would like to find someone who can fasten my top box securely. But again I feel pressured to keep on keeping on. I buy Greg a Snickers as a peace offering. Just in time, because my bike won't start, and we have to bump it. It's not a relaxing way to ride or a stylish way to leave the town.

At last we come to a river; it's wide and clean, and there is a track we can ride our bikes down. There is even a little sandy beach. It's been a long time coming. Modesty is out of the question. I don't care who is looking from the road. I strip off. The sun is warm, but the wind is cold. It doesn't matter. I'm too dirty and too desperate. I go in up to my knees and wash away a week's worth of road grime. It feels so good. I grab my sarong and dry in the sun.

Further down is a pool of shallow water still fed by the river but still and shallow. I learn a valuable lesson, a little too late. It's pretty bleeding obvious really; you'd think there'd be a sign. Still shallow water warms in the sun. It's like a bath, a cool bath, but next to a mountain river it's practically a sauna. I wash my hair in it and then my clothes, then use the river to rinse. The great thing about being so dirty is the relief when you are clean again. I strap my clean wet clothes to my bike. The problem occurs when I put the same filthy bike clothes back on. My hands get dirty as soon as I touch them.

It's no fun wondering every time I turn off my ignition if the bike is going to start again. This time it does, so I can turn my thoughts to how annoyed I am by riding at this speed. I decide tomorrow I will let him go ahead. I'm not doing this anymore; I want a few days off. My bike needs it, and I need it.

I know I need it because when I go through a village and see a kid hitching I ignore him. Usually in a happier frame of mind I would at least wave. Around the corner is a bridge. Before it the mud track has an embankment on either side.

To avoid the muddy rut I go to the left of it and too close to the embankment. My pannier makes contact, and the bike stops dead. I don't though; I keep my momentum and am flung forward off the bike, which hits the ground hard. I'm OK, but the bike has suffered this time. The pannier is bent out of shape, as is the rack; it sticks out at an angle now. The mirror has smashed, and the toilet brush holder tool box is crushed and bent. We lift it up; I can't even do that alone. It's shit. I'm in a really bad mood now; I hate to see my bike getting destroyed. The lid won't fit on the pannier now, and the bastard won't start. We push it to the wooden bridge and bump start it there. I can't do this on my own, and I don't want to do it with Greg. Every time I think I'm going to leave, I find I'm reliant on the company.

I try to find something positive in this predicament. If the bike does make it to UB, it probably won't make it much further. Will it get me back to Europe? I don't know; to Vladivostok? Every day I agonise over this dilemma.

I'm mourning the damage to my bike. I always said I just want to get to Ulan Bator. It all depends on what breaks first: bike, body, or budget. My shock is shot to bits; it bottoms out constantly. I suppose if anything has to break it's best it's the bike, isn't it? It's a hard choice. I just feel sad because it's the end of the trip. I should feel happy because the mission has been accomplished.

There are so many tracks heading in the same direction. Greg, as always, is out of sight. Sometimes I see his tyre track in the mud and know he's up there somewhere. It's not a guarantee, because a track can branch off over a hill and surreptitiously take you in the wrong direction. The sun is out; I'm clean and warm. I should be happy, but I'm not. Up ahead Greg has stopped, as if he could see my need to be cheered up. I've never been good at hiding my feelings. He has stopped by a ger camp where four little girls are standing at the side of the road very obediently. They have clearly been told not to stand on the dirt track but to stay on the grass.

Before I left England I tried desperately to think of something that I could carry that I could give to the local children, something light and typically English.

"Teabags?" said my mother.

"Oh yeah, I can really see their faces light up when I produce a perforated bag of dust out of my tank bag, 'Oooh, but hold on girls, look it's round, and this one is pyramid shaped.'" Chocolate wouldn't travel well. Postcards? Stickers? I opted for friendship bracelets, although they actually came from Indonesia. Another great money-making plan that never happened. I have, since then, met people who give balloons, which I thought was quite a good idea, but the best, although I'm not sure how practical it would be, was a mini photo printer. Take the photo of the locals and give them a permanent keepsake. In a lot of places I've been, I bet they don't have a single photo of their kids, loved ones, and next-of-kin. But I don't have a printer. I only have woven bracelets, and they are a hit. I try to get them to stand by Monklet for a photo and smile, but the smiles are not forthcoming. I dig in my tank bag for bracelets, like Santa looking through the sack on my sleigh. What a great reaction I get. I couldn't take those beaming smiles away with a dead kitten. As I leave, every time I look behind, their newly-decorated wrists are still in the air waving. And now I feel better again.

My ears pop from a change in altitude. I'm not sure whether it's up or down. That's the difference between a throttle and pedals.

Judging by the lack of trees and the cold wind blowing down my cuffs I'm guessing it's up. I expect snowy mountains any minute.

We pass a lot of *ryan* signs without stopping. Greg speeds past them all. It's gone 4 P.M. now, and we haven't had any lunch. When another little community full of promise has been ignored and we are safe from any possible delays or distractions, Greg stops at the side of the track. He asks how I'm doing. My top box, tyres, and clothes bag have fallen off again.

"Not that good actually," and then the dummy flies out of my mouth, the frustration of missing everything in my guidebook. Hurtling to a destination, missing the journey, a bike that's falling apart, the hunger. "I'm sick of this," I kick my top box, hovering above the ground caught on a strap. "I'm fed up of doing this speed, missing everything, I need to go it alone." It all comes out wrong, wrong time, wrong way. I've been good; I kept my mouth shut so often this trip. It doesn't justify my behaviour now, but it proves tantrums fix nothing, they only make things worse. And on top of that we have a fucking audience. I pull my bike apart not looking at anyone. How do you get an audience on top of a barren mountain?

I bang my pannier back into shape, so at least the lid seals now. I take off my seat. I have already come up with a way of bypassing my starter button. I didn't intend to do it here, but under the circumstances I need a bike that will start. Greg could ride off any minute, and I wouldn't blame him. I take off my seat and dig through my pannier to find my spare wire. This could be done so much better without the black mood and the awkward silence. A herder on horseback comes to watch; he dismounts and holds onto his nervous horse. He stands too close, and every time I get up the horse freaks out, and he pulls at its reins to stop it rearing up. I ignore him.

Anger and how not to do motorcycle mechanics. I could write a book about it, or maybe put up a warning sign. Bad karma-canics, go away.

I put a wire from the live of the battery; bypass the block connectors, switch, and relay; and touch it straight to the solenoid, and the bike fires up. The horse rears up and runs off, and the herder runs after it. I don't care; I got my bike to start again. I should care; in fact I do. It's not until later, though, when it's too late for apologies, and I still feel bad about it now, when I think of my first man on horseback when I entered the country and then how I behaved just now. I'm the petulant backpacker on the Indian train who needs a slap and a ticket home.

It's time for a change. I feel relieved now I can start my bike again. I apologise to Greg, I would to the herder too, but he's running across the steppe after his horse. Shit, sorry Mr. Herder. I re-strap everything on the bike, and we are ready to go.

Some tourists in a tour van had stopped to watch as well as I went about my grumpy duties, but still they want a photo before we leave. I'm really embarrassed about my behaviour. And in keeping with the laws of the cosmos after all this work I have done on the bike, it starts on the starter button and continues to for the rest of the day.

We stop for beer; they only have two-litre plastic bottles, and it's not cheap. English prices. We buy one each and carry on. I'm ahead for once, and I hear him hoot. I look around and realise my tyres and top box are about to fall off again. But that's not why he wanted my attention. His beer fell off his bike and exploded, so he's going to go back for another one. It gives me a chance to refasten everything again. It's all I seem to have done today, fasten and refasten my luggage. I'm so tired of it; do I even need to carry these tyres if I'm so near the end of my trip?

Greg returns, and we set off again, and then my beer comes off. It punctures as soon as it hits the ground; a fountain of frothy beer spurts out over the road. I don't even stop. What's the point? It's wasted. As is my money.

We continue towards the National Park of White Lake, and then Greg's other beer comes off. For such a soft road they always find a rock to puncture on. That's such a waste of money. It wasn't even cheap beer. We have wasted six litres of the stuff between us, but I guess that's just the way this day is going.

The road is awful, full of potholes; my forks are banging and my shock keeps bottoming out on this brutal road. There comes a point towards the end of the day when you're really feeling at your most fatigued. As the sun goes down behind you, the shadows disguise the potholes. Too tired to take evasive action, I pound down one after another. I don't mind going slow in mud, but this road is wide. It appears good, which gives the impression we are going even slower than we are. Greg stops at a small store for a beer. I have to admire his determination, but they have none; it's just not meant to be today.

We have a good dinner to eat tonight, all the fresh veggies I bought this morning. It would be so good to accompany it with beer. He is up ahead, I stop one last time, and it's even more expensive. I fasten it well and carry on. White Lake comes into view. Rather than going into the park today, and because it's nearly dark, we opt for a track that takes us to a patch of pine trees. It's not ideal, but we need to get off the road. We have both had enough of it for one day. I pull up behind Greg and park my bike; he looks at my pannier with the two litres of beer strapped on top of it. The look on his face is priceless.

"But you dropped your beer?"

"Yes, and then I stopped and got another one."

So we have a drink, and I apologise again for earlier. I'm cold; I've got a chill I can't get rid of. This is what happens when you don't stop for lunch. I put on my thermals and get in the shelter of his tent. I don't even want beer after all that effort. I stuff down the pasta too quick to taste or enjoy it—too hungry, too cold. I go to my tent.

Nothing tragic happened today, just frustrating, just annoying. It has to be fixed; I want to be on my own.

And that's the bottom line.

DAY 65

TSETSERLEG, MONGOLIA, 143 MILES

That was a cold night. My sleeping bag is done up like a straight jacket. My tent is wet on the inside from the moisture of my breath. It's a bad habit I have, this breathing in the night. It makes everything damp.

The sun rises at the same angle as the hill we are camped behind, so there is no benefit gained by it, other than light, of course. A truck rumbles up the hill and parks close by, three lumberjacks, well loggers I suppose they are, here to take the logs that have already been cut down. They are rolled down the hill recklessly and loaded on the truck. Not a towering pile that needs to be roped down, just enough to fill the bed of the truck, and off they go. Well they can't be accused of being greedy, maybe just lazy. It looks like they might be back, so we leave last night's beer for them by their table stump. I hope they appreciate the effort we went to to get it.

I clasp my hands around my coffee and slurp it quickly. Side stand bread and sausage for breakfast. Like the weather, it's dry and cold, but still filling.

We ride to the road. I see a couple of backpackers actually backpacking. Up until now I have only seen them squashed into the back of vans. Seeing some out in the open is rare, and its the first time I've thought, "Oooh, that's looks fun." Fresh morning, self-contained, off for a hike up a mountain.

There are plenty of tracks along the side of the lake, and soon the little town of Tariat appears on the left, the gateway into the National Park. I branch off to the left, and Greg keeps on his path going straight past. I'm not sure what he's thinking, maybe I am. I'm not going after him. This is the town, this is the compromise. Remember the compromise? The reason we are not in the valley of sacred mountains is because of my compromise to come here. As he continues on, I look over my shoulder at him and he looks at me. If you think compromise is riding past yet another place of beauty you're wrong. I ride into the square, the customary dirt and a gathering of wooden shacks. I go into the store, get water, and wait. I read my guidebook and wait, I get stared at and wait. I ride out to the main road and wait. Then come back and take another route out of town. There is no sign of him anywhere. Where the hell has he gone? I'm ready to split company, but he has my map, the one I can read and pronounce the names. I use it for cross- reference; he doesn't use it at all. I go back to the main road and stop at the highest point and decide I will give him an hour. I use the time constructively. I put oil in my bike and my chain oiler, I download photos to my notebook and do all those things I have not had time to do. That alone feels quite good to do. I listen for his engine note over the sound of the mopeds and then realise I don't actually know what his engine note sounds like; he's always so far up ahead. I ride up the road a bit and decide he must be gone. Oh well, it's not the ideal way to part, but it's happened now. He's not waiting for me, and I'm not looking for him any longer. I ride back to town and ride around in circles. I'm a bit indecisive. I try to formulate a plan. I've got to adjust to riding by myself again, which I am looking forward to. It's just there was no transition period. By giving up looking and chasing, I am now a solo rider again. Due to indecision, rather than intention, I find myself inside the National Park. I see some cyclists, a good-looking Spanish couple. I ask what's the park like; they ask where I am going. I don't know. I think I need to stop for a bit.

I pass volcanic rock that's scattered across the valley floor and has young pines growing up out of it; I wonder when that last eruption happened. I'm riding so carefully, I'm nearly falling off from lack of speed. It's how I perform when I'm being watched; screwing up something I can do perfectly well. The simplest things become an adventure again now I'm on my own. I approach my first solo river crossing; I psyche myself up beyond a level that is useful and go through, managing to fill both my boots again. One day I'll look down and see exactly how that happens. My front wheel seems to have the ability to fan out the water it displaces at the perfect angle to soak me. Bloody trials bike. The Ducati would never do that to me.

I ride down to the lake, past ger camps. The individual gers all lined up neatly with concrete paths leading to the entrances and on to netball courts. This is not why I came. I want wilderness, not the catered for tourist, sterile experience. I suppose this diversion has performed its objective, I'm one again. I go down to the lake, strip, and wash. I seem to have lost all my inhibitions now, I just strip off. I don't even look to see if there is anyone around. I sit in the sun on the banks of the lake, dry off, and read my guidebook until I've got a plan. I'm not staying here. I don't like it. I will head east, but slowly. If I make the town I want to visit fine, if not no worries.

I have a big hill to go up. It didn't seem so big from the other direction. I'm aware again of my vulnerabilities and want to keep my independence. I cross the river much better on the way back and ride to the base of the volcano. I could climb it and view the volcanic lake at the top, but securing everything on the bike seems like too much effort. I turn around and head back out of the park and out of town. I go past the point I waited and head east. All the tracks, and there are a lot of them, start to converge, until its one well-travelled route that leads to a bridge, a single bridge with no other alternative way to cross the river. Where the concrete starts there is a pile of rocks laid out in an arrow, and at the point of the arrow is a piece of paper. A bystander flags me down. I'm not sure I would have stopped otherwise. The paper has my name on it. This is where Greg waited. The note says he wasn't sure if I was ahead or behind, says he waited here, and is now going to Ulan Bator. Well there's the contact. I don't know what he thought about the park. I don't think he ever wanted to go. Well he can happily steam on ahead now, unstoppable: he always was.

I pass the cyclists. They hold out their hands in a confused recognition, half stop, half don't, kind of way. I wonder if they spoke to Greg or read the note. I bet they are really confused. I'm not about to enlighten them with the truth. I've got somewhere to go.

I had read about a gorge; I head to the gorge; I get to the gorge; I stop and eat a sandwich at the gorge; I take photos of the gorge; and just as I'm ready to leave the gorge, a van-load of noisy tourists turns up. Well, I timed that just right. I had my fifteen minutes of solitude. It was a great little picnic spot. I do everything so much quicker now I'm back on my own. Some people travel in groups because they are missing someone. All I was missing was my own company. It feels good to have it back. Once again, the irony of breaking free of people who travel in a hurry, and when I do, I do things quicker without them being around.

Some people might say spending fifteen minutes at a gorge indicates a short attention span. I think it's just an efficient way of using time. I have plenty of it. For me, an uninterrupted, peaceful fifteen minutes to sit, contemplate, photograph, and listen to the river flow down below me is the perfect way to experience it. I bet not one person who spewed from the tourist van, even if it stopped for an hour, got to have the experience I had. Maybe they wouldn't have wanted it. In which case we are all happy.

After a while I come to pristine smooth black road. It's not meant to be ridden on. There are mounds of stones preventing access to it. After what I have experienced in western Mongolia, any attempt to make a road impassable is pointless. It's not too tricky to bump over the mound. It's such a treat. I had forgotten how it was to ride a road and not give it my full attention. I can ride so much quicker into the rain storm ahead now. With smooth roads and tourist ger camps, the Wild West feel has gone. The closer I get to the capital, the more evidence there is of the modernisation that has rippled out. Buses have backpacks strapped on their roofs with pasty faces obscured by condensation peering out of the windows. They display a look of what I like to think is envy. If it is, in a few years time those backpacks will be exchanged for panniers and the sew-on patches for stickers, and this smooth road will be on a Sat Nav programme. I may be a bit late to catch this country untamed, but I'm only just in time. I miss the challenge of the dirt, but while I have a choice I will opt for smooth road over bumps.

Every time my thoughts turn to, what next? I just keep saying to myself Ulan Bator. Just get there. And it works really well. I should have done this weeks ago. It instantly puts my mind at ease. I stop thinking about all the possibilities and go back to focusing on the original goal.

The road is not complete. I come to a smoothed area, which is yet to have its last layer laid. There are miles of piles of chippings. I can just get down the side of them, scraping my panniers as I squeeze past. I'm not sure I'm making this easy on myself or whether I should just give up and go back to the tracks. I'm experiencing every stage of road building. Next comes the smooth black top, sprayed with a liquid tar awaiting its last layer to be stuck on top. Another bump over another mound designed to prevent me from another unfinished surface. As my tyres get soaked in the bitumen, the adhesive surface starts to pick up stones, and they fly off my tyres and stick on my windshield. When a piece of road ends, I go back to the dirt, and every time it looks rideable, I bump up to the new surface and overtake the cars that struggle over the rutted and muddy path at the side. I tend to bottom out as I go over these mounds of prevention. As long as I have enough momentum as the front wheel dives down, I slide on my engine sump protector and see-saw over until the back wheel makes contact and drives me over and onwards. If I go too slow, I get stuck, with the bike pivoting on its belly, and I rock back and forth trying to make the rear wheel make contact and get me off of my temporary pedestal, whilst the cars I passed pass me, no doubt laughing at my predicament. I know I would be.

Ironic really. You can ride absolutely anywhere in this country, no fields, no crops, no fences, you make your own path, but find a proper road, and you're prevented from using it.

The new road becomes inaccessible, and I go back to the track. It's a good surface, and my confidence has reached new levels. I'm riding hard and drifting on the corners in control and loving it. I would never have thought when I wallowed out of my driveway I would be riding in this style. When I overtake buses I give it an extra fist full of throttle to relieve the monotony of the passengers' journey. Well that's my reasoning anyway. It could just be indulging myself in feeling the power of my engine. As I'm hammering along, my right foot comes off the peg and kicks the ground. I look down; there is no right peg. I stop. Both stainless steel bolts have sheared off, and the peg has gone. But that's not all; I look in horror as I realise that the wet bitumen I rode through has gone everywhere. It's covered the engine, it's in-between all the cooling fins, all over the cables, the callipers, the tank, and headlight, it's stuck in the folds of the fork gaiters and covered the rear shock, the panniers are pebble-dashed, it flung up over the top box, and the back light and number plate are smothered. The inside of the mudguards are coated, and even Monklet has splats on his face. It's a disaster.

I'm so annoyed at myself for mistreating something that has treated me so well: it was so unnecessary. Not only is my foot peg missing, but those sheered bolts also hold the centre stand on. Now that, too, is hanging and putting strain on the bolts that hold the other foot peg on.

The bike is so filthy and sticky it is impossible to work on. I walk back and retrieve my foot peg. It wasn't easy to find but not having any pillion pegs, because the pannier rack mounts where they would go, it's really quite important that I get it back.

So I continue with just one peg, dangling my leg. I try to balance it on the brake pedal without pushing it down, but that doesn't work. I was so stupid for riding through that bitumen; you'd think they'd have had a sign.

I have one bolt holding my left peg on, and when that breaks my centre stand will fall off. I know it's only a matter of time. As I bump past some road works, the last bolt sheers. My feet hit the ground, as does the centre stand and peg. I stop and walk back to pick them up. A road worker is standing by them pointing, "Yes, I know, thank you very much." I stomp back to the bike and strap the sticky, bitumen-covered stand to a sticky, bitumen-covered pannier.

It's thirty miles to the town I intended to stop at; the road is finished and accessible. I ride at 60mph for the first time in this country. My feet are dangling, and when my legs get tired, I balance my feet on the sub frame bolts. Two little half inch protrusions from the side of a smooth frame. I look like a jockey heading for a photo finish.

I thought stainless steel was supposed to be tough, that's why I replaced the standard bolts with the stainless ones. It is tough, it's tough to drill, but it's also brittle. It won't stand the impact like the standard ones would have. I do still have the original ones with me, but I have to get the sheered stainless steel studs out first.

It's a sad sight, tar-covered bike bits strapped on everywhere.

On this last bit of road into town, sealed and smooth, for the first time I am able to ride and think about something other than the road. My left hand picks tar out of Monklet's fur. Was it some subconscious deliberate abuse to indicate destination reached, mission accomplished. It's really depressing, and it shouldn't be. I should be euphoric. I sat in my trailer all winter planning a bike ride to Mongolia, and I've bloody done it. Where is the sense of achievement? I think it's trapped under a layer of tar.

In theory, I could just abandon my bike and take the Trans-Siberian train home. It would be pleasant enough, but I'm not going to abandon my bike. It was always prepared in such a way that as a last resort I could, but I'm not out of options yet.

The last twenty miles, instead of taking the usual Mongolian hour, take an effortless twenty minutes.

I go straight to the guesthouse I was recommended weeks ago that is run by an English couple and does bacon and egg butties. But they have no rooms left. So I go to the hotel next door. My bike is locked in a shed; they have no showers, so I have no shower. I scrub the tar off my hands under the cold water in the communal sink. When I go back to the bacon and egg guesthouse, the restaurant is closed. So I wander around the town. There is nowhere to eat. My hotel has a night club in the basement; it has pounding music, primary-colour flashing lights, and tinfoil visuals. It's the only place in town still serving food, and I'm the only one in the place.

So I sit alone, drinking warm beer from a can and eating a stir fry at my table, next to an empty dance floor under strobing disco lights. It's a very strange environment. I half want to get up and just jump around the deserted dance floor like a deranged idiot. Dance as if nobody is watching. Nobody is. Apart from the cook and the two girls behind the bar, there is no one else to embarrass myself to. It would be funny; I don't think there is a risk of someone spiking my unattended beer whilst I'm strutting my stuff. But I will be staying here a few days, and if I play the super stud disco king dancing fool tonight, tomorrow will not result in the kind of stud extraction I'm looking for.

Day 66

The night was deadly silent; it's so good to be alone. For a person who is always craving the opposite to what he has, it's a change to actually be satisfied with my lot. And right now I am, I have missed this. For the last four weeks I've been in the company of others almost constantly. It's no wonder I'm in need of a break. "Everything in moderation, including moderation," my party friend says when she wants to excuse our excessiveness.

So I go back to the guesthouse next door to give it another chance. All the tables are piled with dirty dishes, and the place is full of squawking Americans noisily finishing their breakfast and preparing to cram their ample bodies into the herd of 4x4s with diplomatic plates that are parked outside.

They have the air of the oblivious-to-the-environment US traveller about them. Taking the States with them as they go, eating buttermilk pancakes, Ray-Bans perched on their heads. Their smart shirts and relaxed-fit dress pants are freshly-laundered, ironed, and crisp from air-conditioned travel; clean, comfortable, and sensible loafers. Hearing background voices I understand is strange and annoying. Well, when I say background, it's more an obnoxious wall of chatter, which without the distraction of company, I can give my full annoyance to.

The owner comes over when the last loafer has stepped over his threshold. He apologises for the mess as he clears my table. He has a caring nature, and although I get the impression there isn't a request he hasn't heard or predicament he hasn't seen, he is interested and helpful. More than I dared hope, in fact. Getting a good write-up in the *Lonely Planet* is usually the kiss of death, but the English couple who run this place do so in a friendly, helpful, considerate way. Best of all, it's not done in the money-grabbing—every service has a surcharge—kind of way. He says there is no mechanic to speak of in town, but I am welcome to use his yard and facilities. I haven't even booked a room here yet. I order my long-awaited and much-anticipated bacon and egg butty and eat it too quickly. I'm anxious to get my stuff out of my room and bring it over here to reception until a room becomes vacated and cleaned for me. Then I get my bike out of the shed and ride it over into their yard and find a shady spot where I can work on it.

I take my tools out of my split, crushed, and bitumen-covered toilet brush holder. Then get petrol out of my tank and clean up the tools and all around the area where the sheered bolts are.

The first one comes out easily, easier that I expected. Then I get an onlooker; it turns out he is the maintenance man. After a little observation, he wanders off and comes back with a little screwdriver to help with the extraction. I cut a groove in the bolt with my hacksaw, and the second bolt is out. The next one is too recessed to cut a groove in. It takes a long time. With the speed of an hour hand, it slowly rotates until I can get a grip on it and twist it out the rest of the way. The fourth one has come out en route. Well that's a relief.

The wife comes out to say hello. I try to avoid the conversation she has been having for the last seventeen years, like how long have you been here? And after she tells me, I congratulate her on not adopting the complacency so associated with becoming the *Lonely Planet's* pet.

I continue to clean all the bitumen off; it's a slow and messy operation. The maintenance man has a drill, and I bolt my top box back into place. All the things that have bent, broken, or just deteriorated since I rode with company are now being fixed. I remove the toilet brush holder: Mongolia was too much for it. I have a little CamelBak water container that I have never used. The water in it always tasted funny. It becomes the new tool bag.

It's like meditation; I can focus my thoughts as I restore my bike. I can consider location, destination. All I needed was some time off the road. Dirty hands and shiny wheels, and a bit of me-time is very good for peace of mind.

A gregarious, piss-taking Londoner bounds over; I'm amazed at how quickly I can turn the sarcasm back on. It's been absent for a while. He used to live here, is back to visit after twelve years away. "The place has changed so much," he says. I tell him how I'm recently reunited with my own company and how I lost the Swiss guy. "Did he ride in lederhosen?" he asks. When I mention the French guys on Urals he wonders why I spoke to the French guys at all. He loves his stereotyping, this bloke. He says how this place is based on the church and was originally founded to teach the locals building and carpentry skills but then evolved into a guesthouse. I said I had the feeling it somehow had Christian connections. He asks me how, and I flounder for non-stereotypical observations. He says he will buy me a coffee when I've finished and goes off to take the piss out of someone else.

Later I have a luxurious hot shower, my first in ten days, and the room is lovely: thick duvets with covers that match the IKEA towels. Even a little complimentary cookie.

I have a coffee with the piss-taker; he tells me where I can find a mirror and what the word for it is in Mongolian. He tells me of the Mongolians he met in England, illegal immigrants, and how, with the help of his church, he took them in. Then he asks if I'm spiritual at all. Oh right, I think to myself, here it comes, get ready for the conversion. I nip the conversation in the bud in a well-rehearsed, inoffensive but firm reply I have developed for Jehovah's Witnesses and other preachers. It works like a charm, and we move on to other issues.

I get a text from my mum; she is still waiting on her visa and will be over next week some time.

I bring some beer back to my lovely room. I'm going to stick around for a while, see some of the town, get some culture, visit the museum, climb to the monastery, and see if I can find the statue of Buddha, because I'm not looking for God.

Day 67

Tsetserleg, Mongolia, 0 Miles

I get up from under a big fresh duvet, have a hot shower, and go downstairs for coffee and scrambled eggs on toast. I seem to have temporarily left Mongolia; I'll appreciate it all the more when I go back into it. It's so much better to want to do something than have to do it, and I want a little rest. I know it won't be long before I miss my bike and want a little ride.

I've got the company of the charismatic Christian again. He asks how I financed my trip, mainly because all other topics of conversation seem to hit dead ends. I decided to tell him about the *Deal or No Deal* thing. That topic chugged along a little longer than the others before it spluttered into another silence. Thank God for Noel Edmonds.

I don't really see why it's OK to make fun of the stereotypes of various nationalities, but not the God-fearing. I think taking the piss out of yourself is your rite of passage to taking it out of others. Seems like double standards to me. But that's the hypocrisy of people who love to vocalise their religious beliefs. It's like a penis: it's OK to have one, it's OK to be proud of it, but don't go ramming it down people's throats.

So I wander off to the market to look for my mirror. When I get onto the main road, I see a KTM rider stopped and looking at his map. I run up and say hello. For some ridiculous reason I need to prove my credibility, and I wave my smashed mirror around to show I'm a motorcyclist too. Luckily for me, he is a non-judgemental Belgian. He has come from Ulan Bator, The Oasis guesthouse the Germans in Kazakhstan had told me about. He hadn't seen them, probably long gone by now, but he had seen Greg, which is kind of funny in a relieved sort of way. The place sounds expensive and a Mecca for overlanders. I'm not sure I'm in any hurry to experience that.

He has some trick little accessories on his bike. Incidentally, he has soft luggage, the first rider I have seen without aluminium panniers. I wonder where he puts his stickers. I particularly liked the cable ties that stuck out the ends of the handle bars to remind him of the width of his luggage. If I had them I wouldn't be heading off to market now in search of a mirror.

We have a drink together; he modestly mentions this is a short trip for him; he previously rode around the world for a year or so. He tells of the company he had through the Gobi Desert, how an American in his 60s kept coming off and slowing the rest of them down but wouldn't admit his inabilities. He put the guilt on the others; he is in a hospital in the capital now after a really bad fall. It was clearly something he needs to vent about. I enjoy the venomous accusations; I hate the old guy already.

Refreshed and vented we say goodbye, and I go and look for a mirror. It was very easy. The market has so much mechanical stuff. Annoyingly, all the spares I brought with me are available here. It's like an auto jumble. It's almost frustrating I don't need anything else. I walk round the stalls looking at bike bits and miscellaneous tools. The only thing it lacks is good ol' boys in waxed Belstaffs with flat caps with rollies hanging out of their mouths, talking about obscure British bikes I have never heard of. Instead, the Mongolian equivalent is the nomadic herder with riding boots and long coats tied with a scarf, still with the obligatory cigarette and looking at shock absorbers for Yamaha mopeds. One shop, well I say "shop," they are mainly twenty-foot containers with a counter at the front, behind which are lines of shelves leading into the dark depths where all the good bits lie under a layer of dust, forgotten about, unused and under-priced. Well that's how it is in my fantasies. In reality there is probably a big spider and yak meat. But I do find a Mongolian flag sticker, and now my day is complete. Oh joy, what a conversation piece this will be. It's also very big, perfect for someone who doesn't adhere to the adhesive pastimes of the masses. It is just the Mongolian flag, it doesn't say anything; actually it says "cynical hypocrite."

I also, for the first time, consider the idea of owning some Mongolian riding boots.

I have a wonderfully cynical friend who, when we wastedly wander around the stalls selling dippy hippy clothing, which looks so good from behind blood shot eyes in a festival environment, always says as we try on our ponchos and purple patchwork jackets, "Would you wear it in the Elephant's Head?" It always brings a touch of rationalisation and sensibility before the impulsive purchasing of such impractical clothing. But I think when I go for my next session up in Camden, I might like to put on my Mongolian riding boots and be able to pull it off. I'll let the idea incubate for a while.

On the way back I stop by an Internet café and find I'm very popular on Facebook. Coincidently, during the summer break, reruns have been played, and I was on *Deal or No Deal* last night. Wait till I tell my sunbeam friend.

Back in the yard of the hotel, a trials bike has turned up. I look for the number plate, but it's missing, along with the back light and any indication as to its origin.

At dinner I meet the owner. Well, temporary owner. He flew in, rented a bike, strapped his backpack on the back, and took off. How refreshing. A real adventurer, spontaneous and impulsive. His name is unpronounceable, so I call him Number 6 after his room key. We go to the night club, drink heavily, talk constantly, and laugh raucously.

I once met a man who said of his departed friend, "The only time she spoke bad of you was to your face." Meaning, "Tell the person it concerns their faults, not everyone else." I would love to have someone say that of me at my funeral, but the speaker is as likely to say that as to say, "He had an extensive collection of stickers," but I do try to bear it in mind. However, much like the Belgian today, I needed to vent, and once I started to mention the Touratech twins I couldn't shut my mouth. I probably should have gone and danced off my fury. Once more the dance floor was empty. Will this opportunity ever present itself again?

DAY 68

TSETSERLEG, MONGOLIA, 0 MILES

I contemplate dragging myself up out of bed and down to the all-inclusive breakfast, which is coincidently my hangover food of choice. I've faced greater challenges; I've endured hardships that make this descent to the restaurant seem like a sleep in the park, on a bench with nothing but a limp wrist for a pillow. What does not kill me will only make me stronger, and I won't feel the pain of the thing that does. Seems to me based on that theory that I can't possibly lose. As I stuff my feet into stinking, ripped, and uncomfortable trainers, I trip past the door that says "Number 6" on it and, therefore, must contain a body that feels like mine but hasn't the will or strength to move. The breakfast was worth the effort and so was the ascent back to my bed.

It's time for some culture. It would be wrong to deny myself any longer. I am going to experience something. God dammit! The fresh air will do me good. The experience will enlighten me, and I will return a better man for it—informed and knowledgeably a man of wisdom and understanding, and hopefully I'll have cleared this hangover too.

It's a cloudy and windy morning. I need money. I take my needs to the bank; they put their needs first. My luxurious $100 bill is rejected because of an insignificant rip in the corner. I produce another until they find one they like, then in a petty way, I reject a note they give me because it, too, has a rip in it. The bankers fail to see the humour. Double standards again, silly them.

Then, with Iron Maiden blasting out my iPod, I walk the steps to the Buddah statue. I look down at the town. The experience would be all the better if I had bothered to bring my camera or wear more than just a T-shirt. It wasn't exactly spiritual, but I do miss my bike now. Perhaps it's the physical exertion. Well this is bloody cold. I go back down and try to get into the museum, but it appears to be locked. Culture is eluding me. I'm just not that good at getting it; it's the bane of my life.

I'm going back to my room. On my way I see another KTM; they are popping up like mushrooms. Where is this one from? It's that American from Semey who caught my Tourettes. How irritating.

I've got a duvet calling. I doze for a while.

What's that noise? I know that noise; it's the Touratech twins. What the fuck? The procession is back. My alternative route was fail safe, out of step out on the steppe. But I fell victim to the desire of the bacon butty, and I have to pay the price. The magnetism of the frying rashers brought the hordes into town.

Early dinner I think.

The American and the Touratech twins come in. They don't appear nearly as disheartened by this as I am. Is my solitude such a rare desire?

Number 6 comes down: he's not well.

Listen, you know those people I was telling you about last night, well don't remember, OK. This is them; it's unfortunate.

With blatant brazenness, I ask the Touratech twins for copies of the photos. Well I may as well get something out of this reunion. As last month's memoirs download onto a memory stick, my mum texts me. She has her visa and Trailfinders kept her tentative reservation open. She leaves tomorrow and will arrive in thirty-six hours. FUCK, OK time for some selflessness. Tomorrow I will get on my newly-restored bike first thing in the morning and ride to Ulan Bator and be at the airport to meet her.

DAY 69

ULAN BATOR, MONGOLIA, BY MINIVAN

Next morning, bright and early, I pull open the curtains before the alarm even goes off, to find early is all it is; the sky is low and very wet. Undeterred, I have one more hot water shower, one more rubdown with an IKEA towel, and one more sandwich. I pack up the bike, which is now fully maintained and restored, if not to its pre-Mongolian condition. At least the parts are bolted into their relevant positions, as opposed to strapped and bungeed onto the top of panniers. I say my goodbyes, and in freshly-laundered clothes I go into the pissing wet morning, sit on my soggy sheepskin seat, and press the starter. The engine turns over...and over...and over and doesn't fire. I check the obvious, kill switch, etc., and still nothing. Bugger. I decide the best option under the circumstances is to hope harder and keep pressing the start button. Nothing; check the petrol. Yep, seems to have some. I didn't use it all up getting off the tar. OK, so I wheel it back into the yard, but there is no shelter at all. In a futile attempt, I hang my poncho over a washing line and kneel on a plastic bag. I'm sweating on the inside and getting soaked by the relentless rain on the outside. A row of raindrops hang off my open visor. The next thing to do is check for a spark, but to do that I have to remove my over-size tank. That means I have to take off side panels and seat, but to take off the seat, I now have to take off the spare tyres, which means taking off the top box, which now, due to a broken lock, has to be emptied of sleeping bag, tent etc. and unbolted. All this to remove the tank to get to the spark plug. Fuck that. Not in this weather, in a muddy puddle yard, it is not going to happen. This is not fixing weather. This is plan B weather.

"When does the bus leave to Ulan Bator?" I ask one of the ever-helpful staff

"8 A.M." It is now 8.30.

"But there is a minivan at 2 P.M. Maybe you can get that. You have to buy ticket now, you want? I go buy one for you."

250

No, I don't want, I want my bike to start, but I have to be in Ulan Bator tonight, so this is a time for instant decisions.

"Yes, please, that would be very nice of you."

So Mr. Maintenance man is sent off with my money to buy my ticket, and I decide to give up on the bike. I was allowed to put it in the coal shed, as long as I came and got it before the end of August, when it would be used once again for coal storage.

So, soaked through, I take off my panniers and go back to the restaurant for a cup of tea. Not because I particularly want one, but because at times like this I remember I'm English, and it's what we do in the face of adversity and despair. I reassess my options and retell my story again and again as other guests enquire as to why I am still here. One of the girls from the kitchen comes running up to me very excited. I must follow her now. Oh dear, what's happened?

"Come see, you must come." Apparently there was a traveller outside with long hair and earrings, who looked like me. He is gone now, but I think she wanted to play snap or something. The guests in the restaurant are bemused. "Gotta go, there's another freak in town."

So it's time for a transformation; I have to mutate into a backpacker. I have to go to market to buy a bag, and then if there is enough time, I better dread my hair and pierce my eyebrow. I keep finding myself in market situations looking desperately with limited time. I do find a bag. The choice is basic, get it or not. I only have one option. I get some cigarettes too, for the maintenance man. The rain continues, and this morning's brief freshness has been replaced with inner sweat and penetrating dampness. I'm also a bit stressed about the time and all the things I have to do before I get the minivan.

In actual fact, with this holdall I haven't even switched allegiance to the backpacker fraternity. I'm simply a bag person. The good Christian owners wanted nothing for bike storage and safe keeping of my panniers; seeing as trust deserves trust in return, I give them my keys.

Just like at Sweden Rock Festival, I have to consider all the things I will need for the next week and fill my holdall with essentials.

Once again, I said my goodbyes. OK, Cockney, what stereotypical jokes can you make about my new status as backpacker, because I think I've exhausted all the obvious ones. He gives me one last handshake and one last comment, when I'm already out of the door.

"Graham, try and find Jesus." Well, I have an awful lot of replies for that one, witty, sarcastic, offensive, flippant, factual, argumentative, dismissive, provocative, blasphemous, hysterically heretical, antagonistic, and agnostic, but in my now tried, tested, and well-practiced diplomatic manner, I manage to keep my mouth shut, and if I say anything at all it isn't faithless. And I'm not faithless. I have a strong belief in Karma, and I also believe that everything happens for a reason. I'm not meant to ride my bike today.

I headed for the collection of puddles and mud, which is called the bus station.

I find the minivan, and the bolshie driver insists I sit on the end seat that faces the rear of the van.

"No, I can't. I have to face the direction of travel, or I'll throw up." But graphic visual explanations and even a healthy bribe will not change my assigned seat.

"I'm in seat 5, and at this short notice, I should consider myself bloody lucky to have a seat at all. Now stop whinging bitch and sit there," I think he is probably saying. And when the eleven-seater van has been filled with eighteen Mongolian adults, two babies, and a wet and resentful Westerner, one hour behind schedule we set off.

The space between my seat and the one facing me is just wide enough to get my legs in, due to bags stuffed behind my seat. The back is vertical, and so I adopted the posture of a Ryan Air passenger. I don't have the room to slouch. Personal space goes out the window; there's no room for that in here. I'm glad I'm not fat; two-thirds of my arse hangs off the seat. I'm bolt upright and facing the wrong direction.

I try to turn to see out of the rain-distorted windscreen to at least follow the muddy track and anticipate the direction of the swerving, so as not to bring on travel sickness. This is no trip for runny bum or puking. Well, actually, with a single, swift, window-opening movement from the woman opposite me, I realise puking is actually OK, and that there is an advantage to being in the rear-facing seat, as I'm sure the person in the window seat behind her would agree. When after an hour or so the mud turns to paved road and I can realign, I realise that all eyes are on me. I'm used to being stared at, but I'm also used to having a helmet to hide behind. This is intense head-on, face-to-face staring. All I can do is put on my iPod and look out of the window. We have a brief piss stop, and the bottom half of a plastic water bottle is offered to me. It contains clear liquid. I know exactly what it is. I take a polite sip and offer it back. It's clearly indicated that I should drink the lot. No problem, I shoot the whole lot back in one gulp and simultaneously get a good little buzz and a bit of respect. Now I sit with a nonchalant smile, and I can return eye contact. I wonder if they can tell I'm not focusing.

We pass three laden bikes that are Polish-registered. Our driver hoots and passes with only inches to spare. It's interesting to see how the respect he has for them matches the clearance he had given them. On muddy, potholed roads, in the poor visibility of driving rain, this is really dangerous, and my discomfort is not so bad after all. They look miserable in their waterproofs. Prior to this experience, whenever I passed a tourist bus or minivan and saw the passengers crammed inside, I rejoiced in my freedom and independence. It was as if I had Jesus in my heart. But now I'm happy to be here. I'm getting a new experience, I am plenty experienced in riding in the rain.

It's cold, not freezing, but the wrong side of comfortable. The body contact is actually quite welcome. Babies are held on the breast, on the lap, and eventually on me. I have knee-to-knee, thigh-to-thigh, and eye-to-eye contact, and now I have four little Mongolian feet resting in my lap, and surprisingly, I actually quite like it. Where the hell did this tolerance come from?

I thought it was about a seven-hour journey, but when there is no more light left we stop for food, and a lady with a few words of English explained we are half way. Oh shit.

"Well that means we won't be there until midnight."

"Yes, that's right."

I'm given another shot of vodka. There is quite a camaraderie on this bus, but best of all is the music. A CD plays its local music that everyone is familiar with. The passengers are evenly split gender-wise and with a seventy-year-plus age range. I wonder if there are speakers in the rear. There aren't: it's the perfectly in tune and harmonic voices of my fellow passengers. They sing the chorus so well, not the drunken crooning of a bunch of tourists on the way back from a wine-tasting excursion to their Spanish hotel in Costa Chav. Instead, a from-the-heart, from the bottom of the lungs and gently into the ear, enhancement of a traditional Mongolian folk song.

I smile along appreciatively. I wouldn't have even know what was going on inside these cramped little vans if the bike had started.

My head drops and nods around for a little while squashed in the cramped camaraderie of the commute. I don't think that would have been as evident if it were not for the cold conditions. Heat, I think, would only cause irritability.

I keep my hand on the baby trouser leg that keeps riding up, to keep those tanned little legs warm, and find myself just massaging with my thumb in a kind of lullaby sleep inducing meditational manner. I'm not sure for whose benefit. I'm beginning to feel a slight paternal pang. I wonder where the hell that came from. I wake myself right up. It's followed by a woken screaming kicking baby, and the feeling disappears as quickly as it arrived. I blame it on the cold, the vodka, the singing, the warmth, the buzz, the atmosphere. I've got loads of reasons; are we nearly there yet?

The clue was the adverts. Wait a minute. For the last nine hours, we have been listening to CDs, now adverts? I look over my shoulder and see lights, more lights than I've seen since Russia, more than all the villages I've seen put together over the last ten days. This is Ulan Bator, the destination I looked at for so long; it seemed a world away. It is a world away, and to ride my bike so far seems very ambitious and almost impossible. It was, because my bike sits in a coal shed 300 miles to the west, and although I have made it to my destination, the mission is not completed.

Another area of mud and puddles means we have reached the bus station. It's a lifeless area, not really somewhere I want to be walking around looking for a hotel. A dark voice beside me says, "Taxi," and I take the opportunity while it's there. I have been recommended a hotel from the guesthouse owner. The problem with asking a taxi driver to take you to the posh hotel is the price leaps up. He charges me English prices, but it's gone midnight and I am English and today I'm a backpacker. I'm dependent and at the mercy of the four-wheel shysters.

My first impression of the city is neon lights and karaoke bars, hotels, and pubs—a buzz of excitement, in a haze of humidity.

The hotel is very luxurious. They have their own transport that will take me to the airport tomorrow. The room is actually a suite with a view of all of Ulan Bator. Tomorrow's breakfast is brought up to my room because I will be leaving before the restaurant opens. This suite is bigger than my whole house and furnished better too. I can't imagine anyone else in the minivan today has ended up in such luxurious surroundings.

I'm glad I didn't ride today. I will sort out the bike after my mum leaves. I'm relieved it's safe and under cover; everything will work out. Everything is just fine.

Days 70-73

Ulan Bator to Tsetserleg, Driven in a 4X4

I get to the airport as dawn breaks to meet my mum. In some time zone she passed through it is technically still her 75th birthday. She has bought a big bottle of Jägermeister in the duty-free, which is brilliant, especially because, since I've abandoned my bike, size and weight isn't even an issue. Jäger and mother. You can have one without the other but, like gin and tonic, they simply make the other more bearable.

Seeing as I only got into town seven hours before her, other than a hotel, I have organised absolutely nothing.

Back in our palatial Wi-Fi room, I find some car hire places on the Internet, and then we try to find them in reality. In Ulan Bator it seems everyone is a taxi. You just stick out your hand, and a car stops. The going rate is about 25p per kilometre, and I round it up to avoid any unnecessary confrontation. But the car hire places seem to be gone, and I think the passing opportunist drivers don't want to do a six-day road trip. I decide The Oasis café and guesthouse might be a good place to try. It's not hard to find. As soon as we walk through the gates, there is Greg measuring his bike to crate it up to fly it to Vancouver. I'm glad I didn't stay with him, thinking he was going to Vladivostok.

The Oasis owners are Austrian and try calling some of their connections for me. I can hire a 4x4. I would have liked to have taken my mum to the snowy mountains, but because of the distance I want to do, combined with time I want to do the journey in, the owner will not rent it to me. No point in explaining I'm used to long distances. I have to assume they know the roads better than me. We get nowhere, and on top of that, insurance is almost impossible to get and not worth the paper it's printed on. Anyway, in the event of an accident, comprehension of the language will win over who was actually at fault. This would explain why the trucks here try to kill you, rather than just injure you. It saves a lot of paperwork. On top of that, the implications of breaking down are daunting, and no one will take responsibility for the repair costs. I'm not taking out a dilapidated old vehicle only to be told I'm obliged to pay to have it repaired when it inevitably breaks. The cost keeps mounting until the entire plan becomes unfeasible.

But there is a good atmosphere here; the French hallucinations appear again. There are also several 4x4 overlanders of various nationalities; it's a loud, friendly, upbeat familiar community. And just like the balding straights that all my life have come up to me and said, "I used to have long hair like yours once," I feel the need to mention to every bike rider how I rode here and had a little breakdown. Some insecurity deep inside makes me believe I will have no credibility here without announcing my achievement. Although I come to find that flying out my mum got me more respect than any motorcycle ride I have ever done.

All that aside, the spaghetti is excellent.

We find a car, and it takes us to the tourist office. I'm not really sure what choices we have left now. I can't do buses with my mum, and those four-wheel-drive vans look very uncomfortable, and I see more of them broken down than actually running.

The guy in the tourist office has good English.

"I want a 4x4 with a driver. I want him for six days, and these are the distances and daily destinations. Is that possible?"

"Yes, $60 a day. He will come and pick you up tomorrow."

"And does he speak English?"

"Yes." Well that was easy. Jolly good.

Next morning our driver, Eggy, comes to the hotel. He drives his own Toyota Land Cruiser, which he is fanatical about. He tells me of all the modifications he has done to it: outside suspension, inside entertainment, DVD player, etc. He is friendly and obliging, and we are ready to go.

Before we commit ourselves fully to Eggy, we ask to go to the National Park nearby. On the way there he asks if we want to see the Genghis Khan statue. I had heard of this. It's not in the guidebook, but before I left England my uncle had enthused about it. He had seen a programme about it. He's not known for his memory or recall skills, so for something to make such an impact on him it has to be pretty good, and it is.

As we approach across the hilly grassland, a stainless steel head protrudes above the horizon and pierces the sky. It's so big it's hard to actually grasp the scale. On top of a circular building ,which looks like a mini coliseum, is a 40-metre-high stainless steel statue of Genghis Khan on horseback. It's stunning and brand new too. I get into some serious photography. I've exchanged the freedom of the bike for the freedom of the back seat, and changing lens and settings is all I have to think about now. I look forward to photographing my bike in front of it.

On the way into the National Park our driver cuts into a convoy of cars with a police escort front and rear, and we are waved straight in without having to pay an entry fee. I like this guy.

Eggy is excellent, and he agrees to take us for the rest of our journey. So the overland journey will take a U-turn back to where my bike is waiting for me. It's a compromise on the original plan, but it will still be good, and I can pick up my bike on the way back. Considering how little time and choice we had, it's actually a pretty good scenario.

The next day is mostly driving to a monastery in the town of Kharkhorin. We pass over wild steppe and past herds of yak and ger camps. It's more than authentic; it's a genuine Mongolian experience. Inside the monastery I bump into the Germans, whose 4x4 was where I initially conceived the idea to bring my mother out.

"Ve nu yar moder was coming, ve heard at de guesthouse." There ain't no secrets in this overland community. But it's kind of funny that in this vast empty country I keep bumping into the same people. What does that say about my intrepid adventuring. Perhaps not as groundbreaking as I thought. There is still time, though.

Tonight's hotel is not very nice, it's the only choice; it has no water at all, so we are forced to drink Jägermeister. But of the three fuzzy TV channels, one of them shows Lady Gaga at Glastonbury, so it's not too awful.

I missed a brilliant sunrise; I woke up early enough to see what I missed, but not what I missed. I have no idea what phase the moon is in or how cold the night was. The canopy of stars is now unseen over my roof, not over my head. I have clean nails and cleaner underwear. I can see the appeal on certain levels as I pull on a T-shirt and jump in the back of the Land Cruiser. Today we head back to White Lake.

Inside the 4x4 we are isolated from the country outside. I don't realise it until I stop for a wee and I can feel the wind and become aware of the temperature of the day. My zoom lens protrudes from an electric, tinted window and is quickly retracted before flies and odours come inside our air-conditioned environment.

Our driver and his vehicle combined are a formidable force. All those mounds I rode over he crosses in a skilled and controlled way to drive the new and unfinished road. We cross deep rivers and go up near vertical inclines. I think Eggy enjoys showing off his skills, and I'm really impressed with what he and his 4x4 are capable of. I still see it as nothing more than able transport, and I have no desire at this stage in my life to double my two-wheel vehicle of choice into the security, comfort, and balance of the four-wheel drive.

There is a black sky over White Lake, and I find my old receipt. As the hail batters the gate man, we get in without having to pay again. We stay in a ger camp at the side of the lake, not far from where I had my skinny dip last week; I won't be doing that this evening as the icy wind howls over the rough waters.

The staff are very attentive, taking luggage inside, and the fire they light in the obligatory stove/log burner in the centre is soon radiating heat like a...well, like a radiator really. The warmth combined with the equally obligatory end-of-day Jäger shot, it's not long before I'm happily chilling in a cosy ger.

After a trip to the restaurant ger for dinner, the unattended stove has gone out, so I go off to get some matches. I was mistaken for the sort of person who can only produce heat with the turn of a thermostat dial and was accompanied back to the cold accommodation by the resident fire starter. Patronised and inflamed, we are left in warmth and peace, apart from our vodka-drinking-partying driver next door. They may be good for heat insulation, but designed to be erected out on the isolated steppe, the sound travels right through our end of terrace ger.

I decide that if I sleep without bed clothes, every time the stove needs topping up I will get cold and wake up. I like the idea of staying up all night and keeping the fire burning. It's been four years since I moved from my house with the log burner, and I miss it loads. The only thing I miss more about that house is the shed, which was my own Western ger, although not quite as movable due to its concrete base. But then I didn't find rodents in there like I did in this one. Finding one nibbling at my bread, I made two discoveries: 1. A water bottle is a completely ineffective weapon, unless you want to encourage them to retreat to your spare blanket. 2. More worryingly, said rodent displayed all the characteristics the man in the ger restaurant was impersonating last week to explain the meat being served.

Anyway, I fall asleep, and the fire goes out. I spend a happy hour slicing up logs with my Swiss army knife. I have just my headlight on, so as not to wake Mother. I do look up at one point and realise I have filled the ger with smoke. I open the door and see Eggy being held up by his mate and both staggering to the toilet area. Great, that will be an interesting drive tomorrow. I get the fire alight, but by 1.30 A.M., I think bugger this and shake my blanket vigorously and curl up underneath it.

Day 74

Tsetserleg, Mongolia, Up the Road and Back

At 6 A.M. I light the fire from scratch. See, I'm a fire starter too, and my trail of smoke from the top of my ger is my flag of victory. I am very chuffed with myself.

It has snowed in the night; the mountains are beautiful with their fresh new white autumn hats on. Except it's the middle of August. We didn't have time to get to the snowy mountains, so the snowy mountains came to us. How cool.

Seeing as I have spent my first night in a ger, I have meat and noodles for breakfast to continue in my Mongolian ways. Now if I was to just go out onto the steppe and herd and farm until midday before stopping for a lunchtime vodka break, I'd be living like the locals. Unfortunately, the 4x4 is warmed up with the snow brushed off it, and we are ready to leave.

Yaks wandering through the snow give a little insight into the harshness of this environment during their six-month winter. It must be a tough existence. We have a scenically-enhanced drive today and have to turn up the heater a bit so as not to suffer the hardships of a premature winter. We are heading to the town where my bike is waiting for me; I'm itching to get working on it. Or was that the blanket from last night?

In the few days since I had left it, they had decided they were going to move the coal shed and so, clumsily and heavy-handedly but with the best intensions, my bike had been moved and picked up by things that weren't meant to support its weight. Guards and rails are bent and twisted. I can't be angry. They had put it inside the guesthouse. It's a lovely gesture. So my hope that in a week of shelter it would dry out and fire up was optimistic, but you have got to have hope. It doesn't fire, so I start to strip it down. I hoped in the dark but private storage room I might avoid the inevitable audience. However, as soon as I start work on the bike along comes maintenance man with his soup, and he sits on a pile of cement bags and

259

slurps annoyingly. Whilst the soup burns his mouth, his eyes burn into my back. Damn it.

I have a spark. Good; check carburettor. I have juice running through; OK. I also have a dying battery; I was expecting that. So I get the bike out into the cold sunshine. Now Eggy is keen to help too. I don't work like this. I like to work alone, slowly methodically, stopping lots, considering, thinking. I can't work with someone looking over my shoulder. Every time I stop to think, he's wanting to pull off another part. I don't strip carbs on dusty ground, but he persuades me to, and surprise, surprise, I drop a screw, and we lose it. He had another one; does he think he's helping? Is this for me or for him? Is he being gracious, or is this being done for gratitude? I wouldn't have lost the screw in the first place if I had done it my way. We take it out the front to jump it off the 4x4. Now we have an even bigger audience. But I do find the original screw. I have spark, I have fuel, and it turns over but will not start. I rode it 200 feet from one hotel garage to this one. That was over a week ago. Then I cleaned off the tar, bolted on the bits that had fallen off, and that is all. Why won't it start? I did put in oil. Too much? We have been working on it for five hours, it's cooling down, the light is going, and the bike still isn't. Eggy wants to try bumping it. It's turning over fine. What difference will bumping make?

"It won't work." OK, just to shut you up I will try to bump it. I start to wheel it to the road; no, he wants to do it on dirt.

"The wheel will just lock up and skid." OK, just to humour you we will do it this way. I get on the saddleless bike. No, he wants us both to push.

"Look it's got to have weight over the back wheel." This is futile. OK, come on, let's get it over with.

I put it in second gear and pull in the clutch. We push, we run, I let out the clutch, ready to control the skidding back wheel as it locks in the dirt, but it doesn't lock, it turns the engine over and the engine fires and the bike starts.

What the fuck? I'm simultaneously happy and humiliated. Who would have thunk it? But why? It's beyond any logic I have, beyond any technique I would have applied. I take it up the street, well aware that most fasteners are loose and tank etc. aren't even attached. Listen to that engine: quiet smooth and strong. I'm bemused. So I turn it off and once again it turns over on the starter but won't fire. We put it all back together, push again. Same method, 2nd gear on dirt with no weight over the back wheel, and again it starts. Well, buggered if I know.

At least this way I can get it to Ulan Bator. It has not been a very satisfying fix; it's been a stressful afternoon. The bike is running, but I don't know how or why. What was wrong? And what still is? Nothing has been diagnosed.

Mum has been in the restaurant all afternoon chatting to an English/Malaysian girl who teaches English and lives in Seoul. I love that she can just get on and do this travelling malarkey. I'm cold and filthy but not for long, with a hot shower just up the stairs and the decadence of IKEA towels. And soon, with Jäger in my blood, buzz in my head, bike on my mind, and grease down my nails, the four of us go and have dinner in the night club. I'm not asking if anyone's dancing, I will probably never get the chance to dance here again.

It's arranged that our new friend, Jo, will take my seat in the 4x4 tomorrow, and I'll follow on the bike. It's a perfect arrangement all round. She will keep Mum company and save herself the discomfort of the bus. She has just done a ten-day ger-to-ger hike. I don't think the bus experience would have as big of an impact on her as it did on me.

I go to sleep trying to figure out the bike. This is the second fault that has been fixed, and I don't know how or why. So if it reoccurs, then what? Just bump it? That defies logic too. There is no peace of mind to be gained from a mysterious mechanical miracle. I need explanations and understanding, not blind acceptance that will only satisfy a lazy mind.

DAY 75

ULAN BATOR, MONGOLIA, 307 MILES

You know you are ready to ride when putting on your bike clothes is more thrilling than scrambled eggs on toast. I've had my break; some of it intended, some forced upon me. The ritual of putting my jacket, boots, and helmet on is so exciting. Is any more proof needed that bikes are in my blood?

I remember when I got my first Harley, a 1960 Sportster, I would get shivers of excitement just looking at it. Since the age of ten, when I got a model of an Electra Glide, I was hooked. All through my teenage years, the posters on my wall, the Dave Mann centrefolds out of *Easyrider* magazine, the desire grew. In the early '80s I went to the bike show at Earls Court and bought all things Harley: scarves, badges, all that shit. And when I got home I realised how much money I had wasted. I started a Harley fund. The next thing I owned with that word written on it was going to be a bike. Right out of school I was working sixty hour weeks packing fish and saving up. I even found a girlfriend who shared my passion enough to go halves with me on the purchase. When the bike finally became mine (well ours technically) I would go through a similar ritual as today, preparing myself for the ride and then, just before I went to kick it over, the excitement was so great that I had to take off all my bike gear and run to the toilet. A quarter of a century later, on a smaller bike with a temperamental electric start, about to venture back onto the tracks of Mongolia, the thrill is as fresh as it ever was. Having a passion turns an existence into a life.

So I check over my bike, and with the audience of well wishers, I get on and, with my eternal optimism, turn the ignition key and press the starter button, and it bloody starts. Well, it's beyond me.

Everybody's happy; I suppose I'm happy. Intermittent faults which disappear are not good for confidence in the reliability of your bike. But it's running, and I keep it running whilst I fill up with fuel. I have obviously trapped a throttle cable under that tank because the throttle won't snap back. I have cruise control, and under the circumstance, that's not a bad thing because I don't want to be stalling or turning off the ignition.

And we're off. Bloody hell, look at that. The adventure is instantly back: I'm independent, I'm free, I'm riding again, appreciating all those little pleasures— the feel of the wind in my face, the passing aromas. I have my senses back, and as an added bonus, I can fart at will again. I'm navigating, negotiating the terrain. I'm vulnerable again, out in the big wide open country, and the sky is blue, the day is warming. I've got my fingerless gloves on and my heated grips. Over my shoulder are snow-capped mountains of wild Mongolian weather and in front of me is a 4x4 support vehicle, carrying half my luggage. Hang on a minute, that sounds familiar. Oh my God, all I need now is an extra cylinder and a Scottish accent, neither of which are likely, but I do fall off in the mud, so it's quite an accurate re-enactment.

The melted snow has turned the lower ground to mush, sloppy churned-up grassy mud. My tyres have too much pressure in them. I'm trying to catch up with the Land Cruiser, which is making far quicker progress than me through this bog. With too little momentum, I get stuck in a rut and down goes the bike, the stuck throttle making the engine roar its displeasure as the bike slaps into the mud, which sprays like gravy out of a saucepan when the tin of Bisto slips through your hands. Well that didn't stay clean for long. Neither did I, although I do manage to keep the engine running and lift the bike up by myself.

Over the last week my confidence has gone, and my hardened arse has lost some of its seat endurance. But after a few hours it's like I was never off the bike. I'm up and down the gears, loving the dirt roads, racing the 4x4, beating him on the bumps, but he loses me on the smooth bits, standing on the pegs splashing up the mud. Other than actually being on the back, my mum is seeing firsthand what my journey has been like. Sometimes we are on adjacent tracks, and side by side she can hear the thumping exhaust, see the dirt fly, and best of all photograph it too.

After about 80 miles we stop. Eggy encourages me to kill the engine. Well OK, I suppose we can always bump it, but it starts again on the button and continues to for the next 250 miles and eight hours to Ulan Bator.

Eggy, without fail, honks his horn three times whenever we pass an ovoo. You're supposed to walk round them three times for luck. If you don't have the time, you just honk your horn, and the spirits seem to accept that in this faster pace of modern life you have at least acknowledged their shrine. Now with a fully-charged battery I indulge in the ritual.

Everything happened for a reason. Because of my bike not starting last week, I am now riding the stunning scenery in beautiful weather, I'm escorted by my mother in a 4x4. I'm appreciating the bike all the more, and I don't know if it's coincidence or not, but somehow since I hooted at that ovoo, the day just got a little brighter—not overexposed brighter, just awareness brighter. Maybe it's because I'm not looking through a windscreen.

It's such a contrast to how I travelled this road last time, cramped, facing the wrong direction on the bus, under grey and heavy skies.

It's also a very auspicious day; it's five years since my dad died. If he can see what we're doing, I'm sure under this bright blue sky in this vast expanse of land framed between hills, underlined by rivers, he's looking at me and Mum as she leans out the passenger window taking photos, and he's rolling his eyes and thinking, "Good on ya."

The day is clear and bright, the road is flat and smooth, the land is empty of people and traffic. There on an open stretch of road; in the middle up ahead is a colourful lump. As I approach from a landscape that had nothing to take my attention, I try to work out what the lump is. Various possibilities occur and are rejected as I rapidly approach. Can't be a yak, a cow, or a horse, too big for luggage. Oh my God, it's a body, it's a person lying crumpled in the middle of the road. Not dragged or crawled to the side. As soon as I realise what it is, I'm upon it. There is no sign of blood, but no sign of movement either. Is he dead? Drunk? Dead drunk? Is it an ambush? I have slowed, but I'm not stopping. I look over my shoulder to see what Eggy's reactions are. The 4x4 passes without stopping. OK. Well, I'll ask later.

Greg had told me after we had split up and he rode this road, he came across an overturned vehicle, and two bodies were laid out and covered over. It was the only thing that made him decide to stop that night, instead of going straight through to Ulan Bator. I'm not sure what I just saw, and if I was alone, I'm not sure what I would have done. What could I have done? If he was dead, I can't help him; if he wasn't and I got him to the side of the road, someone who could help would be less likely to see him. I justify my complete lack of involvement to myself, and it's backed up by Eggy's reactions. Like the conversations the Touratech twins had, the miles of dug up roads in Kazakhstan, the intermittent faults of the bike, it's just another thing that happens that I don't understand.

In such predicaments it sometimes helps to ask yourself what you would do if you were someone else, someone you respect. A friend of mine left me speechless when he admitted he asked himself "What would Tony Blair have done"; no wonder his life was such a mess. The Cockney would undoubtedly ask himself what Jesus would have done. Gandhi may be a good role model, but I tend to opt for Vinnie Jones's character in *Lock Stock and Two Smoking Barrels*. It's happened a few times. Leaving a vulnerable girl in California at an inappropriate time, I struggled for words as I got on my bike and just said, "It's been emotional." It was a suitable line in the circumstance, and I got away with it.

It's amazing how quickly I become used to my surroundings. Another ger camp with horses outside, a man on horseback heading for his flock on the hillside, it barely interrupts my daydreams now, barely, but it does. I become aware again of what I am doing and where I am, and along comes that feeling of contentment again. That's twice in the same country in the same month, maybe this is my calling; it's a bloody hard language to learn, though.

As I get nearer to Ulan Bator in-between thoughts of hotels, bike parking, luggage removal, laundry, and what the possibilities might be of getting into Jo's knickers, I realise I'm about to get to my destination. I'd been here a week ago but that wasn't on the bike. This was always the plan whilst I sat the winter in the freezing trailer saving money and researching the trip, whilst telling anyone who would listen I was going to ride to Ulan Bator. It was a world away, and now it's only an hour away, and not only am I about to achieve the dream, but I'm accompanied by my mother on this anniversary of Dad's death. How cool is that? Fuckin' cool, that's how.

As I ride towards the toll booth, which is the city limits, I can see the capital down there in its polluted valley, and all the preoccupations in my mind are replaced with a rush of euphoria. I've just ridden my eBay bike to Ulan Bator. And with the sign above the toll booth saying just that, I get Mum to take a photo of me. There's one for the garage wall. The traffic is horrendous, so I weave off ahead and get to the hotel.

Tonight is Operation Get Laid. It would be the ideal end to the day, the journey, everything; it would just be perfect.

It all goes well; bike is garaged, rooms are booked, Jäger is consumed, meal is eaten, mother is off to bed, bar is attended, beer and cocktails are drunk and so are we, conversations get more personal, body piercings are mentioned but not revealed, but it's a good sign. The bar closes; this is it, we get into the glass lift on the outside of the hotel, isn't this romanti...her floor is reached, door opens, and girl is gone. Doors close again. What just happened? Hang on a minute, that wasn't supposed to...bollocks. Well it was still a brilliant day. And there I was thinking my bike was hard to understand.

Days 76-77

Ulan Bator, Mongolia, 74 Miles

One last day for souvenir shopping in search of the perfect coffee table book and trying on Mongolian riding boots. They just don't have the desired effect. However, seeing as my mum won't be taking any boots home, I can fill her case with maps and guidebooks, which I no longer have a use for.

We may not be driving around in flying cars and have robots for slaves, but in this 21st century there is proof that we are living in the future when I can get on Google in my hotel room, put in "pizza delivery in Ulan Bator," and not only get a number but can connect to it via Skype, and half an hour later a pizza is delivered to the hotel room. We have a quiet night in and kill the Jägermeister.

Another dawn trip to the airport and I'm back to my lone biker status. I book the room for one more night to collect my thoughts. Jo has been in touch from her new hotel. We will ride to the Genghis Kahn statue today. I find myself tidying up the room; apparently it's a recognised human behaviour instinct for coping with loss. I've been told it can be witnessed on *Big Brother* when someone leaves the house.

I don't know why it was a shock to me, but standing in the foyer of a London hotel, surrounded by other hopefuls who had all reached the first stage of the *Deal or No Deal* auditions, everyone was talking about all the other TV show auditions they had attended. Most of them had tried to be on *Big Brother*. I hadn't really thought about what the kind of people I'd meet would be like. They were all TV whores; all they wanted was to be on TV, any TV. I had just, due to a slow winter of work, watched too much TV and got temporarily captivated by the show. Whilst standing in a line for my first on-camera interview, one of the production girls came up to me and asked if I was nervous.

"No, not really; it's just a game show. I'm just glad, looking around me, I'm not an actor and my life doesn't consist of auditions like this for me to earn a living."

I didn't know it at the time, but I think that helped me get through to the next stage. After half the hopefuls had been rejected and I was waiting for my second on-camera interview, I mentioned to possibly the same production girl how many of the people I had spoken to had applied to be on *Big Brother* and how that would be my worst nightmare. I would rather serve a six-month sentence in a Thai prison than be subjected to a summer in that household. I've only seen *Big Brother* in five-second fragments as I surfed for something better, like interference. But I have read several books written by people who were imprisoned in the Big Tiger, as the Bangkok prison is known. It sounds like living hell, but if I had to serve a sentence and the choice was six months in the Bangkok Hilton or a summer in the *Big Brother* house, I can hand-on-heart say I would opt for the former. And after that little rant I got a call to say I'd been accepted onto the show.

If feels a little strange to be on my own again. I remove the tyres from my bike, so I can get Jo on the back. These are things I don't do: tidying up and going out for a ride. It felt like the sort of thing I would do at home (the Essex/Suffolk border region being littered with statues of 12th century Asian warriors).

After a day undercover in the hotel garage, the bike starts on the button in a puff of blue oil smoke. Poor thing, just isn't feeling itself. So why the smoke? Rings? Valves? Maybe it has abandonment issues.

We drop by The Oasis first for a burger and to swap photos with Greg, who is still in residence. His bike is now en route to Canada, and he will be following shortly. Also there are the 4x4 Germans again. They said the Swiss family took the northern route and will be here soon. That's the route I want to take next, so I decide I will come over tomorrow and stay for one night, so we can have a little reunion, swap notes, and have a goodbye party; I reserve a bed in Greg's ger.

I had intended to leave tomorrow, but I don't have to. It feels good to exercise my new liberation and make decisions without having to consult anyone. We are also able to borrow a helmet for Jo, not a legal requirement, but I feel better for her having one, even if she doesn't. She is a good pillion, and we develop a system whereby when we are not in traffic she can rest her feet on my pegs, there being no pillion pegs, and I can perch my feet on the engine bash plate. It's not ideal, but it works quite well. I can make room on my horse for two if I want to.

There is room on Genghis's horse for about thirty. What I didn't realise last time was you can go inside the coliseum and take a staircase up the inside of the horse's tail into its arse, down a narrow corridor, and pop out on top of its head. It is cramped, claustrophobic, and touristy, but some things just have to be done. I think the statue is better appreciated from a distance, but the view from the head is OK.

The advantage of having a passenger is no tripod is needed; Jo takes a photo of me and my bike in front of Genghis and his horse. That will keep my uncle happy.

The ride back is cold, and it rains a bit, but she doesn't whinge. We get to a major junction on the main street through the city, where I need to battle the oncoming traffic to make a left turn. A baton-waving-whistle-blowing traffic cop tries in vain to assert his authority. Jo points out the huge TV screen on the side of a building, which shows the junction we are at, and sure enough, as we move forward we come onto the screen. Not really the distraction you need when you're about to cross five lanes of ferocious oncoming traffic, but at least the impact will be recorded for posterity. Seeing myself on a thirty-foot TV brings back the brainwashed reactions, ride for a ride? deal or no deal?

We arrange to meet for a drink tonight.

My room has been cleaned, but they left the bottle of Jäger. There is a dribble in the bottom; very observant of them. I wring it out and put it back in the bin.

Walking down the main street for my date, I don't feel like a tourist. It's a small city, and I've seen most of it and know my way around now. The sun is low and reflecting off the buildings, and I'm feeling good.

As if we are trying to avoid anything Mongolian, we start in an Irish pub and proceed to a curry house and then on to karaoke bars, mainly because that is all that's left open. It's Saturday night, and every bar we go to closes before we can order a second drink. This is not New York, this city sleeps, and it likes an early night. By midnight we are out on the streets. I walk Jo to her hotel; she flies back to Korea tomorrow. There appears to be no opportunity. As I wander the empty streets back to my room, I wonder what Vinnie Jones would have done.

Day 78

Ulan Bator, Mongolia, 4 Miles

That wasn't sleep; that was passing out. I need to dry out a bit, and I've been drinking every night for...too long now. I also have the first pangs of homesickness. I try and apply logic to it, but logic doesn't cure homesickness.

Of course, I don't want to be working, waking up to an alarm, pushing a trolley around Asda, hoping for a good drying day to wash my bedding. Screw all that. I want to ride my bike round Mongolia, and conveniently, I happen to be in said country, and as if it were planned, I have the perfect bike to travel on, fitted with all the cooking, camping, and other equipment I might need, as well as a map and money. So get over it and get out there. I go down to my bike and load it all up for the first time in ages. Funny how all the stuff I sent back with Mum makes no difference now it's gone, but try and find room to put it back in my panniers and there wouldn't be any.

As I pull out of the undercover parking of the hotel, the security guard gives me a thumbs up, and suddenly I feel better. It's the recognition, the reminder that actually I'm really lucky to be doing this, aren't I?

I ride the four miles to The Oasis. The owner is checking someone else in and speaking German. When she has dealt with them, she says to me, "Feel relaxed, you know everything." Well I don't know if I would go as far as to say that, darling, but I'm pretty sure I don't look relaxed or else why would she tell me to. So I ride my bike over to ger No. 5, throw some stuff on my bed, get out my Russia guidebook, iPod, and go sit at a table in the sun and try to look relaxed.

There are four English backpackers on the table next to me drinking red wine and talking bollocks, not total bollocks, the kind I'm quite fluent in myself and practise whenever I get the chance. I get chatting to them. They have dreads and piercings; I have aluminium panniers with stickers. They have done the usual

Asian backpacking circuit; I have done the usual Asian overland route. They all live in Taiwan and paint a beautiful picture of their adopted country. We drink wine and make jokes and swap email addresses. They invite me to come and stay. "Don't say it if you don't mean it, because I bloody will."

They leave for their flight, and I have a moment to look around me. There are huge Mercedes Unimogs turned into campers, housing families and travelling in convoy as they slowly cross the planet. There are independent Land Rover drivers and various overland bikes, stored, broken, or resting, and two Dutch-registered quad bikes sitting unattended and fully loaded in a way that only a fully sponsored vehicle would be. If I had come from the east to this place I would have felt so disheartened. At least the way I came I genuinely felt like I was doing something unique, and in certain places, at certain times, to certain people, I was. But here in overlander central park only my bike and budget set me apart from the masses, and not very far apart at that.

I catch a bus with Greg into the city to the finish line of the Mongolian Rally. Europeans take very inexpensive cars and vans, and with the sponsorship of companies and individuals, they drive to Ulan Bator. They then give the vehicles and the money that was sponsored to charity.

The downside from the driver's point of view seems to be that the finish line is an unattended car park, and it's crossed over a two week period. So reaching it is a bit of an anti-climax. Greg wants a "Mongo Rally 2010" sticker. I come along for the experience and feel quite disappointed for the Scandinavian drivers, who have just turned up full of excitement and no one to share it with.

The evening consists of the 4x4 Germans, Greg, and I sitting around a cold table outside and drinking beer that won't go down (I think I'm just full). The conversation really doesn't flow; not like it did when we were all exhilarated out on the steppe. Greg has been sitting here for over a week and has one foot on the plane already. It takes more than a scattering of gers and four-wheel drives to recreate the wilds of the west. The homesickness has gone, but I seem to have nothing more to say. Time for some more experiences; I'm ready to move on.

DAY 79

SOUTH OF BULGAN, MONGOLIA, 225 MILES

That's about as close as I want to get to a dorm experience, a six-bed ger, but actually being only half-occupied it was OK. Spiders and beetles crawling over me at night woke me up, but nothing bit me, so live and let live. That's the only problem with felt walls. It provides food and shelter for all kinds of bugs and the things that eat the bugs and maybe even the things that eat the things that eat the bugs.

I collect more email addresses on more scraps of paper and say more goodbyes. Greg gets his taxi to the airport, heading to meet his bike in Vancouver. I slowly prepare myself and my bike to leave. After all this time and so many departures, in certain situations like this one, I still get butterflies. I'm heading for the real back roads. The Swiss family never turned up, so I will make it up as I go along.

The Oasis is to the south of the city. I'm heading north, so by the time I have fought my way through the traffic, the freshness of the morning has been replaced by the sticky dampness caused by a hot engine in stationary traffic. I'm out past the toll booth and ready to have my Mongolian adventure part...I'm not sure what part it is. I've done it with two bikes, solo, on a bus, in a 4x4, on a bike with 4x4 escort, and with a pillion. But this is the only one that's given me butterflies, so it must be important.

As I leave the city behind, I see a camper coming towards me. I turn my head as it passes and see it's the Swiss family. I turn around and speed after them. I don't think I have gone so fast in this country before. I find them stopped in a lay-by. So I get to find out where they went and how the roads are. It's all kind of irrelevant, really, because with four wheels and two kids, their opinion of good is different to mine. Still, I was glad I saw them. I seem to know every European crossing this country or know of them.

I've travelled this road three times now, and it just brings back memories of the people I travelled with. I can't wait to get on some new roads for some new sights, thoughts, and experiences, and no alcohol. I have no peer pressure and no temptations.

Up ahead, just where my map says it should be, is the fork I want off the main road. Back onto the dirt, full tank, a map that is right more often than it is wrong, and once again the sense of adventure and challenge is full on. I stop to reduce my tyre pressures now I've left the paved road. Oh right, I've just realised something. Because of all the weight I carry, my bike is practically vertical when it's on the side stand. I usually try to find a hole to sink it in, and lately it's been OK in Ulan Bator. I thought it was because I sent some heavy stuff back with Mum, but now I'm back on dirt with reduced tyre pressure, I realise that this is the reason my bike is lower and so vertically unstable. All these misdiagnosed things. So maybe my rear shock is not as bad as I thought. Pothole, bang, bottom out, spine shatter, oh yes it is.

It's good to go at my own slow pace, stop to drink water whenever I want, for photos of wildlife, the wild horse drinking from puddles in the road. For a while now, little things that look like baby turtles have shuffled across my path. Now I have the time to turn round and see what they really are. Not turtles is the answer. More like miniature armadillos. Right, well, that's cleared that up. And so concludes the lesson in mistaken Mongolian reptiles.

Once again the dirt road forks. This time it goes either side of a big hill, which is probably not big enough to be a mountain unless it was in Essex. I decide with the help of my map, my compass, and the sun to head in a northwest direction on the right-hand track. It feels strange to be heading west after so long heading east. Then the road splits again. Bugger, there is a limit to my common sense and instinct you know. Stop bloody splitting. I pass the Essex Mountain, and what happens? The tracks all come together again. One went round morning side of the mountain and the other round the twilight side of the hill. There was a ger. So now what shall I worry about? The scenery is OK but not amazing; am I just getting complacent? I want to be doing this diversion, this indirect route out of Mongolia for fun and adventure, not for the hell of it. Where has the awe gone?

Off to the right a town appears, not very big but more substantial than a ger camp. There in the distance is a two-storey brick building. It still amazes me that these tiny, indistinct, unmarked dirt tracks lead to such a significant inhabited area, but maybe that's the way they like it.

So bearings are back, and I continue on, not exactly sure how far I will get today or where I will stay. My panniers are full of food, my hunger can be kept at bay for over a week, but my thirst for only 24 hours. However, there are more rivers than supermarkets, so I think I'll be OK.

There are abandoned truck tyres at the side of the road, which reassure me that this is the route I want to be on. I stop for a drink and realise that this is the first time I have pressed the starter button without hope, just an absent-minded expectation. Confidence in the bike is coming back.

I find myself heading towards a mining town. "That was quick," I think to myself. I had read about this, but in my haste to turn the map in my tank bag prematurely to show my progress, I had lost track of my err, track. So I head towards the mining town. There are lots of piles of the stuff that was dug out in an effort to find whatever they were mining for, I think it might be copper, and there concludes the lesson on Mongolian natural resources.

It isn't a nice town, not a good vibe. Kids pan in puddles at the bottom of piles. Boys ride round on motorcycles holding metal detectors across their laps. Here and there are rusty and abandoned heavy plant and excavating machinery. I stop to get water and draw a silent staring crowd; yeah this place doesn't get many visitors does it?

I find a row of telegraph/power lines, which usually indicates a road, and get out of town; I find a well-travelled road and figure this could be the one. Then a puddle, not just a puddle, a totally flooded road—muddy water of indeterminable depth, which has spread to the banks either side. I decide to take the muddy bit to the left. Big mistake, the mud turns out to be two-foot deep, and I sink down below my axles. Keep going, come on, my chain is covered in mud, the back wheel mainly spins but pushes me forward a little. I head for the higher ground, but that just stops me dead.

I am well and truly stuck. I can't push it, it won't move, it's standing up by itself, so at least I can take a photo. Well I'm stuck here now, and there is nothing I can do. I am totally dependent. I need help to get out of this. Before I have worked out a plan, a minivan comes by full of gold-toothed miners or possibly polished copper. Not the kind of people I really want to be in the debt of. But once they have sailed through the puddle, they stop and produce a rope. I put it round my forks and three of the miners struggle and persevere against a force that won't budge (like a Thatcherite government). The rope is at an angle, and it takes all my strength to not have the bike pulled over. Standing at its side, fighting the angle they are pulling at and with the engine running and bike in gear, slowly it starts to leave the suction it had sunk into. It gains momentum, and then out it pops. Now I'm really at their mercy. I'm in a very vulnerable position. I say, "Thank you," and they repeat "thank you" back to me. I show them my map, and they point back the way I came.

"Really? Back through the mud?"

"No dumb arse, on the other side." I'm pretty sure that's what they said in Mongolian. Well it needs washing anyway, so I turn around and go through the puddle that I now know for sure is not as deep as a minivan, and I ride on through to the other side. I wave and hoot my thanks at them from the other bank. Phew, well that was exciting or something.

Back to the mining town, where there is a little police box with a couple of coppers in it. I take them my map. No one seems to be able to point to where I actually am. This place is not marked at all, but he writes downs 11 km and points, so I go off not quite the way I came. I go the other side of the hill and, oh, would you just look at that? A T-junction and a bridge. If only I'd have gone the twilight side of the hill. Back on the right road, I go through a few puddles to wash off the mud.

Up ahead is a cyclist; he's from Spain. "Need any water?" His English is poor, but he makes up for it in enthusiasm.

"Err, how um, did, da, you, errm, ship, your, eh, bike here?"

"I rode it here."

"Oh wow, like em, ya know, have err, you seen that, um, Ewan McGregor, em..."

I know what's coming; he's very nice, but I just want to ride.

So I say goodbye and head straight into the setting sun. I just don't do that on my eastbound journey, head into the setting sun. Actually it's a pain in the arse. I could really use both hands on the bars, but one is keeping the sun out of my eyes.

I come to fields of crops. Crops in Mongolia? How am I supposed to camp when they are growing fields of wheat? I think it's wheat, and so concludes the Mongolian arable lesson.

It's getting dark. The hills have thrown a much appreciated shadow over me. I find a little spot away from, but still in sight of, a ger camp. I park my bike, put my bike trousers over my reflective panniers, and pitch my tent behind the bike in an attempt to be low profile. Pretty stupid really, when I'm camped in their garden. For the first time in weeks I get out my stove and hide the flame behind the bike. I really don't want visitors, vodka-wielding visitors. I cook my pasta and crouch in the fading light to eat it, washed down with water. My liver is a little confused and probably relieved. Take the night off and maybe tomorrow too. I'll let you know one day at a time.

A full moon rises and illuminates me like a big neon arrow saying "Foreigner camping here." Bugger, but no problem, no visitors.

I lie in my tent; it's like listening to a sound effects tape. The barking dogs protecting the gers and herds in the silent night, the horses whinny (is that what they do? when they are not simmering) and the cows definitely moo. Geese fly overhead, making their call to the stragglers to get back in the chevron formation, but what keeps me awake is the sounds I don't recognise.

DAY 80

ULAN BATOR AGAIN, MONGOLIA, 334 MILES

In the morning, a big mushroom has appeared by my tent. I'm sure that wasn't there last night. I bet that was one of the sounds that startled me in the night: a mushroom popping out of the ground. If I hadn't been around to hear it I wonder if it would have grown so noisily.

A herd of cattle wander past as I dry the dew off my tent and eat a sandwich. Once the tent and sleeping bag are rolled up and in the top box I always feel like I'm more able to make a sharp exit if I need to. I don't need to; the rest of the procedure is done in a relaxed manner. The engine fires up, and I ride off my grassy hillside and back onto the dirt.

I just plod along at 30mph, no rush, no urgency. I just take in the day and surroundings at a pace that feels right. It's so good to be riding alone. A river comes and meets the road. Bugger, that would have been a much better place to stay the night; I stop and wash in it anyway. I love this kind of living. It's taking opportunity of what the land and nature offers when it's available, although I didn't eat the mushroom this morning.

The road ascends away from the river; it doesn't seem that steep, but the bike is struggling. It's really sluggish. When the town of Bulgan appears, the bike is reluctant to descend the hill into it. I stop to take a look and find the rear brake smoking; the mud must have dried and seized it on. It's really hot, and I bet if it was dark the disc would be glowing. Actually it is glowing, I just can't see it in the light.

A mate of mine was sympathising with me once when I moaned about motorists who throw their cigarette butts out of their car windows when they are in front of you. He said especially at night when all the sparks fly up. You know, I think that happens in the day too. In the chart of stupid things I've heard, number one has to be whilst queuing up to get into a Glastonbury at 4 A.M. I bumped into a group who had travelled down from Carlisle in the very northwest of England. They were voicing their dislike for the Scots. The girl said, "The best thing to come out of Scotland was Mel Gibson."

"Well he's not Scottish," we replied in unison. Undaunted she said, "He was in Braveheart."

If I put water on that sizzling disc it may crack, if I don't all I can do is sit and watch the rubber seals burn. Bollocks. I prise the crumbling disc pads away from the disc.

I go into town. Ever optimistic I hope all will cool and be OK. I stop for fuel. "Good morning," the attendant says.

"Good morning, how are you?"

"I'm fine thanks, how are you?"

"Oh, I'm OK." I've deviated from the text book, and he has no answer to that. I could pick it up with, "What lovely weather we are having for the time of year," but I have other things on my mind.

I have no choice but to pass through the little town. It's not bad as they go, it almost has a European village feel to it. With the bike still running, I stop by a litter bin and throw away yesterday's rubbish. People watch from their doorways. I'm not sure if it's a motorcycle rider or considerate disposal of waste that has drawn so much interest.

Out of town on a paved road, and I have no back brake. I stop and change the pads. The old ones are baked brittle and crumbling. I carry spares; it's not a massive problem.

Still no brake; I stop again and pump it hard and watch fluid pour over the disc. Bollocks. The seal around the piston has melted, and it no longer seals. Replacement is the only cure, and I don't carry spares like that.

On top of that, Monklet's helmet has started to crack. It's all going pear-shaped.

Just as the scenery was getting good. Just as the road had turned to asphalt. Shit this is big, very big; turn around big, what now big, new plan big.

My Mongolian show is over; I had decided to do a little encore before I hit the Russian stage, and now it's curtains.

Well, might as well turn round. There is paved road all the way back. But to where? Do I go north to Russia? What is the likelihood of a Kawasaki dealer there? Or back to the familiar UB. I have a couple of hours before that T-junction to think about it. Is this small, black seal going to be the end of my trip? I'm tired, really tired, I'm dirty, I'm hot; researching the next phase of Russia has seemed more like a chore than excitement. Maybe I should just call it a day? After all, I have achieved my goal. Do I ship the bike? Selling it is unlikely and means paying duty and taxes. Scrapping it is just so wrong; bureaucratically the easiest option, but I just can't do that to it. Financially it doesn't owe me much, but I owe it more than a death of disembowelment in a Mongolian scrapyard. All these indecisions, all these options, and no real plan.

I get to the T-junction; I've decided to go back to UB. I stop to get fuel; a girl who was just sitting inside by the pay desk speaks good English. After I have prepaid she comes out to chat.

"Where are you from?"

"England."

"You rode all the way here?"

"Yes."

"Are you tired?"

"Yes, really tired, exhausted, and dirty, and my bike is broken."

"You want hot tea?"

"No thanks, I have water."

"How do you ride if your bike is broken?"

"Carefully."

"Maybe you can get your part in this town. Stay here."

"No, I think I will go to Ulan Bator."

"Your monkey has a pretty smile."

"Thanks."

"He is always smiling?"

"Yes, exactly, he is always smiling." But not me, I'm too tired, too indecisive, exhausted from the road, weary, dirty, unappreciative. Baby, I'm just totally knackered.

If this was an opportunity, I passed it up. Actually as I write I realise of course it was a bloody opportunity. Oh well.

I don't like this part of Mongolia. It's paved and industrialised. It has train tracks and even signposts.

As I head south it gets hotter. I have to stop to take linings out of my jacket and trousers. There is a deafening sound of crickets when I take off my helmet and turn off my engine. I eat a bit of sausage, and some stray dogs approach. I've heard stories of how vicious they can be, but they don't seem threatening, I throw them some sausage. It's nice to have company for lunch. Without so much as a bark of thanks, they turn tail and wander off. See ya then.

I'm entering Ulan Bator for the third time now. The first was with relief, the second with elation, and now it's with despair. Am I just tired today or tired of riding completely? I've just had a week off.

I've just ridden to UB on a bike the total value of which is £2,000. People spend far more than that on their two-week holiday and don't mourn its loss at the end of the fortnight. I still have money in the bank. Why don't I just let go of the bike and go play another game with the money. That sounds good. I've used these 300 miles constructively, and I have a plan.

I approach the city just in time for rush hour. I'm riding far too aggressively for one brake and after such a long day on the road, as well as being sleep deprived.

I try to slow myself down. Despite it all, I'm not hurt. Don't mess yourself up now, when you're so close. I overtake a car on a bridge. I should have given a warning hoot; it's the way it's done. I don't bother, and as I overtake him he swerves into my path to overtake the bus in front of him. I jump over further. We may have made contact. I jerked so violently out of his way, I'm not sure if I was jumping or I was pushed. I stay on the bike and blast out of the situation too fast for a heavy bike with only one brake. I make it back to my guesthouse. I should have done it slowly, more carefully. I just wasted a life.

The Swiss and German drivers are surprised to see me; the tide mark of mud one third of the way up my pannier tells a better story than any sticker does.

They offer me a shared ger with a deathly ill and incoherent Frenchman, who has spread his possessions over every bed. Dying and inconsiderate; I'm not staying here.

I don't like sharing, never have. I hate dorms, no matter what form they come in. Backpacking twenty years ago I hated them, and I still do now. I get a ger to myself. I shower and rehydrate, clean clothes, and then call Andy in England; he will send me a calliper. I have got the ball rolling, and now I have to stop here until I get a brake.

DAY 81

ULAN BATOR, MONGOLIA, 0 MILES

I sleep for twelve hours in my own personal ger. I must have been tired, and I can't make good choices with a tired mind.

I realise I'm just exhausted. The week off with Mum was not a week off. It was just different travelling.

Right, decision time.

Do I ship it, abandon it, store it, fix it, or sell it? Am I out of bounds, homeward bound, or onward bound?

The best way I know to figure out my next step is to meditate, and bikes are my medium.

The chop always evolves into its next carnation after a relationship ends. And when I eventually emerge from the shed with scarred and greasy hands from grinding, welding, and polishing, as I push the bike into a new season with mirror-blinding, shining aluminium and an engine that's fresh and ready to pull, and a mind that's clear and focused, that's when I know we are ready to go off and do it all over again.

So I sit in the sun with a hose and clean all the mud off. It takes a long time, but I have a lot of time. Then I take off the calliper to clean it up and assess the damage. The seal isn't a flexible rubber "O" any more, it's a crunchy crumbling "C" burnt, charred, and useless.

The owner has connections. I can ship it home from here, he can make a crate and everything, but it's not cheap. He also knows someone who may have a seal. I try to call the guy, but he only speaks Japanese or Mongolian, so that doesn't go very far. Every time I hear an engine I look up. I don't want to have to share my ger. I like having it to myself.

I need to find the DHL office to get the address for Andy to send the seal kit to. There are some charity workers in the restaurant, expats, come for some sticky cake. They say their office is right by the DHL office, and they give me a lift. I try to make conversation and understand what it is they do, but somehow I'm just not getting it. I think they think I'm stupid. I think the explanation of their job description is lacking. But I appreciate the lift. The DHL depot is a big, flashy modern building, which gives me hope; they say the package should arrive in about four working days.

I walk the main street and look at a few guesthouses. If I'm sitting around for a week, I want my own room. They are either fully booked, no bike parking, or too expensive. I walk the entire length of the city. I find one that meets my needs, and they will have a room free in two days, so I book that. I've walked miles, my trainers are so uncomfortable, but like my spare tyres, I can't seem to throw them out, although my tyres have far more mileage left in them than my footwear.

I take some back streets to the manufacturing side of the city, where gers are made. As I walk past I can see the various stages of construction. The trelliswork sides that hold the flared spokes of the roof, which lead to a circular wooden apex hub. I can see the way the felt and canvas is wrapped around it and the wooden floorboards. Tepees, igloos, gers, or mud huts, ancient indigenous accommodation does not seem to have corners in its architecture. Maybe it's to do with Karma. What goes around comes around.

Having travelled seven time zones ahead of British summer time now, I've acquired all the information I need by the time Andy has woken up. He will send me the calliper off his own bike to save time; to the address I have texted to him. What a star. It will cost more to send an entire calliper but I can't screw it up like I could trying to fit a seal in a calliper that could turn out to be warped anyway. It has already begun its journey before I have walked back to my ger. But it's not my ger any more, not just mine. A German couple, Geron and Bern, have turned up on BMWs.

My new roommates are good company, they have humour, and that's all you need. I righteously decline beer from them and vodka from the Swiss family—my little self-imposed detox. They try to make me go for kebab. I say no, no, no.

DAY 82

ULAN BATOR, MONGOLIA, 0 MILES

"Listen to what your body is telling you." That's what my doctor friend is always saying. You don't have to have a medical knowledge. Your body already does, and you just have to listen. Mine is whispering, "More sleep." Everything happens for a reason. Like it or not, I'm not going anywhere for a while so relax, rest, and recharge.

Strange how when you have a regular power source to charge your camera batteries there is nothing to take photos of. My box of charges, transformers, and converters takes up more space than my noodle supply and is heavier too, but it is used more. One day a single USB cable will charge everything, but until then, the space that used to be filled by cassette tapes is now full of plugs and leads. It's a little bit of the modern day that won't be missed when the future gets here.

Three in the ger is fine. I can handle that, but now we are joined by a very smelly Dutch cyclist. I know how hard it is to keep the BO at bay on a bicycle. The pad in the crotch of your cycling shorts becomes a sponge of obnoxious stench. I used to wash mine as soon as I stopped for the day when I cycled in India, and they would dry overnight. In cooler climates, you don't sweat any less, but the option of overnight drying disappears. However, I was at least aware of my smell and would do something about it whenever the opportunity presented itself. There is opportunity here, but it's always difficult to tell someone they stink. Much easier to discuss it with others in hushed whispers so the offender is kept unaware. What a silly practice that is.

My German roommates, or germates I suppose they are, have got here via Russia and now have the whole of Mongolia and Kazakhstan ahead of them. So it's time for them to change their tyres. They are really struggling, so I go off to buy them some washing up liquid to ease the tyre over the wheel rim. We had all watched tyre changing videos on YouTube before we left. I had even mounted my first set of tyres myself, but our efforts aren't a patch on the videos now we're YouTubeless. Geron is sweating and struggling. Even with my extended tyre levers, the tyres don't pop onto the rim like they do on the videos. I really admire his patience. Even when he nips the tube and has to take the tyre off again to mend the puncture, still he keeps his cool.

They abandon their old tyres. I suppose I should too. I'm pretty sure I will go to Vladivostok now; I have to come up with something. In this environment the second question asked upon greeting a new arrival is, after origin, destination. "I don't know" is not a satisfactory answer. The advantages of Vladivostok are I get to travel the Trans-Siberian Highway. I will have successfully gone as far as I can across Eurasia, from the Atlantic to the Pacific, and there are cheaper shipping options from there than there are from this land-locked country. It makes sense really. Plus I can take advantage of my outrageously expensive multi-entry Russian visa. Bern, in an effort to stop my indecision, tears the pages out of her Russian road atlas for me from Lake Baikal to the far southeast. Like my Mongolian map, this, too, is written in Cyrillic, which is just fine with me.

No one can agree on the length and condition of the new Trans-Siberian Highway. Somewhere in the back of my mind I remember hearing 5,000 kms from Vladivostok, but I don't remember who told me or where I was when I heard it, so that figure is irrelevant really. But regardless of the length of the dotted line of under construction road on my loose pages, I think I can now safely discard my old tyres.

Inspired by our stinking roommate, I decide to scrub and wash my bike jacket and trousers. There is little else to do, and I feel like being productive. I can trace my calliper's progress on the DHL site: it's in Germany at the moment.

Geron has been bump-starting his BMW since Moscow. The dealership there had said it would take eight weeks to get him a new starter motor in from Germany. I'm not sure if that's a Moscow thing or a BMW thing. I would have thought you could walk from the Bavarian Motor Works to Moscow in eight weeks; so he got his new one sent here and he, too, is experiencing the new found joy of a starter button again. I sit in the sun and watch my clothes dry. I work out my budget and how it is going, from the extremes of Sweden Rock and £10 beers to the wilds of Mongolia, where progress was so slow that a tank full of petrol would last two days and camping was free and frequent. I have averaged £40 a day over twelve weeks. Which is another reason to carry on eastbound. I think I'm establishing a plan.

The man who can fix things has turned up to take my calliper away. I think he either has the seal or he doesn't. They are without doubt people of incredible ingenuity, but I don't believe this is something that can be made or bodged. But not sharing my cynicism or my language he smiles and takes it away with him. I'm not confident he can fix it, and I'm not that worried either. I'm glad I've got another one on its way. I don't know how willing I would be to let this one out of my sight otherwise.

I decide to wander off; it's so easy to not move away from the familiarity of this self-contained holiday camp. I don't want to be eating expensive Western food; it's good, but I like Mongolian food. I find a little café and get some yummy noodle soup. I love noodle soup and saving money, as well as getting away from the comfort zone for a while, so I am tripley satisfied and leave a tip because I will definitely be back.

The owner is here late tonight. She is awaiting the arrival of twenty-six Koreans. She tells me of her fifteen years here and the changes she has seen, the increase in the city's population and the decrease of the country dwellers.

Ulan Bator's population has increased by a third in the last three years to almost a million people. There are problems with alcohol and pollution. I remember from the view I had from the hotel, it seemed most houses had gers in their tiny dirt yards. It's what they move into during the winter months, ironically the "tent" being a better heat insulator than the house. In the winter people burn anything to keep warm: plastic bottles, old tyres. And the smoke sits in the valley. Eyes stream all day, and your throat is permanently sore she says. In Germany they have a pollution table, and when the level reaches 50, warnings are issued, no one is allowed to drive and windows are kept shut. By the same scale the winter level in Ulan Bator hovers around the 1,200 mark. That has got to reduce your life expectancy.

The touring bus of South Koreans arrives. They are very loud, very enthusiastic, and very excited. I make a swift escape to the ger. But sleep is futile. They sing and clap their hands, so I get up again and sit in the restaurant with the Swiss guys and my laptop. They download episodes of *Shaun the Sheep* for their kids to watch as they drive through China, and I look at my calliper's movements. Some of the more excitable Koreans come into the restaurant to ask us if we would watch them rehearse some songs they will be singing to the children of an orphanage tomorrow. Well, why not?

"Go ahead." And so procedes the thigh-slapping, hand-clapping, joyous renditions of how Jesus is the way to happiness. Oh dear. When they have eventually shared all the joy that is in their hearts, we politely clap, and I tell them that I'm sure the orphans will love it. They are so incredibly over-excited; I think spontaneous combustion is quite a likely conclusion to the night's events. I go to my ger at midnight, checking where the fire bucket is, and spend the next two hours listening to clapping, singing, giggling, and door slamming. What I didn't know was my fellow gerees were also lying there seething, with earplugs and iPod earphones pushed in deep. At 2 A.M. I got up to use the toilet block with the intension of politely suggesting it might be a good time for them to shut the fuck up, but thankfully for all of us, it was time for them to say their prayers and go to bed.

It was their one and only night in a ger on their week's tour of the country. I think they should be allowed to enjoy it, despite their lack of consideration. For the love of God!

DAY 83

ULAN BATOR, MONGOLIA, 0 MILES

Throughout the sleepless night my fellow gerees had been plotting their revenge of revving bikes and general morning rowdiness. But the Koreans were up again at 6.30 A.M., and apart from a few puking hungover stragglers in the toilets, they were fed and back on their bus before most of the lazy overlanders were even out of bed.

I'm glad I wasn't rude to them last night. It was a one-off, and it's not like I have to work this morning. They weren't deliberately offensive, just bloody annoying. I don't know whether it's the race or their joy for their love of God, but they are actually hard to dislike. Anyone that polite and bubbly is going to bring out the best in me, even after a night of sleep deprivation.

Before last night the only contact I have had with any South Koreans was cycling through a gorge in southern China. When I was catching my breath at a vista point a group of Korean tourists stopped in their minivan: four very cute girls came over to chat. The only part of the conversation I remember was them saying, "Oooh yoo zo strong," and I have a photo of them standing by me on my bicycle, and I'm wearing a very big grin.

I drink my coffee and check on my calliper's progress. This morning it's in Seoul. Well there's a coincidence. I think Jo said it was only a three-hour flight, so it might get here today.

A very frail old American has turned up; he has just got out of hospital. Oh right, I know who he is. I don't tell him I met his Belgian riding partner. His bike has been stored and covered up, he is retrieving some stuff out of the panniers before it is shipped home for him. He can barely walk, let alone ride. He seems nice enough but is so weak. I help him cover his bike back up, and he gives me some chain lube. So much valuable stuff is discarded here: tyres, food, spare parts.

I soak my chain in lube; it's just at a time it could really use it after the muddy ordeal it went through.

Having discarded my tyres I am now keen to get rid of any other unnecessary weight. I decided last night whilst I was lying awake I could do without my top box now, and its contents could be put in my new holdall. So I spend a happy few hours pratting about with my luggage, only to decide actually I do need the top box, and anyway, it really doesn't weigh that much.

An English couple turn up in a Land Rover. I saw them here on my very first visit. They had attempted the northern route I had taken, and their vehicle is broken too. The body is held to the chassis with ratchet straps. In fact, the whole thing is falling apart.

The driver is a big brummy bloke; he is very matter of fact and easy going. His unruly bleached hair and scruffy clothing resemble his Land Rover, which in turn reflects his whole attitude. Not concerned with appearances or presumptions, he's a very unassuming likable person. I know of a Christian Cockney who could do well to learn a lesson or two from him.

I'm surprising myself at how I'm adapting to this communal living. I have even cancelled my guesthouse booking. I'm unbothered by the comings and goings in the ger or even the flies as I lie on my bed and doze. I really am in a very relaxed state. "Just relax," that's what I was told to do when I got here.

The Swiss family are off; I doubt our paths will cross again. Another goodbye, another email address.

Still in my weight-saving mode, and in honour of my absent English riding buddy, I decide to "completely unpack and repack my panniers." I discover some pineapple chunks and olives I didn't know I had, but know I don't want. I also refresh my memory as to what I am actually carrying.

My brake calliper is returned; nothing can be done with it. "Well thank you for trying." I'm not surprised. I suppose that can go where the pineapple chunks were. I never get any extra space.

Geron and Bern couldn't find the big market on their last attempt, so I offer to go with them. As we walk down the street our Dutch roommate cycles past heading for the train station. So it would appear we are three again. Somehow I end up buying riding boots, exactly the same ones I saw when my mum was here. I can't be accused of impulse buying. They are a black suede finish, stop below the knee, and there are two straps with buckles at the top. They have furry insides. To try them on I am given a plastic bag to put over my foot. "Mongolian sock," says the stall holder. From what I can understand, there are two types of materials used to make the boots: one is horse, the other is dog. The ones I am keen on are dog.

"Dog?" I ask.

"Dog," he confirms and then adds, "Good dog." Well if it's a good dog how can I possibly say no.

We look at ger furniture as if we were going to buy something for our home.

It's Friday night, I've completed my alcohol-free week, my calliper is still in Korea, so I will be here for the weekend, and I think it's time for a beer. We sit outside, it's almost like camping. We pull snacks from the panniers of our ever-present bikes, and our tent is a ger. There is a bright orange sunset, followed by a big moon. I wish we were experiencing this out on the steppe, but actually this is good. The bike is clean, lubed, and ready to go, if not able to stop. I'm happy with my new Vladivostok plan, and I'm clearly well-rested now, because in my deep relaxed sleep I'm dreaming about all sorts of weird shit. I only hope I'm not talking in my sleep.

Day 84

Ulan Bator, Mongolia, 0 Miles

Weekends, the blight of the non-working man. When the people who keep the world functioning take a break from all their hard work for two days it disrupts the lives of those of us whose life is a permanent vacation. My calliper is having a weekend city break in Seoul.

It's a cloudy morning. Geron and Bern are going to visit a temple; I saw it from the balcony of the hotel. I read about it; I decide I can live without the experience. I think it's the perfect morning to go to the supermarket and buy a bottle of Chilean red wine. I am right. It is. It's very quiet here today. One of the quad bike riders arrives and starts going through his piles of equipment. He's not easy to talk to. They were going to break a world record apparently. The bikes had been abandoned for two weeks whilst they took the train to Beijing. I asked if it was the world record for "longest unattended quad in Mongolia," but I didn't get a comprehensible answer.

I speak to my daughter, who wants Monklet to have a Facebook page. I spend the next two hours creating an email account for him, only to discover I made his date of birth too young and he is not eligible for an account. When I try to change it, it's too late. Warning bells ring somewhere in a cyber-pedo-alert security chamber, but a few hours disappear whilst I'm doing it, as does the red wine.

I go and get some noodle soup, come back, and doze. It rains; it's a very lazy day, self-indulgent and dull, and I decide only another bottle of red will really do the day justice.

Geron and Bern were thoroughly unimpressed by the temple, as they thought they were going to see the big Genghis statue, so they want consolation noodle soup; I decide it would be the perfect trip to christen my new boots. We all go back there in the evening and drink a few beers.

I am pretty happy by now.

Some scouts have arrived at The Oasis. They are fully-grown adults, in shorts, with scout scarves and scout caps, and shirts with patches sewn on. I'm not sure of their nationality, but they are European. What must the locals make of them? I mean tourists generally are a victim of ridicule out here and deservedly so, but this isn't a fancy dress party. There's being proud of your status, but have some etiquette. They are a great source of entertainment to us, and we take the piss relentlessly and perhaps a little too loudly. They will have their revenge.

Geron had been to the supermarket and comes back with some beers and vodka, and that's when it all starts to go very wrong.

Having managed to avoid all the invitations of vodka binges, from western Russians to nomadic Mongolian herdsman, only to fall victim to the transparent poison in a guesthouse with the German couple.

Geron was pouring massive shots, and we laughed loud and long, and I never once listened to my body. I have no recollection of what was said, but we were clearly being incredibly witty and at some point for some ridiculous reason I went and bought another bottle of Genghis Khan Vodka.

We are joined by the peroxide, Land-Rover-driving, brummy. And we all become even funnier than we were before.

The next thing I remember, I am on all fours on my bed.

Day 85

Ulan Bator, Mongolia, 0 Miles

I should have stuck with wine, shouldn't have had the beer, should have kept away from the vodka, shouldn't have had more vodka. Stupid, stupid, stupid.

Aaarrrgghh, what time is it? What time did we go to bed? Where is my stuff? A second bottle? What happened to it? Oh no. I feel awful. Why am I awake? Why am I alive? What can be done?

I need to go to the nice porcelain toilets inside. I'm not using the pit toilets. I may be some time.

I pass the breakfast area. Coffee? Food? No way. Back to my bed.

Every hour the brummy comes and wakes me up.

"Piss off." It's bad enough I feel this way, at least let me sleep through this self-inflicted agony.

At midday I tell myself I'm feeling better; my body is being petulant and won't listen to me. I struggle pathetically with a sun shade; all I want to do is sit outside in the shade. It's a complicated operation and clearly beyond my capabilities. I have my bag of supplies from my bike and go through them looking for something that I may want to try and eat. It is pointed out to me that the breakfast stuff is still available. I try toast, but it's too hard to chew, and swallowing is impossible.

Geron and Bern are going to the market. I seem to be suffering more than the others; it was that head start I gave myself. Do I voice it to justify my condition, or keep quiet and look like I can't take my drink? And does it even matter? I'll sleep more, I think, or maybe not. We have a new germate straight off the plane from Holland. She is pretty. I discover she is the affable contingent of the arrogant, sponsored, Dutch quad fraternity.

I can't sleep; I go and throw up. It's a rare occurrence, but if you are going to mix the grape, the grain, and the bleeding vodka, it's to be expected. I think I may feel better now.

Geron and Bern are back from market and packed up. They are leaving today. Did I know that? Rather them than me, but I'll miss them, when I stop thinking about my hangover.

"Feels so good not to be carrying my spare tyres anymore," said Bern as she gets ready to get on her bike. I wonder how many people say that as they leave this place. Hopefully, I'll be saying it tomorrow.

I have the ger to myself. I can sleep undisturbed, but I know this is going to be a 36-hour hangover; it has all the traits of a day-and-a-half of suffering.

I have a craving for sausage and mash. I know it's available in the Irish pub, so I get the bus to town. As I go in, the charity workers are coming out; I say hi. I can see they still think I'm stupid. Today their assumptions are more accurate, or at least my protests are more subdued.

I find a quiet corner to sit in and order steak and chips. It's hard to swallow; I should have stuck with the sausage idea.

The evening gets cold; the Dutch are not home. I am exactly in the frame of mind Greg was when I got here. It's time to leave. I light the stove, and it fires up remarkably easily. The ger heats up very quickly; it's too hot. I have to lay on top of my bed, then I start to sweat and I have to get up to open the door. I have put on way too much wood. I can't go to sleep until it calms down and I can close the door. I hope this is my last night here. I can't do another circuit of meet, greet, befriend, and leave. It's my turn to go somewhere.

Day 86

Ulan Bator, Mongolia, 0 Miles

It's that, "Oh I feel so much better, but I could feel so much better" feeling.

To the DHL website. No change. It's still in Korea. This will not do. I'm going to the office. Anyway, I need to send my riding boots home. They are no good for riding in and too big to carry. Go home good dog.

DHL want £75 to send them back. They only cost £25. They also say my package will be here at midday. I go to the post office and send them back for the price they cost me. That'll do.

The post office is more like a department store—so many rooms, so many different aspects to the whole mail phenomenon. I manage to buy a box and have to go to the other counter to get it taped shut, then another one for a customs form, and on to the counter where I pay for my postage. I am then led behind the counters and through a few doors to an x-ray machine, and I get to watch it go along the conveyer belt, and sure enough, on the screen are my boots. The man seems satisfied and stamps my customs form. I get a copy, and the longwinded but straight forward process is complete.

I have absolutely nothing else to do. I can only wait. So I go back home.

The Dutch quads are leaving; they most definitely have a superior complex. Usually when someone leaves they at least say goodbye. It takes more than four wheels and handlebars to have a sense of balance. They seem to have imported some women. They are perched on the back, lidless and generally unprotected, whilst the riders are togged up in helmets, suits, and boots. How very gallant of them.

The brummies want to go to the Irish pub, so we all take the bus. The place is full of westerners, and I'm sitting with three Brits, eating fish and chips. I like Ulan Bator as a city, but I'm very ready to leave. I've had my break, had my rest, had my relax, and now I'm just bored and frustrated.

I go to the DHL office, impatiently sitting on the couch whilst customs detain my package and charges me 50% duty. There is no point in arguing; I just want it. I read in-house magazines on corporate expansion and worldwide domination, of obedient employees rewarded with in-print recognition, and mutual back patting for an upward moving graph. It's all so career and company orientated, its everything I'm not; but I'm glad their weekend is over, and the world is moving again. My eyes are peeled for the courier to arrive from the airport. It's the first time I notice that the yellow and crimson of a Buddhist monk's attire is similar to DHL uniform. I look at them expectantly like I'm looking for enlightenment, when all I want is to lighten them of their load. Why is a monk in a DHL office? To collect his package I assume; I don't know. I didn't ask. The office closes at 6 P.M. The employees start to leave, but I don't budge. A courier carrying a brake-sized box comes through the doors waiting to be locked at 6.30. It's my brake, and it is fitted and bled by 7.30.

The waiting is over. I've got two days left on my visa. I won't be seeing any more of Mongolia. I've got one last night in a ger, and I have it all to myself. The nights are cooling down, and I'm heading to Siberia. I am prepared, and my bike is prepared. I light a fire and lock my door. I'm pleased and surprised I survived the dorm environment. Sometimes you don't have to go anywhere to make discoveries. Four weeks ago I was dying to see the inside of a ger. Careful what you wish for.

Tomorrow I start stopping again.

Day 87

Kyakhta, Russia, 231 Miles

"Feels so good not to be carrying my spare tyres anymore," I would almost definitely say to someone if I were not the lone ger man. But the trainers remain, although relocated due to a slightly different packing technique. I'm so used to my system. I know everything I carry and where it goes, and I notice when something is not there. Both my toothbrush case and comb are missing, and I search and find. The comb was hidden between the cracks in the wooden floorboards. I would not have seen it if I hadn't been looking. I'm so proud of my organisation and methodical packing. I can only apply this now I can go at my own pace, travelling alone.

I'm not facing much today that I don't already know. Even though I haven't done this border before, it will be my third entry into Russia, so for those reasons I'm not suffering too badly from the butterfly effect.

My breakdown perspective before I left was if something breaks that stops me in my tracks, I simply wait for that thing to arrive from home, and in that time I will get to know whatever village, town, or area I am in. The place I ended up not being able to leave was the final destination; whilst I came up with another final destination.

"Final destination." It always makes me smile when the plane touches down and the arrival is announced over the speakers. "Wishing you a pleasant stay in the city you have just landed in or a pleasant onward journey to your final destination." Well it's the grave really, isn't it? All of us will finally end up dead. But thank you for your kind wishes for my continuing transit to my death. Perhaps that's why it's called an airport terminal. It's all making sense. Maybe I'll call my next book *En Route to My Final Destination* and try to avoid the last chapter.

I'd forgotten how friendly the Mongolians are once you leave the city, all hooting and waving. Actually I don't remember that. I pass a truck, and the driver is particularly animated. I glance behind. My daypack that contains my trainers is dragging along behind me. If I hadn't put the ratchet strap through the arm straps it would be long gone. It's been dragging for a while. It's worn through in places. So much for my new packing method.

I wave at the trucker as I pass a second time with a more secure load. It's definitely cooler. I don't know if it's the altitude, the climate, the season, or the day. But I have liners I can put in my clothing, thermals, thick gloves, and scarves. It can cool more; I will be OK.

It's so good to be back in the green hills, the herders on horseback, the gers; I'm going to miss this. I have to come back. I thought the mosquitoes were going to be unbearable, but they were scarce. I thought the roads would be impassable, but as long as the rain stays at bay they are OK, and I thought it was going to be wild, and it's as wild as I choose it to be.

I can't even do a paved road from the capital to the border without making myself stressed. I can only afford to put in 10 litres of fuel when I need 15, and I'm wondering if I can make it. I have my first and only stop check in this country and have to pay a road toll, only 25p, but it was allocated for noodle soup. Why do I make myself ride this way? Doing constant calculations on distance, fuel used, and money left. I could have changed another $10 and worried about something completely different. When I'm not calculating, I'm remembering Russia, the lack of road signs, the constant police checks, and how I can't find my way out of cities. Then I remember shezlic, the meaty shish kebabs, and everything seems better. I ride on my bike, but really I travel on my stomach.

The mountains are looking more rugged as they head off into the horizon. It's exciting; I've been deprived of this.

I briefly consider going to see the girl at the petrol station who liked Monklet's smile, but my visa is ticking, and I blast straight past.

I'm getting closer to the border. With only 50 kms to go, I take a wrong turn. It's a pretty little market town looking down into a wide valley; the kind of place I would maybe like to stay, but I have to leave. I haven't had time pressure at all this entire trip. I don't like it.

This road seems to have all the Mongolian scenery condensed into one short journey. I pass sand dunes in a mini Gobi Desert, then pines and rocky hills, and once again open plains with ovoo and shrines positioned perfectly, where the skies double in size and trees have autumnal colours. Photo time again. Back in road mode.

I know I'm going to miss Mongolia. I would love to return sometime. My only regret is I will never be able to visit Mongolia again for the first time. Will I ever get that awe of the wild or only a memory of a feeling I once had.

I have 30 kms to go; I have enough fuel, so I stop for noodles, which I eat in a rush because I heard the border closes at 5 P.M. and I can't be stuck another day. It turns out the border is right around the corner, so I have more fuel and indigestion than was necessary.

The exit from Mongolia is straightforward. Very drunk Mongolians try to help me. If Russia lets them in, in their paralytic state, I think I'll be OK. I haven't drunk in two days.

Something changes instantly when you leave. I know I say that about every border crossing, but I get my exit stamp from Mongolia and at the next barrier are blonde-haired, white-skinned Russians. I didn't realise it, but for the last month any hair colour but black and any skin rather than wind-torn, sun-dyed, dark and weathered with blushed cheeks have indicated western traveller, and therefore a minimum of a nod of acknowledgement was offered. Now I have to physically stop myself from smiling at every western-looking person. They all look like me again (well you know), but they are native.

I'm handed the now familiar customs declaration form, but the lady only has Russian language ones, and she loves it. I, however, have an old one in English, so I know what to put in what box. Ha ha, you can't stop me that easily. A Dutch driver comes the other way. I let him copy my form. He thanks me by name.

"How did you...oh right, you know everything about me, don't you?" My passport number and currencies and quantities I'm carrying, I willingly shared my confidential information. And the sadistic customs woman will have to wait until tomorrow for her perverse thrills. She stamps my passport and points at the calendar, December 1st. "Oh don't worry, I have to be home by Christmas." She laughs; I really don't think I want to be in Siberia in December. Through the barrier, and I'm in Russia again and am able to fill my empty tank for a nominal fee.

I hadn't really intended to stay in this border town, but with another time zone at the border I'm too late to get insurance, and I'm not going to ride in Russia without it; too many tales of incarceration, impoundment, and fines.

The only complication checking into my hotel is that they want me to park my bike over the road at the police station, but the police don't seem so keen on the idea. I lock it up beneath my second floor window. I'm sure I will hear if anyone messes with it in the night.

I wondered if I would ever get so far out that places like Russia on a second or third visit would become familiar, when on my first entry it all seemed so foreign. But now it's not that I feel closer to home, I just feel used to being away from it. Mongolia lies in its own shadow just a fence away; the roads here are still dust, but the accommodation has been upgraded from cloth and felt to wood and corrugated iron. But the difference is children play in the streets, just like at home; out on the wild steppe of Mongolia there were no streets to play in. I didn't realise those things were missing until I saw them again. Although water is still drawn from roadside pumps, it is transported in Ladas, as opposed to horse and cart. I think they still have some catching up to do.

I find a pizza parlour, where some TV music channel is playing. The time is 3 P.M. in Moscow where it is broadcast from, but it's 8 P.M. here, and the realisation of the size of this country is dawning on me. Whilst it's dusk in Siberia, they haven't long had their lunch in the capital.

My room seems to have no electric. How am I supposed to charge my phone? I look for my headlight in my tank bag, it's not there. I know where it is, it's on a headboard in a ger in Mongolia. Shit. I remember my comb but forget my bloody headlight. Mr. Methodical has no one to blame but himself. Damn it.

I fall into a deep sleep and so the knocking at my door takes a while to bring me back to consciousness. Oh, that will be the prostitute, I suppose. I find some clothes and sheepishly open the door with annoyance and a little intrigue. Two women, wow. I recognise one; it's the hotel receptionist, with her translator. "It's OK, I can't afford two and anyway I have a phrase book."

Turns out my bike is not safe outside. I have to get dressed and follow a man on a bicycle to a gated and dog-guarded barn. I ride lidless, without insurance or underwear, and leave it there; it will cost £1.75. Well that seems reasonable. And there I was thinking I was going to get screwed.

Day 88

Baikalsk, Lake Baikal, Russia, 343 Miles

Redeeming my organisational skills, I find my Post-it note from Kazakhstan, written for me in Russian by an embassy employee asking for motorcycle insurance. I show it at reception, and it starts a four-way heated discussion, and eventually a very vague map is drawn for me. Actually it's not so much a map, more a squiggle; it could just be a rune. So I walk into town and see what is around. I can't read the signs, but banks are always easy to spot, so I go into one.

"This is a bank," says the teller.

"Yeah, I know."

"Go to administration." It seems to be the answer to most of my questions. I go to a big building. A cleaner who doesn't clean looks at my note, and with the same enthusiasm he applies to his cleaning, he nods something negative. So I go to another bank, the teller points up; I go upstairs and find an unlocked door. A woman sits behind a desk, and I show her my note. From a drawer she pulls out a blank insurance certificate and without emotion starts to fill it in. I have enough joy for us both. I searched through a town I don't know, with signs I can't read, and communicated in a language I can't understand, and I got what I wanted, two months insurance for £15. Whoopee. I'm well chuffed with myself.

I give a thumbs up and a big smile as I go back past reception. Their rune was useless as a map, but it at least signified that I could find an insurance place in town, and I did. So it was a good sign.

It had rained in the night so I was glad that my bike was kept undercover. The dog is restrained, and in just T-shirt and jeans I ride it back to the hotel. Without my helmet on it sounds quite rattley. And when I check the oil I find it is very low. On the rough Mongolian tracks I kept my speed down, but whizzing along at 65mph all day yesterday it really burnt away quickly. Is there such a thing as a worry-free trip? I go from calliper worries, to visa expiration, to insurance, and now back to the bike.

I try not to think about it. I'm in the land of cheap oil. As long as I carry some and keep an eye on the level, what can possibly go wrong?

Mongolia looks like a dream this morning, as I leave this Russian border town and look over my shoulder for one last glance at it. There was a layer of misty cloud between the hill tops and the land below. Out of the corner of my wind-glazed eyes I have one last fleeting glimpse to say goodbye. I really can't tell if that image behind me is real or not. It's in my camera, in my memory, deeply imbedded in my mind, but when I turn to look it's gone, like a memory jog of last night's dream, when today's busy schedule won't give me the time and peace to recall those soft-focus streams of images. My mirrors won't reflect it without the same blur with which my memory recalls it. And even the postcards don't depict it. Mongolia has an elusive life. It captivated me, but I can't capture it. It lies somewhere in a past time. It can be visited, but it can't be transported. Even its eagles don't fly over the border to Russia. In years to come they may tame the environment like America did in Alaska, but they could never tame the climate. How can you stop snow in August with modernisation?

Once again I'm heading in a direction that is not the usual. I'm north, and then I'm west to Lake Baikal.

Kazakhstan and Mongolia always filled me with trepidation, but with only the Trans-Siberian Highway to go, it's only my excessive oil consumption that concerns me. But everything I do now, every place I see, is a bonus beyond the original plan. No one is expecting me to be anywhere at any time. I have a visa for three months, bike insurance for two, and medical insurance for one, and the money hasn't run out yet either.

The skies are brightening but with a chill. The sun has lost its strength, I have ridden into autumn. Riding into fall, as opposed to falling when I ride. Not on these asphalt roads.

This trip became my longest bike trip six weeks ago in time spent, but as of yesterday it became my highest mileage too. I broke the 11,750-mile mark that I did on my Alaskan trip.

I manage to bypass Ulan-Ude and stop at a café for some lunch. It's a miserable experience. I get some grey ham slumped over a lump of potato. I get white sugarless coffee, the complete opposite to how I drink mine, and I get tea too. On top of that I'm being stared at blatantly by the other diners. When I go to get up, my jacket on the back of the chair makes it fall over backwards, just to bring even more attention to myself, in case someone was distracted by their plate of gruel.

It's a relief to get out. When it comes to built-in misery the Russians really excel themselves. From the decor, food, inhabitants, and furniture there wasn't a single positive thing about that place. But a frame of mind can change around the corner from the seat of a motorbike. Where the road meets the river an old man sitting on a rock turns and waves, and that's all it takes. With an unnecessary twist of the throttle, all is well inside helmet land again.

I ride for five hours on good road with road markings and signposts. There are laws and assumptions that people will obey them; indicators are used as are lanes. It's so much easier to drive this way. My map is in Cyrillic, like the sporadic signposts, and I know exactly where I am. I just can't pronounced it; it's all such a novelty. Has the hardest part been done?

I'm on a road of frustration, so close to Lake Baikal but barely getting a glimpse of it. The Trans-Siberian Railway hugs the shore, and the road runs parallel to it but is separated by a strip of changing aspen and pine trees. Although it's pretty, I came here to see a lake. Every track that leads down to the shore has unavoidable puddles across them, and I have a fear of deep puddles now and the muddy sides of them. So I turn back to the main road. Bern recommended this road to me. If she thinks this is good, she must be loving central Mongolia right now.

I stop to buy some smoked fish, it is still warm but impossible to eat without getting very smelly fingers. Maybe that is why the girl at the stall is hardly wearing anything. Must save on the laundry.

Knowing I'm going to be turning back at some point feels like I'm stretching an elastic rope attached to my bike. How much further am I going to ride around this lake before I'm pulled back in a more familiar easterly direction. I follow signs to a hotel, and with the ease of an English-speaking-girl I get an OK room.

The place seems dead. The girl tells me in summer they are busy and in winter, too, for skiing, but now is autumn, and why would anyone come in autumn?

"Yeah sorry, I'm a bit late."

I'm sitting in my room with my back to the window and notice a change in colours on the wall. I'm missing the sunset.

So I hurry down to the shore, and the lake reveals its beauty. I catch the end of the daylight as a spectrum of pastel colours across the sky are reflected in still, clear water. The inevitable rubbish is on the ground. However, sitting on a log on the stony shore, looking straight ahead at the silhouetted mountains on the other side of the world's largest freshwater lake, plastic water bottles don't concern me.

DAY 89

60 km East of Ulan-Ude, Russia, 268 Miles

I have a book designed specifically for the needs of the single-language traveller, like myself. It is called a "point-it" book and has pictures of everything you might need from guns to tampons, neither of which I have pointed to yet. If you need a charger for your iPod or even your phone it won't work. It's a bit old. However, if you need a betamax tape or a needle for your gramophone it's just the job.

I take my point-it book to the restaurant and point at eggs and then at toast.

"No toast," says the waitress; I point at a loaf.

"No."

"I'll just have eggs then." I sit and look at the pictures in my book until the eggs arrive with two slices of bread and butter. Whatever.

Indecision is the curse of my days now. Just where should I wander to? It's always been "what next?" And now I'm heading west, I wonder should I head home, but what about the highway east? Should I camp tonight or get a hotel? How much further should I keep going round the lake if I'm going to turn around at some point?

The lake's uniqueness is its volume, and that is contained in depth rather than surface area. So unless I'm going diving I'm really not going to appreciate that aspect of it. It contains one fifth of the world's fresh water. If it were emptied, we would all be standing a foot deep in water; which while it is still contained within the banks of the lake can be drunk without any need for purification, except ironically, where the rivers of Mongolia flow into it. Mongolia may be an organic country, but it doesn't have much in the way of sewage treatment, so what flows into Russia isn't quite as pure as the driven Siberian snow.

It occurs to me I don't even like lakes that much; I would not describe myself as a lake fan. Mountains yes, but not lakes: I seem to be drawn to them. The Aral and

Caspian Sea are both lakes too. Well this is the mother of all lakes and far superior to other great lakes. I think I can move on now.

I speak to a friend of mine in the States. He is in a bar, drunk. I tell him of my quandaries. I'm not sure he helps at all, but the banter is good. I decide to check out. Whilst I have been deliberating, a mist has come down, and so any hope of seeing the lake now in-between the trees and through the mist is pretty slim. I'm glad I took the sunset opportunity last night.

On the subject of pretty, slim, and chances, as I'm packing up the bike the hot towel girl calls me back to my room, and I follow her up the stairs, completely distracted from the fact all my valuables are on the bike unattended and the keys are in the ignition. I point at the towels, which I left on the spare bed, and I'm free to leave. Bike, oh yes, where was I?

Sometimes the same road in the other direction can be a completely different experience; however, this is not the case with this road. It remains as frustrating and disappointing as it was in the other direction yesterday.

My little helmetless ride yesterday morning made me aware of my engine rattle. It's almost a clunky slap, and I'm wondering if it is the bottom end. I'm accumulating evidence to prove my theory, and there is no shortage of reasons.

Sentiment should not be a decision maker. It is pointless to ship the bike anywhere when the transport costs are more than the replacement costs, just so I can have the bike in my garage and say where I went on it. I will have to settle for a blown-up photo and a number plate on the garage wall. That's how I can afford to do these things. If I had an 11-grand BMW I wouldn't be able to come here in the first place; not that I would want to be seen on a BMW; even by people I don't know. My bike and everything on it was all bought to be disposable, it was all bought for a one-way trip. It was never meant to own me. But the bond of my two-wheeled travel companion has become very strong, and it will be so hard to just abandon it.

"Thanks for the ride; see ya." A one-trip stand?

Now I ride without spare tyres, I've lightened my load. I consider all the spares I brought with me, the inner tubes, so heavy and bulky, the levers and cables, all the dehydrated food I haven't touched. At least I have a use for my wind-up torch now. I can pull off a sticker-festooned pannier and jump on a plane, and instead of giving my money to a shipping company, I can buy another bike in another country. Wouldn't that make sense? Can I think about something else now?

I stop to get some more fish from the smoked fish girl. I thought I might get a bit more recognition from her. I'm wearing the same as I was yesterday. Disappointingly, she isn't. It's a lot colder this morning. I divert off to the shore to eat my smoky lunch; it's choppy today, not the reflective smoothness of last night. I can't turn the bike around on the narrow path, so I ride onto the sand and get stuck; I keep stalling the engine under the strain of a sunken back wheel. Just what a rattling engine and slapping piston doesn't need.

I dig with my flapping sole and create some kind of ramp and gracelessly bump back onto the track.

Back on the road I get one of those flashes of brilliance, born of sober morning thoughts: most unlikely. Based on the theory of: "I have had the same broom for twenty years, five new brushes and two new handles but it's the same broom." What if I take the essence of the bike, its individuality, the oversize tank, the one-off pannier rack, the spotlights, and lever protectors, etc. It would make for a small crate, cheap shipping, and would turn the next KLR into an overlander like the one I have now. I wouldn't mourn the loss of a tired shock or burnt out spark plug. I keep its identity and leave the frame and engine numbers behind.

This is a completely brilliant idea, and now I can find something else to occupy my thoughts, I mentally build a crate with all that I will keep. I'm worry-free again.

Oh wait.

The engine noise is getting worse.

Still not entirely satisfied with my Lake Baikal experience, I decide to go and look at a delta that feeds into it. I head round a little peninsula, with fishing villages of tiny wooden shacks and gardens of grass, as opposed to the standard dirt. It's very pretty, but I still can't see the lake, and now I can't see the delta either; just a neat line of fishing boats high and dry on the stony shore. Deltas are best witnessed from above and deep lakes from beneath. Being on the same level I'm not really scratching the surface of all that it offers.

I take off my helmet and ride with my head bowed down towards the engine. It sounds awful, really ill. I turn heads, not from my exhaust note now, but from the singing metallic chinking from within my crankcases. I'll be lucky to make it to Ulan-Ude, let alone Vladivostok. Shit. Just as I find one solution, I get a new problem. The stress in my back is aching, and I limp along and get to the outskirts of the city. I call my KLR buddy, Andy, in England and describe the sounds and symptoms and ask his advice. In desperation for a diagnosis, I even hold the phone to the running engine, the cost of the phone call running higher than the revs. He says if it is big ends they will go soon, if not already.

I take out the filter. It's not really metally. Two guys pull up in a van.

"Ah England, Chelsea, Beatles. Do you need help?"

"What's Russian for magnet?"

I look in my point-it book, and there is no magnet. I check both my phrase books and nothing. I'm so busy looking at books, they decide I stopped for a reading break and leave me to it. I drain some oil to check the magnetic sump plug. It's not really a pyramid of swarf. I'm slightly reassured. I put the same oil back in and some new too, then by-pass the city. I ride out until the shadows of pine trees cross the road, which follows the river. This would all be idyllic if I was not waiting for the termination of my engine; seeing the crankshaft pierce the casings like an alien out of a chest.

I follow a track into some pines. I am relatively well-hidden, so I make camp. I am in a clearing of recently logged trees. The lumberjacks have left some clothing and equipment behind. I hope they won't be back for it tonight or too early in the morning.

The stove won't light, and I can't heat what was to be my first boil-in-the-bag meal of Lancashire hot pot. I dispose of the stove fuel and replace it with fuel from the tank and "woof" I have ignition and soon boiling water and a good and effortless meal. Well the food preparation was effortless, if not the heating method.

It's always scary camping alone. I have full phone signal so send a few texts. The forest is so quiet that when there is a noise it makes me jump. I have put my phone on silent. I do it every night because I'm eight hours ahead of the UK now. When it lights up with a reply even that makes me jump. Oh God, I'm not going to sleep tonight am I?

DAY 90

CHITA, RUSSIA, 380 MILES

Like a terminal patient, it's always a relief to see the light of a new day has arrived when I've camped alone in the wild.

As I eat some breakfast I try to appreciate my surroundings. The rising sun casts a rippling light on the tops of the pine trees as they sway silently. I like the solitude and tranquillity of the forest. What I don't like is the unknown and my lack of defence against it. Every time I have entered Russia I have been asked by customs, "Guns? Narcotics?" I laugh it off, as if I'd be that stupid. But I don't really know what is out here. I have a rock by my tent, and sleeping with my Swiss army knife open no wine cork will ever defeat me. I don't think it is adequate protection. Perhaps if I was viewing the tree-covered hills from the deck of my log cabin not only would the view improve, but the feeling of vulnerability would be left on the forest floor.

I'm wondering what this road to Vladivostok is like. I tell myself it can't be any worse than anything I have already ridden. It's the engine I should be worried about. But it starts up, the choke increases the revs as the engine warms, and along comes that tinny reverberating sound. It makes me cringe. I can't pinpoint its source, the whole engine sounds like a bag of nails. At least it started. I wouldn't want to be stuck here.

Relief keeps coming, with a packed bike and not being discovered, and again when I find my way back to the road. The sun was in my eyes when I came down this track, and it is again now. It's an early start. Heated grips and fingerless gloves are perfect balance for a clear autumn morning with a fresh chill. I slowly accelerate up to 60mph, independent, self-contained, and feeling good.

I see a motorbike coming the other way, but very fast. We wave and turn our heads to try in that nanosecond to indentify number plates and nationality, but neither of us brakes. Bummer really, because I want to know how far Vladivostok is and how much of the road is paved.

I think of the people I have met and the invitations I have to go to stay in Seoul and Taiwan, and that starts me singing *Yellow Rose* to myself by Roger Waters, with its Chinese-Taiwanese themes. It's as if my undistracted mind is focused with either perception or empowerment because another biker with flags flying comes towards me. I brake and turn to meet him. Oh right, I've heard of this guy, a crazy Chinese guy with no luggage except a massive subwoofer on the back of his bike and his daughter wearing a cardigan and open-face helmet—no camping gear, no food, no water, nothing. Riding round the world and on the road for seven years, but he appears to go home for lunch. He is the epitome of amazement. We take each other's photos and swap emails. Not really much to say to each other. There are lots of questions, but I prefer to have this encounter shrouded in mystery. He wears a multicoloured cotton jacket and trousers with fringes on the cuffs and trouser legs; he says he pulls one off at every country he visits. I'm in awe, he tells me he is for peace; I show him Monklet and tell him Monklet is for smiles.

It was a surreal encounter. I feel so much better. If he can make it, so can I. I'm glad I am going the other way; I bet he's a pain in the arse to travel with, always borrowing something. The ambiguity of his quest occupies my thoughts as I pass though the sort of scenery I expected of Siberia. I look down at a wide river winding past a scattering of lakes, patches of pines, and undergrowth, which break up the lush green meadows. Unfarmed and untamed, I don't think scenery gets any wilder.

Despite my early start, the day has flown past: it's time for a sausage stop. I have some shade and am hidden from the road, so with no urgency or impatient companions I once again re-fasten my tank with its ever-breaking support brackets.

I notice the exhaust is a little loose in the cylinder head. So I decide to use my spare exhaust gasket to replace the old one. But there is no old one, gone. I fit the new one and clean myself up with fizzy water. I spend over an hour eating, fixing, and cleaning. I've missed this selfish free time. As I pull back onto the road I'm thinking, does that engine seem quieter now? So was that noise transference from the exhaust valve, amplified through the pipe not insulated by a gasket? Is that why the sound reverberated all around? Have I fixed it?

Why am I the prophet of doom? Why is every problem considered terminal? The engine still knocks, but now it's just a top end low revs under strain noise. I can live with that, the engine won't die with that. Is that all it was? I don't so much ride with confidence as much as wait for this easy fix to reveal itself as blatant optimism. But the bike continues. I can cope with excessive oil consumption. Anyway, how far is it to Vladivostok?

Some might say a little knowledge is a dangerous thing. In my defence, I would say an expert is someone who knows more and more about less and less. I shall continue to collect my many experiences and learn a little from them all. OK, I misdiagnosed my engine noise. The reward for displaying such symptoms of pessimism is relief.

I'm still in anticipation of the road ahead, not really sure what to expect, but that's half the fun isn't it? That's why I left home—the element of the unknown. I'm glad this feeling still exists. If I knew it was a smooth road all the way how dull would it be? It would be nice to know how far I have got to go, though.

The road isn't perfect, but it's perfectly acceptable. It's an ideal temperature, and I'm happily heading east. After 12,000 miles I wouldn't describe Siberia as endless, it seems anything but. It's vast, but the end is near, I'm just not exactly sure how near. It's hilly, it's flat, it's pine-covered, and then barren; it's varied in a slow sort of way. All the time I'm riding into autumn; yellow slowly turns to orange, like a three-day sunset. Turn away and you notice the change when you look again.

I stop for another golden photo opportunity and finish off the smoked fish because it's making my panniers smell. I put some more oil in the bike and forget to put the oil cap back on. I notice before I'm in top gear that it's spraying everywhere. I turn around, trying to ride with my foot over the filler hole, which has an oily mist pumping out of it. I know exactly where to find it; it will be by those golden aspen trees. I have a film of oil over the right-hand side of the bike now, smoking off my quiet exhaust, and now my stickers are even stickier.

Other than burning oil there is a variety of smells, the pines of course, and cellulose from the newly-painted Armco. There is the smell of boiling liquid tar being poured into potholes. The vats are heated by burning logs and transported in diesel trucks bellowing black exhaust. And then there is the fish. I just can't get the smell of it out of my hands.

Unlike the Mongolian wilderness, this is not so accessible. A V-shaped trench had been gouged either side of the road, making a swift exit into the woods impossible.

I plod along past the occasional village, most of which are unmarked and unnamed, so I'm not really sure of my progress. When I come to a sign, I stop to turn my map page over, and a jeep pulls up behind me.

"Where 'av ya bin, where are ya goin?" usual banter, but stinking of vodka. He is a big man, bearded, weathered, and looking just like the kind of build suitable for surviving such a climate. I tell him I don't speak Russian, but that doesn't stop him. He gives me directions for when I reach Chita, something about a roundabout and taking a right. I do at least get that much, then he shakes my hand. If the contact is useful for no other reason it at least reminds me how wasted the other motorists are. But actually, although I'm used to it now, with only a few exceptions people stop because they have the time and the interest and they just want to be of help. These people walk into my life and become a brief part of my journey. It's human contact without clear communication but with the best of intentions.

Jet fighters appear, flying in tandem and doing loop-the-loop. They swoop into my field of vision and keep my attention until they disappear into the haze.

I find some waste ground, some abandoned buildings turned rubbish tip. I've had my eye open for such a place for a while, so I do a sneaky oil change. A military truck comes by; they are just young lads.

"Help?"

"No thanks," I smile and nod, just look the other way please. I point at the planes.

"Yes, up in the sky, that's what we do." They proudly acknowledge.

As I approach the grey of Chita's industrial side, I can see the smoke-belching chimneys, and I face the daunting task of finding the centre and a hotel. I see a sign: 2,165 kms to Khabarovsk, and now I know because it's another 700 kms from there to my new final destination. A quantity at last; a whole new set of calculations I can do in my head.

I come to a roundabout and assume it's the one the drunk was telling me about, so I take a right and for a while it works: it gets me going in the right direction towards the centre. I follow a river and then a train track to a station, and there is the big central square. Its very grand; extravagant modern buildings line the wide clean streets, neon lights and a vibrant atmosphere. It's Friday night, and it feels like a city ready to party. It's such a contrast to the sullen suburbs I just came through. I stop to check my guidebook. Some Finns in a camper van approach me. They would like a photo. They had seen me earlier apparently, but I'm preoccupied. They got me at a bad time. I need a room first and foremost.

A local biker stops and tells me to follow him. We pass a grand hotel. I'm not sure what is going on there, but on the steps are maybe twenty stunningly beautiful women, all in evening dress and photographers snapping away at them. They look like supermodels, every one of them. I'm not preoccupied about finding a hotel now. How come whenever the scenery is spectacular I'm obliged to catch up with a bike in front? First he takes me past where the bikers meet and then to a hotel and tells me to come and meet them all later. You are never alone for long in a Russian city if you're riding a motorbike.

I have hot water; I wash myself, my hair, and my clothes, and still I can't get the smell of fish out of my fingers.

I've gone through another time zone. They don't need it. It is still light at 11 P.M., and the sun doesn't rise until 8.30 A.M.; they are just showing off.

I walk the streets but can't find food; the restaurants are filled with fat middle-aged women dancing between the tables. I walk towards some promising lights and find myself in a high-rise housing area; it's not got a good feel to it. An inadequate car revs its little engine and spins its wheels, the international sign of a small dick.

I find a café, and with my choice words, I order exactly what I want. It is busy, with well-dressed diners around large tables, their conversation stimulating enough that I can go unnoticed at my window seat. Then the music is turned up, and they all leave their tables and dance around the restaurant. It seems so contrived. I'm glad I'm invisible. I get out as soon as I've finished my last mouthful. Unfortunately, my visibility does not come back. As I go past the bike meeting place I can't seem to catch an eye, and as for the non-stop parade of beautiful women, I'm so past getting laid now, they can sense it, I'm sure. I project it. It's hard to be blasé and nonchalant when ya gagging for it. I'm the shaking, sweating, cold turkey junky in the pawn shop, desperate to sell my last bracelet to the uninterested proprietor. He doesn't care I need a fix, and there's no point in it coming off my wrist.

Fireworks wake me up in the night; I've got a very strong feeling I've missed something significant happening here tonight.

Day 91

Chita, Russia, 0 Miles

I'm going to have a day off; there are lots of sights to see, and I've got a really lovely room to stay in and avoid them.

The hotel breakfast is buffet-style, mostly attended by stewardesses and pilots. You know you're staying in a good hotel when you have clientele like this. I don't really recognise most of what I put on my tray, but I save the sweet for last.

When I have consumed most of what I brought to my table, I pop the sweet into my mouth. It's a cube of butter, and I can't get the taste and greasy coating out of my mouth. I suck in my cheeks and try to swallow, but my mouth has just been saliva-proofed with a layer of grease. I'm trying to think what facial expression would be described as "butter wouldn't melt." Mine is more "butter wouldn't ingest." I don't even have any coffee left to rinse it down with. On top of that, I have to pay £7 for the privilege because my room didn't include breakfast. Well, if I'd have known that...

Spending a morning in my room writing is as enjoyable as riding when there is no time pressure. I even wear my glasses. It's a bit like dressing for the part, although my sight is definitely deteriorating. When Bern gave me this map of Siberia, she mentioned she could not read the print. It looked fine to me, but it's true, when I glance down to my tank bag I just can't focus on it. I hold my finger on the blurry word, but even on these deserted roads I can't hold my gaze long enough to focus before I have to look up to check I'm not about to trundle off onto the tundra.

The problem with a day of writing is it's not easy to write about. And having struggled through it, at the end of the day when I write my diary, I have to write about writing about writing and that's when I know it's time to find another subject matter.

I wander out to see some sights; it's warm and sunny, and it really brings out the beauty in the place. I haven't brought my camera out with me so the statues,

312

arches, and architecture have to be committed to memory. But, apparently, they weren't.

I find a bustling market. I always like them, especially if I'm looking for something in particular, but I'm not. So I wander aimlessly and buy some supplies from the supermarket. I can't find an open Internet café or any Wi-Fi so I end up going to the grand hotel which I passed last night, and they are happy to let me sit in their foyer and use their connection. It's another exercise in the self-awareness of a pink laptop.

Today is just lazy; I eat in my room and look at maps. I'm not lonely or wanting for anything much. I could have left today but I'm quite content not to. Maybe it's because the festival season has finished at home now. I know there is nothing else I would rather be doing and nowhere else I would rather be. Happily alone in Siberia, I never would have thought it.

DAY 92

SOMEWHERE NEAR MOGOCHA, RUSSIA, 457 MILES

I can't believe I slept until 9 A.M. It's that time zone lag. I only take one day off, and the butterflies breed in my tummy. I've never experienced such a continual thrill of nerves on any previous trip. I suppose it's a good thing. If no other trip provokes such trepidation, will it seem bland? Won't be doing the Lake District next year then.

I remember to take my supplies out of the fridge. The tomatoes have frozen, but they will probably travel better that way, maybe. I diligently write down all the major city names in Cyrillic so that I can recognise them in a glance should a signpost grace my path at a fork or roundabout. I decide to take the same way out of the city that I came in. I know it was not the quickest, but I also know getting out is always harder than getting in (there were once a generation of Siberian inhabitants who would agree with that, I think).

I stop to treat my engine to some 98 octane fuel and then manage to get completely lost and ride round endless Soviet housing blocks and onto dirt roads. 30 miles later I am at the beginning of a highway that began 10 kms away from where I started. That was a waste of super power fuel. And there is the sign, in Cyrillic, for Khabarovsk. I'm still unsure how much of this road will be paved and how readily available fuel is. It's cold; the engine seems to like the cool air, and I have to put on my proper gloves. No more posing in fingerless gloves, and I'm wearing my scarf, as opposed to my bandanna.

In places the road is so new there are no white lines and no Armco. It's brand spanking new—President Putin's gift to Russia apparently. The only worry is, with road this new, when will I get to the bit they haven't done yet? Apart from that dodgy area in Dagestan, this has been the only other time a really fast bike would have been any use at all on this trip. But to conserve my ever increasing oil consumption and knocking engine I just plod along at my usual 60mph. I stop every 100 miles for fuel, just in case the fuel stations run out with the asphalt. There are some very big, modern American trucks coming the other way. One of the drivers waves at me. I'm not used to this at all, and although I catch it, I don't have time to return it. The driver has just completed a long and lonely road back into civilisation, and I have only just left the city. Human beings aren't a novelty to me yet.

Things are really cooling down. When I stop for my lunchtime soggy, thawed tomato and sausage sandwich, I have to put on my linings and fleece. All these clothes usually sit behind me in a bag offering back support, but now I'm wearing them I may be warm, but I can't lean back and give it the easy rider position anymore. Autumn has arrived here, with orange ferns in the undergrowth and yellow aspen amongst the pines. It's a little scary being so far out; there is some traffic, but nothing much in the way of any form of life.

Back in western Russia every fourth car wasn't a Lada, but here every car has a paper temporary number plate in the window and is right-hand drive, even though they drive on the right. There is a massive migration of imported second-hand cars from Japan, personally and commercially imported. The further east I ride, the left-hand drive Lada becomes a rare sight. These are fast cars, reliable, and being right-hand drive it means the drivers can pass me even closer, despite the wide open road ahead. Bastards.

The scenery is pretty—hills and trees, not really barren wasteland, just untouched and for most of the year I would imagine uninhabitable. I'm not feeling so good; it's coming on in waves, maybe something I ate. That damn tomato. I haven't had a hot meal in two days. It's so much effort ordering from a menu I can't understand. I have to be in the right mood; hunger usually being the best motivator. I make myself stop at a café; it has some trucks outside, so it can't be that bad, can it? All heads turn; they always do. Sometimes it's OK, sometimes I feel like screaming and sometimes I just can't face it. I point meaningfully at an item on the menu. "Nyet" is the response; it means "no." I still can't pronounce it right, and God knows I've heard it enough times. It's the most frequent answer to my requests.

"Stroganoff," the miserable bitch says.

"Da," I reply, meaning "Oh yeah, great, that will be perfect." I drink my black sweet tea and out comes some dreary meat on top of some watery, bloated rice, and it's barely warm. "This, darling, is utter shit. You should be ashamed of ya self serving up such inedible tripe. It's a waste of fairy liquid getting this plate dirty with such fowl-looking slop, assuming you bother to clean them at all, or is this just the last lot of rejected leftovers? This isn't a place of exile now you know, I don't have to be here, I have choice." If only I spoke Russian. It comes with bread. Great, more bread. Everything I eat is either between or accompanied by bread. I push it away so as not to be put off my tea and walk out. I paid upfront of course. Places like this the world over would never chance leaving the bill until after the meal. It's such an awful experience; I just want to get away. I don't bother to top up from the large galvanised tanks of fuel out by the stinking and no doubt frequently-used pit toilet. I just leave. Now I really feel rough. Nothing I can put my finger on, just need a nice room, a good bed, warmth, and familiar food, but not bread.

I can't tell where I am. Fuel stations and civilisation in general have dried up. So much for writing down the town names; the only one that is ever signposted is Khabarovsk in ever-decreasing distances. A town is signposted. I can't read the name. I only know it in Cyrillic but said town is down 11 kms of dirt road. I don't need this, but I don't need to run out of petrol either. I overtake a car because I'm eating his dust, I hit two rocks in a row really hard, the suspension bottoms out, and the front wheel now has more flat spots than an engine at altitude.

I get my fuel. God, what is this place? It's got the now almost obligatory Soviet housing blocks, but it's so desolate: not uninhabited, it's just had a joy bypass. I chance getting some supplies. Soon as I'm here, I find a...well, it's a shop. It's a faded sign over a doorway in a grey concrete block. I walk through, and there is a bunch of musty, royal blue couches and armchairs, and beyond, a few shelves of dull and uninspired packaged food.

A young girl is sitting at a counter looking as stuffed as the couches. She shouts for her mother, and I think granny comes. I can't find water. Every transparent liquid I see is vodka. I find lemon water. I'm really feeling bad now. I go get my water bottle off my bike and show it to them. They find me fizzy. I hate cooking and brushing my teeth with fizzy water. Bread and chocolate, that'll do I guess. I decide to rid my pocket of the ever-swelling pile of coins. I count out 50 roubles. It takes a while, but there is no rush for anything in this place. Urgency is not anywhere to be seen. I make a gesture like I can pull up my trousers now, and it raises a slight smile, and they follow me out, to check I'm leaving? Three generations of utter boredom watch me mount my tired dirty steed. Maybe they're pleased I'm leaving, maybe they're envious, and I leave into the unknown and leave them in their complacent familiarity.

The sun is going down; shadows are getting longer. I have to find a place to camp. So much of the tundra each side of the road is just a boggy...well, bog really. I cannot, dare not, get the bike stuck again, not out here, not on my own. I don't like the places I'm finding, and I'm running out of daylight. I go down a dirt track, the entrance to which is blocked by a mound of stones and rocks. It goes to a kind of quarry, an excavation for the use of building this improved highway. It will have to do.

Dry mud is impossible to get tent pegs into, and I'm far more exposed than I would like. In this vast expanse of wilderness there are surprisingly few places to actually camp. Now I've stopped, I have nothing to concentrate on but the way I feel. My bottom explodes, and I think I'm going to throw up. This is not really the place to feel like this, especially being on my own. At 9 P.M. it's dark. I put on my thermals and get into my sleeping bag. I can't face food. I can hear the Trans-

Siberian Railway on one side of me and the occasional vehicle from the road on the other and pure silence in between...

I wake in the night because there is something outside the tent. By the time I have wound up my torch and unzipped my sleeping bag and inner and outer tent the source of the noise has long gone, but I'm not going to just lie there in the unknown. I at least want to know what is going to attack me, man or beast. What beasts are out here anyway? Bears? Siberian tigers? Those vicious marmots with the sharp pointy teeth? It rains a little in the night, but it's mainly that infinite star canopy that I see when I brave the outside in my long underwear for yet another piss. It's a long and lonely road this, very long and very lonely.

DAY 93

CLOSE TO BELOGORSK, RUSSIA, 515 MILES

When the daylight comes there is a sheet of ice on my seat and top box. Not frost, ice. God it was cold last night. Siberia, cold? Who would have thought it. You'd think someone would have said something.

But I feel better, just a pounding head. That's fixed with forcing myself to drink 2 litres of water whilst I dry the ice off the tent and make a peanut butter sandwich and swallow an Ibuprofen. Back to the road.

You would think after all these miles and all these different terrains I would know how to ride appropriately, but I go too slowly and too cautiously over the mound of stones which were put there precisely to stop me being this side of them in the first place. The rear wheel spins and buries itself. I'm stuck, again. I manage to push the bike back and put it on the side stand. I kick the stones around a bit and then breathlessly attack the new hurdle with more speed and determination, if not more confidence.

So I start my ride today with breath that mists up my visor and a sweat under all my layers of clothing. I'm back on the road 430 miles further down it than I was this time yesterday. Well that warmed me up. I continue east. I was kind of looking forward to this autumn ride but an autumn ride is one thing, out for a few hours and then home for a whisky or cuppa tea, but getting out of an icy tent, waking up to a frozen seat, and riding for twelve hours in clear blue, but still cold skies, isn't so much an autumn ride: it's a big chill.

But today for the first time making an appearance from the bottom of my pannier is the heated waistcoat, plugged into the auxiliary socket especially fitted to accept its plug of warmth and comfort. I didn't even know I was going to Siberia when I packed it. Like everything else, it was bought on the cheap, and I don't have the thermostat for it. I usually just turn it on and off, but that's not a necessary practice, not out here. I leave it on constantly, and it's wonderful. It warms the whole of my body, even the extremities. I figure that as soon as the heart pumps the blood around the body, as long as there is warmth around the heart, then the blood will warm and then in turn warm up its destinations. But best of all is the collar. It's so toasty, and I push my neck against it to feel the electric warmth. It's better than a hug. The problem is it makes me sleepy.

It's only the third time I've worn it. The first was in Canada, a consolation on a rainy day for the scenery I was missing. The next was on a 300 mile ride to northwest Wales one New Year's Eve. I was stuck behind a row of cars in the fast lane of a dual carriageway doing exactly 70mph. Knowing I'd been pushing my luck a lot on that ride, I tried to remain patient and not undertake, but I didn't try hard enough and flew past them on the inside, just as the leader decided to pull into the slow lane I was occupying. Swerving, braking, and accelerating all in a heartbeat, I took evasive action and avoided contact. I sped away. In my mirrors flashed a blue light. One of the cars was an unmarked police car. Bollocks. I pulled over in a lay-by; he was most perturbed.

"Wait there," he said and went to deal with another motorist who had pulled into the lay-by behind us both. I'd been riding for a while, so I unplugged myself from the bike and walked around a bit to stretch my legs. When the plain-clothed cop came back to me I was composed and ready to justify my actions. It turned out the motorist he had been speaking to was the self-righteous, law-abiding citizen who had created and led the fast lane procession. The moralistic wanker was so disgusted at the police car's erratic driving to catch me after my unlawful riding practice, that he had taken it upon himself to stop and get the cop's number to report him. By the time the officer had returned to me he wasn't in the frame of mind to prosecute, he wanted an ally to back up his actions, and he vented to me about this idiot who had caused this incident in the first place. Well yes, officer, I agree entirely. I never even had to admit or explain my conduct; he only wanted my details in case he needed a witness, should the threat of him being reported become a reality. I hadn't witnessed any of what went on behind me after I accelerated away from my near-miss manoeuvre, but I agreed wholeheartedly to back him up all the way should I be called upon to do so. After that encounter I didn't need to turn my heated clothing back on for quite a while.

I do calculations in my head, miles to kilometres, distances to days. I look forward to significant numbers: halfway down the highway, 13,000 miles travelled since home. But then there are no exciting numbers due, and I realise, apart from pump attendants, shop assistants, hotel receptionists, and ugly old hags who dirty plates in the name of food, I haven't spoken to anybody in over a week. There aren't even any police checkpoints like there were in the west. I guess it's not a desirable place. "If ya wanta come here, feel free, we ain't gonna stop ya." I'm not stopping at cafés any more either. Too many bad experiences. In fact, I'm not eating at all. I'm listening to my body, and it's not telling me it's hungry.

I have a green, aluminium water bottle. It's strapped to the front of the bike. I have never put water in it, but it became quite useful for oil storage now topping up the oil level has become a daily task. Today the vibrations and bumps got the better of it, and it sprung a leak, so it's time to discard it. But it came all this way; it feels disrespectful to just unceremoniously dump it. I struggle to put sentiment aside. There will come a time when I will knock the dents out of my panniers. Will I mourn the loss of those souvenir impressions I collected en route too?

It takes so long to cross a page of the map. Gratification does not come quick with these immense distances between areas populated enough to be given a name. OK, I admit it, Siberia is a little bigger than I first thought, not endless but definitely prolonged. But it's bright, and it's sunny; it's a dry ride. I bet this must be a miserable motorcycle experience in the wet.

I don't have many songs in my head, and I don't have many thoughts either. I'm not travelling some inner path to self-awareness, I'm just trying to use a *Delicate Sound of Thunder* to get a Lady Gaga song out of my head. Most of today's riding has been done in a daze; concentration levels are low, not distracted, just low. I don't need concentration; the road is smooth and there is no traffic, no police, and no livestock wandering the road—just a smooth black ribbon of asphalt.

I make my mileage, so focused now on my destination I miss the turn off to a town I half wanted to see. The half of me that didn't care is pleased for the lack of diversion, and the half that did want to see it checks the guidebook again and decides it's not really that interesting after all. So I am wholly in agreement, I'm informed, I know what I'm missing, and I don't care. A democratic decision has been reached between my two minds.

Shadows are my only constraints. When they reach a certain length I have to stop. 515 miles. Today has been my highest mileage day so far. Yesterday held that title for one day. Considering the hard seat and slow speed, that's pretty good. This ain't no tourer, but with the additional padding of thermal underwear and lined trousers, my arse has more mileage in it.

I find a river, a big, brown, slow-moving silent river, and although judging by the amount of rubbish left behind, it's a popular spot, it's late, and I take a chance and camp there. I cook a ready meal; all these emergency things I bought from home are getting used now I'm at the end of the journey and haven't had an emergency. When I go to wash my plate in the river I find it's really warm, un-naturally warm, like a warm patch in a public swimming pool, and I wonder what secretive Soviet experiment upstream has generated such heat in this stealthy flow of gravy brown water. In fact, it's not totally silent. In the night it makes the occasional "plop" for no apparent reason.

DAY 94

KHABAROVSK, RUSSIA, 429 MILES

The night seemed cold, but there was no frost on my seat, just low energy levels I suppose. This could be my last night's camping, and I have so much food left, so extravagantly, I make beans on toast for breakfast. Well, beans on blackened bread eaten with burnt fingers.

There is a sandy track from the river to the road. I hate sand. Once again I'm breathless and sweating by the time I get to the road; it's a great warm up, work out, or am I just out of shape from three months of throttle twisting?

I have a full tank, so the day starts with 100 non-stop miles. A truck overtakes to wave at me, then slows for a second chance as I pass it, and up he comes again. This is getting a little annoying now. When he pulls in at a café, he indicates that I should stop and have a drink with him. I pass the opportunity by. The less contact I have, the less I want: I'm focused on the road ahead.

It's going to be another high mileage day. Adventure will never find you on the road if you don't stop to let it catch up. From dawn to dusk I ride, getting closer to my destination, but nothing gets close to me.

Now I have started to empty my panniers of food, I am really into shedding weight. I discard my olive oil, and later I find a few cloves of garlic I was carrying. Oh yes, that will really make me go faster.

Sometimes the road runs with the train track, sometimes with a river, and sometimes it runs alone. It's the only variety available. As the day progresses my shadow slowly emerges from behind me until I can see it out of the corner of my eye. Sometimes I try to take photos of its perfect definition of my riding position, but when I hold a camera I lose the pose.

The distance markers are beginning to represent years. When it's at 1,914 I think to myself that was when the First World War started, then 1,939 the Second, and it occurs to me all that could happen again in this century we've only just begun. When it gets to 1,965, the year of my birth, I start to associate the years with events in my life. Each new number is about forty seconds away, perfect for my attention span. It starts with schools attended, houses lived in, and albums released. Then into the 1,980s and girls I was seeing, places I travelled to, and bikes I owned. It is a real memory exercise. The 2,010 sign was missing, but come 2,011 all I know for sure is I'm going to see Roger Waters in May, and then 2,012 and beyond I realise I have no clue where I will be living, house or country, no plans whatsoever. And I think that's the way I like it.

At kilometre 2,161 I've long since stopped playing the year association game; it's stopped being fun once I passed my expiry date. I've reached Khabarovsk, and I cross a massive bridge over the equally massive Amur River. It's the river that divides Russia and China, but clearly not at this point, unless I've gone very wrong. Instant sensory overload, there is so much to look at. My mind has really gone numb, slowed right down. There is no end-of-the-road celebrations; I'm thrown into civilisation with no time to consider what I've just done.

There is traffic and things to think about like finding a hotel, once again negotiating my way into the centre of a foreign city. And once again I manage it perfectly, without one single wrong turn or one signpost understood. I'm so glad I'm not one of the satellite navigation generation and I can find my way using a black and white map in a guidebook. For the first time the temperature warning light on my bike has come on. Turns out the wire has come off the fan. If my body had a temperature warning light it would also be illuminated. The thermals are no longer needed but not easily removed.

The streets in Khabarovsk are hilly, a little San Francisco-like. I have heard good things about this place and have been looking forward to seeing it; I may be taking a day off. These hills are no good in traffic for a hot and tired engine. The top end knocks like a hammer banging nails into shipping crates; I hear ya knocking, but I can't commit. The first hotel has no rooms, the second I can't find, the third has no rooms, nor the fourth. The fifth is a railway station resting house, and I can't leave my bike unattended here while I go and find the reception. The next one has expensive rooms, but it's late, I'm tired, and this is what credit cards are for.

They have secure bike parking and the promise of a much-needed registration of my visa, and there is a sign that says Wi-Fi. So I walk the four flights of stairs to my room. Laundry? No, I'll be OK. I've got one more pair of underwear. I'll just have a shower. The shower holder is loose, and the water sprays everywhere. I go get my Swiss army knife to fix it but slip on the wet floor and go down hard. Arrggghh. It's a quick fix, but now my shoulder and back are wrenched and bruised. I shouldn't have to do this in an expensive hotel. No Internet—I have to go down two floors to get reception, by reception.

Anyway, I'm hungry. I walk to the café I saw by the station. It closes at 8 P.M., and it's gone 8 P.M. because I have crossed yet another time zone. I find a fast-food place. The burgers look bad, and I've had enough of meals between bread. Well, there was a big sign for a supermarket by the hotel. I'll get something there, but I can't find it either. OK, last resort, the Chinese restaurant, but it's full, not even a table for one. Shit. Back to the station, and I get a kebab. It's actually pretty good, but I'm eating and walking and not really enjoying it. Back at the hotel, and the Internet is slow and keeps cutting out. I'm really not having a good time.

That's been the problem every time. If I read about a place and like what I've read I will have expectations. This guidebook must have been written by a really optimistic or patriotic researcher because, more often than not, I only find disappointment. If I wrote the next edition it would be so cynical visitors would be pleasantly surprised by what they saw, if they bothered to come at all.

DAY 95

NORTH OF SPASSK-DALNY, RUSSIA, 322 MILES

With cool air and city noises drifting through my open window, I sleep really well. Maybe I should move to the city. Not this one though, with its population of half a million inhabitants. Khabarovsk is officially the world's coldest city. There are certainly plenty of autumn leaves blowing around the streets, but the temperature of this place is mainly reflected in the white, blancmange-consistency scrambled eggs and potato pancakes for "included" breakfast. How difficult is it to heat food in this country? Obviously very.

There is no way in hell I'm staying another night, but I'll take a walk around the city.

I'm sure it was pure coincidence putting Guns 'N' Roses's *Chinese Democracy* on my iPod as I walk down to the river, the far bank of which laps against Chinese shores. The sky is the deep blue of high altitude, and it complements the spires of the church. If it wasn't for the golden domes on top, the spires would fade into the firmament. It's worth a few photos, but I feel it's more because I ought to than an uncontrollable urge to capture the architecture. It's the same with the city in general. After a few hours I feel I have walked around enough. My feet certainly do. OK. Been there, seen it, done it, back to hotel. Check Internet. "Nych." I have to pay for another log-in code if I want to get online today as well.

"What do you mean, as well?" OK, don't bother, "Is my visa registration done?" Suddenly no English is understood. No surprise. No registration. I make one of the easiest decisions I've made in a while. I leave.

760 kms left to go to Vladivostok—the end of the country, the end of the trip. I'm not going to make it today: it's already midday.

Slowly it occurs to me, I don't think I really like Russia that much. Everything has been disappointing. Sochi was just a rich city, fine if you've got money. The coastal road there was just crawling trucks pumping black clouds of diesel exhaust into the air and down my lungs. The Caucasus Mountains were littered, and the "attractions" were little more than building sites. The Altai was tacky, touristy, and as with every place that has seen any kind of life, littered with plastic bottles and any other discarded trash. Then Lake Baikal, when I could see it was, again, left like there was a dustmen's strike. The Trans-Siberian Highway was good. I'm really glad I got to do it, but there is nothing I have seen that makes me want to come back. The women are beautiful, absolutely stunning, but that's only because they're not covered in discarded plastic bags and smashed vodka bottles. As a point of transit, a gateway to Kazakhstan and Mongolia, it was fine, but as a destination in itself it's been lacking.

As I leave the city, like every country since Poland, people sit on stalls and sell their wares at the side of the road. It's large mushrooms this time, from sex to watermelons, from fermented mare's milk to wicker baskets, they have sold what they had to offer. I like that. Although the English lout in me desperately wants to stick his foot out and kick over a bucket of 'shrooms, not in a nasty way, it would just be so much easier than making contact with a melon. Of course I would never do such a thing, but, man, those buckets are soooo kickable.

This road feels different to the Trans-Siberian. I can't put my finger on it, and then I realise I'm going south. After west, it's my least travelled direction. I would never notice it on the M25, but on such a significantly easterly trip, a change in direction alerts my internal compass, but it's OK; today it's the right way.

When I stop on a side track to have my lunch, someone has shat right there. Problem is now I'm down on it, now I've decided I don't like it, I can see fault with everything. I move on and find a river to stop by; it's OK, but again, rubbish everywhere. They have no pride in their country. You can boast the biggest this, the highest that, but if all you see is trash where ya promote natural beauty then it will always fall short of its potential.

I could use some stimulation. I'm getting a little tired of my thoughts, now they are going in a downward spiral. They are not deep, or funny, or even interesting. I think I'm winding down; I fill my tank, possibly for the last time. I'll still need more oil, though.

With 300 kms to go I find a motel; it will be nice to have an early finish, 6 P.M., have a proper meal in the restaurant, and sit and read my guidebook. I deal with the bolshie babushka at reception, and she takes me to a room, but she can't get in. Lots of knocking, many keys, and twenty minutes later she opens the door to reveal a drunken, unconscious guy on a bed with the TV blaring.

"I'm not sleeping here." I want a private room for that price. "OK, give me my money back." What a complete waste of time.

Back on the road I'm scanning for a possible camp site. There are some nice little hills, but I think everyone thinks that, and they have been made inaccessible. I follow a track into waist-high grass. I'm hidden from view. Yeah this is better than some shared box of a room. The sun is going down, but it's still warm. I take off my shirt and light mozzie coils and spray myself in my skin-melting DEET.

When I went to buy this stuff before I left, there were three choices in the shop—weak, medium, or strong. Let me see, I thought. Do I want to get bitten a lot, a bit, or not at all? So I went for the strong.

Everything has been used so sparingly, and consequently I have lots of everything left. Only the life of the engine is limited, and while I boil my rice, of which I still have one-and-a-half bags, I contemplate again what is causing the excess oil consumption. Rings, valve guides? Seals? And what's the rattle? Broken valve spring? Timing chain? Piston slap?

My boil-in-the-bag chicken tikka masala is so good. The emergency food is better than my usual efforts. All the heat, cold, bumps, and abuse have done nothing to take away its yumminess.

I consider all the options I may have, as far as bike shipping goes and whether I will head east still or back west. The budget has been fine. I don't want to blow it on pointless shipping. My house has not sold whilst I have been away. What a waste. I could have had it rented out, and someone else could be financing an extended journey.

I drive myself crazy sometimes with preplanning. Everything is considered in advance: camping, food, piss stop. It's having too much time and too little distraction. It's one thing to be organised, but this is bordering on OCD.

To prove to myself it's not a problem, I leave my dishes unwashed and my teeth unbrushed. I'm a rebel without compulsion.

DAY 96

VLADIVOSTOK, RUSSIA, 171 MILES

Everything is dew soaked, and in the time it takes to eat, wash up, and pack, the sun still has not risen above the bush I had camped behind. So I roll up a soggy tent and ride back through the long grass, following the indirect route I made last night, back to the dirt track.

I still get a thrill from that start of the day ride, rested and refreshed, packed up and geared up. The engine fires, and I look around me to see if it has alerted anyone as I put on my gloves. I do my high kick to get my leg over the luggage, get my balance, kick up the side stand. Reduce the choke, pull in the clutch, clank down into first gear, and wobble off down the dirt, looking through a dew-soaked screen to see where the road is. Check for traffic with a look beneath my chin guard like butter wouldn't swallow, bump onto the smooth surface and into the new day. Maybe the last day.

Today is the day I go as far as I can. Today I reach the Pacific, or to be specific, it's the Sea of Japan, but if you're talking the seven seas, then it's the North Pacific.

I pass four hotels in the first half hour. I don't care. I saved money camping and definitely ate better than I would have in their restaurant.

A car overtakes me inquisitively close and then slows so I have to pass on the inside. A camera is pointing at me; I don't mind; I haven't had this for a while. I'm almost posing, almost, but I'm still assuming the position.

The road starts to descend, there are some lovely hilly bends; I am really going for it. I haven't leaned for quite a few days, and that was only on a roundabout. I'm flashed by a truck. I brake hard and upright the bike; around the next corner is a speed trap. I know they heard the revs drop, but there is nothing they can do. I don't want to get stopped now, not so close to the end, and be fined money that could be better spent on a hotel.

327

It occurs to me, possibly a little too late, that I can shoot video on my phone. It's small and easy to hold in my left hand as I ride. I have a little go as I wind down the hill. Monklet's tail flaps in the wind and wraps round the heated grip, and when I look back at the footage of oncoming trucks and leaning bends, it's one of those sequences that appears better than the reality. Three months of road and thirty seconds of video footage—that was a flash of belated brilliance.

I find myself going through a polluted, slum-ugly city, full of red traffic lights and pedestrian crossings. This is where the ugly people are sent. Where's the eye candy? Everyone is so sullen, it reminds me of home. I'm sure I could have bypassed this place. I must have drifted off and missed an important sign. The signs I see now are leading me against my sense of direction, down dirt roads and under railway bridges, but the masses are going that way too. It's a messy diversion, but it pops me out at the main road again, and I inadvertently got to see a place I will happily never see again.

I've only done 100 miles by lunchtime; I thought I would be in Vladivostok by now, based on the previous high mileage days and no traffic lights. I didn't want Mongolia to end, but I do Russia. It's not the riding that bothers me; it's the country I'm riding in.

I find a litter-infested layby; it has receptacles that resemble bins, but only to me, because no one else has used them. I finish the last of my food, use my last wet wipe, and dispose of last night's rubbish.

50 miles to go. I'm not nervous nor elated, not happy or sad or depressed. Not numb, disappointed, not excited or stressed, not anything, just relieved I suppose, no feeling of achievement.

Just a badly-packed, dew-soaked tent, a pile of smelly clothes, incomplete paperwork, and the worry of what to do with my bike now. Did I come too far? Should I have stopped sooner? Left wanting more? Or felt like I've had enough? Funny how the fun has gone.

A police check at last. I hand him documents so enthusiastically, before he even asks for them he has his hands full. He clearly can't read what they say and hands them back to me too quickly. "But look, I got insurance." I'm on my way again in less than a minute. Well, that was uneventful.

On the road into Vladivostok there is a big concrete sign announcing the name of the city. It's a standard thing, but in this case it's worth a photo. I cross three lanes of unforgiving traffic, and conveniently, there is a car stopped, so I ask the driver if he can take a photo of me, which would be great if he hadn't cut the "K" off the side of the photo. It's a sign; it sums up Russia—"could be better."

The happening part of the city is at the end of the peninsula. By accident I find my first choice of hotel, but I can't find the entrance. I ask at a car wash, but it appears to be gone. It can't be good for business. One of the first rules of being a successful hotelier must surely be "have a door." All the best ones do.

Apparently babushkas can be found at the train station holding signs for rooms to rent. I wander around the area trying to look homeless, but no one approaches me. I try a second hotel and am given a map to a third. No bike parking, but a quiet street. It will do nicely, although I have to pay for a three-bed room. Before I can check in I have to write an explanation as to why my visa has not been registered yet. I have no hesitation in naming the premises of empty promises in my alibi.

I head for a café with Wi-Fi and treat myself to my first beer in ages. I hear some English from the table next to me, a Yorkshire man on business. The waitress makes him aware that I'm English too. He gives me a wine gum and says he can help me with the shipping of the bike and takes my email address and phone number. I haven't spoken to anyone in nine days; I'm finding it difficult to shut up and to be coherent too. The combination of the two is not doing me any favours.

The Wi-Fi goes before I can check flight prices, and the beer goes to my head.

My bed is so uncomfortable; I do the Goldilocks thing on all three beds, then lean the first one up against the wall and sleep on the floor. My head is too occupied with shipping to think about what I've just done.

I remember reading once: there are goal seekers and the goal celebrators. The goal orientated, they are the mad ones; they are going crazy, and they are creating their own craziness, and then the craziness has its own momentum: they move deeper into it, then they are completely lost. The other type of person is not a goal seeker—he is not a seeker at all, he is a celebrator. Celebrate! You are breathing and you are alive, and you have consciousness—celebrate it! Then suddenly you relax, then there is no tension, then there is no anguish. The whole energy that becomes anguish becomes gratitude; your whole heart goes on beating with a deep thankfulness—that is prayer. That's all prayer is about: a heart beating with a deep thankfulness.

I read this when I was trying to get into the knickers of a particularly spiritual girl. She turned out to be playing for the other team. But at least I learned a little wisdom from the bad romancing.

I passed my goal weeks ago. What the hell does that make me? I ran right off the pitch, out of the stadium, so what's the score?

Day 97

Vladivostok, Russia, 16 Miles

I got some silent texts in the night; the Yorkshire man, true to his word, said someone will be contacting me with a view to shipping the bike. Well that's a good start.

Vladivostok is a city of Wi-Fi, it's transmitted across the entire city. All I have to do is buy a card, scratch off the number, type it into the home screen, and the world awaits my perusal until my credit runs out.

I look up flights. The prices are so expensive. Getting anywhere from here is going to cost a lot of money. I decide I must be doing something wrong and head out to find a travel agent. She speaks really good English and finds me a flight tomorrow for £800; it's cheap because no one wants to fly on September 11th anymore.

I walk down to the docks. You never know, I might find an English-registered ship that has room for a bike on board, and maybe me too. I'm up for that. But all I see are gunboats; it was always a long shot. I do find a souvenir shop and look for stickers, but fridge magnets is as close as I can get and a set of Russian dolls, the first I have seen. One of those prefixes I just knew but don't associate with a country. Like Panama hat, Bermuda shorts, French fries, Scotch whisky, Turkey breast, and Greece nipple.

Back home a single room has become free. It's on the other side of the hotel, so I can't see my bike, but I can see the harbour and docks. I have an amazing view until I hang up my tent to dry.

I had noticed a shipping agent building next to the hotel. I try to communicate with the security guard, who is very enthusiastic but not very helpful. I am passed on to two fat, gold-toothed ladies, who are extremely cheerful and make hand gestures to enquire whether I'm considering flying or shipping. "Oh wavy hand, definitely wavy hand." I am led through the depths of the building, and then we stop by a window.

"Yul Brynner," says the lady.

"Oh right, it's Yul Brynner's house." I read it was round here somewhere, and it's not Rory Bremner, which I kept saying by mistake.

I'm taken to the office of a man who has a very large desk: it's unfeasibly big. There are infinite possibilities of what you could do with a desk that size. I could turn it upside-down and put my bike on it and sail it home. The man also has a very large world map on his wall. I would really like to trace my route on it, but it's behind me, and I should be looking at him. As if there are not enough distractions in his office, he also has a balcony with a view almost as good as the one from my room. He points to a building by the train station and says I should go there and writes in Russian what I should look for and ask for when I find what I'm looking for.

I think I have just spoken to someone quite important, judging by his office, or possibly just wealthy and inadequate. Either way, I head in the direction he pointed with my piece of Cyrillic-inscribed paper. I pass old women holding "room for rent" signs. Where were they yesterday?

I find the shipping company and am told to wait for Yuri. It's a name I've heard of. All roads apparently lead to him where the shipping of a motorbike is concerned. Whilst I'm waiting, Eugene calls me, a connection from the Yorkshire man. He gives me some options and will call me back.

Yuri arrives; he takes me to the Korean ferry terminal to get prices. It's an option, I suppose. He also has some Americans who have a container going to Houston, and I can put my bike in there. He tells me if I abandon the bike here, I will not be able to get another Russian visa, as the conditions of the temporary import would be breeched. My stomach does that thing it does when things look bad. I don't like Russia that much, but I don't want to burn my bridges to Kazakhstan and Mongolia. I can't scrap it or give it away, and it costs more than it's worth to ship. It's 5 P.M. on a Friday night. I have got so much information going through my head.

I have the contact number of the "Iron Tigers," a Vladivostok bike club. I was going to call them anyway, but Yuri knows them and where their shop/clubhouse is. So I jump on my bike and follow him through rush-hour traffic, trying to keep landmarks in mind. I follow him for half an hour all along back roads that I will never remember. We are miles from the city. As I ride I think to myself I will just give the bike to them; they can have it. Maybe they can give it to someone in need, for all the good deeds that bikers have done for me this trip. I'll just walk away from it. "I gave it to a bike club." That's a good ending; that will do.

The Iron Tigers are somewhere between a gang and a club. If this were the west they would most definitely be classed as a gang. We are very east, and the biker camaraderie is as strong as it can get. I have the number of the president, but I meet André, the second-in-command. I think he is. Him and Yuri talk at length in

Russian. I stand around hopefully and try not to let my attention wander, which is never an easy task, especially considering all the data input I've got today. Nothing is sorted, and Yuri leaves. How the hell am I going to find my way back?

So I ask André my options, and he invites me upstairs into the club house.

Put me in a Hell's Angels clubhouse, and I would not be this composed, but I'm in a bit of a situation, and I amaze myself how I can step up and deal with it.

First I lay my gun on the table and then chop out two halacious lines of cocaine, whilst André shouts at one of the topless women in a dog collar to bring some whisky. Would also be a perfectly acceptable end to the journey.

He does offer me a beer, but I know I have to find my way back to my hotel at some point, through fearsome traffic. I need to be alert and on my guard, so just a line, if you please, my good man.

He speaks good English in a unique voice. There are some bikers who, from a suit or a prison uniform, still scream biker. This is not the case with André. He is not a small man, but his face is not hardened; his tattoos, if he has any, do not show. His hair is blond, and his demeanour, whilst assertive, is not intimidating. Sometimes the best way of showing who you are and what you do is by blending in.

He doesn't want my bike.

"It is of no use to us without Russian registration, and anyway, we have 200 bikes already."

God, I can't even give the thing away. He tells me for 8,000 roubles he can organise the bike to be crated and put on a train to Moscow. That's good, that's less than £200, but I still have to get myself to Moscow, and its 10,000 kms away. I do have a connection there, the Russian girl I met at the Ukraine Bike Show; from Moscow I could ride the bike home. André says I will live in the clubhouse for a week until I fly to Moscow. There is no question of trust. I am a biker, therefore entitled. That's how it works here. He has three Belgians and a Frenchman staying here at the moment. But they will be shipping to Korea shortly; their bikes are currently clearing customs. It takes a few days.

The club is off to a party for the weekend, but I can stay here if I don't mind being alone. "Mind being alone? You don't mind me being here with your 200 bikes then, unknown to you and unaccompanied?" I explain today I have been given so many options, I have to go back and process them all. I thank him, pick up my gun and my helmet, and give him a hug and a soul brother handshake, and head for the stairs.

Just as I get on my bike to leave, the Belgians and Frenchman arrive. They are frustrated at the time it is taking for their bikes to be cleared through customs, before they can be put on the ferry to Korea. The Frenchman says there is another ferry port option; it is a 250 km ride from here. Word has it the customs procedure there is straightforward. He has an email from a British guy who got his bike shipped back to England on a ferry from South Korea. So I follow him back inside the clubhouse, so he can retrieve the information off his laptop for me. André tries again to get rid of the beer, but there are no takers.

"It's like my bike," I tell him, "you can't give it away."

"You must drink in Russia," he says, "It is the only way to cope with Russia." That makes a lot of sense and is very good advice. Why did I not get told that until I was in the far eastern part of it? It should be stamped on the visa, not be kept a Siberian secret.

With the information I need, I again say goodbye and head out in the direction André gave me. It sounded quite easy, but when I found the main road, he had told me to go right. I know it's left, and I take a left and head back to the city. His English was very good, so I can excuse him not knowing his left from his right. Finding my hotel is not too difficult, which is just as well because I don't know what it's called and my map is in my room.

I get on the Internet, and I call an English phone number on Skype. A woman answers.

"Hello, this may sound a bit strange but I am calling you from Vladivostok. I have been given your number by a Frenchman who rode with your son through Mongolia. He said you know of a way to ship a bike back to the UK from South Korea."

I was speaking to supermum. She reeled off numbers and names, companies and costs, routes, duties, times, and procedures. She said her son will be home later and to call again then. Every option I've been given today has made me want to run away. This one sounds good. Not only is it financially viable, but I get my bike back home too. I also get to ride through another country, and I have already been given an invitation to stay with Jo if I'm ever in Seoul. It's not the end of the road at all.

I need food. I've drunk beer on an empty stomach whilst I have spoken to her. André said it was a necessity. Who am I to argue?

I find a pub with shite beer and shite service. The menu is in English, and I still order shite. Back in the room I speak to son of supermum. He bombards me with more information and will email me yet more. My new bed is more comfortable. I think I might have a plan, a new plan, a new country. Everything happens for a reason.

Day 98

I go down to the café to get my coffee and look out of the window to check my bike is still there. It is, so I can continue to figure out what I'm going to do with it. It would be most inconsiderate of it to go missing after all the effort I'm making not to give it a watery disappearance, the consequences of which Eugene clearly explained to me. Anyway, I refuse to push it off the end of Eurasia into the Sea of Japan, even though Japan was its place of birth.

I call the shipping office in Korea. I speak to someone helpful, but the man I want won't be there until tomorrow. The progress is teasingly slow. Can I or can't I? Shall I just go to Korea anyway?

If I do end up taking it to Korea, I think perhaps a clean is in order, so I take the bike to the car wash I saw the other day. I have barely ridden 100 feet the wrong way down my one-way back ally and coming the other way is the Frenchman with a Belgian buddy. What are the chances?

We have a longer chat this morning; sounds like his riding buddy through Mongolia rode like Greg did, when he wanted to ride more like I did. If we'd have met we might have found a world of joy. I could go to the clubhouse and stay there, but they leave tomorrow, and anyway I like my new little room with its big view and stolen Internet connection. And in my ever contrary way, now I have the option of company, I don't actually want it.

The car wash guy remembers me, and without language, it's arranged I will give him a back hander if he power washes my bike. He sprayed it with something that, if the bike colour were not impregnated in the plastic, then I think it would have taken the paint off. It took off a lot of the grime, and if it had been done properly it would look amazing, but only the part of the wheels that were showing got sprayed and trying to get him to squirt his toxic load on the inside of the mud guards was painful. It's so shiny where the magic, cough-inducing spray was blasted but so the same where it wasn't. This, I think, is the way Russia is. Whether it's scenery, officialdom, photos, or bike cleaning, "could be better" is the mission statement. Even with my limited abilities and attention span, my "that'll do" attitude would put me in a class of perfectionists in this place.

Still the bike looks 90% better than it did, and he is very happy with his disproportionately large kickback. After such high pressure aquatics, it's always a relief when the bike fires up. I'm done in no time. If I had known it would have only taken fifteen minutes, I would have arranged to meet the Frenchman at whatever café he was off to.

There is nothing much I can do, because once again, it's the weekend and the people who make things happen are helping themselves.

This place appears to be quite a holiday destination, even this late in the year. I wander through the pedestrian zone where music is pumped through speakers on lamp posts with incredibly good sound quality. George Michael has never sounded so good, and I wonder if they play requests. The streets are full of courting couples, who become unsuspecting victims of clubs and restaurants that prey on such vulnerable sources of income. I observe cynically, I'm either in self-conscious sobriety or the drunken letch, although this evening I'm in-between. I smell shezlic on the air. I follow my senses to an open barbequing area and order hunks of meat dripping in bloody juices. The stall holder is very excited about my earrings, and we have a conversation in Russian. I only have individual words, but they are appropriate and witty and delivered in the right order. Oh look at me, I'm integrating.

I sit at a plastic table and people-watch whilst I fill my stomach. Finding food I want, managing to order it, and then it actually living up to its expectations is a rare occurrence. Times like these have to be appreciated. I see a couple having an argument and lean back in my plastic seat with a feeling of satisfaction.

Day 99

Vladivostok, Russia, 0 Miles

I go to get my coffee, but they won't give it to me. It takes a phone call and translator to tell me that until I bring back yesterday's cup I can't have another.

When it's the appropriate time in Korea I speak to my man at the ferry terminal. It's a difficult conversation, but I think we understand each other; he will email me some instructions.

I had scanned and copied all my bike, passport, visa, and insurance documents before I left home and emailed them to myself. So it was easy to send my Korean man what he needed. I love it when my organisation skills pay off. That was also why I got all my visas before I left. A reoccurring theme in my research was the frustration of waiting for a visa for one country whilst the one you have for the country you are in runs out. I knew there would be enough bureaucratic delays that were beyond my control, so I might as well deal in advance with the ones I knew about.

I get a text from a friend at home. "Off out for a ride, wantta come?" I've been gone over three months now, the whole of the summer, did you not notice? I text back, "I've been away all summer. I've ridden to Vladivostok," his reply is "All that way but you won't come out for a ride." I'm not texting back; he'll figure it out.

I'm just PC boy today, in front of my little computer in my tiny room with my massive view. I eat crisps, chocolate, cinnamon rolls, and have an altogether unhealthy day.

I've been in contact with the Americans with the container to Houston; the price has dropped, because basically anything is better than nothing as far as they are concerned. Eugene has called and is pleased I am making progress. My contacts are contacting me; something is going to happen, I can feel it.

I've never researched any part of this trip as much as I have researched the next leg, mainly due to free stolen Internet connection and nothing else to do, and also because this was never in my plan. I need to figure it out a bit. Korea? I never even considered it, never. All I know about Korea I got from *M*A*S*H*. I research ferries, currency, maps and routes, insurances, customs, whether a carnet de passage is needed for my bike, and other regulations. Until I get off the ferry I don't even know what side of the road they drive on. But I've utilised the Internet like never before. I've even found pictures of the ferry I hope I'm going to be getting. I think my little pink notebook has paid for itself now.

I'm glad I'm of the age where I'm old enough to continually be in awe and appreciation of the ease the Internet has brought to every aspect of my life; yet, thankfully, young enough to be able to figure out how it works. Maybe not with the built-in instinctive ability a child of this century has that allows them to do in a single click what takes me eight left clicks, two right clicks, a copy, paste, and scroll down, but hey, I'm still saving time, I think. Where would I be without it? Probably out on the streets. Actually I should do that anyway.

I try and find a bookshop, but I can't. It's a lovely city to walk round though, hilly and scenic, and there is a monstrous bridge being built, joining the peninsula to the mainland. Two pairs of V-shaped concrete pillars are the only evidence of it so far, but they alone show the vastness of the project. If the design is in keeping with the architecture of the rest of the city, this structure will be Vladivostok's Sydney Harbour Bridge. It's a significantly beautiful Russian city and a mere 6,000 mile drive from the capital.

I have a reply from Korea when I get back. They need the bike dimensions. I don't have any form of measuring device. I hit the streets again. Not much is open. I find a pharmacy; they have a cloth tape measure, but it's the shop's one. I show the loitering security guard what I need. "Nych," but he gets the assistant. "Nych," but wait, the boxes of surgical support clothing come with a free paper tape measure. A box is opened, and I am given one for free. Some poor fat bastard won't know their circumference now.

My tent has dried out and is wrapped tighter than it has ever been wrapped before, and my thermarest is compressed like a passenger in a Mongolian minivan. This is all a rehearsal for getting as much luggage secured on my bike, under lock and key, as possible, assuming the bike is accepted to get on the Korean, Hyundai, and Kia car ro-ro ferry to Southampton. The authorisation from Mr. Big is still pending. Well it may be granted by now, but my Internet connection is...it's gone. I'm going to Korea anyway, I have to; to my north is frozen and impossible Siberia, to the south China and North Korea: not countries of easy transit. To the east I have now run out of land. Eurasia has reached its end, and I'm not going back the way I came. I don't go back, I go forward.

I read that only international ATMs in Korea will dispense cash on a foreign card. So that was a nice little worry for the night.

DAY 100

ZARUBINO, RUSSIA, 154 MILES

I have now completely forgotten how awful it is to get up and go to work. I'm so immersed in my little travel world. The worries and "what ifs," the problems that come with a transient life style, and not the first consideration of how much worse life would be if I was actually working for a living.

I go and find a cash machine to get money out, as opposed to going to work to actually earn the stuff, although that reality is looming. The first one offers me dollars or roubles, brilliant, except it has no dollars to dispense. I get Russian money and take it to a babushka on the street holding a piece of crumpled cardboard with a dollar sign drawn on it in black marker. No brightly lit signs and pictures of flags with buying and selling rates. Well, I suppose it keeps the overheads down. She rummages around under her skirt and produces some dollars and stuffs my roubles... well, I'm not exactly sure where.

There are pigeons all around this pedestrianised area, and the two benches at my side are occupied by sleeping, homeless drunks, bearded and filthy. They have also forgotten how awful it is to get up and go to work. It's strange how international money transfers are going on in the street right next to them. One of the benches is actually free; the drunk has fallen off in his night and lies on the pavement beside it.

I want more money, I need more money for all the costs I will incur both sides of the ferry trip, before I am free to hit the streets of Korea in search of an international ATM. So I chance my luck and stick my card in another hole, enter my series of numbers again, and out pops more currency. I love this.

Back to the babushka who is beginning to smell a rat, but it's just the sleeping tramp next to us, I think.

OK, job done. Pack up. My visa registration is waiting for me. I'm ready to go. I know there are better ways out of this city, but I want a particular photo: my bike on the hill, looking down at the harbour with the unfinished mega bridge, which isn't spanning across it yet, in the background. I look forward to seeing a photo of the finished project; I have no need to return to see it.

Being on a peninsula, it's not difficult to find my way out. I contemplate one more picture by the Vladivostok sign, but it would only be staged and the bike is clean now and it would lack authenticity.

It's a tricky little place to get to this tiny village that happens to have a port that takes freight and hopefully me to Korea. But with a little skill and with the help of my brilliant map, the right towns keep appearing in the right order. It's a pleasant temperature, hilly roads, the engine is coping, if not reassuring, at least not noticeably complaining. I should be enjoying it; I'm just worrying about the next thing, always the next thing. There is no relief from having my money changed or visa registration received, no comfort in being here a day before the ferry leaves. I'm just thinking what if I don't get a ticket, what if I don't clear customs? This will probably continue into Korea until the bike has left my possession and I can sit in a bar in Seoul clutching an e-ticket and knowing it's all over. And then perhaps I can paint a picture of achievement and fulfillment because for now those things are eluding me.

The riding, I have always said, is the easy bit. I seem to have my distribution of mileage verses bureaucracy wrong at the moment. I did high-mileage days of nothing but bike, eat, and sleep across the Trans-Siberian Highway, and now it's all paperwork and research. But that's how countries are when you reach their end. Ferry ports by their very nature are on the coast, along with customs and freight agencies. Be kind of pointless having a ticket office in the middle of the Siberian tundra.

I get to the port thirty-six hours before the ferry leaves, in case there is a problem. There is a problem; I'm here too early. They won't sell me a ticket; the customs lady is not even working today. "Nyet" then "no" in English, says the miserable old bag behind the glass. Like I don't know what "nyet" means. "No what? No ferry? No ticket? Don't just say 'nyet' you sour old boot." But "nyet" is the answer to everything I try and ask. I cross the causeway towards the village. It's a bad bit of road. I hit a pothole badly. Ouch, I always feel my bike's pain when this happens. I wonder if it feels mine. With something that resembles help from a couple of drunken youths (oh God, has it gone midday already?) I am pointed down dirt roads to a building that doesn't say hotel or anything at all. But it is a place to stay. The price is outrageous. I'm too tired to argue—always a struggle, always another hurdle.

Why, in this empty hotel, am I given a room facing the car park? Why can't I be facing the bay, the harbour, the rocky islets, which the sun will set behind, the causeway, and the ferry terminal? I point at my eyes and the window, and the demanding foreigner is led with much resentment across the corridor.

With cooler clothes on I ride back to the building, which I will refer to as the terminal. I hit the pothole again. Now I have the assistance of a boy breathing vodka fumes all over me. Just because he has five words of English, the babushka delegates her negativity to him. She seems to think he would get me to understand why she won't sell me a ticket, in fact, why the answer to all my questions are "no."

"Me time, you time," he keeps saying, pointing aggressively at a clock.

"This me time no you time." Oh piss off, boy.

I go to get supplies. I haven't eaten, and somehow it's become 3 P.M. A guy looks interestedly at my bike as it's parked outside the slightly convenient store, like everyone has from Manningtree to Siberia. When I come out of the shop with sausage, bread, and cheese his wife or daughter (he is either lucky or younger than he looks) speaks English and asks the usual questions, but today the answer is, "I left 100 days ago today, 20,000 kms. Yes, all the way from England. Perhaps you could help me." And they follow me to the thing that isn't a terminal, and once again, I hit the same pothole, and once again, my forks bottom out and front tyre sighs as it's dying breath gets prematurely closer. I must be really tired. It reminds me of a poster I once saw in America.

1. I walk down the street.
There is a deep hole in the sidewalk. I fall in.
I am lost...I am helpless. It isn't my fault.
It takes forever to get out.

2. I walk down the same street. There is a deep hole in the sidewalk. I pretend
I don't see it.
I fall in again.
I can't believe I am in the same place. But it isn't my fault.
It still takes a long time to get out.

3. I walk down the same street. There is a deep hole in the sidewalk. I see it
is there.
I still fall in...it's a habit...but, my eyes are open, I know where I am.
It is my fault.
I get out immediately.

4. I walk down the street.
There is a deep hole in the sidewalk. I walk around it.

5. I walk down a different street.

The babushka is interrogated. I mean why the hell is she here if there is no boat and she won't sell tickets? Make her do something useful. Once again she explains something in Russian, but this time I get the translated information I need. Come back tomorrow is the gist of it. I kind of guessed that, but now I know for sure.

The girl of unknown relationship to the man asks me, because she cannot understand how and why I would come so far without the native language, "How do you manage; why do you bother?" I don't really have an adequate explanation. I didn't mean to come here. I didn't expect to be here. If I said "for fun" she would know I was lying. Yes I'm tired, yes it's nearly over, no I'm not always alone. It's not the sort of description of a journey that would make someone envious. I'm sure she left pitying me. Well that's a pity.

After all these miles, the roads I ride I don't see, that's not why I go down potholes. It's not my fault. This is the downside of research. All I have is knowledge of the potential problems, and I don't have any solutions, just worries. If I hadn't spent the weekend researching, I would have trundled down here the day of the ferry and probably have got on it blissfully unaware of all the possible things that could have gone wrong. Just like I have approached every other obstacle, unresearched and dealing with the situation as it occurs. I'm beginning to question the comfort of the notebook; it may be working against me.

Later that evening I walk across the causeway, then down to the water. I sit on the shore and drink a can of cheap beer and watch the sea soothingly lap against a tide mark of rubbish. I'm so close to North Korea; I think those hills in the distance are probably part of the secretive country. I indulge in the luxury of leaving the can on the ground and walking away, across the endless line of plastic bags and discarded bottles of vodka, water, and all liquids in between. My careful disposal won't make any difference to anything. When in Rome trash the place like the locals do.

I walk on to a kebab shop. Oh look, there's that pothole. They have no kebabs or any food at all. I've really had enough of Russia. If one more person says "nyet" to my perfectly reasonable and undemanding request...it's dinner time, it's a kebab shop, what is it I'm not getting, other than a kebab?

So I walk back in a humid sweat with another beer from another shop. I don't want to buy from the same shop. They may think I have a drinking problem. I find that my second choice, the hotel café, does not sell food either. The receptionist indicated walking back the way I came, but I'm all hot and sweaty now. So, lidless and just in a muscle shirt for the first time this trip, with a lovely little two-beer buzz, I ride back across the causeway. I miss the pothole.

I find a café where briefly the "nos" and "can'ts" stop. Wow, this is all getting really poignant. At last a good experience. Little things like a willing helper at the restaurant are nice touches. He goes through my point-it book with me, and I get fish, bread, salad, and soup, and it's oh so cheap. They added it up wrong, so I correct them and pay the extra. It's nice to be nice, smiles generate smiles, and I should know this by now. The ride back is even better, two miles, less than that, but the sun is going down behind a rocky island, and the sea was lapping like it does, and I love to ride lidless and buzzed. What pothole?

DAY 101

DON CHENG FERRY, SEA OF JAPAN, 3 MILES

A new packing strategy is needed: I have to pack a bag to take onboard. Still in my discarding-anything-I-don't-need mode, I use the last of my washing powder, hang my underwear on my mirrors, and put on my wet but clean T-shirt.

When the cleaner barges into my room without so much as a knock I decide it's time to either leave or lose my tenacious smile. Why is she here anyway? To check the toilet still stinks?

When I cycled round India I would come across screaming western backpackers whose teddy was thrown out of the pram and whose dummy lay next to it. They had been there too long, and it was time for them to leave India; they were getting nothing out of it. Nothing positive. It's a trying place. For the same reason it's time for me to leave Russia. I'm trying to, but guess what? The bike's electrical fault has made another appearance after a month's absence. Once again the start button does nothing. Oh great. I use my auxiliary live wire from the battery and touch it to the solenoid; I have contact and ignition. I take my last ride down the causeway, and I hit the pothole. Oh for fuck's sake!

So the day so far has gone from the electrical terminal, to a front wheel with indeterminable damage, to the not-really-a-ferry-terminal. Nobody is home; a uniformed girl takes my phrase book and looks at every page and eventually points at a word that is translated as *food*. Could you not have mimed an eating motion? It's a different logic. Everyone is at dinner, so I stand around. A car pulls up, and the man who helped me order in the restaurant last night steps out. He shows me his address book and points at an address in Liverpool.

"Oh you have a friend who's a scouser?"

That's all he wanted to show me. He says goodbye and goes about his day—one small positive gesture in a day of obstruction.

Behind that guard is a door; behind the door is a toilet.

"Toilet?"

"Nyet."

Nyet, nyet, bloody nyet! Say nyet one more time, I dare you, I double dare you. I go piss up a wall. When Mrs. No is back from lunch, she sticks her hand through the window of her cubical. What? What does that mean? The answer was apparently "passport." Well why didn't you say so, fair maiden? I'm so sorry my powers of telepathy are somewhat subdued today.

Then she wants 250.

"250 what? Dollars?"

"Nyet."

"Credit card?"

"Nyet, rubelies."

Every word you say annoys me. I give her money, and she indicates that I should go into the port. I get on the bike and start it with my jump wire, but the guard won't lift the barrier.

"Nyet."

Oh what, the port's full is it? I have to wait for some reason before I can enter. I stand in the shade of the wall; it stinks of urine.

Some Koreans turn up with polite intrigue, questions, and conversation. I instantly know I'm going to like Korea. I share my dislike for this country with one of the men, who wholeheartedly agrees with me.

A woman in casual dress and with a shopping bag comes and asks for my documents. And who are you? A passerby?

I'm waved inside the port without my documents. I ride around, and the only people about seem to be deaf mutes. I find a lady in uniform who blanks me; I turn my bike around and shout at her, "HELLO?"...

"HEY!"

I'm totally blanked. There are signs in English telling you what not to do: no smoking, $30 fine; no rubbish, $30 fine; but no signs telling you what to do. Customs? Immigration? Nyet.

Bugger this. I try and ride on the ferry, and finally I get a reaction.

"Wait, it will not leave till 7 p.m.; now is 2 p.m." OK, fine, that's all I need.

So I park my bike in the sun to dry my pants that are hanging off it.

Sometimes it's my life line, today it's my washing line. I sit in the shade and put some Motorhead on my iPod and swear into my voice recorder. Motorhead is the perfect music when you're fuming with attitude, filled with hate for the authoritative establishment, and you're ready to explode. I'm so ready to get on that boat and wave goodbye to Russia with one fifth of my hand.

And then a long overdue and so needed angel arrives in the form of an overland motorcycle with a Canadian on it. And he knows who I am. He met Geron and

Bern, the Germans I shared a ger with in Mongolia, and passes on their best wishes; he's been on the road for sixteen months. He doesn't have many stickers. Interesting. He is equally burnt out on Russia. The hours pass, and the conversation flows. We are of the same age, with the same lone traveller observations, feelings, and humour. Nothing is a problem anymore. It's not halved; it's diminished. We may even have camped in the same quarry on the Trans-Siberian Highway. He said in the movies it's always the quarry where people are shot; I'm glad I didn't make that association when I was unzipping my sleeping bag to see what the noise outside my tent was.

At some point during our carefree conversation, Mrs. Shopping Bag has returned my documents. We get covered in dust as the ferry is unloaded of Korean imports and diggers drag race up the dock. His trip is over too. He's just flying from Korea to San Francisco and then riding back home up to Canada; what some people would regard as the dream ride of a lifetime. For him it is the home straight. But don't we just love to understate that stuff, us overlanders. I just have to ride across Korea from coast-to-coast over the mountains to a port on the west side, and maybe my bike will be homeward bound too.

The foot passengers are in a big waiting room inside what is most definitely a terminal. It consists of a vending machine and hard plastic seats which, if they sold burgers there, would encourage you to leave as soon as your food was eaten. But burgers are not an option and neither is leaving: not yet. Being the only two vehicles to be boarding we are in the privileged position of being able to sit outside all day in the sun and dust. With our trips nearly over we hardened, hardcore overlanders don't even notice discomforts any more. Well after the scheduled departure time we are called to the ticket office, which is in front of the rows of seats of terminal discomfort. At first we try to communicate through a glass window but are soon invited into the actual office. VIP all the patient passengers must think; well that's what I think anyway. Wrong again. There is a problem, due to an Englishman making such a fuss two weeks ago with refusal to pay certain fees. Now all payments: bike freight, my boarding pass, Korean customs fee, disembarking fee, compulsory insurance, and carnet deposit have to be paid up front, but they won't take credit cards or roubles. Even my cabin was at risk; I may be hard core, but come on. I Googled the cattle class accommodation, and I simply can't sleep in those conditions, darling. Anyway, the bike freight is way more than the accommodation, so it's easily justified.

"I'm in Russia; what currency do you want?"

"US dollar." Oh for Putin's sake. "672 of them."

For an hour or more I deal with this idiot boy in a shiny suit, who is helped by a lovely translator.

"I was an English teacher, but since my husband left me I have to do this job to pay my bills. I should not be here. They bring me in to translate when there is a problem, and the foreigners always shout at me, and it's not my fault. I'm translator only, I am here to sort out problems, I am not the cause. I don't like to work with this young man, but what can I do? I have no choice."

Said young man is copying my comments into a chat box on his computer in Korean characters, and I assume he is communicating with the powers that be at the port of our destination. They respond. There is no compromise and only two solutions, one of which is not an option.

It's announced. "So it would seem you will not be getting on this ferry tonight."

Oh yes I will. You can't just make up the rules, costs, and currency as you go along. I offer you payment in several forms, but you won't accept it. I go to the ATM to get more roubles, and then the boy pulls a $100 bill out of his shiny trouser pocket. I take it from him; with that and my emergency dollars I can make the amount needed. It's painful. I give him roubles at my exchange rate and take his name and mobile number because he has not heard the end of this. It's done. Receipts are stamped, and invoices are signed; bill of lading is issued; freight paid. It's progress but not as we know it.

Now the Canadian has to go through the same procedure to procure his first-class cabin. Hey, it's not for me to justify. He is quite a charmer; I could learn something from him. How does he manage this after so long on the road? I watch, I learn, I have a go. I point out to her that her predicament is not helped by the fact she is at the end of the road, everyone is out of patience by the time they get here. If we had met people like her along the route we wouldn't be so jaded.

I am out of currency; my dollars were for emergencies, but when it looks like I won't be boarding the ferry it becomes an emergency. More hours pass, and just when my emergency noodles are about to be taken from the panniers and cooked, we are asked to board. My early arrival was unnecessary, as we are the only two vehicles on the entire ferry. Four polite, helpful Koreans in red boiler suits ask where they should fasten the straps to secure my bike; it's so refreshing, though bolshy Russian officials scream for my passport.

"Look, I've been here for twenty-four hours before I entered the port. I've been in the port for eight hours sitting around. Now is the most important part of the day. I have to supervise the securing of my bike for its journey to Korea. Now shut up and let me unload my bag, then you can see my passport."

Oh yes, it is so time for me to leave.

"Go to customs," they demand.

Do you realise how flawed your system is? All the Kalashnikovs, drugs, lucky Siberian tiger foot charms, and other contraband are in the panniers, which you haven't even looked in. I have just a fleece and toothbrush in the bag that you will be X-raying. So my bike is once again left in the care of the unknown, my bag is X-rayed, and I get the sixth stamp next to my Russian visa. I am free to leave. An even number; this isn't au revoir, it's goodbye.

"Have a good trip. Please visit Russia again."

"Nyet."

The ferry is Korean-run and I'm greeted on board with a bow and a smile.

"You are the motorcyclist, your room is this way, and this will be the restaurant. Here is your meal voucher."

Wow. What a difference a smile makes: a polite, happy, helpful culture. I knew it; I knew I wasn't tired of travelling. I was tired of the country I was travelling in. Everything is good again, and even the guy that collects the dirty plates loves his job and accepts the tray joyously. People smile and say hello, and I just realise I am going to Korea. I was simply getting out of Russia, but now there is a destination to look forward to. A new country I never even thought I would end up in with my bike.

Goodbye, Russia; goodbye pothole; I'm off to ride a different road.

Day 102

Socho, South Korea, 1 Mile

I get to share the Canadian's first-class cabin. I leave him sleeping and go and get a coffee. Whilst I'm sitting at the table, the Korean guy I spoke to at the port yesterday comes and gives me some meal vouchers. I don't know if they are spare or he bought them especially as a gift, but I just know I'm going to love Korea.

Breakfast looks a lot like dinner, only with a fried egg, which I eat with chopsticks.

I go up to the top deck; there is no one up here. I sit up against a big thing that ships often have on their decks, probably a hydraulic oil storage house or some such nautical storeroom. I put on my shades and my iPod, and whilst seagulls fly level with the boat, the music plays in my ears and fills my head, which disperses Russia and all its stresses. Eventually only good memories of Russia will exist, like recollections of school days, when detentions, homework, and the displeasure of uniforms are not conjured up in those half-remembered days. But for now I only have relief that I have left it all behind. Siberia was beginning to look like a place that was impossible to leave. It does have a reputation.

In the afternoon I sit on the floor and chat to my roommate. First-class cabins don't actually have seats. He says he doesn't want to get back into the rut he was in before he left. Things will be different on his return, although he will go back to the same work initially to get some income and top up his funds. I know this pitfall all too well. If you want to avoid that rut, you have to exercise great willpower. Like a recovered junkie out of rehab going back to his group of old friends, the ritualistic old habits are hard to avoid. The honeymoon period of reunification after a break up with nothing resolved, after the thrill of the post-break-up sex—the same pitfalls await. If you want to avoid that rut it's best to go down a different road. I can speak with authority because this

347

has happened to me several times. That's the great thing about experience; you recognise a mistake when you make it a second time.

My phone is dead; I have no Wi-Fi, no currency, and I've just used the last of my Mongolia-purchased peanut butter. It's late afternoon, and there is no evidence of any land.

I go back to the top deck and stare ahead until misty mountains appear on the horizon. In this late afternoon haze, as Korea rises out of the sea, it is clear that it is everything Russia isn't. Short of swimming, the approach from the ferry has to be the slowest introduction. Tall buildings appear, then fishing boats, harbour, docks, advertising posters, roads, signposts…and finally people, a slow orderly procession into the immigration area.

It's polite, it's friendly, it's helpful, efficient, smiley, and best of all it's in English, the signs, and everyone speaks it to some degree. Right from getting off the ferry it's all so organised, straightforward, logical, achievable, and our situation isn't even that simple. My Canadian friend is putting his bike on a truck to a crating agent to have it flown to the States, thereby avoiding the riding paperwork by remaining in transit. I have to get temporary insurance and plates and permission to ride in Korea, and it is done painlessly and professionally. I even get given some money back because I pre-paid too much in Russia. All this with a bow and a hand shake, no shouting, no pointing and demands. No "nos." I'm even allowed to use the customs Internet because I haven't checked it in three days. I go straight to the reply from the shipping company. I have been granted permission to put my bike on their ship for a bargain $500. I have cleared immigration and got all my personal, motorcycle, and riding documentation completed. Everything is wonderful; I'm escorted to the ferry to unload my bike. That was the sixth ferry crossing of this overland trip and, for me, the last one. For the KLR there is one more to go; a forty-day voyage back to the UK. I'm not even sure which way round the planet it is going: Panama Canal or Suez Canal.

The bike, being manufactured in Japan, has practically completed its lap of the globe; the tank from California is only an ocean away from its origin. Various parts are celebrating a variety of landmarks like birthdays as their journey continues.

It's dark now and a new country and night time: never my favourite combination. The Canadian's bike is put on a truck, and he is leaving with it, so it was a very quick and distracted goodbye, when we thought we would be sharing a room and a few beers tonight. But his company arrived at the right time, and it's only the unexpected efficiency of the country that has meant we are going our separate ways so soon.

I suppose now that will be my last chance meeting with another overlander. I'm leaving that lifestyle behind, for a while. So off I go on my own again, totally on my own. The negativity I carried with me in Russia has been replaced with respect, gratitude, and even enjoyment. Out of the port I ride, with fork-lift drivers and customs officials waving as I leave.

Right outside, on top of a high-rise building, is a motel sign, and I can read it because it says "motel" in English. I ride round the corner and park undercover and am greeted by the check-in guy, who shows me exactly where to park in view of the security camera. Then I'm taken to the reception. He, remarkably, just assumes I want a room, unlike turning up at a hotel or guesthouse in Russia, where they wonder what you want.

"How much?"

"40,000 won."

Shit, that sounds a lot, but it is £22. OK, I'll take it.

I'm given a toothbrush and razor and take the lift up. I'm not expecting much. It's gorgeous, big TV, massive bed, air-conditioning, clean, and spacious. No built-in Soviet misery here. It's wonderful. There are shampoo bottles in the bathroom and lotions and moisturisers and all sorts of things, kettle and fridge. The great thing about being deprived such things is now I appreciate them all the more.

Out of the window I can see the ferry I've just got off and the town I'm about to go into. Out on the street I can look around me without fear of falling down an open drain. There is all sorts of cool stuff: dried fish and octopus, chillies and seaweed. I try to get a sim card, but the Korean phone system seems unique to them. They don't even have sims in their phones. I don't really understand it, but I accept it. I know in this polite helpful country, if it were possible it would be done. I find the international ATM, and it works and dispenses large quantities of large denomination notes with very large numbers on them, but they, too, are easy to read and understand. So now I have money. I completely wuss out, and instead of going for something local and traditional, I go get burger and fries. Everyone smiles. The manners, the politeness, the gratitude for my business, it's all so refreshing; a smile generates a smile. I want to stop people just to tell them how much I love their country.

I would really like to prolong this visit, but I must remember I have a sickly bike, and I have been lucky enough to be granted permission to put it on a privately-run freight ship. I don't want to push either.

Day 103

Pyoungteck Port, South Korea, 260 Miles

Hotels with complementary products are such a rare occurrence for me; I have to indulge. I utilise my shampoos and all things cosmetic, then I hit the streets.

I need to get three things before I leave. I manage only to get breakfast. The map and phone card I ask for and cannot get, but the negative responses are accompanied by apologies and explanations. All contact is pleasurable, and the breakfast is orgasmic. Ground coffee, freshly-baked muffin with a perfectly cooked egg, cheese, and ham. Whilst I'm eating that I see a roll with bacon on the outside, which I just have to have too, "for the journey," I justify to myself. I just didn't specify which journey and eat it before I walk back to the hotel.

Some of the tour shops have some interesting pictures of local sights in their windows. It's a little frustrating. I would like to ride around more; see the country. I have to remember I may have the time and the money, but the bike is sick, and just because it's running now doesn't mean it will continue to, so let's head straight for the shipping company.

Funny how, knowing I have to ride across the country, I don't have a trace of butterflies, I don't even have a map. Just some names of towns to look for and some road numbers. It's the ideal riding temperature, and there are so many signposts that it's hard to pay attention to the road. The road runs south alongside the beach. It's clean and welcoming and not a bottle in sight. Welcoming, but not exactly accessible. There is, along its entire length, an impenetrable fence with barbed wire coiled along the top, apparently to keep out the North Koreans who might swim south. So guarded gateways are the only way onto the beach.

There is a strong military presence; I don't know if it's just manoeuvres or daily duties. There are frequent convoys, and helicopters fly over head. I find myself singing the *M*A*S*H* theme inside my helmet. It's better than my rendition of *The Great Gig in the Sky*, but it's still not painless. There are lots of checkpoints, which consist of several armed soldiers behind banks of sand bags. I'm not stopped, and somehow they don't look that intimidating. With their painted faces and thick glasses they just look like dirty bell boys, not really fighting machines.

There is not a single bit of doubt in my mind; the route is straightforward and well-signposted. I would like a map but I don't need one.

I'm riding slowly, enjoying the road, obeying the limits, as do all other drivers. It's great to be stress-free.

It's hard to find something that would sum up Korea in a photo, something to stand my bike in front to say "I rode it to Korea," but that's the only complaint I have. My helmet is worry free, the ride is wonderful; this is how it should be, not fretting about all that's to come.

But of course, once I get the feel of how the road and regulations work, my mind is free to wander. It occurs to me I could get a flight on Sunday. I would cross the International Date Line, and it would still be Sunday when I arrive in Denver, therefore, my daughter's birthday party. It's only a thought for a minute because as soon as it occurs to me I know, I don't think, I just know with absolute certainty, that that is what I'm going to do. It's perfect. I've ridden as far as I can, without carnets and without huge freight costs and with a bike that's now using more oil than petrol.

I stop at a sort of food hall; the toilets are clean, the queues are orderly, and no one pays me any attention. My bike doesn't even get a glance. I'm not stared at; I'm not special anymore. I love the anonymity. I order noodle soup. I can read the menu, and I get service with a smile.

I ride over the mountains. I even got to lean my squared-off and mutated tyres over onto their precipice edge.

It's a densely populated country; the towns are large and close together, but the road and infrastructure is perfectly adequate. Everything functions. I go past ski resorts with hotels everywhere; no hint of snow yet, not like a Mongolian August.

Bikes aren't allowed to use the motorways, but that's fine by me; I'm happy to use the truck-free main roads. Town by town, I run down my list of landmarks and across to the west coast as the sun is going down.

OK, I've had more adventurous rides and more challenging, but what I really needed was a pleasurable one, and that's exactly what I got.

After all, this really is the end of the trip, and I've totally run out of superlatives. I want uneventful.

It's a big industrial port. There are lots of choices, and I don't even have an address, just the name of my man who I've been emailing. I see a storage area of new cars. I stop to ask a security guard. Not only does he speak English, he calls my man and gives me the phone.

"Ah, Mr. Field, I've been expecting you all day."

"Sorry, I've been riding."

"I suggest you get a hotel tonight, and I will meet you at 9 A.M. tomorrow." My thoughts exactly. Mr. Security then draws me a map to the hotel that it is recommended I stay the night in.

In this one I get a complete goody bag at reception, and the room has a balcony and massive TV, DVD player, microwave, and computer. It's just so lavish. But with sincere apologies, I'm told the restaurant is closed. So I wander down the street and find an empty Chinese restaurant. They turn off their TV and open up for me. I'm given a fixed meal and help myself to beer out of the fridge. They feed me up. Every dish I empty, I'm offered a refill, not to charge me more, just to make sure I'm fed to my liking. These two ladies have taken waitressing to a level of mothering in the way they look after me. One of the ladies shows me she has a tattoo on her back too. They don't speak English, but they don't have to. I know I'm welcome, and I just can't stop smiling in this country.

I get some supplies because I have to do laundry. I wash jeans, socks, and T-shirt and hang it on my balcony using my fire escape emergency abseiling rope as a washing line. This practice is probably frowned upon, but so are dirty undies.

Day 104

Seoul, South Korea, 3 Miles

My clothes are still wet, but I put them on anyway. Then I go through my panniers. I throw out the noodles I brought from England and never used once, along with Ukrainian rice, Russian tins of salmon, Kazakhstan baked beans, and all the rest of the emergency food that I have carried all this way.

The food is replaced with bike clothes and all the things I don't need any more and some things I do but forget to take out, like Marmite. It's amazing how my panniers swallow up so much stuff, now I don't have all this space-consuming food that wasn't consumed. Next time I'll know different. I can travel so much lighter. I'm not sure I'll even take a stove next time. And all those spares, two inner tubes that take up so much room—I never got so much as a puncture, let alone gouged tyres and ripped tubes.

I'm off; the last three miles of the trip, and I'm still using what's left of my tank full of cheap Russian petrol. Practicality overruled sentiment, and Monklet had to witness the end of the road travelling in the holdall, bungeed on the back seat. His work here is done. I arrive at the terminal. Beyond the fence are lines with new cars and 4x4s waiting to be exported. It looks like a Waitrose car park.

Security comes and greets me; they insist I come into their break room for a coffee. I would really rather stand in the sun to dry my wet jeans and T-shirt, but I can't refuse their hospitality. Mr. Man arrives right on time, and I'm instructed to ride my bike through the barrier and into the compound of a million shiny cars.

At the dockside are huge ferries, ships, whatever they are, that hold 6,000 cars and one dodgy motorbike; they leave every day all over the world. That's a lot of cars. There is a brilliant model of one in a glass case with the side cut out to show the multiple levels inside. It holds trains too. I want to take a photo, but I'm a tourist in a professional logistics operation, and just taking one of my bike before I leave it causes busy men to impatiently stand around.

I have to show Mr. Ferry loader how to start my bike. I keep the jump wire a secret and show him how to bump it Mongolian-style, and it doesn't work. Well, you get the idea. I pat my bike goodbye and glance at the mileage. It's another too brief parting of ways; see ya in Southampton in November. I padlock my lid onto the seat, and without time for a second glance, I'm taken to a big office where juice is brought in for me to drink whilst the prepared paperwork is gone over with me.

I'm told how lucky I am and that these requests are seldom granted permission. I feel lucky, I feel honoured. He tells me how three Belgians and a Frenchman arrived unannounced the other day, and although he tried, he could not get the authority to let them ship their bikes. He was genuinely saddened that he was unable to help them.

Those Belgians and the French guy had all that time whilst they were in the Iron Tigers' clubhouse to prearrange their shipment. They had a two-day wait for their bikes to clear Russian customs before shipping to Korea. This is one of the benefits of being a lone traveller with time on my hands and without the distraction of company. I'm thinking that all my advance research and concerns were justified, and I've really fallen on my feet here.

When Mr. Man has completed my paperwork, I collect my holdall, and he drives me to the customs broker, an older man, who is happy to see me. I have the documents he needs, and he quickly and efficiently deals with it all, whilst coffee is brought in for us; then he offers to drive me to the bus station.

It's a long drive, but he insists, and then he helps me sort out my express ticket to Seoul. When I shake his hand with both of my hands and all my gratitude he giggles. Is it because I've just come from Russia or are South Koreans the loveliest people on the planet? You may need vodka to cope with Russia, but a smile will suffice in Korea. And I'm never given a reason not to wear one.

God I need a wee. There's a lot of beverages in this export business. All of this has only taken an hour-and-a-half, and it's done. I can see why everything you pick up has a "Made in Korea" sticker on it. They are a "can do" nation; I just haven't seen where they "do it." I've seen no evidence of manufacturing on my brief journey across the country. Somewhere there must be a very big industrial zone.

The bus is clearly marked, on time, and clean and modern. I take my seat, with my only possession next to me, my holdall—no helmet, no tank bag, no thick armoured jacket. I am no longer an overland biker; I'm a bus passenger, and I'm happy and relaxed. I almost have to make myself proud of my achievement. The exporting of the bike was so straightforward, it's easy to forget that I played any part in it at all. Without a fight, without a struggle from one ferry to another, from coast to coast, it was a smooth operation. Getting here, that was the tricky bit; that and discovering that here is where I should go, where I should stop—where the journey ends. But the journey never ends. This is not my final destination, not yet.

The bus takes the express highway. I look out at the paddy fields; I push myself back in the seat with an incredible feeling of well-being, relief, and general elation. I get out my notebook full of names, numbers, routes, and costs and make some calculations. 14,844 miles from my house to here. I have got this far on £5,200; that is exactly £50 a day, my original grab-a-number estimated budget. I feel the euphoria flood over me.

I still have my feet on the ground. Under the seat in front of me, actually, there is a problem with my new and only form of transport. My trainers have been on the way out for a while; in fact I only brought them along for the Sweden Rock Festival back in June, and they are still with me, and they stink, but now with wet socks inside them it's pushed them over the edge. They are offensive. I have to get rid of them, but that means taking them off in a shop to try the new trainers-to-be on. It's going to be embarrassing. Another tricky operation I have to contemplate.

I call my daughter and tell her as soon as I get to Seoul I will be booking a flight, and she will be the first to know when I'm going to be there. She pointed out that, actually, I will be the first to know.

Seoul is massive, with huge multi-lane highways. The biggest buildings I see say Kia and Hyundai on them. I feel like a country bumpkin on his first trip to the city as I take photos out of the bus window—always the telltale sign that you're not a local. I'm not; I'm a total tourist here, and I don't care.

At the Seoul bus terminal I find socks. My holdall is so heavy. I suppose I'm not used to actually carrying my luggage. I have some time to kill until I meet Jo (who is about to become a victim of saying "come visit if ya ever in the area"; don't say you weren't warned, cus I bloody will).

I go into a Starbucks to use the Wi-Fi to look up flights. I hate Starbucks, I hate that I should be intimidated and confused by an order board when all I want is a coffee. I hate that it comes with choices I don't understand, I hate the customers who smugly order their fifteen syllable beverage which costs three times it's worth and then tip. I hate that they dictate what music I should buy and listen to, and today I hate that, after all the hypocrisy and humiliation on my part, I still can't get online. Bloody multinational, corporate brainwashing, market controlling, coffee shop.

I have to give my phone to the taxi driver, so Jo can tell him where to go. It takes ages. Come on, this call is going via England. It's costing me a bomb. We drive for a long while, through a tunnel, and still the city continues. What I was taking photos of from the bus was just the business side; now I'm at the sights and entertainment side. Jo meets me under a large and unique statue; he couldn't have been much of a taxi driver to not know where this place was.

It's good to see Jo again, a familiar face in a foreign city.

"Look, I'm going to be a needy guest. I have got to get some trainers; I can't contain the odour emanating from them anymore, and I need a travel agent too. Then we can celebrate."

She has it all under control. We drop off my stuff at hers and go to her local travel agent; it's over £1,000 to fly to Denver. No way. Chinese New Year is about to start, and everyone is flying everywhere, and everything is booked. There is no choice, I'm told. But there is; I'm going back to the Internet. We get trainers, cheap, new, and uncomfortable; they will be fine. The shop's display is mainly outside on the street, which is a relief for all concerned. Back to Jo's and get online. I find a flight for £750 that'll do nicely. I just book it. Knowing the demand and lack of choice, I can't afford to hesitate; the opportunity is there. In my experience it's best to take that opportunity, if it's there. I get a text from the Yorkshire man, now in Bangkok; Eugene in Vladivostok is worried about me. He tried to call my hotel, but they said I left. I call him; sometimes you can't consider the cost. He says he thinks I'm a very brave man for what I have done. "What, paid 750 quid for a flight? Oh the trip, well thank you and thanks for your efforts too. They helped me make this decision, and I'm very happy with it."

And that is the last scenario I contemplated. I'm in Seoul, I have an e-ticket, I have company, and I have a cold Corona in my hand with a lemon in the top.

"OK, Jo, I've stopped being needy; just one more thing."

I put my damp and minging socks along with my rancid trainers in a sealed plastic bag and throw them out. They were the ones I wore on TV; no wonder they are knackered. I've landed on my feet a lot in them. Now they are left in Seoul. (There's a joke there somewhere but I can't find it.)

I have thirty-six hours R&R in Seoul, as they probably said in *M*A*S*H*.

Jo has got me on the guest list of the British Embassy so we can go to their bar for Friday night drinks.

It's full of expats, predictably. We meet a guy who looks like Prince Charming out of *Shrek*. He has a motorbike too, and apart from nationality, we have absolutely bugger all in common. They are all nice enough, but they are workers, not travellers. They wear English football shirts; they have worries like getting their dental treatment done before their subsidised oral benefits are withdrawn at the end of the month. It's just too trivial for me to even make an effort to empathise. They continue with the benefits of changing the end-of-month bowling from Tuesday night to Thursday night.

It's only interesting because it's so alien to me. My mind was blown in Mongolia, numbed in Siberia; I don't want to be the boring traveller who can only talk of his Eurasia motorcycle trip. But it's the answer to the question of "What are you doing here?" Apart from "I have absolutely no idea," it's all I can think of to say.

It's like I told the Canadian on the boat: have one travel story, tell it well and concisely, and have a punch line; don't be a travel bore. I haven't prepared one. I try the walking to the ger to ask for directions story, but it falls flat..."So, how much is a root canal going to cost you?" One of the guys tells me how he kissed Jo at a New Year's party and how hard it is to get close to her. "It depends who you are," I reply, meaning "Lucky you," but it was interpreted as "I got further." Oh God, I've found myself in a macho, one-upmanship conversation. I need another drink.

Luckily, Jo has other plans; we walk down by a manmade river lined with courting couples, through markets of gift-packed spam and dried fish. Jo mentions how she hates to be touched. Is she excusing herself for the Ulan Bator lift incident or explaining it, perhaps just preparing me for later?

"How did you fare with getting your nipples pierced then?"

It's an open and honest conversation; we walk down streets illuminated with a thousand signs in Korean characters. Now this is what I wanted; this is real, so is the discomfort of my new footwear. We eat in a restaurant where the food is brought raw and you cook it yourself on a grill in the centre of the table. I bet this place is great in the winter. We are the only westerners; I could never do this on my own, even if I had found the place. I wouldn't know how it works or what to order.

We go to a Jägermeister bar, but both admit we are too full to fully appreciate the experience. The bars blend into each other, as do the people we meet in them and the things that were said. But the country doesn't merge into a string of borders crossed. It's got individualism like they all do, and furthermore, I would just like to say I'm actually very, very drunk. What time is it? Has America woken up yet? I need to send a text.

Day 105

Various Locations, 1000s of Miles

Jo knocks on my door.

"They are leaving in half an hour."

"Who are? What? The plane?"

Some guys at the bar last night invited me to go hiking with them; did I say I was going? I'm sure it seemed like a brilliant idea at the time.

It's out of the question. I've got a hangover to get over, and I'm not doing it with fresh air and exercise. I'm on holiday, don't ya know?

Jo is off to work. It would be very easy to slob around in her apartment all day watching *BBC World*: oh will ya look at that, some miners are trapped in Chile. It appears that barring a few African tribes, I'm the only one who was unaware of the South American subterranean disaster. I could eat Mexican food, surf the Internet, and talk on Skype too, but I have less than twenty-four hours here, and I am going to see how many of them I can fill. I'll just check my email.

There is a very informed overlander network, and with the help of horizonsunlimted.com, it still amazes me how close-knit and supportive everyone is. I got an email from the Finn I met in Kazakhstan, who rode his BMW back home from working in Korea. He had heard from the Frenchman I was coming here and sent me some good routes to ride. Unfortunately, I didn't get the email until today.

I got forwarded emails from helpers and people who know people. We're all out there doing our thing, sometimes struggling, always learning, and occasionally in a position to help. It's been a trip of people's generosity: from a bed and a home-stay on the first night in Germany, to an expat English teacher's spare room on the last night. This isn't couchsurfing in a virtual world; this is real life hospitality given by genuine people and appreciated with more than a ticked box and positive

358

feedback. People are not commodities: you can't trade real life experiences on the Internet like goods on eBay.

The Internet is there to make life easier: not as an alternative to life.

I find a back road café, where I sit on the floor and eat shellfish noodle soup with chopsticks. It's a long and relaxing meal, after which I'm ready to see Seoul.

My bag that dragged behind me along a Mongolian road is now useless: the holes have joined together. I put my fist through the bottom of it to show the luggage seller in his subway shop exactly what the problem is. He finds it most amusing, and whilst the smile is still on his face, I knock the price of a new one down 5,000 won. Then I wander the streets of Seoul and buy gifts, take photos, and even find some stickers.

Whilst I struggle with the map in the underground station, an elderly man asks if he can be of assistance. He takes me to the platform I need. He tells me he is a retired government official and asks me, "What work is it that you are engaged in?" Hmm, that's a tricky one. My immediate reaction is to lie: after all I'm not exactly sure how long the train will be and how good his comprehension of English is. Anyway, if I name my previous occupation I may find myself back in the rut I was in before. I'm a writer. I'm an artisteeeest.

My last day ended with an invite to a girly night out. Now that's how to end a bike trip: going bar hopping with seven girls, and I'm the only guy.

That's how to celebrate 15,000 miles, 14 countries, 10 time zones, and 6 ferries all on an £800 eBay bike. That's the great thing about knowing someone in a strange country; without Jo my trip would have ended alone in a hotel being a tourist—but not this trip, not this time. We meet the other six at a bar in the university area. I was invited to come here last night. In one of the drunken conversations with a drunken expat, I seem to remember the phrase "It's like fishing with dynamite" being used.

So here I am with seven girls of various nationalities, all of whose first language is English, the common denominator being that they are all English teachers. The conversation is not all shop and not all travel: it's varied, stimulating, and entertaining; and I'm being particularly attentive to figure out who is married, who has boyfriends, and who is available. The girl I'm most attracted to is the furthest away from me, but that's not why she looks so good. She has long black hair worn up and thick-rimmed glasses, with the prettiness that you just know, with the removal of her glasses and the shake of her head, her hair will cascade down with shampoo-commercial bounce and her beauty will be striking. I direct my conversations, wit, and Canadian-learnt charm in her direction. It's received well with polite laughter. I love it when a girl finds my jokes funny and she's not even drinking. Slowly the others eliminate themselves as possibilities with rings on their fingers or work in the morning. But not Miss Pantene: she still has potential, until, that is, she gets up to go to the bathroom, and I see she is eight months pregnant. Bollocks.

Every time we move to another bar, we lose a girl, but the bars are good, the beer is excellent, and the company is perfect. When we are down to five, we get another taxi to another part of town, and tipsy innuendo floats round the car.

If I had left a girlfriend at home, she would never have believed that I had travelled so far and remained faithful. If I was on a mission to see hundreds of beautiful women of various nationalities, under all manner of circumstances, and not get laid, I would win a fucking award. But that's life. Life on the road is like a festival, when your two favourite bands are playing simultaneously on different stages; you can't do it all. It's not a matter of making the right decision, it's about making the best of the decision you made.

Like the ideal country, the ideal scenario does not exist. Too much company: party too hard. Too little company: think too much. Got a partner: long for freedom. Got freedom: lose confidence. Share a bed for too long, and I lie awake staring at the ceiling thinking of empty roads and new experiences. An empty road will reflect the choices you made in life brighter and clearer than any mirror or shrink ever will.

It's hard to sum up a journey that hasn't ended. When was the last day? I couldn't even decide when the first one was. My life has always been about bikes. Before I owned a spark plug spanner, before I was old enough to have a licence, I bought a non-runner off a scrap merchant. From the *Easyrider* magazines of the '70s to my first Honda SS50. Doing my Star Rider course in freezing February weather. Rallies and bike shows, importing classic old Harleys in the late '80s. Attending drag racing meets and Moto GP weekends, where like armchair travel, I found myself spectating, when I wanted to be experiencing. Customising and touring, speed and handling, reading and dreaming, feeling the wind, the rain, the heat, the power, the thrill. Staring wide-eyed through a visor, crouching low or sitting upright hanging off my apes. Grabbing for the clutch, knocking it down a gear whilst glancing over my shoulder; opening the throttle and stealing the empty road ahead from a startled motorist. Sunny country lanes, like the back of my hand: looks like bad road positioning, but I know where the manhole cover is.

It's in my blood; it defines who I am.

It never really stops. The methods of transport change, from dodgy bikes to dodgy trainers to plane to hire car. There is no end. It may be the trip of a lifetime, but I have a lot of those. I steer my life in this direction. Sometimes I reap the benefits, sometimes I mourn the losses. But if I don't take advantage of the freedom I have, then the price I paid to have it is too high.

Sitting on the plane it really sinks in that it's over. I'm temporarily bikeless, so this is what motorcycle emptiness is. What am I going to do now? From a springtime of lists and the preparation, to the final research in a Vladivostok hotel room arranging the parting of ways at a South Korean logistics company; I won't see my bike again until it is standing upon Southampton Dock. I've met riders who have done more and spent more, taken longer and ridden harder, but on such a small budget I managed a long-time dream whilst dreaming up new dreams.

I have delays in Tokyo and LA, where I try to hold on to what I've been doing. I look out the window at the Hollywood sign as we come in to land. The images of the trip pass through my memory like they flash across my screensaver—the most realistic movie I've ever seen. I wonder if Korea could be the one. I'm not sure; it ticks a lot of boxes. Too bad I couldn't have spent more time there.

No one country is perfect. If it was everyone would want to go there and then the perfection is gone, ruined by overcrowding and strict immigration laws.

When I get to Denver, my daughter's mother, Brigitte, finds it hilarious that I still think I'm going to find perfection somewhere. But I do; I really believe it. Perfection is everywhere: it just doesn't stay for long. You have to keep looking; you have to have hope. Where would you be without hope? What's next, always what's next? I have the option of going back. I could pick things up where I left them. I can go forward, I can tread water, and I have a few obligations in a world of oysters.

I'm happiest when I'm searching for happiness. Forever the optimist. Always searching for greener grass.

EPILOGUE

SPRING 2011

Adventure is right outside your front door. I could have been going to Asda, but I went the other way. All you have to do is go outside and stop: adventure will come and find you.

Consider the daily commute to work; a familiar, repetitive, and uneventful journey, but get a puncture one morning, a change in routine, get out of the car at a point you would usually pass by, and something out of the ordinary is going to happen. Something already has. It will quite likely involve meeting someone new, even if it's the AA man. It may be a local you haven't spoken to before. In general, people like to help, especially in a situation they can relate to.

I will always pick up a hitchhiker in pissing rain in honour of the man who stopped for me because he cared more for me than he did his upholstery. And with that contact, even if it's only help with a spare tyre, comes a new experience, and that is my definition of adventure. New experiences; you don't have to take a husky-driven sleigh to the North Pole. You just have to stop somewhere new, and something new is already happening to you.

Good people exist everywhere; they just don't go door to door. Well some do, but that's different. But even stinking of vodka, BO, or smoked fish, a little human contact can be the high point of the day. You meet the best people when you're not planning to. It's spontaneous, it's refreshing, it puts faith in human nature, and it's everything couchsurfing isn't. It's real life, and it's always been out there. You just have to stop and let it in.

At the beginning of November, I got a call from an ocean freight company on the south coast of England, mainly pointing out that they wanted money, and as an afterthought, that I would receive some kind of service for that fee. My bike was due to be cleared through customs on Friday, in fact it was, but having no concept of how far Essex is from Southampton or what customer service is, they returned my call too late for me to pick it up. So on the Monday I drove down to the docks. The last mile took an hour, the cause of which was a security man at the dock entrance telling cruise ship passengers where to park. Is this the first time a cruise ship has docked here? Have you never thought of developing a better system?

When I find the freight company, again cash money is demanded immediately. I didn't pay the Korean freight until two weeks after I had left the country; they were quite happy to trust a transient non-resident.

A car transporter driver moans to me about how he, too, has driven his empty truck all the way from Essex to pick up some cars that were picked up last week and will be driving all the way back empty too. He walks me to the pickup point. I have to explain I had ridden my bike to Korea."

"Any ag?"

"No, no agro."

"Good on ya."

At the pick-up point where, despite the email announcing my arrival, the high-visibility-clad dock worker had no idea I was coming or where my bike was. His phone didn't work, either, so he couldn't get in touch with someone who might know. Whilst he struggles with his limited communication skills, I'm told to bring my van over. After much looking, my bike is found; it's just outside the undercover parking where it had been stood in the rain all weekend. The ramp I was assured they had before I left home doesn't exist, and I'm not allowed to drive my van in or, indeed, strip my panniers, etc. off in the compound. So I go all the way back and park my van back where it was before I was told to move it, then push my bike out of the compound. A plank is located whilst I take off panniers and load them in the van. Health and safety forbid the dock hands from helping me to push the bike up the ramp. I do persuade him to put his steel-toe-capped foot on the end of it to stop it slipping.

"So ya rode it to Korea, eh?"

"Yeah, that was easy compared to today's fiasco."

I get my gate pass, and just to prove how inefficient and flawed their system is, I drive out the dock without stopping or showing it.

How the hell does this country function? Everybody wants money, but no one provides a service worth paying for. No wonder they want money up front.

The lap is complete. I stop by Andy's; the two KLRs are together again. We make tentative plans to do the Pan-American Highway next year. We have already started the research.

The Germans got to Ulan Bator the hard way, via the Gobi Desert, in just five weeks. It sounded like a tough ride, but they were always good riders. The bikes were shipped back to Hamburg and deteriorated more on the snowy and salt-covered 400 km journey home than all the previous miles they had endured. They made an impressive DVD about it. No wonder they were always charging batteries.

Greg rode down the west coast of the States, and upon arrival at the Mexican border, decided he had neither the time nor the money to get to South America so headed east and shipped his bike home.

The Touratech twins completed their trip to Ulan Bator, and the bikes were shipped back to Austria where they bought them off the sponsors and performed their presentation. A few of their photos made it into the Touratech catalogue.

Number 6 was so inspired by the overlanders he met, when he got back to Holland he kitted up his KTM and headed to Africa.

Bern and Geron rode home safely to Germany and later did a little ride to Albania.

The Czechs located, bought, and exported a container full of gers back to Europe; I would love to own one.

The Canadian says the sixteen months away seemed like they never happened and is thinking another trip may be in the pipeline.

Did I make the right decision to keep going after Ulan Bator? In hindsight, absolutely. Russia was hard work, but it made South Korea all the more rewarding.

The KLR is still my only bike legally on the road, so it's been my winter bike and has still not been stripped to source the reason for the oil consumption, and as for it not starting, it was a one-off. It's been suggested it may have been the automatic decompression mechanism that stuck and prevented the valve from shutting properly and, therefore, not enough compression for the bike to start. It sailed through its MOT without as much as a clean, the only problem being I had forgotten what the registration number was, which was a bit embarrassing after so many miles and forms.

It needs some TLC, and when I finish this paragraph that's exactly what it is going to get.

It's great to have it back in the garage; the map page is still in the tank bag, which I put my red wine in when I ride back from the Co-op. It shows the way to Vladivostok in Cyrillic.

When I rode it to see some friends, they seemed to think my return justified the opening of some champagne. Whilst we drank, their teenage daughter came downstairs with her phone in her hand. She looked up from some important texting and said, "Hi, how was it?"

"How was what? Everything?" I said, struggling to sum it up so concisely.

"Yeah, everything."

"Em, well, it was good."

"Cool," she said, and carried on texting.

Other Books from Road Dog Publications